OXFORD MODERN LANGUAGES AND LITERATURE MONOGRAPHS

Ghost Stories in Late Renaissance France

Walking by Night

TIMOTHY CHESTERS

OXFORD
UNIVERSITY PRESS

OXFORD
UNIVERSITY PRESS

Great Clarendon Street, Oxford OX2 6DP

Oxford University Press is a department of the University of Oxford.
It furthers the University's objective of excellence in research, scholarship,
and education by publishing worldwide in

Oxford New York

Auckland Cape Town Dar es Salaam Hong Kong Karachi
Kuala Lumpur Madrid Melbourne Mexico City Nairobi
New Delhi Shanghai Taipei Toronto

With offices in

Argentina Austria Brazil Chile Czech Republic France Greece
Guatemala Hungary Italy Japan Poland Portugal Singapore
South Korea Switzerland Thailand Turkey Ukraine Vietnam

Oxford is a registered trade mark of Oxford University Press
in the UK and in certain other countries

Published in the United States
by Oxford University Press Inc., New York

British Library Cataloguing in Publication Data
Data available

Library of Congress Cataloging in Publication Data
Library of Congress Control Number: 2010940306

Typeset by SPI Publisher Services, Pondicherry, India
Printed in Great Britain
on acid-free paper by
MPG Books Group, Bodmin and King's Lynn

ISBN 978–0–19–959980–6

1 3 5 7 9 10 8 6 4 2

For my parents

Table of Contents

Acknowledgements

Warm thanks are due first of all to Wes Williams, who supervised my work on ghosts when I was preparing it as a doctoral thesis. His insight, wisdom, generosity, and patience knew no bounds. I should further like to thank my examiners, Terence Cave and Neil Kenny, for the care with which they read my script, and for their comments and suggestions. Ian Maclean and John O'Brien were already owed my thanks for their generous help over the years; my debt to them doubled when they kindly agreed to act as readers for Oxford University Press. Thanks also to Richard Mason, for his unfailing attention to detail when copy-editing my text.

I also wish to acknowledge a number of institutions that helped me to complete both thesis and book: the Arts and Humanities Research Council, which awarded me four years of postgraduate funding; Exeter College, Oxford, which offered me a place to read for my Master's degree; Balliol College, Oxford, where I moved to pursue my doctoral studies; Queen's College, Oxford, which appointed me a Laming Junior Fellow; and Royal Holloway, University of London, where I have enjoyed the warm support of my colleagues since January 2007.

To the following friends and colleagues, my thanks for their invaluable advice and encouragement: Ben Brice, Emily Butterworth, Marianne Closson, Richard Cooper, Catherine Cramp, Agnieszka Gratza, Joe Harris, Anna Holland, Ann Jefferson, Pierre Kapitaniak, François Lecercle, Alex Marr, Thibaut Maus de Rolley, Richard Scholar, Noel Sugimura, Rowan Tomlinson, Kate Tunstall, and Lydia Wilson. Of course the responsibility for any blunders committed, or insights omitted, is mine alone.

I took my title from the English translation of Ludwig Lavater's treatise on apparitions, *Of Ghostes and Spirites Walking by Nyght* (1572). Lavater thought that certain types of people were more likely to see ghosts than others. One such category was scholars, their eyes blurred and minds addled by years of nocturnal reading. Though I myself have never seen a ghost, I think I know what he means. Writing a thesis, and then turning it into one's first book, can be a haunting business. Four people above all have endured and supported me in this troubled state, and to them I owe special thanks: Tessa Escárzaga, my parents Graham and Anne, and my sister Anna.

T.G.C., June 2010

A Note on the Text

Early modern orthography has been respected in all cases, except for the following modifications:

- The distinction has been made between /i/ and /j/, and /u/ and /v/.
- Abbreviations (and '&') have been resolved.
- Modern accents have been added in ambiguous cases (à, là, où, etc.).

In those cases where long or obscure passages of original French text might present difficulties to non-specialist readers, English translations have been provided. These can be found in footnotes. Unless otherwise stated, all translations are my own.

Introduction

This book describes the end of one ghost story, and the beginning of another. Transitional in this as in so much else, the sixteenth century was a period of far-reaching transformations in ghost narrative in France. Whereas medieval ghost stories were overwhelmingly clerical in origin and written in Latin, their Renaissance successors were increasingly likely to be composed in French and, as the period went on, secular in flavour. And whereas the purpose of the medieval ghost narrative was largely devotional, Renaissance ghost tales fed a far more varied market, and were apt to offer readers more worldly titillations. Although it was arguably not until the late eighteenth century that the ghost story came to be recognized as a discrete genre within European fiction (and first in the English 'Gothic' before a later flourishing in France), several of its features were already embryonic by the year 1600. What these features were, and how this came about, is the subject of this book.

Insofar as its main object is narrative, this study employs the methods of literary criticism. But ghosts are also a topic in intellectual history—a history with which stories, like any other product of the mind, often stand in dialogue. Literary texts do not exist in a vacuum. This was especially true in the Renaissance, where the boundaries between literature and other forms of discourse were so porous that to speak of 'literature' at all can sound historically naïve. As can be seen from the sheer variety of textual sources considered in what follows, ghosts slide across such boundaries with particular ease: from devotional treatises to tracts on New World cosmography, from commentaries on biblical episodes (such as the raising of Lazarus or the apparition of Samuel to Saul) to collections of *contes* or *histoires prodigieuses*, from juridical demonology to sectarian polemic, or from popular pamphlets to Rabelais's *Tiers livre*. As ghosts, and ghost narratives, move from one discourse to another, they frequently change shape. This protean quality makes them an attractive quarry to the student of the period, but it also renders them peculiarly difficult to grasp, irreducible as they are to a fixed or stable form. For this reason it will be necessary in this Introduction to set out more precisely the linguistic, textual, generic, and chronological terrain across which ghosts and ghost stories will be tracked in what follows.

LANGUAGE

First there is the problem of words. 'Ghosts' in this study means apparitions of the dead. The use of this term would be as straightforward as it sounds were it not that early modern French, while disposing of several approximating terms, has no direct equivalent. Instead the texts considered in this study employ a varied and sometimes bewildering vocabulary, and it is striking how much the problem of terminology exercised some Renaissance experts on the subject (while others mix up terms with no regard for consistency). *Fantosme* (or less often *fantasme*), etymologically related to Greek and Latin 'fantasia', was sometimes used. This stressed the role of the imagination, and could—though need not necessarily—imply that the witness is in error (as in English 'phantom pregnancy' today). *Vision* and *esprit* could both refer to a range of spiritual phenomena that included the appearance of dead souls (especially when used as part of the formula 'les esprits qui reviennent'), but could just as well apply to angelic or demonic visitations. *Apparition* usually described the event rather than the thing itself, and so was frequently conjoined with other terms (as in the title of Noël Taillepied's 1588 *Psichologie, ou traité de l'apparition des esprits*). *Lutin* was a relatively popular word, and might refer to a whole spectrum of fairies, will-o'-the-wisps, hobgoblins, and devils. At the other end of the sociolinguistic scale, learned writers sometimes naturalized the Latin terms *manes*, *lares*, *lemures*, or (where the ghost is particularly hostile) *larves*. These labels do imply visitations from the dead, but the taint of paganism or heterodoxy (all four terms describe the spirits of dead ancestors who have become household gods) meant that their use never became widespread, and was usually confined to humanist discussion. *Ombre* and *idole*, although slightly less recondite, had a similar savour, and were the preferred choices of humanist tragedians (such as Étienne Jodelle or Robert Garnier) and the poets of the Pléiade when evoking the shades of the pagan underworld. *Spectre* (calqued on Latin 'spectrum') was a neologism in the period, popularized in the mid 1580s by the humanist magistrate Pierre Le Loyer.[1] More concerned with the medium of apprehension (i.e. sight) than the origin of the spirit itself,

---

[1] On Le Loyer's 'spectre', see pp. 144–8.

the term did nothing to suggest a visitor from the dead. *Revenant* does exactly this; but this term came later, a mid eighteenth-century coinage.[2] None of this should be taken to imply that, lacking a single word, Renaissance French writers had no notion of ghosts. It was rather that, in order to capture that sense, it was necessary to resort to more circuitous formulae, such as 'une âme qui revient / apparaît, l'esprit d'un mort', etcetera. This makes for an important difference. In English, to utter the word 'ghost' is usually to evoke a spirit whose identity has *already* been established as the soul of a dead man or woman. By contrast, the less decisive terminology available to Renaissance French authors tends to emphasize the provisional, and therefore arguable, status of ghosts that was in fact common to both England and France in this period. As we shall see in the first part of this study, the Reformation polemic over the appearance of souls from Purgatory contributed in no small part to this sense of the return of the dead as a contested event—open to doubt, discussion, and debate. Demons were often supposed (and not only by Protestants) to assume the shape of dead men in order to deceive their grieving relatives. In France especially, the lack of a specific term suggests that apparitions of this kind were regarded as phenomena whose precise identity and cause *remained to be determined*. By using the English 'ghost', then, this book sometimes supplies a value, and a degree of interpretive confidence, where none exists in its source. The reader should be aware of this mismatch. In those cases where to speak of a 'ghost' would do especial violence to the source, the less specific 'apparition' has usually been preferred.

Not that 'apparition' either comes entirely without drawbacks. Like 'vision' and 'spectre', 'apparition' points both at the thing perceived and the mode of perceiving. Apparitions appear. More specifically, they appear to the senses: they are seen and heard, sometimes even touched. To this extent a further distinction needs to be made between ghosts and extra-sensory experiences of the dead, whether in dreams, ecstatic visions, or vague apprehensions of a presence. These kinds of categories were active in the period itself, though the faculty psychology in which they were based differs from our own conceptual framework. The customary classification followed the well-known hierarchy established in Augustine's commentary on Genesis. Augustine distinguishes between three types of 'visions':

---

[2] See A. Calmet, *Dissertations sur les apparitions des anges, des démons et des esprits, et sur les revenants et vampires de Hongrie, de Bohême, de Moravie et de Silésie* (Paris: Debure l'aîné, 1746). In Calmet 'revenant' strongly implies a ghost that was embodied. On embodied ghosts, see below pp. 205–46. For further discussion of the terminology of ghosts, see below pp. 70, 144–7.

visio corporalis, perceived through the senses, *visio spiritualis*, when presented to the imagination without a body (as in dreams and ecstasies), and *visio intellectualis*, which involved 'visions' apprehended neither through sensory experience nor the imagination. This last category of vision was the highest and the purest, since it bypassed the—potentially distorting—mediations of the lower faculties. By contrast, the apparitions discussed in this study belong to the humblest rank of *visio corporalis*. As Stuart Clark has shown in a recent study, experiences of this kind were more than usually difficult to distinguish from optical illusions, tricks, impostures, and other 'vanities of the eye'.[3] This problem of perception was felt all the more acutely in an age that, thanks to the rise of philosophical scepticism, placed less and less trust in the evidence of the senses. To that extent, the early modern witness to apparitions of the dead was faced not only with a doctrinological problem—is this a spirit from Purgatory?—but also with the question of whether anything of the kind had truly appeared at all. If 'ghosts' raised questions of religious understanding, 'apparitions' threw out a challenge to an entire epistemology.

The lexical mobility characteristic of ghosts and apparitions, and connected to the kinds of theological and epistemological uncertainties outlined above, was also occasioned by the shifting tectonics of language use in the period. Toward the last third of the sixteenth century ghosts began to be discussed in French as well as Latin. Something of this change can be glimpsed in a moment in Pierre de Larivey's 1579 comedy, *Les Esprits*. The play owes its title to a scene in which the protagonist Severin, a miserly father in the Plautine mould, returns home from business in town only to find his house in uproar. Unbeknownst to him, his dissolute son is inside drinking with friends and mistresses. Severin's cunning servant, Frontin, provides the son with an alibi by persuading his master that the building is haunted. With the help of an accomplice, Monsieur Josse, Frontin then proceeds to arrange a mock exorcism, in which Severin is forced to play a leading role. Magic wand and book of spells in hand, Josse approaches the house and instructs the terrified old man as follows:

> M. JOSSE: Or, je vais commancer ma conjuration; dictes après moy:
> *Barbara piramidum sileat miracula memphis.*[4]

But Severin has other ideas:

---

[3] S. Clark, *Vanities of the Eye: Vision in Early Modern European Culture* (Oxford: Oxford University Press, 2007), ch. 6 ('Apparitions: The Discernment of Spirits').

[4] P. de Larivey, *Les Esprits*, ed. by M. J. Freeman (Geneva: Droz, 1987), p. 112: 'M. JOSSE: Right, I'm going to begin my conjuration. Repeat after me: *Barbara piramidum sileat miracula memphis.*'

SEVERIN: Je ne sçaurois dire cela. Faictes vostre conjuration tout seul si
             vous voulez, et parlez françois... peut estre qu'ils [les esprits]
             n'entendent pas latin.
M. JOSSE: Il vaut mieux.[5]

Severin's failure to repeat the words of Josse's conjuration reinforces a
sense of his comic degradation. For those spectators or readers learned
enough to recognize in the Latin little more than a garbled quotation from
the poet Martial, his absurdity is only deepened further.[6] And yet
the suggestion that the ghosts in his home 'n'entendent pas latin', while
comic, is not wholly ridiculous. Severin's statement registers an important
diminution in Latin's prestige as the normative language of ghosts. Perhaps this explains why his relieved tormentor, now dispensed from
performing a sustained charade in Latin, agrees ('il vaut mieux').

    This shift towards French was a new development. During the Middle
Ages vernacular treatments of ghosts had been rare, with learned discussion largely confined to a latinophone ecclesiastical elite. When the change
came, it was by no means total, with French coming to rival rather than
surpass Latin as the medium of choice. Sixteenth-century churchmen
continued to conduct exorcisms in Latin. Latin was also the language of
several late-century learned works on ghosts, some of which proved
enormously successful. For instance, publishers continued to print editions of the Swiss minister Ludwig Lavater's influential ghost treatise *De
spectris* (1570), some illustrated, well into the second half of the seventeenth century. That the Latin edition of this bestselling treatise so
comfortably outran its vernacular translations should warn us against too
vaunting a claim for a French revolution in language usage. Such examples
notwithstanding, the growth in the number of vernacular texts on ghosts
remains a striking feature of the period, which had witnessed an increasing
prestige accorded to French across a range of learned discourses. Within
theology, it was clear by the close of the Council of Trent (1545–63) that
Reformers had largely succeeded in forcing the polemic over ghosts
into the vernacular. Counter-Reformation defences of ghosts in French,
written by Jesuits like François Feu-Ardent, or Franciscans such as Noël
Taillepied, figure prominently in this study.

    Beyond theology, too, the use of French as a medium of learned exchange
had gained ground following (to cite two well-known staging posts) the

---

   [5] Ibid.: 'SEVERIN: I can't say that. Do your conjuration on your own, if you please, and
speak French. Perhaps they [the spirits] don't understand Latin. M. JOSSE: That would be
best.'
   [6] See R. Cooper, 'Pierre de Larivey astrophile' in *Pierre de Larivey (1541–1619):
champenois, chanoine, traducteur, auteur de comédies et astrologue*, ed. by Y. Bellenger
(Paris: Klincksieck, 1993), pp. 97–118 (p. 99).

edict of Villers-Cotterêts (1539), making French the official language of administration, and the flourishing of vernacular humanism propounded in Joachim Du Bellay's *Deffence et illustration de la langue française* (1549). Such was the pace of change that by late century there had emerged a large class of what might be termed professional vulgarizers (such as Pierre Boaistuau, François de Belleforest, Gabriel Chappuys, Antoine du Verdier, or François de Rosset), who made their living by producing vernacular translations, digests, and anthologies of works across a whole range of subjects. These were aimed at the literate, but not necessarily Latin-speaking, gentleman reader, who was now given access not only to the wranglings of sectarian polemic, but also to issues relating to law, medicine, cosmography, and history; when in less studious mood, this new category of reader was also able to enjoy new vernacular genres such as the *histoires tragiques*, the *histoires prodigieuses*, as well as the seemingly limitless profusion of sensationalist pamphlets (the so-called *canards*) peddled by hawkers in the street. Ghosts appeared across this intellectual territory, often in new and unusual guises quite distinct from those of purgatorial polemic. The current study aims to provide a survey of ghosts and ghost stories in this emerging vernacular field, which is considerably larger than previously supposed.

TEXTS AND BOOKS

It will by now have become clear that the evidential basis of this study is the written text in print. As with the emphasis on vernacular material, this focus on textual mediation needs underlining from the start, since it has led to some unavoidable exclusions. One is that of oral ghost traditions, still alive today in certain parts of rural France and doubtless bearing traces from centuries before.[7] Neither has there been any attempt to recover, from behind the written text, the so-called 'popular' ghost beliefs in the manner of the 'annaliste' tradition of Le Roy Ladurie's *Montaillou*, the archival anthropologies of Natalie Zemon Davis, or, more recently and for the medieval period, of Nancy Caciola.[8] This is not to say that popular

---

[7] The great classifiers of folklore Arnii Arne, Stith Thompson, and Vladimir Propp, recognized the recurrence of ghosts in folk tales without theorising about them in detail. For a more recent study in this tradition, see D. Buchan and E. Ivres, 'Tale Roles and Revenants: A Morphology of Ghosts' in *Western Folklore*, 45 (1986), pp. 143–60.

[8] E. Le Roy Ladurie, *Montaillou, village occitan de 1294 à 1324* (Paris: Gallimard, 1975), ch. 26 ('Folklore et revenants'); N. Zemon Davis, 'Some Tasks and Themes in the Study of Popular Religion' in *The Pursuit of Holiness in Late Medieval and Renaissance Religion*, ed. by C. Trinkaus and H. A. Oberman (Leiden: Brill, 1974), pp. 307–36; eadem., 'Ghosts, Kin, and Progeny: Some Features of Family Life in Early Modern France' in *The Family*, ed. by

beliefs about ghosts find no place whatsoever; it is rather that, where these do appear they are usually mediated through the unflattering lens of written—and so by definition—learned opinion.

As Caciola has argued in the medieval context, this lens is generally unreliable, and perhaps never more so than in the second half of the sixteenth century.[9] This was the era of the witch craze, and one where men and (especially) women still attached to the vestiges of rural paganism—or suspected of being so—suffered large-scale persecution. Little surprise in such circumstances that urban, educated authors should have been so keen to set their own discussions of supernatural topics apart from the fireside 'fables' or 'bourdes' (tall tales) of the peasant population. One example of this discursive elitism can be found in the *Essais* of Montaigne, himself no friend of the witchcraft persecutions. His chapter 'De la peur' (1.18) opens with an immediate dismissal of peasant fears associated with ghosts or, as he puts it somewhat derisively, 'les bisaïeux sortis du tombeaux enveloppés en leur suaire . . . des Loups-garous, des Lutins, et des chimères'.[10] Although elsewhere in the *Essais* Montaigne is more indulgent towards peasant super- stitions surrounding ghosts, witchcraft, and magic, his characterisation of 'le vulgaire' and its beliefs needs to be treated with caution.[11] Sympathetic or not, such cursory anthropologies are likely to reveal less about the true content of rural beliefs in the period than the ideological bias of those who conduct them.

A. S. Rossi, J. Kagan, and T. Hareven (New York: Norton, 1978), pp. 87–114; N. Caciola, 'Wraiths, Revenants, and Ritual in Medieval Culture', *Past and Present*, 152 (1996), pp. 3–45.

[9] Caciola has written persuasively on the ways in which historians are prone to reprodu- cing medieval or early modern hierarchies between religious norms on the one hand and superstitious 'exceptions' on the other. See Caciola, 'Wraiths, Revenants, and Ritual', pp. 3–4; eadem., 'Spirits Seeking Bodies: Death, Possession, and Communal Memory in the Middle Ages' in *The Place of the Dead: Death and Remembrance in Late Medieval and Early Modern Europe*, ed. by B. Gordon and P. Marshall (Cambridge: Cambridge Univer- sity Press, 2000), p. 68 (for the useful anthropological concept of the 'normal exception').

[10] M. de Montaigne, *Essais*, ed. by P. Villey (Paris: Presses Universitaires de France, 1965), p. 75: 'great-grandfathers issued from the tomb wrapped in their shrouds . . . were- wolves, goblins, and chimeras'. As with all subsequent references to Montaigne, this translation is taken from M. de Montaigne, *Complete Works*, trans. by D. M. Frame (London: Everyman, 2003), p. 62.

[11] In the more sceptical chapter 'C'est folie de rapporter le vray et le faux à nostre suffisance' (1.27), Montaigne concedes that he has no authority to dismiss popular beliefs in the supernatural: 'Si j'oyois parler ou des esprits qui reviennent, ou du prognostique des choses futures, des enchantemens, des sorceleries, ou faire quelque autre compte où je ne peusse pas mordre . . . il me venoit compassion du pauvre peuple abusé de ces folies. Et à présent, je treuve que j'estoy pour le moins autant à plaindre moy mesme' (*Essais*, p. 179): 'If I heard of returning spirits, or prognostications of future events, enchantments, sorcery, or some other story that I could not swallow . . . I felt compassion for the poor people who were taken in by these follies. And now I think I was at least as much to be pitied myself.' *Complete Works*, pp. 160–1.

This same insistence on textual mediation has also entailed caution of a more far-reaching kind. The present study proceeds as if the ghosts discussed here had no existence beyond the texts in which they figure. This approach involves more than simply refusing to believe what our ghost narratives describe (though in the case of this author it happens to mean that too). More precisely, it entails suspending the very question of veracity altogether. No attempt has been made in this book to reach behind the text and offer rationalizing explanations of 'what really happened'. Bracketing the referent in this way does not stem here from any Derridean conviction that 'there is nothing outside the text'. Nor need the refusal to obey our modern, scientific impulses arise from any ethical anxiety about projecting one's own values on the belief systems of the past. Indeed there are some cases in this study where it would be extremely interesting to know the truth behind a given ghost narrative, if only that were possible; as we shall see, sceptical observers at the time often asked this very question. The problem is rather that, except in only a very few cases (for example, that of the notorious Orleans hoax of 1534, described in Chapter 1, where the 'ghost' was eventually revealed to be a friar gadding about in the rafters of a church), rational causes are irrecoverable at this distance from events. Instead we must attend not to the event itself but to the textual trace that has outlived it—to what it reveals about attitudes to ghosts, and changes in ways of representing them in stories.

The transmission of those stories involves a further form of mediation. This is the mediation of the book as a physical commodity. It was suggested earlier that this study stands in the borderlands between literary criticism and intellectual history. Since in this period the chief medium of both ideas and narrative was print, the current study has often had recourse to an adjacent third field, namely the history of the book. However ethereal its subject, written discourse on ghosts does not float free of the concerns—financial and profit-driven as well as intellectual, polemical, or aesthetic—of the printers, publishers, and booksellers who produce and transmit it. Their changing sense of the market for ghosts— as a topic of learned discussion and as a subject for narrative—both responds to, and partly powers, the transformations mapped out in these pages. Understanding the material fortunes of the book (who printed it? along with what else? in what format? with what notion of its readership?) is essential if we wish to reconstruct the 'horizon of expectation' of those who read ghost stories in this or any period.[12]

[12] The phrase is borrowed from H. R. Jauss, *Towards an Aesthetic of Reception*, trans. T. Bahti (Brighton: Harvester, 1982). For the landmark theoretical justification of this

This emphasis on material history may represent this book's most important contribution to the related area of witchcraft studies. For one of the questions to which it seeks an answer is also fundamental to any history of the witch craze: what is 'la démonologie?' Even if this term was not available to French authors of the period, can it be said nonetheless to describe a field of enquiry of which they themselves were aware?[13] In other words, did late Renaissance readers recognize demonology *as* a discourse— with, for instance, its own distinct type of expertise, vocabulary, or set of heuristic operations, or a certain attitude towards narrative evidence? By ignoring the commercial circulation of books on the topic, and the reading habits of those who bought them, existing studies on witchcraft have somewhat neglected this question. It is notable that Stuart Clark's otherwise magisterial *Thinking with Demons*, for instance, takes no account of the market for books on witchcraft and magic, or of the questions of who read them, how, or why.[14] Clark's thesis belongs to a *mentalités* tradition that tends to suppress the differences between microscopic cultural communities, or discursive fields, in favour of a macroscopic *Weltanschauung* common to them all.[15] By contrast, the material history of demonology—and what that might tell us about its rules, limits, and ambitions— remains largely unexplored.[16]

methodology, which inspired its application in this study, see D. F. McKenzie, *Bibliography and the Sociology of Texts* (London: The British Library, 1986).

[13] James I's *Daemonologie* (1597) was not well known in France, and it is arguably not until Gabriel Naudé's *Apologie pour tous les grands personnages qui ont estés faussement soupçonnez de magie* (Paris: F. Targa, 1625) that a French author coins a term—'démonographes'—to describe a body of *writers* whose business is demons; see Naudé, *Apologie*, sig. avr. Even though we find isolated instances of the word 'démonologie' in the seventeenth century, for instance François Perreaud's *Démonologie ou traitté des démons* (Geneva, 1653), it is not until the nineteenth century that it enters common usage.

[14] S. Clark, *Thinking with Demons: The Idea of Witchcraft in Early Modern Europe* (Oxford: Oxford University Press, 1997).

[15] Witchcraft and the occult have been fertile grounds for historians of ideas. For a full bibliography, see *Thinking with Demons*, pp. 726–72. See especially, since Clark, R. Muchembled, *Une histoire du diable: XIIᵉ–XXᵉ siècle* (Paris: Seuil, 2000). For a similar long view of ghosts, see R. C. Finucane, *Appearances of the Dead: A Cultural History of Ghosts* (London: Junction Books, 1981) and J. Delumeau, *La Peur en Occident (XIVᵉ– XVIIIᵉ siècles): une cité assiégée* (Paris: Fayard, 1978), pp. 75–87. Recently, in *Vanities of the Eye: Vision in Early European Culture*, published during the preparation of this book, Clark has transferred the pure *mentalités* approach to apparitions and discourses of perception across the early modern period in Europe. See also S. Clark, 'The Reformation of the Eyes: Apparitions and Optics in Sixteenth- and Seventeenth-Century Europe', *Journal of Religious History*, 27 (2003).

[16] For discussion of what forms such a history might take, see T. Chesters and T. Maus de Rolley, 'Le Diable et le bibliothécaire: la classification des ouvrages démonologiques dans les catalogues bibliographiques aux XVIe et XVIIe siècles' in *Styles et partages du savoir (1500–1700)*, ed. by F. Lavocat and F. Lecercle (forthcoming 2011).

By attending not only to the authors of the texts considered in this book but also to the industry responsible for the transmission for those texts, what follows seeks to go some way towards writing that history. This study argues that early modern French readers did in fact construe demonology as something like a discrete discursive category, but that it remains doubtful whether a single term is sufficiently supple to allow for the many subdivisions, distinctions, and overlappings that make up this patchwork field. The literature on ghosts makes this amply clear. Although it cannot be denied that the return of the dead and episodes of witchcraft often appear in similar discursive contexts (necromancy, sciomancy, demonic illusions, narratives of widows' bereavement, and so on), or that both may be connected to a growing crisis of religious and epistemological confidence, many authors, printers, and booksellers considered in this study took special care to set their writings apart from the business of hunting witches. That they did so in such numbers has prompted me to propose, for example, a new subdivision of demonological writing, namely 'pastoral demonology' (discussed in Chapter 2): though clearly related to writing on witchcraft, this textual corpus pays attention less to criminal than to devotionally productive spiritual encounters. It is further suggested, in the later part of this book, that a similar dissociation between witchcraft and ghosts can be found in the growing number of secular, politically moderate authors who publish on apparitions. By revisiting the discursive category of 'demonology' through the history of the book, and seeking to be more precise about the distinctions, tensions, and criss-crossings between its constituent parts, this study hopes to contribute to the ever growing body of work on the early modern paranormal.

GENRE

'Ghost narrative' in this study means narrative in prose. The decision to exclude theatre and poetry may appear regrettable. After all, those two genres play host to the best-known ghosts of the period, from the shade of Antoine in Jodelle's *Cléopâtre captive* or Égée in Garnier's *Hippolyte* to the apparition of Du Bellay in Ronsard's 'Élégie à Louis des Masures'.[17] Naturally, these have also attracted the most critical attention. In the context of theatre, Olivier Millet has contributed two important articles on the figure of the ghost and especially its centrality within the neo-Senecan

---

[17] E. Jodelle, *Cléopâtre captive*, ed. by K. M. Hall (Exeter: University of Exeter Press, 1979); R. Garnier, *Marc Antoine; Hippolyte*, ed. by R. Lebègue (Paris: Belles Lettres, 1974), pp. 111–15; P. de Ronsard, *Oeuvres complètes*, ed. by P. Laumonier, 20 vols. (Paris: Hachette, 1914–75), x, 362–70.

prologue.[18] To Millet's findings have been added a number of studies by François Lecercle, focused on the most famous of all ghosts on the French Renaissance stage—that of La Taille's Samuel in *Saül le furieux*—and recent work by John Nassichuk.[19] Poetry has proved a slightly less attractive haunt for ghosts, although Jean Rousset showed long ago the ubiquity of phantoms and apparitions within so-called 'baroque' verse, shaping as they do a vision of flux, impermanence, and death.[20] Marianne Closson's *L'Imaginaire démoniaque en France: genèse de la littérature fantastique (1550–1650)* has provided an extremely thorough inventory of ghosts and demons in both genres.[21] My study owes an especial debt to Closson's comprehensive survey, since I have been dispensed from the need to enlarge my literary corpus.

But the decision to exclude this body of literary materials is not only related to the existence of previous work on the subject. A more important factor is in play: namely, the location of so many theatrical and poetic apparitions in the classical tradition of *prosopopeia*. To reiterate: the purpose of this book is to chart changes in late Renaissance ghost narrative against the background of sixteenth-century thinking about ghosts and apparitions. It is my view that the markedly generic character of *prosopopeia* usually leads away from contemporary intellectual developments and instead to an encounter with classical literary tradition. The truth of this claim is demonstrated most clearly with respect to the protatic ghosts of sixteenth-century neo-Senecan tragedy. But for one or two notable exceptions (Shakespeare's *Hamlet* being one, La Taille's *Saül le furieux* another), it is the debt to Seneca, rather than the emergence of new thinking about ghosts, that determines the shape and character of the

[18] O. Millet, 'L'Ombre dans la tragédie française (1550–1640), ou l'enfer sur la terre' in *Tourments, doutes et ruptures dans l'Europe des XVIe et XVIIe siècles*, ed. by J.-C. Arnould, P. Demarolle, and M. Roig-Miranda (Paris: Champion, 1995), pp. 163–77; idem., 'Faire parler les morts: l'ombre protatique comme prosopopée dans les tragédies françaises de la Renaissance' in *Dramaturgies de l'ombre*, pp. 81–100; see also C. Martinez, 'Fantômes, oracles et malédictions: figures du temps tragique' in *Le Temps et la durée dans la littérature au Moyen Âge à la Renaissance*, ed. by Y. Bellenger (Paris: Nizet, 1986), pp. 139–51.
[19] F. Lecercle, '*Saül* et les effets de spectacle' in *Les Tragédies de Jean de La Taille*, ed. by F. Charpentier (= *Cahiers textuel* 18, 1998), pp. 25–2; idem., 'Les Bénéfices de la trahison: impératifs de foi et exigences dramatiques dans le *Saül* de Jean de La Taille' in *Il tragico e il sacro dal cinquecento a Racine*, ed. by D. Cecchetti and D. Dalla Valle (Florence: L. S. Olschki, 2001), pp. 17–54; J. Nassichuk, 'Jodelle and Garnier: Ghost Prologues from Seneca to the Renaissance' in *Haunting Presences: Ghosts in French Literature and Culture*, ed. by K. Griffiths and D. Evans (Cardiff: University of Wales Press, 2009), pp. 43–59.
[20] J. Rousset, *La Littérature de l'âge Baroque en France: Circé et le paon* (Paris: Corti, 1953), ch. 4 ('Le Spectacle de la mort'). See also, in this tradition, C. Blum, *La Représentation de la mort dans la littérature française de la Renaissance*, 2 vols. (Paris: Champion, 1989).
[21] Geneva: Droz, 2000.

ghostly stage prologue.[22] This disconnection between ghosts on stage and ghosts in theory explains the little attention accorded to theatre in these pages.

In poetry, too, the motif of *prosopopeia* stands relatively remote from the concerns of new vernacular writing on apparitions of the dead, tending instead to reach back to ancient models, especially epic. Take the famous example of Ronsard's 'Élégie à Louis des Masures', published in 1560. Halfway through that poem the shade of Du Bellay, who had died the same year, appears to the sleeping poet.[23] The ghost is hideous in appearance, 'have et descharné, planté sur de grands os', fleshless, hairless, its stomach opened out and crawling with worms. These images are Ronsard's own, probably manufactured from the visual stock of the late medieval *danse macabre*. But another motif gives away the essentially classical force of the encounter, as the poet tries to embrace Du Bellay three times, only to see the ghost slip his grasp ('Trois fois je le voulu en songes embrasser, / Et trois fois s'enfuyant ne se voulut laisser / Presser entre mes bras...') ['Three times I tried to grasp him in my dream / And three times fleeing hence he avoided / My embracing arms...']. This thrice-thwarted embrace, commonplace in writing on ghosts in the Renaissance, is borrowed from an episode in Virgil's *Aeneid*, where Aeneas similarly fails to clasp the ghost of his dead wife Creusa.[24] The allusion would not have been lost on Des Masures, the poem's addressee: only months before he had completed his French translation of the *Aeneid*, a project that had occupied him for well over six years.[25] In this context, and although Ronsard was clearly affected by the premature death of Du Bellay, the apparition might be read as a kind of in-joke, even a celebratory toast to Des Masures's literary achievement. Du Bellay had been the foremost theoretician of vernacular translation. Now invited as the guest of honour at his own poetic wake, he enters a conversation between poets about the future—or afterlife—of Pléiade *imitatio*.

---

[22] In her classic study on folkloric influences in the time of Shakespeare, Katherine Briggs concedes that, in the case of ghosts in the theatre, the power of the Senecan model also left little room for incorporating popular beliefs in the return of the dead. See K. M. Briggs, *The Anatomy of Puck: An Examination of Fairy Beliefs among Shakespeare's Contemporaries and Successors* (London: Routledge, 1959), ch. 9 ('Fairies and Ghosts').

[23] P. de Ronsard, *Oeuvres complètes*, ed. by P. Laumonier, 20 vols. (Paris: Hachette, 1914–75), x, pp. 362–70.

[24] Virgil, *Aeneid* 2.792–4. Virgil himself is imitating Homer (*Iliad* 23.99–101), where Achilles tries and fails to embrace the shade of his great friend Patroclus. Ronsard repeats the motif 'Prosopopée de Louis de Ronsard'; see *Oeuvres complètes*, vi, 40–3.

[25] The first four books of Des Masures's translation had appeared in 1554. The rest of the work was published as Virgile, *L'Eneide*, trans. by L. des Masures (Lyon: J. de Tournes, 1560).

To engage in such a reading is not to diminish the value or interest either of this poem or of the many other instances of *prosopopeia* in sixteenth-century French verse. It is rather to claim that they are usually best understood not with reference to the theoretical developments described in this book, but from within the well-charted territory of Pléiade poetics.[26] As with the theatre, the exceptions are striking. One chapter in this book includes the famous moment at the end of the 'Hymne des Daimons' in which the poet tells how he once fought off a host of demons with his sword. As is well known, Ronsard's hymn is in large part a vulgarisation of Psellus-Ficino's treatise on spirits, *De daemonibus*. To this extent, 'Les Daimons' occupies a similar discursive space to, say, Le Loyer's *Quatre livres des spectres* in a way that the 'Élégie à Louis des Masures' does not. For this reason, then, it is the only verse ghost narrative to be considered in this study.

APPARITIONS OF THE LATE

The question of Pléiade poetics and the imitation of ancient models finally brings us to my chosen period label, 'late Renaissance France'. Invoking 'the Renaissance' is not a neutral choice these days: in anglophone literary critical circles, 'early modern' has become the preferred term, such that deviating from it now calls for explanation. In the context of a study on ghosts, one obvious attraction of the term 'Renaissance' is its figurative proximity to notions of recrudescence or revival. The metaphor according to which Renaissance humanism 'resurrected' the language, texts, and ideals of the ancient world is commonplace in the period itself. Du Bellay's *Les Antiquités de Rome* are full of such instances, such that humanist archaeology becomes a kind of necromancy in which the poet conjures the spirit of a revered cultural precursor:

> Rome n'est plus: et si l'architecture
> Quelque ombre encor de Rome fait revoir,
> C'est comme un corps par magique savoir
> Tiré de nuit hors de sa sépulture.[27]

---

[26] See G. Castor, *Pléiade Poetics: A Study in Sixteenth-Century Thought and Terminology* (Cambridge: Cambridge University Press, 1964).
[27] *Les Antiquités de Rome*, v, 5–8, in J. Du Bellay, *Oeuvres poétiques*, ed. by H. Chamard, 8 vols. in 9 (Paris: E. Cornély and others, 1908–5), II, 8: 'Rome is no longer: and if in its architecture / Some shade of Rome can still be seen, / It is like a body by occult art / Pulled from its sepulture at night.'

The image of the 'ombres', 'manes', 'idoles', or 'esprits' of ancient Rome floating north and revivifying French letters and culture was attractive to Du Bellay and the Pléiade even if, as later critics such as Malherbe will imply, such 'magique savoir' entailed from the beginning a factitious transplantation. Although the Pléiade poets receive only limited attention in what follows, the fact that such a prominent group of writers exploited the ghost as a way of thinking about reviving the 'spirit' of ancient letters in the period goes a large part of the way to recommending 'the Renaissance'.

Setting aside a portion of Chapter 1 sketching out the theological prehistory of ghosts in the late Middle Ages, the chronological territory covered in this book stretches from 1546 (the date of Rabelais's *Tiers livre*) to 1614 (the date of François de Rosset's *Histoires memorables et tragiques de ce temps*). Given the historical trajectory described by that arc, perhaps finally the 'Renaissance' proved less compelling than its melancholy companion: 'late'. All ghosts are—by definition—apparitions of the 'late', and those considered here reveal a special, poignant kind of lateness. In France in particular it is the lateness of a mood, of certain habits of hopeful thought and feeling, coming to an end with the outbreak of civil war. Of course, whether expressed in the burgeoning volume of sermons on the Antichrist, the vicissitudes of the historian Louis Le Roy, the scepticism of Montaigne's 'Apologie de Raimond Sebond', or Ronsard's pit-gazing *Derniers vers*, this crisis went far beyond the figure of the ghost. Indeed, a veritable horde of monsters, demons, witches, and prodigies joined ghosts as the expression of an outlook that, whether or not articulated in religious terms, was *eschatological* at root.[28] These were 'late' times—perhaps the very last—and the florescence of the 'insolite' that they brought in their train occasioned some of the most troubled, and troubling, documents of all European thought.[29]

Not at the beginning looking forward, but out on the end looking back: it is above all because of this temporal orientation that 'late [Renaissance]' has been preferred to the more up-to-date 'early [modern]'. This is not to say that, viewed from our own twenty-first-century perspective, the narratives that feature in this study bear no connection to what came after. The recent theoretical notion of 'spectrality' has at the very least its lexical

---

[28] On the extraordinary explosion of such phenomena in the second half of the sixteenth century, see Jean Céard's classic study, *La Nature et les prodiges: l'insolite au XVIe siècle en France* (Geneva: Droz, 1977).

[29] Terence Cave's *Pré-histoires: textes troublés au seuil de la modernité* (Geneva: Droz, 1999) provides an outstanding model for reading the anxieties just described. The front cover of Cave's book is adorned with an image drawn from the illustrations to Conti's *Mythologiae*. It is of a shrouded figure, not unlike a ghost.

roots in this era; the text that coined 'spectre', Pierre Le Loyer's *Quatre livres des spectres* (1586), is examined in detail in Chapter 4 of this book.[30] By the end of the same period today's readers may also begin to glimpse a number of narrative motifs recognisable from the nineteenth-century ghost narratives of Nodier, Gautier, and Potocki, or of Freud's theory of the Uncanny. One is the space of the haunted house—a new narrative scenography that emerged out of Protestant efforts to wrest control of lay domestic space (as described in Chapter 2). Another related preoccupation (described in Chapter 6) is an increasing association between ghosts and sexual secrets. The differing characterisations of male and female witnesses to ghosts, or the relationship between ghosts and male friendship, may also be of interest to students of gender and sexuality in later periods. In these and other ways it is hoped that readers with no specialist interest in the sixteenth and early seventeenth centuries may still derive some profit from what follows. In the end, though, this study has fought shy of trumpeting a founding moment or an epistemic shift. This is in large part a question of historical tact. The birth of the modern ghost story (if that is what it was) meant the death of so much else.

The book is divided into three parts. Part I ('Ghosts and Religion') considers the ghost as a figure within theological reflections on Purgatory, intercession, and the authority of the priest. Chapter 1 offers an overview of sixteenth-century religious debate around these topics, and traces the stakes of that debate back to the Gersonian tradition of *discretio spirituum*. Conducted through a blend of narrative exchange and exegetical polemic, the debates considered here establish important points of connection between ghosts and a range of intellectual and moral concerns explored in subsequent chapters: the nature of ghostly bodies, ubiquitism, the legitimacy of communing with the dead, and the memory of souls. Chapter 2 narrows its focus to two of the most important theological works to be published on ghosts in the second half of the sixteenth century: the Swiss minister Ludwig Lavater's *Trois livres des apparitions des esprits* and the *Psichologie* of the Franciscan Noël Taillepied. Both

---

[30] The idea of spectrality was first developed in J. Derrida, *Spectres de Marx: l'État de la dette, le travail du deuil et la nouvelle Internationale* (Paris: Éditions Galilée, 1993), and has since produced a plethora of theoretical reflections on ghosts. See, notably, N. Royle, 'Phantom Review', *Textual Practice*, 11 (1997), pp. 386–98; *Ghosts: Deconstruction, Psychoanalysis, History*, ed. by P. Buse and A. Stott (London: Macmillan, 1999). For an excellent survey of more recent developments, and the related notions of 'hauntology' and 'the phantom' (as theorized in particular by Nicolas Abraham and Maria Torok), see C. Davis, 'État présent: Hauntology, Spectres, and Phantoms', *French Studies*, 59 (3) (2005), pp. 373–9. See also, by the same author, *Haunted Subjects: Deconstruction, Psychoanalysis, and the Return of the Dead* (New York: Palgrave, 2007).

texts are considered as examples of what might be termed 'pastoral demonology'—a body of work concerned less with witchcraft and magic (as in juridical demonology) than the spiritual regulation of lay domestic space. Variously constructed as masculine (Lavater) or feminine (Taille-pied), that space—the haunted house—became the theatre in which the early modern reader must overcome the twin temptations of false doctrine and despair.

Part II ('Ghosts Beyond Religion') examines the return of the dead in non-theological contexts. In so doing it challenges the view, common among historians of Reformed societies, that religion was necessarily the dominant perspective from which ghosts were viewed in the period. Chapter 3 presents an overview of the increasingly large volume of secular writing on ghosts. It shows, first of all, how even a biblical episode such as the apparition of Samuel to Saul (I Samuel 28) becomes a fashionable topic among non-theologically trained writers, and is increasingly re-garded through the prism of classical necromancies such as those re-counted in Lucan's *Pharsalia* or the *Life* of Apollonius of Tyana. This chapter then goes on to explore some of the ways in which, through the rise of the bestselling *histoires prodigieuses*, ghosts begin to acquire other intellectual associations. These associations include, but are not limited to, those between ghosts and prodigies (Pierre Boaistuau), ghosts and friend-ship (François de Belleforest), and ghosts and stoicism (Bénigne Poisse-not). Chapter 4 develops this reflection on ghosts beyond theology with special reference to arguably the period's most important—and certainly most voluminous—treatise on ghosts and apparitions, Pierre Le Loyer's *Quatre livres des spectres*.

Part III ('Stories') takes up in detail the question of narrative. Rather than consider particular discursive frameworks (Chapters 1 and 3) or their particular instantiations in an author or authors (Chapters 2 and 4), this section takes two archetypal ghost narrative models and follows them as they move between discourses, authors, and texts. Both involve different conceptions of what constitutes, if anything, a ghostly body. Chapter 5 examines the common story in which a witness to an apparition assails it using a lance, spear, or sword. Occurring most notably in Rabelais's *Tiers Livre* and Ronsard's 'Les Daimons', this narrative motif mobilizes, and plays upon, a whole series of (principally) theological opinions according to which ghosts are invulnerable to physical violence. Chapter 6, staying with bodies, effects a move from violence to sex. In doing so it replays a shift of emphasis notable in the period itself. The rise of the secular ghost narrative described in Part II opened up a very different, and altogether more prurient, perspective on the twin theological concerns of female spirituality and private, domestic space considered in Part I. As a result, the story in which a (female) lover returns—in the body—to her living companion becomes a form of ghoulish erotica. Exploited notably by Le Loyer himself, as well as by François de Rosset and a number of early seventeenth-century pamphlets or *canards*, the theme of 'Revenant Lovers' brings us to the brink of the modern.

PART I

GHOSTS AND RELIGION

1

A Religious Controversy

GHOSTS AND PURGATORY

Ghosts in the Middle Ages were priestly business. Acting in concert with the clergy, their task was to promote solidarity between the living and the dead. The theological framework for this relationship was the doctrine of Purgatory.[1] Embryonic in the writings of Augustine and Gregory the Great, and developed further by Aquinas, Church teaching on Purgatory was formalized at the Councils of Lyon (1274) and Florence (1438–9). The doctrine held that, at the moment of death, the souls of only very few men and women deserved to proceed immediately to Paradise or Hell. A tiny number of holy personages, such as saints, might enter heaven at once, whereas those guilty of serious transgressions, such as sodomy or suicide, were damned without appeal. But the majority were guilty of 'light' or venial, rather than cardinal, sins: to borrow a memorable phrase from the twelfth-century *Vision of Tondal*, these men and women were 'the wycked but not very'.[2] Once their faint stains of indiscretion were purged away, it was believed, these souls would be admitted to the beatific vision. The term of their purgation varied as a function of their transgressions while alive. And because it was believed that remission for minor sins could be obtained through the offices of the living, dead souls would return as ghosts to plead for intercession.

As Jean-Claude Schmitt's excellent study of ghosts in the Middle Ages has shown, tales of such returns abound in medieval sermons, and in

---

[1] The bibliography on Purgatory in the Middle Ages is extensive. See in particular R. Ombres, *Theology of Purgatory* (Dublin: The Mercier Press, 1978), pp. 39–45; J. Le Goff, *La Naissance du Purgatoire* (Paris: Gallimard, 1981); M. Vovelle, *Les Ames du purgatoire, ou le travail du deuil* (Paris: Gallimard, 1996), pp. 18–92 (on the iconography of Purgatory); P. Marshall, *Beliefs and the Dead in Reformation England* (Oxford: Oxford University Press, 2002), pp. 6–46.

[2] The description is that offered by the angel to Tondal. See S. Greenblatt, *Hamlet in Purgatory* (Princeton: Princeton University Press, 2001), p. 62.

books of *miracula* and *mirabilia*.[3] Indeed, so extensive was the medieval clergy's attachment to stories of apparitions of the dead, Schmitt claims, that the Church effectively fostered a 'banalisation' of the ghost.[4] Ghost narrative in this period certainly conforms to an insistent model. First the dead soul would return, in various different guises, to request a favour of a living relative or friend. The details of this request might be specific to its own—perhaps troubled—history: the restitution of stolen goods, reburial, or the proper implementation of dying wishes. At other times, the ghost would demand more general remedies: requiem masses, almsgiving, penance, pilgrimage, or the paying of indulgences. The second phase of the story describes, often in careful detail, the requisite acts of redress or devotion performed by the living. Once action had been taken and the purgatorial term commuted, the souls would return, finally, to thank their intercessors. Hundreds of ghost tales in the period obey this simple threefold pattern. Whether this 'banalized' procedure, and its repetition in narrative, robbed ghosts of their power to frighten or disturb is doubtful, and remains a subject of debate among social historians of death.[5] But however imperfectly secured within what Schmitt terms (adapting a phrase of Philippe Ariès) an 'imaginaire apprivoisé', ghosts were certainly able to shoulder an important psychological burden for those mourning their dead.[6] As departed souls were unchained from the bonds of Purgatory, so those they left behind were freed from morbid attachments to the grave. Ghosts were the agents through which parishioners conducted the multiple transactions—emotional, social, and financial—that made up the work of mourning in late medieval Europe.

With the advent of the Reformation, the status of the ghost was irredeemably transformed. The Lutheran and Reformed churches struck hard at the doctrine of Purgatory, and viewed associated beliefs in return from the dead as little more than the crude instrument with which a

---

[3] J.-Cl. Schmitt, *Les Revenants: les vivants et les morts dans la société médiévale* (Paris: Gallimard, 1994); see also Le Goff, *Naissance du purgatoire*, pp. 241–6. On popular beliefs surrounding the return of the dead in the Middle Ages, see E. Morin, *L'Homme et la mort* (Paris: Seuil, 1970), pp. 132–56 (on 'la survie du double'); E. Le Roy Ladurie, *Montaillou*, ch. 26 ('Folklore et revenants'); C. Lecouteux and P. Marcq, *Les Esprits et les morts* (Paris: Champion, 1990); N. Caciola, 'Wraiths, Revenants, and Ritual'. For an excellent anthology of medieval ghost tales, see *Medieval Ghost Stories*, ed. by A. Joynes (Woodbridge: Boydell, 2001).

[4] Schmitt, *Revenants*, p. 161.

[5] R. A. Bowyer contrasts the domesticated ghosts of the Middle Ages with their later, more terrifying, counterparts in 'The Role of the Ghost-Story in Mediaeval Christianity' in *The Folklore of Ghosts*, ed. by H. R. Ellis Davidson and W. M. S. Russell (Cambridge, NJ: D. J. Brewer, 1981), pp. 177–92. Marshall dismisses this opposition in *Beliefs and the Dead*, p. 262.

[6] Ariès opposes 'la mort apprivoisée' of the earlier Middle Ages to 'la mort ensauvagée' of later periods, including our own. See P. Ariès, *L'Homme devant la mort*, 2 vols. (Paris: Seuil, 1977).

corrupt priesthood extended its influence into the afterlife.[7] The hopes and fears that ghosts engendered among the common people were denounced as the vehicle for a host of clerical abuses. Luther's Halloween protest against the much-despised traffic in indulgences, the ninety-five theses nailed to the door of the Castle Church in Wittenberg on 31 October 1517, was only the most famous in a long line of objections to ghosts and what they stood for. Protestant critics also accused the priesthood of exploiting popular belief in ghosts in elaborate exorcisms, lavish burials, and exorbitantly priced prayers or masses for the dead. Such objections both emerged from, and served to reinforce, the soteriological bedrock of Reformation thinking. Beliefs about Purgatory were fundamental to the question of how it was supposed that men were made 'right before God'. For Protestant theologians, the idea that the intercessions of the living might improve an individual's standing before his maker represented the worst kind of Pelagianism. Man was not justified before God by his works, and still less the works of others on his behalf; rather, justification was achieved, according to the famous Protestant slogan, *sola fide* (by faith alone). To the extent that their new strike against Purgatory obviated the need for institutional mediation, the Reformers marginalized ghosts, along with the clergy they once so lucratively served.

This sketchiest of outlines must put aside the complex question of how the new doctrine was actually received among the laity of Europe. As recent social historians of England and other Reformed societies have shown, the precise impact of Protestant teaching on lay attitudes to death and the afterlife is still a matter for debate. In the English context Keith Thomas and others have taught us that the Anglican Church would not have changed such deeply rooted beliefs and practices overnight, and was forced to settle for a centuries-long campaign of negotiation and compromise.[8] In France, where the dissemination of Protestant teaching was a perilous and uncertain business, the picture is no clearer. There, belief in Purgatorial apparitions was still encouraged in orthodox Church teaching. But it is difficult to imagine

---

[7] The clearest guide to the polemic in England is P. Marshall, 'Fear, Purgatory, and Polemic' in *Fear in Early Modern Society*, ed. by W. G. Naphy and P. Roberts (Manchester: Manchester University Press, 1997), pp. 150–66.

[8] See K. Thomas, *Religion and the Decline of Magic: Studies of Popular Beliefs in Sixteenth- and Seventeenth-Century England* (London: Weidenfeld and Nicolson, 1997; first ed. 1971), pp. 587–606; Marshall, *Beliefs and the Dead*, pp. 245–64. On the specific question of ghost belief in Anglican communities, see J. Bath, '"In the Divell's Likenesse": Interpretation and Confusion in Popular Ghost Belief' in *Early Modern Ghosts: Proceedings of the 'Early Modern Ghosts' Conference held at St. John's College, Durham University on 24 March 2001*, ed. by J. Newton and J. Bath (Durham: Centre for Seventeenth-Century Studies, 2002), pp. 70–8; B. Lewis, 'Protestantism, Pragmatism, and Popular Religion: A Case Study of Early Modern Ghosts' in *Early Modern Ghosts*, pp. 79–91.

that ordinary men and women, otherwise faithful to the preaching of their priests, were not shaken by the mockeries of Protestants among them. Whatever the real reception of theological debate within the lay community, learned observers were in no doubt that, ideologically speaking, the return of the dead had become something of a crux. In 1575, François de Belleforest remarks that although belief in ghosts constitutes in itself 'une chose indifferente'—that is, it is not and never has been an article of Catholic faith—such belief 'traine apres soy une queüe qui n'est pas de petite importance'.[9] This is an understatement: the question of whether the dead could come back to the living went right to the heart of how man might save himself.

The *queüe* or 'tail' described by Belleforest, and the swathe it cuts through the apologetic, polemical, satirical, and exegetical writing of the period, is the focus of this chapter. Underlying all these modes of discussion was the troubled question of ownership. To whom did the figure of the ghost—and by extension the community of the dead—rightfully belong? To understand early modern claims upon such ownership, it will first be necessary to take another backwards glance: towards late medieval discussions of *discretio spirituum*, from which the clergy of that period claimed to derive their authority on apparitions more generally. As we shall see shortly, the *discretio spirituum* was primarily concerned in that period less with ghosts than with discerning the spiritual agencies at work in visions and mystical prophecy, that is with the task of distinguishing between divine and diabolical possession. But in spite of this difference of emphasis the ideals and principles of discernment would exert a considerable influence on the Catholic theology of early modern ghosts, and on the Reformers' attempts to dispute that theology. The following section examines the ideological foundations of priestly *discretio* as expressed by one of its leading proponents, Jean Gerson, and some aspects of its legacy in sixteenth-century France.

DISCRETIO SPIRITUUM AND THE MEDIEVAL LEGACY

'Try the Spirits': Jean Gerson

Late medieval theologians derived their authority on visions from the Pauline idea of *discretio spirituum*, or the 'discerning of spirits'.[10] This

---

[9] P. Boaistuau, F. de Belleforest, and others, *Histoires prodigieuses*, 6 vols. in 2 (Paris: veuve G. Cavellat, 1597–8), III, p. 359.

[10] The tradition of *discretio spirituum* has its roots in the early Church. For a succinct summary and bibliography, see J. T. Lienhard, 'On "Discernment of Spirits" in the Early Church', *Theological Studies*, 41 (3) (1980), pp. 505–29.

derivation was founded on three key scriptural *loci*, all tirelessly repeated in pre-modern discussions of the matter. According to Paul, Satan often transforms himself into 'an angel of light' (2 Corinthians 11:14). As a consequence, those visited by visions must 'believe not every spirit, but try the spirits, whether they are of God: because many false prophets are gone out into the world' (1 John 4:1). But the power to try (*probare*) the spirits is not given to everyone. Only those possessed of *discretio spirituum*, one of the charismata, or spiritual gifts, enumerated by Paul (1 Corinthians 12:10), can be trusted to distinguish reliably between good and evil spirits. A priest inherits the gift of discernment as he is anointed to his office. It falls to him, therefore, to pronounce on the divine, or diabolical, origin of visitations to his flock and, as their confessor, to decide what course of action should be taken when they occur. The shape of this argument, with its basis in the Pauline and Johannine epistles, is ubiquitous in theological writings across Europe in the later Middle Ages. Nancy Caciola's recent *Discerning Spirits: Divine and Demonic Possession in the Middle Ages* has provided a rich account of this discernment corpus, from the early 'proto-discernment' treatises of Henry of Freimar or Nicholas de Dinkesbuhl, to the late fourteenth- and early fifteenth-century works of Henry of Langenstein and Pierre d'Ailly.[11]

Most celebrated of all, however, are Jean Gerson's two short texts on the subject, *De distinctione verarum visionum a falsis* (1401) and *De probatione spirituum* (1415).[12] Gerson's tracts were composed against the background of a furious polemic over the legitimacy of the Avignon papacy, fuelled in no small part by the visions of a lay mystic, Bridget of Sweden, portending its imminent collapse.[13] Following her death in 1373, Bridget had become, in Caciola's words, 'the first test case for the discernment of spirits, for her death initiated an intensive debate at the highest levels of

---

[11] N. Caciola, *Discerning Spirits: Divine and Demonic Possession in the Middle Ages* (Ithaca: Cornell University Press, 2003). See also Schmitt, *Les Revenants*, pp. 182–6; R. Voaden, *God's Words, Women's Voices: The Discernment of Spirits in the Writing of Late-Medieval Women Visionaries* (York: York Medieval Press, 1999), especially Ch. 2 ('Seducing Spirits').

[12] Complete translations can be found in P. Boland, *The Concept of 'Discretio spirituum' in John Gerson's 'De probatione spirituum' and 'De distinctione verarum visionum a falsis'* (Washington D.C.: The Catholic University of America Press, 1959), pp. 25–38 (*De probatione*) and pp. 76–145 (*De distinctione*). All English references are to this edition. Latin references (provided in italics where relevant) are to J. Gerson, *Joannis Gersonii doctoris theologi et Cancellarii Parisiensis opera omnia*, 5 vols. (Antwerp: sumptibus societatis, 1706), I, pp. 37–43 (*De probatione*), and I, pp. 43–59 (*De distinctione*).

[13] For more detailed historical background, see Caciola, *Discerning Spirits*, pp. 274–319; C. Roth, *Discretio spirituum: kriterien geistlicher Unterscheidung bei Johannes Gerson* (Würzburg: Echter, 2001); D. Elliott, 'Seeing Double: John Gerson, the Discernment of Spirits, and Joan of Arc' in *The American Historical Review*, 107 (2002), pp. 26–54.

ecclesiastical culture over whether she was a true saint who prophesied in God's voice or a herald of the Antichrist possessed by the Devil—and how one might tell the difference'.[14] The difference certainly mattered: it is a sign of Bridget's divisive power that the visionary had been canonized no fewer than three times, in 1391, 1415, and 1419, by three different pontiffs.

Gerson wrote his most influential work on discernment, *De probatione spirituum*, for submission to the second phase of the deliberations on Bridget at the Council of Constance in 1415. Alarmed at the growth of unfettered lay female spirituality, the author, then chancellor of the University of Paris, cautions his fellow clergymen against the prophecies of mystics. He begins in familiar terms by describing the qualifications required of those who wish to try the spirits. It is possible in some measure, he claims, to acquire the requisite knowledge through study of Scripture or private revelation. However, neither of these methods, which he calls—respectively—academic (*doctrinalis*) and empirical (*experimentalis*), are adequate in themselves.[15] Rather, he goes on, the would-be spiritual investigator must also have received the gift of what 'the Apostle called the discernment of spirits' (*quod Apostolus nominavit discretionem spirituum*).[16] This third method Gerson terms official (*officialis*), and is bestowed upon the clergyman by virtue of his office (*ex officio*).[17]

Having established the authority of the clerical investigator, Gerson moves on to the classification of the spirits. The task of *discretio spirituum* is to distinguish between four categories: the spirit of God (*spiritus deus*), the good angel (*spiritus angelus bonus*), the evil angel or demon (*spiritus angelus malus*), and the spirit issuing from the witness's own—human— nature (*spiritus humanus*).[18] In order to decide which of these has taken possession of the visionary, the clergyman must ponder six questions:

Quis?   Who has the revelation?
Quid?   What does the revelation mean?
Quare?   Why is it said to have taken place?
Cui?   To whom did the witness look for advice?
Qualiter? What kind of life does the visionary lead?
Unde?   Whence does the revelation originate?[19]

Later we will see how, in the early modern period, the attention of those wishing to try the spirits falls primarily on the external characteristics—shape,

[14] Caciola, *Discerning Spirits*, p. 278.
[15] Boland, *Concept of 'Discretio spirituum'*, p. 25; Gerson, *Opera omnia*, I, p. 38.
[16] Boland, pp. 26–7; Gerson, I, p. 38.   [17] Boland, p. 27; Gerson, I, p. 38.
[18] Boland, p. 38; Gerson, I, pp. 42–3.   [19] Boland, p. 30; Gerson, I, p. 39.

colour, sound, gesture—of apparitions. It is notable in Gerson's sequence, by contrast, that the greater part of his focus rests on the witness him- or (more usually) herself. Who is she? Why does she allege she has experienced a vision? In whom did she choose to confide? What kind of person is she? Gerson affords this last enquiry (*qualiter?*) especial weight, going so far as to urge an investigation of the 'individual's entire personality: his education, habits, likes, associates; also, whether he is rich or poor, for in the one we may suspect pride or secret sensuality, in the other, deception.'[20] So preoccupied is Gerson with the question of *qualiter?* that at moments in the treatises it seems to have eclipsed all the others. Later in the *De probatione spirituum*, attempting a further, pithier, definition of *discretio spirituum*, he simply states: 'Discernment of spirits ascertains the kind and manner of life led by the person who claims to have visions' (*quae visiones se habere dicit*).[21]

As is suggested by the word 'claims' in the definition just quoted, at the heart of discernment lies a hermeneutics of suspicion.[22] The advantages of that hermeneutics, based on unforgiving scrutiny of the visionary narrator, are especially clear in the context of the campaign to discredit Bridget. For if neither the sensual rich nor the deceiving poor are above suspicion, then women, Gerson would claim, are least trustworthy of all. Invoking a favourite commonplace of the discernment tradition, he repeats the warning from Paul's second epistle to Timothy against 'silly women [*mulierculae*] laden with sins, led away with divers lusts, ever learning, and never able to come to the knowledge of the truth' (2 Timothy 3:6–7).[23] Towards the end of his tract Gerson expands upon the passage in 2 Timothy by describing how a woman 'itches with curiosity', and is often prone to 'continual conversations', entering into 'lengthy accounts of her visions'.[24] He claims that there is 'scarcely any plague more harmful or incurable than this': even if nothing more sinister occurred than a great waste of precious time, 'it would give abundant satisfaction to the devil'.[25] So pervasive is the misogyny of *De probatione spirituum*, Caciola has argued, that Gerson goes further than his precursors in the discernment tradition by implicitly diabolising all female prophecy.[26]

Gerson's other tract on discernment, *De distinctione verarum visionum a falsis*, seeks to turn this suspicion of women mystics to more positive ideological account. In it he shows how potentially errant female spirituality

[20] Boland, p. 30; Gerson, I, p. 39. [21] Boland, p. 36; Gerson, I, p. 40.
[22] The same point is made, in different terms, in Voaden, *God's Words, Women's Voices*, pp. 66–71.
[23] Boland, p. 37; Gerson, I, p. 42. [24] Boland, p. 36; Gerson, I, p. 42.
[25] Boland, p. 36; Gerson, I, p. 42. [26] Caciola, *Discerning Spirits*, pp. 302–6.

might be brought under the control of male ecclesiastical authority. Gerson lists a number of virtues (humility, patience, charity, love of truth, etcetera) that the witness must exhibit in order that her story be considered trustworthy. The most important of these Gerson calls, tellingly, *discretio*. This *discretio* is not that of *discretio spirituum*. By discretion here Gerson explains that he intends primarily 'flexibility', 'willingness in accepting counsel', or, in other words, subservience to the will of one's confessor. This pliability is expressed in various forms of moderation.[27] Gerson makes especially clear his distaste for excessive fasting, for example (a practice long associated with Bridget of Sweden). An associated, and arguably more important, requirement of this secondary—feminine—*discretio* is that the visionary remain moderate in her words, and refrain in particular from speaking of her experience to anyone but her confessor. Here the meaning of 'discretion' is close to its modern sense of 'the ability to keep a secret'.[28] Both for Gerson and generations of his successors, the model here is provided by none other than the Virgin mother herself. In contrast to the shepherds who spread the news of Christ's birth announced to them by the angel Gabriel, Mary did not rush to tell others but 'kept in mind all these words, pondering them in her heart' (Luke 2:19).[29] Her example is doubled by another witness to Gabriel, namely her cousin Elizabeth, mother of John the Baptist. Gerson explains that neighbours continued to call Elizabeth's son by his given name Zachary (i.e. after Elizabeth's husband) 'because his parents had not gossiped or talked lightly about the boy's name'.[30] In this way Mary and Elizabeth's discreet refusals to boast of their visionary experiences provide an exemplary corrective to Paul's 'silly women'.

Taken together, Gerson's twin tracts on discernment form something of a loop in which, thanks to its double meaning, *discretio* is effectively

---

[27] Boland, pp. 86–92; Gerson, ɪ, pp. 48–50. The sense of *discretio* as 'moderation' is already found in the *Rule* of St Benedict (c. 480–547), where it appears to have been derived in turn from Cassian (c. 360–430/5). Lienhard writes that '*Discretio* has come to be considered the typical Benedictine virtue'. See 'On "Discernment of Spirits" in the Early Church', p. 527.

[28] Gerson's specification of *discretio*'s meaning to the ability to keep a secret was thus not as self-evident as it may appear to modern readers. This sense of 'discretion' developed later in France, and becomes especially visible in seventeenth-century discussions of courtly manners, *honnêteté*, and the art of polite conversation. See M. Maître-Dufour, 'Une anti-curiosité: la discrétion chez Mlle de Scudery et dans la littérature mondaine (1648–1696)' in *Curiosité et Libido Sciendi de la Renaissance aux Lumières*, ed. by S. Houdard and N. Jacques-Chaquin, 1 vol. in 2 (Paris: ENS editions, 1998), pp. 333–58.

[29] Boland, p. 83; Gerson, ɪ, p. 46.

[30] Boland, p. 85; Gerson, ɪ, p. 47.

inscribed within the terms of its own definition.[31] We saw earlier how *De probatione spirituum* lodges *discretio* in the figure of the priest, and makes *discretio* a matter of discerning the person and habits of the witness. On reading the *De distinctione verarum visionum a falsis*, however, it transpires that discretion is no longer only a requirement for confessors, who must know how to discern between true and false prophets, but also for would-be prophets, who must be able to discern between true and false confessors. This becomes a convenient arrangement within which the discerning clergyman is defined as he who ratifies only the visions of the discreet witness, the discreet witness as she who confides her secret only in the figure of the discerning priest. It takes one to know one: looked at in this way, the encounter between confessor and mystic is clearly regimented as a mutually validating union of male ecclesiastical discernment on the one hand and moderate female lay spirituality on the other. Gerson's writing on the subject discloses the self-reinforcing, indeed intensely circular, logic of late medieval spiritual discernment.

This logic was to serve Gerson and his colleagues well, helping (as he saw it) to restore masculine clerical authority to an all too 'effeminate age'.[32] As we shall see in the next section, the notion of *discretio spirituum* was one to which early modern Catholic theologians would continue to appeal for their authority in matters of not only visions (as in Gerson), but also apparitions of the dead.

Mouvements, Marques: Pastoral and Demonological Discernment

The *discretio spirituum* of the late Middle Ages, especially in its Gersonian form, exerted a lasting influence on the theology of early modern France, though its various strands are not easily disentangled. As religious and political contexts shifted over time, so too did discernment's theatres of application. As we have seen, Gerson's early fifteenth-century tracts on the subject emerged out of the debate over women's prophecy during the Great Schism. During the sixteenth century, arguments over female visionaries and mystics receded, probably as a result of the more pressing threat to the Church posed by evangelical and Calvinist Reformers. Some inspired women, such as the Rheno-Flemish mystics or Teresa of Ávila in Spain, continued to flourish outside France. But in France itself the

---

[31] On the duality of *discretio*, see also M. Sluhovsky, *Believe not Every Spirit: Possession, Mysticism, and Discernment in Early Modern Catholicism* (Chicago: University of Chicago Press, 2007), p. 172.
[32] See Caciola, *Discerning Spirits*, pp. 307–9.

relationship between female mysticism and clerical discernment would only resurface with the so-called 'illuminist' circle of Mme Acarie and Pierre de Bérulle in the early years of the seventeenth century, and later in the work of Jean-Joseph Surin, Madame Guyon, and Antoinette Bourgignon.[33] To the extent that *discretio spirituum* originated as a response to the female mystic, the story of early modern discernment thus appears an interrupted history. Far from disappearing from the sixteenth-century scene, however, *discretio spirituum* shifted into other spheres. As it did so, the Gersonian sense of 'spirit', and its associations with true and false prophecy, also began to change.

It is possible to distinguish two sixteenth-century developments of Gersonian *discretio spirituum*: these might be termed the pastoral and demonological strands. (A third, hybrid branch—which I have termed 'pastoral demonology'—is discussed in Chapter 2.) In the first, the focus of discernment became the inner spiritual life of the ordinary layman or, especially, laywoman. This form of 'pastoral discernment' is a feature of much Counter-Reformation writing, most notably Ignatius of Loyola's *Spiritual Exercises* and the devotional manuals of François de Sales.[34] A less well-known example is the Italian Serafino da Fermo's short *Trattato della discretione*, translated into French in 1581 as *Brief discours de la différence des esprits*. Composed in the vernacular and dedicated to a lay noble-woman, Gioanna Ursina de Gonzaga, Da Fermo's little treatise is a response not to the oracles of female visionaries but to the false prophets of the Reformation, and the spiritual uncertainty to which his flock had been exposed.

In the early part of his work Da Fermo voices an eschatalogical anxiety prevalent in Catholic writing of the period: that the spread of heresy marked the approach of the last times. One indication of this, he explains, is the alarming increase in demonic activity, 'par ce que nous sommes proches de voir preparer le siege et la venuë de l'Antechrist'.[35] Faced with

---

[33] On the discernment of spirits and seventeenth-century mysticism, see S. Ferber, *Demonic Possession and Exorcism in Early Modern France* (London: Routledge, 2004) pp. 91–4 (on illuminism) and pp. 140–7.

[34] On Ignatian discernment, still practised today, see J. J. Toner, *A Commentary on Saint Ignatius' Rules for the Discernment of Spirits* (St Louis: The Institute of Jesuit Sources, 1981) and T. M. Gallagher, *The Discernment of Spirits: An Ignatian Guide for Everyday Living* (New York: Crossroad, 2005). On discernment in François de Sales, see F. Charmot, *Ignatius Loyola and Francis de Sales*, trans. by M. Renelle (London: Herder, 1966), Ch. 6 ('Discernment of Spirits').

[35] S. de Ferme, *Brief discours de la différence des esprits, recueilly des oeuvres de Reverend Pere Seraphin de Ferme, chanoine regulier et predicateur excellent*, trans. by N. Dany (Rheims: Jean de Foigny, and Paris: Nicholas Chesneau, 1581), sig. Av[r]. The Italian original appeared in Venice in 1541.

this demonic presence, Da Fermo urges upon Gioanna and his readers a form of spiritual watchfulness, such that they might always be ready to 'bien discerner entre le mouvement de Dieu d'avec celuy de l'esprit maling'.[36] Formulations such as this, scattered throughout the treatise, recast the spirits of Gersonian *discretio spirituum* in a slightly different mould. In Gerson, to distinguish between spirits was to discern the divine or diabolic origins of mystic prophecy. In Da Fermo, spirits are to be understood rather as a disturbance ('mouvement') in daily moral life. Here spiritual influences have become internalized as vicious or virtuous impulses to be resisted or embraced. While writers like Da Fermo and St François preserved Gerson's interest in the regulation of female spirituality, their conception of spiritual agency thus marked something of a shift. Understood in this way, pastoral discernment becomes an exercise in domestic spiritual discipline, which a woman would undertake with the guide of her confessor. (We shall see in the closing chapters of this book how, in the hands of later secular writers, the connection between the spiritual encounter and the everyday desires of ordinary women would find itself exploited for titillating, rather than edifying, ends.)

A second development of *discretio spirituum* in this period can be found in late sixteenth-century demonology. Here the object of attention is not women who claim divine inspiration (such as Bridget of Sweden), or the spiritually uncertain laymen and women of pastoral discernment, but those accused of witchcraft. Perhaps it is unsurprising that Gersonian *discretio spirituum*, with its implicit diabolisation of female spirituality, should have branched out in this direction. Nancy Caciola concludes her *Discernment of Spirits* with the suggestion that 'witchcraft is an extreme but logical conclusion of the shifts in the interpretation of possessed behaviours engendered by the discernment of spirits', arguing that the discourses of demonology and discernment are both predicated on the same misogynist fear of inversion in the sexual hierarchy.[37] Caciola supports her case by remarking on the centrality of Gersonian *discretio* to the early witchcraft theory of Johannes Nider. Picking up the same thread in the second half of the sixteenth century, she also notes that French publishers began to print the *Probatione spirituum* together with Jacob Sprenger's seminal textbook on demonology, the *Malleus maleficarum*. While it is possible that Caciola overemphasizes the place of misogyny in the formulation of early modern demonology (to which it is hardly specific in the period), there is no mistaking the marked appropriation of *discretio*

---

[36] Ibid., sig. 19ᵛ.   [37] Caciola, *Discernment of Spirits*, p. 318.

spirituum in writing on witchcraft and the pact.[38] The demonological works of late-century theologians, such as Sébastien Michaëlis, Pierre Crespet, Martin Delrio, and Juan Maldonado (known in France as Maldonat), all continue to employ the language of discernment.[39]

Demonological discernment differs from both its Gersonian and pastoral variants in two important respects. One again concerns the question of what is meant by the 'spirits' of *discretio spirituum*. Most demonologists approached the term not as an agent of mystical possession (as in Gerson) or of inner spiritual disturbance (as in Da Fermo), but as an external apparition apprehended through the senses. The reports of witches' confessions circulating as a result of the persecutions, many of which contained vivid accounts of demonic appearances, doubtless contributed to this shift. In their stories, and for those tasked with interpreting them, spirits were beings one could see, hear, smell, and even touch. Connected to this change in emphasis were a number of implications for the ways in which spirits were investigated. Whereas the focus of Gersonian and pastoral discernment rested exclusively on the personal virtues and habits of a witness, the attention of demonological discernment was drawn increasingly towards the external characteristics of the spirit. And whereas Gerson proposed six questions (*quis? quid? quare? cui? qualiter? unde?*), demonological *discretio* usually concentrates its focus on four aspects, or 'marques', by which apparitions might be discerned. Although not categorized at the time according to any stable terminological scheme, it is nonetheless possible to identify a recurrent implicit typology: this referred commonly to affect, form, comportment, and doctrine.

The capucin friar Noël Taillepied provides a typical example of this scheme in his 1588 *Psichologie, ou traité des apparitions des esprits*.[40] *Affect* concerns the emotional impact of an apparition on the witness. Fear giving way to consolation or joy indicates the presence of a good spirit, Taillepied argues; the reverse should make us wary of an evil apparition. Inasmuch as discernment through affect locates the spirit's identity internally, that is within the emotional life of the witness, it shares certain features with its medieval and pastoral variants. Unlike this first 'marque', however, the

---

[38] On the sometimes oversimplified relationship between demonology and misogyny, see Clark, *Thinking with Demons*, ch. 8 ('Women and Witchcraft').

[39] S. Michaëlis, *Pneumalogie, ou discours des esprits, en tant qu'il est de besoing pour entendre et resouldre la matiere difficile des sorciers* (Paris: Guillaume Bichon, 1587); P. Crespet, *Deux livres de la hayne de Sathan* (Paris: G. de la Noüe, 1590); M. Delrio, *Disquisitionum magicarum libri sex* (Louvain: G. Rivius, 1599); J. Maldonat, *Traicté des anges et demons*, trans. and ed. by F. de la Borie (Paris: F. Huby, 1605).

[40] See N. Taillepied, *Psichologie, ou traité de l'apparition des esprits* (Rouen: Jean Osmont, 1602, first ed. Paris: Guillaume Bichon, 1588), pp. 287–8.

second, third, and fourth elicit an increasingly forensic scrutiny of the spirit itself, making the object of study its colour, shape, sounds, words, and deeds. To this extent discernment becomes external in its focus. *Form* denotes the guise in which the spirit appears before the witness. Taillepied explains that benign spirits are usually thought to be white in colour, with angels taking the form of doves, lambs, and saintly personages; lions, bears, dogs, toads, snakes, and cats usually indicate the presence of an evil spirit. *Comportment* bears on the behaviour of the spirit towards the witness, and requires close attention to posture, countenance, and gesture. Finally, *doctrine* involves the question of how far this behaviour, and the spirit's instruction to the witness, obeys or diverges from the teachings of the Church.

The other respect in which demonological discernment differed from its variants was in its categorisation of spirits. Like Gersonian and pastoral discernment, demonological *discretio spirituum* aimed to differentiate between angels and demons. But it also sought to distinguish between both of these and a category not discussed explicitly in either of the other discernment traditions: namely ghosts, or souls returned from the dead. The task of distinguishing between ghosts and demons was especially important, since it could sometimes mean the difference between salvation and perdition. The Limousin priest Claude Durand issues a characteristic caution when he writes that 'il faut apporter beaucoup de prudence lors qu'une ame revient'.[41] The demon often tricks men under a mask of religion and piety; consequently, those visited by spirits of the dead, he urges, must 'consulter les hommes prudents et spirituels qui peuvent avoir la discretion des espritz'.[42]

A vivid illustration of this principle in action occurred in 1566, when a young girl from Laon, Nicole Obry, was possessed while visiting her grandfather's grave. Obry had not long been at the graveside when a demon raised the old man's body up, told her that he was suffering in Purgatory, and asked her to recite prayers for his soul. When she granted this request, and thereby showed herself complicit with the Devil's wishes, he left the old man's corpse and possessed her body in turn. What happened next is well documented, as people flocked from all over Europe to watch the successful exorcism performed at Laon Cathedral.[43] But the primal scene of Obry's possession continued to trouble demonological commentators. Jean Maldonat, lecturing at Clermont a few years later

[41] C. Durand, *Le Purgatoire des fideles defuncts* (Poitiers: Anthoine Mesnier, 1605), p. 252.
[42] Ibid., p. 252.
[43] On Obry's possession, see I. D. Backus, *Le miracle de Laon: le déraisonnable, le raisonnable, l'apocalyptique et le politique dans les récits du miracle de Laon, 1566–1578* (Paris: Vrin, 1994); Ferber, *Demonic Possession*, pp. 23–39; Sluhovsky, *Believe not Every Spirit*, pp. 19–23.

in 1570–1, cites it as perhaps the most notorious instance of the change-
ling's powers of deception and disguise. It was also a conclusive indication
that neither the *vulgaire* (common people) nor women (except the Virgin
Mary, for Maldonat as for Gerson the exception that proves the rule) were
reliable discerners: Obry had taken a demon for a ghost.

Even for the experts, Obry's grandfather (or the Devil in his guise)
remained a problematic apparition, since interpreting this figure hinged
on the broader question of Purgatory. So far in this discussion discernment has featured as an exclusively Catholic notion. So it was. Demonological writers from the Reformed Churches, such as Lambert Daneau,
never employ the language of discretion (except ironically), viewing it as a
form of priestly self-promotion. This is not to say that Protestant writers
did not attempt to distinguish between good and evil spirits. Indeed, in
many cases their conclusions are identical. For instance, when Daneau
reports the case of a young witch whose familiar first appeared to her as 'un
homme laid noir et ord', he would have been every bit as likely to have
'discerned' a demonic presence in this figure as his Catholic counterparts.[44] Here, as in many questions relating to witchcraft and the pact,
sectarian difference counted for relatively little.[45] With ghosts such as
Obry's grandfather, however, matters were more difficult. This spirit
could not be classified according to the predictable dictates of colour,
and did not choose its shape from the standard demonological bestiary of
dogs, snakes, toads, and cats. Nor was this Paul's 'angel of light'. To return
to the last of Taillepied's four 'marques', the only clue to be discerned
raised the vexed question of doctrine.

Given the theological differences that divided Protestants and Catholics
in the period, to make doctrine a criterion of discernment was merely to
beg the question. By appearing as a ghost from Purgatory and requesting
prayers for the dead, Satan had been able to exploit the young girl's
Catholic piety to take possession of her body. For commentators faithful
to traditional Church teaching, the Devil's concern to undermine faith in
Catholic precept only served to confirm its fundamental truth. Furthermore, it was only because ghosts exist and ask for intercession, they
claimed, that the demon chose to make its approach in that form rather
than another. Protestant theologians reached the inverse conclusion: any
spirit found promulgating popish doctrine could forthwith be denounced
as demonic through and through. In cases such as Obry's there was no

---

[44] L. Daneau, *Deux traitez nouveaux . . . le premier touchant les sorciers . . . le second contient une brève remonstrance sur les jeux de cartes et de dez* [1574] (n.p: 1579), p. 123.
[45] On the relative unimportance of sectarian difference in early modern demonology, see
Clark, *Thinking with Demons*, ch. 35 ('Protestant Witchcraft, Catholic Witchcraft').

need for Protestant 'discretion', since the Reformed view of spirits exclud-
ed the very possibility that the dead might come back to the living. Later
on in this book we shall consider some of the ways in which the very
intractability of this binary dispute, whereby one party merely inverts the
propositions of the other, encouraged those outside theology to suggest
new modes of thinking about ghosts in the second half of the sixteenth
century.[46] But first it will be necessary to examine some of the ways in
which debate over ghosts was conducted in the early years of the Reformation. There we shall see cases of *discretio spirituum* taking on an added
urgency, as priestly practice tried to stave off the Protestant challenge.

NARRATIVE POLEMIC

Discretio in Action: Montalembert's
Merveilleuse Hystoire (1528)

The early years of the Reformation in France produced no theoretical mono-
graphs on the question of ghosts. Even in Europe more generally, it seems not
to have been until Johannes Rivius's *De spectris et apparitionibus umbrarum*
of 1541, or Peter Martyr's polemic on the raising of Samuel (1564), that the
subject takes shape as a discrete intellectual concern.[47] In the absence of
specialist treatises, one prominent medium for debate was narrative exchange,
between Catholic accounts of hauntings supposed to prove the truth of
ghosts and Protestant debunkings that sought to undermine them.

One early Catholic apology for apparitions of the dead, and a powerful
example of Gerson's *discretio* in action, was Adrien de Montalembert's *La
Merveilleuse Hystoire de l'esperit qui nagueres s'est apparu au monastere des
religieuses de sainct pierre de lyon*, published in Paris by G. de Bossozel in
1528.[48] Little is known of Montalembert, who simply describes himself as

[46] On 'inversion', see especially Chapter 2, pp. 97–9.

[47] J. Rivius, *De Conscientia libri III... Eiusdem de spectris et apparitionibus umbrarum,
seu de veteri superstitione liber I* (Leipzig, 1541); P. M. Vermigli, *In Samuelis prophetae libros
duos... commentarii* (Zurich: C. Froschauer, 1564).

[48] This text has received relatively little attention. It was the subject of some interest in
the mid eighteenth century, Nicolas Lenglet Dufresnoy having published it in his *Recueil de
dissertations anciennes et nouvelles, sur les apparitions, les visions et les songes*, 4 vols. (Avignon:
J. N. Leloup, 1752), I, pp. 1–90. See also A. Gachet d'Artigny, *Nouveaux mémoires
d'histoire, de critique et de littérature*, 7 vols. (Paris: Debure l'aîné, 1749–56), VII,
pp. 175–256. For a nineteenth-century reading, see S. Clerc, 'Un exorcisme à Lyon au
XVIᵉ siècle' in *Revue du Lyonnais: esquisses physiques, morales et historiques*, ed. by L. Boitel
(Lyons: L. Boitel, 1835), II, pp. 81–9. Moshe Sluhovsky provides a brief account in *Believe
not Every Spirit*, pp. 17–19.

an *aumosnier* in the court of François I. Housed in a fifty-six-page quarto and accompanied by sixteen woodcut illustrations, his text purports to offer the true account of a young nun haunted by the ghost of her best friend. Judging by contemporary historical sources (some of which are drawn on here), it appears to have at least some basis in fact.

The setting for Montalembert's story is the Abbey of Saint-Pierre-les-Nonnains in Lyon (today the site of the Musée des Beaux Arts). Following its reformation in 1524, this beleaguered institution was still struggling to restore its reputation among a population long scandalized by the life of its nuns.[49] One of the sisters who left at the time of the reform, taking with her a number of valuables from the sacristy, was Alis de Tésieux. Once outside, Alis sold first her loot and then, when the money ran out, her body. It was not long before she was struck down by a venereal disease. Horribly disfigured, Alis removed to an isolated village where, repenting to the Virgin and praying for her soul, she died 'habondonnee par tout le monde'.[50]

Two years later in the spring of 1526, Alis's ghost begins to haunt a young nun who had stayed behind at Saint-Pierre, Anthoinette de Grolée.[51] The spirit cannot be seen, but first announces itself to Anthoinette by kissing her on the lips as she lies in bed; the dead nun then accompanies the young girl wherever she goes, making her presence felt with a series of raps under the floor. Concerned at the disturbances, the Abbess of Saint-Pierre calls in Barthélémy du Bois, acting deputy to the absent Archbishop of Lyon.[52] Du Bois arrives, accompanied by the author, Montalembert, to conjure the troubled spirit. After the dead nun's remains are returned to the abbey, and following a long series of 'benedictions, excommunications, interdictions, coniurations, interrogations, oraisons, suffrages et

---

[49] The royal decree ordering the abbey's reform was issued on 29 October 1524. See *Catalogue des actes de François Ier*, 10 vols. (Paris: Imprimerie Nationale, 1887–1908), v, p. 622.

[50] Montalembert, *Merveilleuse Hystoire*, sig. Cii^r.

[51] The text describes Anthoinette as 'natifve du Daulphiné', though the Grolée name was well known in Lyon at this time. The early seventeenth-century historian of Lyon, Claude de Rubys, alludes to a 'rue de Grolée' and a 'hôtel de Grolée' in the city; see his *Histoire veritable de la ville de Lyon* (Lyon: Bonaventure Nugo, 1604), p. 313. The genealogist Samuel Guichenon mentions a Jean-Philippe de Grolée, 'aumônier de François Ier', who may have been personally known to Montalembert. Guichenon also refers to two sisters, Philiberte and Jeanne de Grolée, as having been nuns at Saint-Pierre in the 1520s. I have found no record of Anthoinette. See S. Guichenon, *Histoire de Bresse et de Bugey* (Lyon: Jean Anthoine Huguetan and Marc Anthoine Ravaud, 1650), p. 115.

[52] The Archbishop of Lyon in 1526 was François de Rohan. According to one nineteenth-century historian, his suffragant was Barthélémy de Lucques, and Montalembert has mistakenly translated his name, Du Bois, from Latin *de luco* (i.e. 'wood'). See M. A. Péricaud, *Notice sur François de Rohan, Archévêque de Lyon* (Lyon: A. Vingtrinier, 1854), p. 24 n. 1.

absolutions', many of which Montalembert reproduces (in both Latin and French), the soul of Alis de Tésieux is finally released into Purgatory.[53] Now appearing in visible form, larger than in life and surrounded by light, she bids Anthoinette and the nuns goodbye. Thirty-three deafening knocks ring out from the abbey, representing each of the thirty-three years Alis had been condemned to spend in Purgatory, a sentence now commuted to just thirty-three days.

Though never explicitly invoking the priestly prerogative of *discretio spirituum*, the *Merveilleuse Hystoire* remains nonetheless an exemplary performance of clerical authority, most notably in its appropriation and validation of private (female) supernatural experience. In many respects Montalembert embodies the ideal practitioner of Gersonian discernment, and Anthoinette de Grolée its ideal witness. The haunting of Anthoinette begins in the intimate space of the girl's bedchamber, as the ghost plants a kiss on her lips: 'luy fut advys que quelque chose luy levoit son queuvre-chef tout bellement, et luy faisoit au front le signe de la croix, puys doulcement et souef en la bouche la baisoit'.[54] 'Let him kiss me with the kisses of his mouth' (Song of Solomon 1:2): this *osculum oris*, something of whose sensuousness Montalembert renders in his phonemes ('doulcement et souef en la bouche'), belongs to a rich mystical tradition deriving its authority from the Song of Songs.[55] Anthoinette would have doubtless been aware of this tradition, central as it had long been in promoting the conventual union between Christ and his Christ-brides. But in spite of this sanctified heritage, she remains exemplarily discreet in her response to the apparition, not rushing to tell others of her experience but rather 'pensant à parsoy, que ce pourroit estre qui lauroit baisee, et de la croix signee'.[56] The young girl's circumspection *à part soi*, with its clear parallels in Mary's response to Gabriel in Luke 1:29 ('And when she saw him, she was troubled at his saying, and *cast in her mind* what manner of salutation this should be'), recurs later in the text when, having witnessed another of Alis's appearances, Anthoinette falls to her knees, 'considerant à part soy la façon de ceste apparition: et ainsy sans mot sonner, prenoit garde quelle devyendroit. Puis sen alla coucher, sans en

[53] Montalembert, *Merveilleuse Hystoire*, sig. Bii[v].

[54] Montalembert, *Merveilleuse Hystoire*, sigs Ciii[v]–Civ[r]: 'it seemed to her that something was lifting her veil right up, and making the sign of the cross on her forehead, and then gently and softly kissing her on the mouth'.

[55] On kissing, the Song of Songs, and mysticism in the French Middle Ages, see Y. Carré, *Le Baiser sur la bouche au Moyen Âge: rites, symboles, mentalités* (Paris: Léopard d'Or, 1993); for Renaissance interpretations, see M. Engammare, *Qu'il me baise des baisers de sa bouche: le cantique des cantiques à la Renaissance* (Geneva: Droz, 1993).

[56] Montalembert, *Merveilleuse Hystoire*, sig. Civ[r]: 'wondering in her heart who this could be that had kissed her, and signed her with the cross'.

parler à personne'.[57] The insistence with which Montalembert underscores the girl's exemplary discretion marks her out decisively from
Paul's—and Gerson's—'silly women'.

When Anthoinette does eventually tell of what she has felt and seen, the
news passes up a tightly controlled chain of ecclesiastical command: first to
the abbess, then to Du Bois and to Montalembert himself. Not that the
disturbances at Saint-Pierre remain secret for long: the author tells how, as
he and Du Bois walk down the hill towards Lyon to perform the exorcism,
they see a large crowd assembled outside the abbey walls. But the rabble
pressing at the gates, and the circulation of unofficial narrative—or 'bruyt'—
it threatens to set in motion, are never allowed to intrude upon proceedings;
Montalembert devotes great care to describing how he and Du Bois manage,
by way of a clever ruse, to gain access to Saint-Pierre through a side door,
unnoticed by the crowd.[58] The importance attached to the bedroom scenes,
and the dangers represented by prurient public interest in the story, renders
a large part of the drama that of the story's own transmission. The hero of
that drama is of course the author himself, who manages the transmission
of the tale and its interpretation. Its culmination is the scene of the first
woodcut, in which Montalembert is shown presenting François I with the
text we are about to read.[59]

Firmly secured in the official channels of *discretio spirituum*, what began
as a moment of bewildering intimacy in a young girl's bedchamber is
safely transformed into a national public lesson. Beyond the self-reflexive
show of ecclesiastical muscle described above, the text serves several
purposes at once. Most straightforwardly perhaps, it may have been
intended as an apology for Saint-Pierre itself. Still tarnished by its former
scandals, despite its recent reform, the Lyon convent that is the setting for
the narrative badly needed to restore its reputation: the absolution of the
sinful nun serves to enact, as it were metonymically, the institutional
purgation of the abbey.

The text also functions as a devotional manual. Montalembert writes in
the dedication to François that he is telling Alis's story for the 'edification
de tous bons et loyaux crestiens'.[60] Unlike the exclusively clerical readership
imagined in Gerson's *De probatione spirituum*, the *Merveilleuse Hystoire*
envisaged a broad audience. This much is clear from the decision to write
in French, rather than Latin; it also explains the presence of woodcut

---

[57] Montalembert, *Merveilleuse Hystoire*, sig. Miv[r]: 'considering in her heart the manner
of this apparition: and so without breathing a word, she wondered what would become of
her. Then she went off to bed, without speaking of this to anybody.'
[58] Ibid., sigs. Div[v]–Ei[v].
[59] Ibid., *Merveilleuse Hystoire*, sig. Bi[r].
[60] Ibid., sig. Ai[v].

illustrations.[61] The early images, of the dying Alis praying to the Virgin, closely resemble the popular devotional tradition of the *Ars moriendi*. Bossozel specialized in printing illustrated devotional texts and may here have reused his existing stock. The remainder of the illustrations (these clearly custom-made) serve to clarify some of the more difficult theological aspects of the story they accompany, especially those relating to Purgatory. While the narrative describes the ghost as manifesting itself only through touch and sound, Bossozel's woodcuts represent Alis visibly, as a skeleton dressed in a nun's habit; the ghost endures the traditional paraphernalia of Purgatory in the form of the chains around the figure's waist and feet. Later, as the nuns of Saint-Pierre begin to intercede on Alis's behalf, the skeletal appearance of the ghost is gradually diminished. This gradual transmogrification is clearly meant to mark the progress of the dead soul's deliverance from Purgatory. Similarly, whereas the early illustrations feature Alis submerged waist-deep beneath the ground, once released from her penance she gradually rises. Motifs such as these combine to produce a vivid visual analogue for the sometimes complex relationship between Purgatorial and earthly time.

A further, related, function of the text is as a weapon against heresy. As the dedicatory woodcut suggests, the *Merveilleuse Hystoire* is intended as a vindication of Church practice before the king and his lay subjects. But as Montalembert's appeal to 'loyaux cretiens' implies, the Christian community in 1528 could no longer be deemed to constitute a single, unitary readership. Montalembert states in the preface that his account was partly aimed at, in his words, 'la confusion et extermination de la Secte damnable des faux Heretiques Lutheriens et leurs Sectateurs'.[62] This anti-Lutheran colouration deepens during the priests' interrogation of the ghost. Suspecting that the knocking may be that of a visitor from Purgatory, Du Bois asks the spirit for confirmation: 'Dy moy, adjure par les haulx noms de dieu sil y a veritablement aucun particulier lieu qui soit appelle purgatoire, où quel puissent estre toutes ames qui par la justice divine la sont condamnees? Respond que ouy.'[63]

As if to reinforce the point, Montalembert here adds, repeating the terms of his preface, 'par ceste responsce est confuse et condamnee la

---

[61] On Bossozel's woodcuts, see R. Brun, *Le Livre illustré en France au XVIe siècle* (Paris: F. Alcan, 1930), p. 267.

[62] Montalembert, *Merveilleuse Hystoire*, sig. Bii[r]: 'the confounding and extermination of the damnable Sect of false Lutheran Heretics and their Sect Members'.

[63] Ibid., sig. Jii[v]: 'Tell me, swear by the most sacred names of God whether there is any particular place which be called Purgatory, where all souls condemned by divine justice might be? It replies that there is.'

damnable assertion des faulx hereticques luteriens'.[64] There then follows a series of questions relating to all those practices (pilgrimage, almsgiving, Mass, etcetera) that, according to Catholic doctrine, accelerate a soul's term in Purgatory. In this way Du Bois's interrogation effectively calls upon the ghost to validate one by one all those clerical procedures vilified by the Reformers. As it does so, Montalembert gradually clarifies the meaning of the mysterious encounter in Anthoinette's bedroom. 'Qu'il me baise des baisers de sa bouche': the ghost's kiss was finally to be read as the seal of approval for Christ's one true Bride, the Roman Catholic Church, and the various rituals by which it cemented the continuing allegiance of its followers. At a time when the Song of Songs was becoming increasingly associated with evangelical spirituality, Montalembert's symbolic appropriation must have seemed all the more striking to his contemporaries.[65]

La Merveilleuse Hystoire stands as an early instance of a vernacular ghost story attempting to respond, in a manner comprehensible to the general population, to an assault on the doctrine of Purgatory that was gathering dangerous pace. To a certain degree it may be possible to attack Montalembert's grasp of Lutheran teaching as confused on this point. Luther's early objections to Purgatory were made on account of the abuses it engendered, with indulgences singled out for especial condemnation; it was not until the Schmalkaldic Articles of 1537 that he went as far as to deny the very existence of Purgatory. Even after this date Lutheran confessions tend not to reject the doctrine outright, whatever their objections to requiem masses and papal claims to the power to remit sins.[66] Nonetheless, Montalembert would not have been unusual in ignoring such niceties. The Bull *Exsurge Domine* of 1520 condemned a number of Luther's supposed propositions on Purgatory.[67] The authorities in Rome had clearly recognized a strong tendency in Lutheran circles to imply, if not to argue openly, that Purgatory itself was nothing more than a papist fantasy. To this extent the story of the haunted nun, with its vivid illustrations, its familiar structure, and its Gersonian heritage, offered a timely counterblast to the Protestant naysayers.

[64] Ibid., sig. Jii^v.

[65] Engammare (in *Qu'il me baise des baisers de sa bouche*) notes the presence of the *Song of Songs* in the correspondence of Guillaume Briçonnet and Marguerite d'Angoulême (later de Navarre) in the early 1520s (pp. 446–9), as well as in Marguerite's biblical theatre and spiritual poetry (pp. 474–8).

[66] For a recent and more detailed study of Lutheran attitudes towards death and remembrance, see C. M. Koslofsky, *The Reformation of the Dead: Death and Ritual in Early Modern Germany, 1450–1700* (Basingstoke: Macmillan, 2000), pp. 19–39.

[67] See Ombres, *Theology of Purgatory*, p. 48.

By the time Montalembert wrote his *Merveilleuse Hystoire* at the end of the 1520s, Lutheranism was gaining ground in France. The related, though less militant, evangelical ideals of Jacques Lefèvre d'Étaples, and Guillaume Briçonnet's experiment in the diocese of Meaux, had begun to spread. It was not long before they reached Orleans, where a young Jean Calvin was studying law. As we shall see in the next section, events in that town were to play a commanding role in shaping sixteenth-century attitudes to ghosts. Having looked briefly at the Lutheran position, however, and before turning to Orleans, it will be necessary to evaluate the stance on ghosts and ghost narratives among the francophone reformers of the 1530s, 1540s, and 1550s.

Protestant Responses: The Ghost Hoax

What Montalembert called 'la damnable assertion' against Purgatory, and against what some held to be clerical superstitions surrounding apparitions of the dead, continued to win supporters in the middle decades of the sixteenth century, and far beyond the confines of Luther's Germany. The Italian Protestant Bernardino Ochino summed up the feeling of many in his *De Purgatorio dialogus* of 1555. Ochino's dialogue opens by likening the Catholic clergy to the Gaderene demoniac (Mark 5: 2–5; Luke 8:27), camped ghoulishly among the dead from whom they suck their living.[68] A similar emphasis characterizes francophone theology of this period. Texts such as Jean Calvin's *Institution de la religion chrestienne*, Guillaume Farel's *Traicté de Purgatoire*, and Pierre Viret's *Disputations chrestiennes* (to name only the best known) all impugn the Catholic doctrine of Purgatory, along with the funerary and commemorative customs with which it was associated.[69]

These writers varied their angle of attack. Calvin and Farel largely limit themselves to what they deemed a lack of scriptural foundation for Purgatory. Much of their argument hinges on what they claimed to be the apocryphal status of the book of Maccabees, often cited by Catholics in support of prayers for the dead.[70] Having thus disposed of what they

---

[68] B. Ochino, *De Purgatorio dialogus* (Zurich: J. and A. Gesner, 1555), p. 1. Grévin and Chandieu launch similar accusations against Ronsard, 'jadis poëte, maintenant prebstre', in Protestant polemic of the mid 1560s. See p. 198.

[69] J. Calvin, *Institution de la religion chrestienne*, ed. by J.-D. Benoit, 5 vols. [1536] (Paris: Vrin, 1960), III, ch. 5 ('Des supplémens que les Papistes adjoustent aux satisfactions: assavoir des indulgences, et du Purgatoire'); G. Farel, *Traicté de Purgatoire* (n.p., 1543).

[70] The key passage is 2 Maccabees 12:41–6, where Judas Maccabeus prays for the souls of slain Jewish soldiers. On Reformation debates over Maccabees and the canon, see Greenblatt, *Hamlet in Purgatory*, pp. 138–40; A. E. McGrath, *Reformation Thought: An Introduction* [1988], 3rd edn. (Oxford: Blackwell, 1999), p. 152.

deem the only biblical support for the practice, they conclude that the doctrine of Purgatory must be, in Calvin's words, 'une fiction pernicieuse de Satan'.[71] Viret, for his part, builds on Calvin's notion of Purgatory as fiction in his extended satire on Catholic visions of the afterlife.[72] His *Disputations chrestiennes* argue that the 'cosmographie infernale' described by medieval accounts of voyages into the afterlife should be given no more credence than the classical underworlds of Homer or Virgil.[73] 'Théophile', the author's mouthpiece, reserves especial scorn for the popular idea that there may exist terrestrial portals into Purgatory, such as the volcanic 'soupirails' at Mount Etna in Sicily or—particularly— Iceland's Mount Hecla. Long associated with ghostly apparitions, these were privileged landmarks in the Catholic geography of the afterlife.[74] As for Hell, over whose existence there is no doubt, Théophile concludes that the true penitent worries less about where it is to be found than what he or she must do to avoid it.[75]

The assault on Purgatory was nourished by a strong anticlerical tradition for which concrete abuses, rather than questions of doctrine, were the principal focus of attack. A favourite target in the period is the monk or priest who seeks to stage hoax apparitions (*contrefaire l'esprit*). Stories abound of Catholic clergymen who exploit the mysteries of the Church by staging ghostly hauntings; at least two readers of Montalembert's

---

[71] Calvin, *Institution*, III, p. 150.

[72] P. Viret, *Disputations chrestiennes, touchant l'estat des trespassez, faites par dialogues* (n.p., 1552). The sections of Viret's dialogue concerned with Purgatory have recently been re-edited; see P. Viret, *La Cosmographie infernale*, ed. by C. Calame (Paris: Éditions de la différence, 1991). References are to this edition.

[73] Viret, *Cosmographie infernale*, p. 46.

[74] Sixteenth-century cosmographers and theologians make frequent reference to the cries of dead souls emerging from Hecla, and to ghosts visiting the local Icelandic population. In some accounts, the typographic proximity between Iceland and Ireland merge Hecla with another celebrated gateway to Purgatory, Saint Patrick's hole. See J. Ziegler, *Schondia* in *Quae intus continentur: Syria...Palestina...Arabia Petraea...Aegyptus... Schondia*, etc., ed. by J. Ziegler (Argentorati: apud Petrum Opilionem, 1532), sig. 93ʳ; O. Magnus, *Historia de gentibus septentrionalibus* (Romae: apud Ioannem Mariam de Viottis Parmensem, 1555), p. 62; L. Surius, *Histoire ou commentaires de toutes choses memorables, avenues depuys LXX ans en ça par toutes les parties du monde, tant au faict seculier que Ecclesiastic*, trans. by J. Estourneau (Paris: Guillaume Chaudière, 1571), sigs. 182ᵛ–3ʳ (on Etna), p. 183ʳ⁻ᵛ (on Hecla); S. Maiolus, *Les Jours Caniculaires, c'est à dire vingt et trois excellents discours des choses natureles et surnatureles*, trans. by F. de Rosset (Paris: R. Foüet, 1609), pp. 76–9, 633. On the geography of Purgatory in the Middle Ages, see Le Goff, *Naissance du Purgatoire*, ch. 6 ('Le Purgatoire entre la Sicile et l'Irlande').

[75] For more on early modern arguments over the location of Hell and Purgatory, see P. Marshall, '"The Map of God's Word": Geographies of the Afterlife in Tudor and Early Stuart England' in *The Place of the Dead: Death and Remembrance in Late Medieval and Early Modern Europe*, ed. by B. Gordon and P. Marshall (Cambridge: Cambridge University Press, 2000), pp. 110–30.

Merveilleuse Hystoire, one no less a figure than Cornelius Agrippa von Nettesheim, pronounced its author guilty of just such a deception.[76] Other writers, such as Erasmus in his celebrated colloquy, *Exorcismus sive spectrum*, or the *conteurs* Philippe de Vigneulles and Bonaventure Des Periers, make the priest himself the target of a hoax, as others exploit his excessive superstition.[77] One of Vigneulles's *Cent Nouvelles nouvelles*, set in the town of Metz, tells the story of a nightwatchman and a gatekeeper who succeed in persuading a priest and his two companions that the gatehouse in which they are staying is haunted by spirits. Bellowing through pipes tunnelled into the bedroom, and pulling at their bedclothes, the hoaxers terrify their guests, whose credulity soon becomes the talk of the town. Des Periers's narrative, included in his *Contes ou nouvelles recreations et joyeux devis*, runs along similar lines. The son of a widowed innkeeper, frustrated at the way some local Franciscans are exploiting his mother's hospitality, devises a cunning ruse ('cautelle') to evict his unwelcome guests. A calf is set loose in the monks' bedchamber at night. Convinced that the animal's frightened lowing is the moaning of a spirit, the Franciscans pack their bags, never to return. Both Vigneulles's and Des Periers's characters owe much to the popular tradition of the trickster, whose cunning is as much to be admired as their victims' credulity despised. On the whole, however, most anticlerical narratives on the theme of the ghost hoax cast the priest himself as swindler and, in what would become a recurrent topos of anticlerical satire, revel in his unmasking as a charlatan and fraud.

One text that arguably did more than any other to set the trend for narratives of this kind can be found in the correspondence of Erasmus. Following the controversy that had broken out on the publication of his *Exorcismus sive spectrum*, the Dutch humanist returned to the subject of ghosts in a letter to the English bishop, John Longlond. It appears that Longlond had written to Erasmus warning him of the hostile reception the *Colloquia* had received among the more orthodox elements of the English

[76] H. Cornelius Agrippa von Nettesheim, *De incertitudine et vanitate scientiarum et artium* (Paris: Ioannes Petrus, 1531), sig. 64ʳ. Péricaud mentions a Lyonnais contemporary of Montalembert's, Claude Bellièvre, whose *Lugdunum Priscum* contains a note on the haunting at Saint-Pierre. According to Péricaud, who edited the text, Bellièvre alleges that 'cet exorcisme fut un jeu concerté par quelques religieux ou par le prieur du couvent' ('that exorcism was a hoax played by some religious or by the convent superior') but is reluctant to name names. See Péricaud, *Notice sur François de Rohan*, pp. 23–4, n. 4.
[77] D. Erasmus, *Opera omnia* (Amsterdam: North Holland, 1969–), III (= *Colloquia*, ed. by L.-E. Halkin, F. Bierlaire, and R. Hoven), pp. 417–23; P. de Vigneulles, *Les Cent Nouvelles nouvelles*, ed. by C. H. Livingston (Geneva: Droz, 1972), pp. 216–18; B. Des Periers, *Contes ou nouvelles recreations et joyeux devis* [1558], ed. by P. L. Jacob (Paris: Garnier, 1872), pp. 274–5.

clergy. In his reply of 1 September 1528, Erasmus reaffirms his allegiance to clerical institutions and ceremonies, but steps up his reproach of those who abuse them. Rather than revisit the text of the *Colloquia* directly, he turns instead for his evidence to two recent instances of clerical malpractice.

The first story tells of a priest who tricks his congregation into believing the local graveyard to be haunted by dead souls. Erasmus describes how the priest had fixed lighted candles to a number of live crabs, and set them loose at night to crawl among the graves. Confident that no one would dare approach the mysterious lights, he then preached to his parish that the graveyard was haunted by unquiet souls who had returned to demand indulgences. The hoax (*fucus*) was eventually discovered when one or two of the creatures, which the priest had failed to collect, were found wandering the graveyard with their candles still attached.[78] The second narrative features the same hapless villain, who takes to haunting his niece's chamber at night, dressed up as a ghost. His hopes that the niece, whom Erasmus describes as 'bene nummata', will hire him as an exorcist are dashed when, unbeknownst to him, she calls instead on a drunken male companion to lie in wait with her one night. The conclusion of the story is played for laughs:

> Here comes the spectre, as usual, making some sinister sound or other. The exorcist awakes. He jumps to his feet, not yet sobered up, and goes on the attack. The spectre does his best to frighten him away with ghostly voices and gestures, but he replies, still full of drink, 'If you are the devil, I am his mother.' He takes hold of the impostor, beats him repeatedly and would have killed him had the ghost, recovering his normal voice, not cried out 'Spare me! I'm not a spirit, but Master John!' On hearing this familiar voice the niece jumps out of bed and separates the combattants.[79]

As is commonly the case in such narratives, physical violence provides the means by which the identity of the—all too embodied—hoaxer is restored. Or, as the English translator of Ludwig Lavater's great ghost treatise *De spectris* would later put it, 'in case spirits which have bodies do wander (that is conjurers, priests, whores, and whoremongers, which faine

[78] See D. Erasmus, *Opus epistolarum Des. Erasmi Roterodami*, ed. by H. M. Allen et al., 12 vols. (Oxford: Clarendon Press, 1906–58), vii, pp. 460–7.

[79] 'Adest spectrum solito more, nescio quid triste mugiens. Excitatur exorcista. Prosilit nondum sobrius, aggreditur; ibe spectrum voce gestuque deterrere parat. At ebrius ille, 'Si tu es' inquit, 'diabolus, ego sum mater illius', et correptem impostorem fuste dolat, occisurus ni mutata voce clamasset, 'Pace, non sum anima, sed sum dominus Ioannes'. Ad vocem agnitam mulier exilit e lecto pugnamque dirimit.' Erasmus, *Opus epistolarum*, vii, p. 462.

themselves to be spirits) there can be no better conjuration invented than to bang them well with a cudgel'.[80]

Frequently reproduced, translated, and imitated in later writing on apparitions, Erasmus's letter to Longlond dignified the anticlerical ghost hoax as a suitable subject for satire.[81] Whether the priestly counterfeiter stages his hoax in the public space of the graveyard, or insinuates himself into the privacy of a woman's bedroom, his unmasking remained, for all its comedy of demystification, a serious business. According to many critics of the Church, scandals of this kind were rife. Erasmus does not name names, places, or dates in his letter; other writers are more incriminating. Protestant polemicists often cite the outrage said to have occurred in Berne in 1509, for instance, where four Franciscan monks had faked the appearance of a spirit, and in Clavenna where, according to Johannes Stumpfius's Helvetican chronicles, a priest had assumed the guise of the Virgin herself in order to sleep with a young girl.[82] But perhaps no hoax was more notorious than that which was visited upon the mayor of Orleans in the spring of 1534.[83]

---

[80] L. Lavater, *Of Ghostes and Spirites Walking by Nyght*, trans. by R. H. and ed. by J. Dover Wilson and M. Yardley (Oxford: Folio Society, 1929), p. 215.

[81] The letter appears to have influenced Marguerite de Navarre, with whose *Heptaméron* XXXIX (the story of a chambermaid who fakes an apparition and is discovered by her master) it shares a number of narrative features. It also inspired a number of natural magicians, notably Giambattista Della Porta and Jean Prévost, both of whom recommend the lighted crabs (or in Prévost's case tortoises) as a trick for frightening unsuspecting guests. See G. Della Porta, *La Magie naturelle ou les secrets et miracles de la nature* [1565] (Paris: Rouvray, 1993), p. 148; J. Prévost, *La Premiere Partie des subtiles et plaisantes inventions. Contenans plusieurs jeux de recreation, et traicts de souplesse, par le discours desquels, les imposteurs des bateleurs sont descouvertes* (Lyon: A. Bastide, 1584), sig. 50ᵛ. Other non-clerical ghost hoax episodes can be found in C. de Bourdigné, *La Légende joyeuse de Maistre Pierre Faifeu* [1532], ed. by F. Vallette (Geneva: Droz, 1972), ch. 26 ('Comment il fist une finesse pour coucher, en la chambre de sa mere, avecques sa chambriere'); H. Estienne, *Apologie pour Herodote* [1566], ed. by P. Ristelhuber, 2 vols. (Paris: I. Liseux, 1879), I, pp. 268–9 (on a chambermaid whose imposture is discovered by the humanist scholar and printer, Josse Bade); A. Tyron, *Recueil de plusieurs plaisantes nouvelles, apophtegmes, et recreations diverses* (Antwerp: M. Huyssens, 1596), sigs. 84ᵛ–90ᵛ ('D'un povre estudiant qui venoit de Paradis, et d'une riche paysanne, qu'il trompoit à merveilles'); A. de Boufflers, *Le Chois de plusieurs histoires et autres choses memorables tant anciennes que modernes, appariees, ensemble, pour la pluspart non encores divulguees* (Paris: J. Mettayer, 1608), Book 3, ch. 77 ('D'un bon homme contrefaisant le gobelin'). For more on the ghost hoax as a narrative genre in the sixteenth century, see E. Butterworth, 'The Work of the Devil? Theatre, the Supernatural, and Montaigne's Public Stage', *Renaissance Studies* 22 (5) (2008), pp. 705–22.

[82] Cited in L. Lavater, *Trois livres des apparitions des esprits* (Geneva: F. Perrin for J. Durand, 1571), Book 1, ch. 8.

[83] The Orleans scandal has received recent attention in discussions of changing attitudes towards burial practice in the period; see P. Roberts, 'Contesting Sacred Space: Burial Disputes in Sixteenth-Century France' in *The Place of the Dead: Death and Remembrance in Late Medieval and Early Modern Europe*, ed. by B. Gordon and P. Marshall (Cambridge:

In the early months of that year, the mayor had been in dispute with the local Franciscans over a piece of woodland that they claimed was rightfully theirs. During this period his wife, Louise Moreau, died. When it tran-spired that the dead woman, who had developed Lutheran sympathies during the last years of her life, had requested a simple burial, at virtually no expense, alongside her father and grandparents, the *cordeliers* took further offence. Accounts of what happened next vary. The basic facts are these. Several monks, under the leadership of a certain Colimant, decided to engineer an elaborate hoax designed to spite the enemy mayor. Hiding high up in the rafters of the local church, a novice, named Halecourt, pretended to be the ghost of the deceased woman. When Colimant and his accomplices came to interview the spirit, the ghost revealed, by way of a series of knocks, that Louise was damned for Lutheran heresy and would only stop her disturbances if her body was exhumed and buried elsewhere. However, it was not long before the company gathered in the nave of the church began to grow suspicious when the ghost, with ever-increasing vehemence, refused to allow any of its members up to see it. When the rafters were checked and Halecourt was eventually discovered, the matter was taken up with the king and the chancellor. The court demanded that the perpetrators be arrested, ques-tioned, and eventually tried at the Parlement de Paris. There Colimant and his co-plotters were found guilty of the fraud. Fortunately for them, politics came to the rescue. Intervening between the moments of arrest and punishment, the *affaire des placards* had broken out, and with it a good deal of anti-Lutheran sentiment. The king was in no mood to humiliate the clergy. To the dismay of Protestant observers, Colimant, Halecourt, and their accomplices were spared the gallows.

Writing in his *De praestigiis daemonum*, translated into French in 1567, the German demonologist Johann Weyer recalls the furore of the scandal at Orleans.[84] Weyer himself had been in the town at the time of the events, attending to the children of Noël Ramard, physician to the king and his sister, Marguerite de Navarre. Such was the notoriety of the case, Weyer claims, that 'un esprit d'Orléans' had entered popular French parlance as a phrase denoting a hoax, a prank, or a tall story.[85] Judging by the range and the profile of responses to the case, Weyer may not have

Cambridge University Press, 2000), pp. 131–48. See also G. Berthoud, *Anthoine Marcourt*: *réformateur et pamphlétaire du Livre des marchans aux placards de 1534* (Geneva: Droz, 1973), pp. 124, 142–3.

[84] J. Weyer, *De l'imposture et tromperie des diables, des enchantements et sorcelleries*, trans. by J. Grévin [1567] (Paris: Jacques du Puy, 1569), pp. 364^v–7^v.

[85] Weyer, *De l'imposture*, sig. 367^v.

exaggerated the impact of the affair. Antoine de Marcourt, writing late in
1534 in his anonymously published *Livres des marchans*, is among the first
to mention it, alongside a similar case at Evreux; two years later, in 1536,
the case was discussed further at the disputes of Lausanne.[86] In a passage
that appears to confirm Weyer's claim, Jean Ménard, writing in his 1542
Déclaration de la reigle et estat des Cordeliers, lists the episode of the 'esprit
d'Orléans' among the most outrageous Church abuses of the last two
hundred years.[87] Marguerite de Navarre certainly knew of the scandal; one
of the stories in the *Heptaméron* (XLIV) features a certain 'Coliment', a
villainous priest doubtless named after the hoaxers' ringleader.[88] Mention
of the affair is made in Calvin's correspondence and Sleidanus's chronicles,
in Beza's *Histoire ecclésiastique*, as well as in a number of references
throughout Henri Estienne's *Apologie pour Hérodote*;[89] it almost certainly
provided the inspiration for George Buchanan's satirical comedy, *Francis-
canus*, translated into French in 1567;[90] and a sly allusion to the scandal
can also be found in Rabelais's *Tiers Livre*.[91] Among Catholic writers
seeking to make the case for the reality of return from the dead, response
to the episode remained more muted. According to Delrio, however, 'la
cause d'Orléans' was so far-reaching in its implications that it was enough

[86] A. de Marcourt, *Le Livre des marchans* [1534] (n.p., 1541), sigs. Cvii^r–Cviii^r;
A. Piaget, *Les Actes de la dispute de Lausanne, 1536* (Neuchâtel: Secrétariat de l'Université,
1928), p. 168.
[87] J. Ménard, *Declaration de la reigle et estat des Cordeliers, composée par ung jadiz de leur
ordre, et maintenant de Jesus Christ* (Geneva: [J. Michel], 1542), p. 111.
[88] See G. Toothil, 'A Note on Frère Colimant (*Hep*.XLIV)', *Bibliothèque d'humanisme et
Renaissance*, 33 (1971), pp. 151–3.
[89] Calvin's account of the incident, written to aid the preparation of Johannes Sleidanus's chronicles, is published in J. Calvin, *Ioannis Calvini opera quae supersunt omnia*, ed. by
G. Baum et al., Corpus Reformatorum 38 (pars posterior) (Brunswick: C. A. Schwetschke,
1863–1900), pp. 39–42. For the account in Sleidanus, see his *Histoire de l'estat de la religion
et republique*, trans. by R. Le Prévost ([Geneva]: B. Richard, 1557), sigs. 133^v–4^r; Estienne,
Apologie pour Hérodote, I, pp. 25, 269, and II, pp. 299, 397; [T. de Bèze], *Histoire
ecclésiastique*, 3 vols. (Antwerp: J. Rémy, 1580) I, pp. 17–19.
[90] G. Buchanan, *Le Cordelier, ou le Saint François*, trans. by F. Chrestien (Geneva: Jean
de L'Estang, 1567), p. 51.
[91] The reference in Rabelais is made as Panurge tries to persuade his companions to
return to the bedside of the dying Raminagrobis. Because the old man had earlier chased
away a party of monks, Panurge fears for his salvation: 'Nous le induirons à contrition de
son peché; à requerir pardon es dictz tant beatz peres, absens comme praesens. Et en
prendrons acte, affin qu'après son trespas ilz ne le declairent haereticque et damné comme
les Farfadetz feirent de la praevoste d'Orleans'; F. Rabelais, *Le Tiers Livre* [1546], ed. by
J. Céard (Paris: Livre de Poche, 1995), p. 221: 'We'll lead him into contrition for his sin, to
ask pardon of the most blessed fathers, absent as well as present—and we'll put it in writing,
so that after his death they won't declare him a heretic and damned, as the hobgoblins did
with the provost's wife of Orleans.' As with every subsequent reference to Rabelais in this
book, the translation used is F. Rabelais, *The Complete Works of François Rabelais*, trans. by
D. M. Frame (Berkeley: University of California Press, 1991), p. 321.

to lead the faculty of theology in Paris into an official reassertion of its belief in ghosts.[92]

The Catholic reply to the Protestant onslaught on Purgatory, and on related customs of commemoration and remembrance, was made on several fronts and most forcefully by Jesuits.[93] In 1563, the Council of Trent reaffirmed the doctrine of Purgatory as an article of faith.[94] After this date the volume of texts composed in defence of Purgatory increased considerably, whether as the subject of a complete monograph or as part of broader apologies for Catholic belief.[95] Writing of the two most influential treatments of the subject after Trent, by Bellarmine and Suárez, one recent historian of the period has called this the 'Golden Age of Catholic writing on Purgatory'.[96] Much of this corpus, though by no means all, continued to appeal to popular belief in apparitions of the dead as a means of persuading the wavering laity. For some late-century Counter-Reformation theologians, the proper response to Protestant vernacularisation was to resist replying in kind, and prefer Latin as a medium. Hence ghosts became an important ally in Peltanus's *Doctrina catholica de Purgatorio*, widely read in France, and in the Latin treatises on apparitions of the Flemish Jesuit, Petrus Thyraeus.[97] For the most part, however, the favoured language of persuasion became French. Catholic polemicists and preachers such as Melchior Flavin, Jean Lambert, François Feu-Ardent, René du Pont, and Pierre Crespet all appeal to common experience of ghosts to defend the

[92] M. Delrio, *Les controverses et recherches magiques de Martin Delrio P. et Doct. de la Compagnie de Iesus*, trans. and ed. by A. du Chesne (Paris: Jean Petit-Pas, 1611), sig. Rviii[v].

[93] For a detailed study of Purgatory in the Counter-Reformation, see H. W. Sullivan, *Grotesque Purgatory: A Study of Cervantes's "Don Quixote" Part II* (University Park, Philadelphia: Pennsylvania State University Press, 1996), ch. 3 ('The Theology of Purgatory in the Counter- Reformation'), especially pp. 79–101.

[94] Trent's 'Decretum De Purgatorio' is reproduced with an English translation in N. P. Tanner, *Decrees of the Ecumenical Councils*, 2 vols. (London: Sheed & Ward, 1990), II, p. 774. See also Ombres, *Theology of Purgatory*, pp. 48–9; Vovelle, *Ames du purgatoire*, pp. 92–111.

[95] By far the most influential were the disputational writings of Bellarmine and, in particular, Suárez.

[96] Sullivan, *Grotesque Purgatory*, p. 79.

[97] T. Peltanus, *Doctrina catholica de Purgatorio, animarum sedibus* ([Ingolstadii]: ex typographia Weissenhorniana, 1568); P. Thyraeus, *De variis tam spirituum quam vivorum hominum prodigiosis apparitionibus et nocturnis infestationibus libri tres* (Coloniae Agrippinae: ex off. M. Cholini, sumptibus G. Cholini, 1594); idem., *Loca infesta, hoc est de infestis ob molestantes daemoniorum et defunctorum hominum spiritus locis, liber unus...Accessit eiusdem libellus de terriculamentis nocturnis* (Coloniae Agrippinae: ex off. M. Cholini, sumptibus G. Cholini, 1598); idem., *De apparitionibus omnis generis spirituum, Dei, angelorum, daemonum et animarum humanarum liber* (Coloniae Agrippinae: ex off. M. Cholini, sumptibus G. Cholini, 1600).

reality of Purgatory.[98] Their task was far from simple. As another Counter-Reformation theologian, Claude Durand, remarked ruefully in his *Purgatoire des fideles defuncts*, 'plusieurs mesme des Catholiques à peine se peuvent persuader que telles apparitions soyent veritables'.[99]

Scandals such as the Orleans affair did not help, and it was possibly as a result of that episode, and others like it, that extended clerical ghost narratives like Montalembert's *Merveilleuse Hystoire* became rare in the second half of the sixteenth century.[100] This is not to claim that Catholic theologians ducked narrative exchange altogether in this period. Not a few responded to Protestant accusations of ghost hoaxes with a counter-charge of their own: that Calvin had faked a resurrection at Geneva in 1538 so as to bolster his status as a charismatic leader. The Catholic chronicler, Laurentius Surius, tells how Calvin had persuaded a poor man to have himself borne into his congregation on a bier, as if recently deceased.[101] Then, at the right moment, the chief Protestant minister would miraculously revive him. All went according to plan until, at the critical moment, the volunteer suddenly died for real. God had intervened, explains Surius, 'de façon que Calvin fut trompé luy-mesme, et fut cogneu que ce qu'il vendoit pour parole de Dieu, n'estoit que mensonge et chose controuvée'.[102] 'True' accounts of returns from Purgatory, not unlike the medieval ghost narratives described at the beginning of this chapter, also appeared in theological writing of the second half of the sixteenth century. The texts of Flavin and Lambert contain a number of typical examples, and were collected together in Taillepied's *Psichologie, ou traité de l'apparition des esprits*. However, unlike Montalembert's *Merveilleuse Hystoire*, these narratives tended to be brief, and betoken nothing like the clerical

---

[98] M. Flavin, *De l'estat des ames après le trespas, et comment elles vivent estans du corps separees, et des purgatoires qu'elles souffrent en ce monde, et en l'autre, apres icelle separation* [1579] (Rouen: Romain de Beauvais, 1605); J. Lambert, *Discours evangeliques et instructions chrestiennes et catholiques* [1582] (Paris: Guillaume Bichon, 1586); F. Feu-Ardent, *Semaine des dialogues, ausquels entre un docteur Catholic et un Ministre Calvinic sont paisiblement examinez et confutez quatre cens soixante et cinq erreurs des Hereticques* (Paris: Michel Sonnius, 1598); R. du Pont, *La Philosophie des esprits* (Paris: veuve Guillaume de la Nouë, 1602); P. Crespet, *Discours catholiques, de l'origine, de l'essence, excellence, fin, et immortalité de l'ame* (Paris: Claude Chappelain, 1604).

[99] 'Even many Catholics can scarcely be convinced that such apparitions are true'. Durand, *Purgatoire des fideles defuncts*, p. 46.

[100] Montalembert's own text is re-edited once in 1529 (Rouen: Rollin Gaultier) and again, without illustrations, in 1580 (Paris: Jean Pinart). The disappearance of the visual apparatus of devotion in Pinart's edition suggests that the publisher may have been attempting to exploit the growing vogue for sensationalist *canards*, which his text resembles.

[101] Surius, *Histoire ou commentaire de toutes choses memorables*, sigs. 201ᵛ-2ʳ.

[102] Ibid., sig. 202ʳ: 'such that Calvin was himself tricked, and it became known that that which he traded as being the word of God, was nothing other than a lie and a counterfeit thing'.

self-assurance we find at the beginning of the period. Overall, and as we shall see in more detail in Part II of this book, the business of producing sustained ghost narratives of any length was taken up by writers at one remove from the once dominant priesthood: in the *canards*, for instance, or Catholic demonologists such as Pierre de Lancre. By the end of the sixteenth century and into the seventeenth, it seems that accounts of demonic possession, rather than the ghost narratives that had served so well during the Middle Ages, were to become the Church's ideological weapon of choice.[103]

As Catholic confidence in sustained ghost narratives dwindled in the second half of the sixteenth century, and as it became clear that the strategy of merely restating the priestly prerogative of *discretio spirituum* was unlikely to prevail over an increasing anticlericalism, theologians increasingly found themselves drawn instead onto exegetical ground. The arguments over Purgatory are too varied and too complex for consideration here. But the debate over scriptural support (or lack of it) for the return of the dead was by comparison relatively circumscribed. One of the most important biblical episodes was that of Samuel's apparition to Saul in I Samuel 28, conjured up at Saul's behest by the woman of Endor. We shall postpone discussion of this narrative since, as will become clear in Chapter 3, debate around that episode ranged far beyond theology. More pertinent for our purposes is the evidence provided by the New Testament. Since, following the fourth session of the Council of Trent (1546), only ordained members of the Church were permitted to interpret the Gospels in print, this guaranteed a certain exclusivity to theological opinion, even if this restriction was respected only by upholders of traditional Church doctrine. Discussion of two New Testament episodes recurs in the polemic: the appearance of the risen Christ to the disciples in the locked room (Luke 24:36–43; John 20:19–29), and the story of Lazarus and Dives (Luke 16:19–31). Each of these biblical *loci* inspired countless sermons and commentaries, and the following discussion of sixteenth-century readings makes no claim to be exhaustive. What follows aims rather to complete our survey of sixteenth-century theological writing on ghosts by providing a flavour of these (often tortuous) exegetical discussions, and what they reveal of the period's attitudes to the return of the dead.

---

[103] The possession of Nicole Obry in Laon (1566) was discussed briefly above. The later sixteenth and (especially) seventeenth centuries saw an increase in such cases, with those of Marthe Brossier (1598), Louis Gaufridy (1611), and the possessions at Loudun (1632–8) and Louviers (1642–54) among the most prominent examples. For further discussion and a comprehensive bibliography, see Ferber, *Demonic Possession*.

GHOSTS IN THE NEW TESTAMENT

Walking through Walls: The Locked Room

Strictly speaking, not a single ghost appears in the New Testament story.[104] Where the subject of ghosts is raised at all, they are usually associated with instances of human error. When, for example, Christ walks on the water, the disciples cry out in fear, having mistaken him for a 'spirit'. (Matthew 14:25–6; Mark 6:49). The Apostles' Greek word here is φαντασμα, retained as 'phantasma' in the Vulgate; the lexical proximity to 'fantasy', also preserved in sixteenth-century French translations of the same term (variously 'phantosme' or 'phantasme'), underscores the sense of error and misperception.[105] Variations on the same theme resurface with the appearances of the risen Christ. When the holy women see Jesus in the garden, he senses that they too may have mistaken him for a ghost (all the more likely since they believe him to be dead), and tells them not to be afraid (Matthew 28:10). And when their sighting is reported to the eleven, the disciples suspect—again wrongly—that what the women have experienced was a vision in a dream (Luke 24:11). The connection between ghosts and error is most explicit of all in the final verses of Luke's Gospel, where the disciples themselves, gathered together in the locked room, mistake the risen Christ's glorified body for a spirit (πνευμα). Jesus corrects them at once, urging them to 'handle me and see; for a spirit hath not flesh and bones, as ye see me have' before requesting, as further proof of his embodiedness, that they bring him food to eat. This performance of Christ's corporeality, made still more explicit in John's story of doubting Thomas (John 20:24–9), takes especial care to invoke— the better to head off—attempts to dismiss the Easter narrative as nothing more than a dubious ghost tale.

According to Schmitt, the scriptural association between apparitions and error had played a significant role in what he calls the early Christian Church's 'refoulement des revenants'.[106] Seeking to wean new heathen converts off what was then deemed a superstitious animism, early prose-lytizers often had recourse to the episodes just cited. However, by the sixteenth century, when Counter-Reformation polemicists found themselves

---

[104] The appearance of Moses and Elias in the transfiguration on the mount (Matthew 17:1–3; Luke 9:30–3) is a marginal case. For most medieval and early modern commentators, the exceptional status of these figures placed them outside the category of 'ghosts': these were no ordinary dead, and Christ no ordinary witness.

[105] Lefèvre d'Étaples has 'phantasme', the Geneva Bible 'phantosme'.

[106] Schmitt, *Les Revenants*, ch. 1.

embroiled in a polemic over Purgatory, the very same biblical evidence was frequently turned around to prop up the reality of ghosts. Taillepied and François Feu-Ardent are among a number of Catholic writers who argue, for instance, that the disciples' reaction in the locked room, far from disproving the existence of ghosts, testifies rather to their own faith in their reality. Why else, if ghosts did not exist, would they ever have supposed that a ghost was what they saw? According to some commentators, the response Christ offers them ('a spirit hath not flesh and bones, as ye see me have') may even amount to a tacit endorsement of that faith. Thus Martin Delrio voices a widely held opinion when he remarks that Jesus could easily have reproached his followers for their credulous belief in apparitions of the dead, 'ce qu'un bon maistre comme luy, vraye lumiere du monde n'eust negligé', but refuses— revealingly—to do so.[107] Feu-Ardent, like Delrio, concludes from this that while the disciples were mistaken in this specific case, 'neantmoins ils n'erroient point en la proposition generale et universelle'.[108] Protestant polemicists clearly felt the force of this argument and tended to duck it by adopting a more capacious reading of Luke's term, $\pi\nu\epsilon\nu\mu\alpha$. Thus Calvin maintains in his commentary on Luke that the disciples thought they saw not the dead soul of their master, but rather an image of the resurrection.[109] Lavater, and Beza after him, observe that the apostles may have taken Christ not for a ghost, but for an angel or a demon.[110]

If the narrative of Christ's appearance to his disciples had implications for belief in the return of the dead, it also formed the theoretical basis— common across the confessions—on which all spirits, whatever their origin, were held to be incorporeal in nature. As we shall see in later chapters, disagreement over the embodiedness of spirits was not uncommon in the period, especially among non-theologians. But within theology Christ's words to the Apostles ('a spirit hath not flesh and bones, as ye see me have') made for a broad consensus on the matter. The Dominican Sébastien Michaëlis, writing on Luke 24 in a chapter of his *Pneumalogie* entitled 'Si les esprits ont corps', is quite categorical on the incorporeality of spirits: 'Il y a antithese entre un corps et un esprit si bien que la consequence est tousjours necessaire negativement de l'un à l'autre: tellement que si une chose est corps il s'ensuivra quand et quand qu'elle n'est

---

[107] Delrio, *Controverses magiques*, sig. Riii^r: 'the which a good master such as he was, true light of the world, would not have neglected to do'.

[108] Feu-Ardent, *Semaine des dialogues*, p. 84: 'nonetheless they erred not in the general and universal proposition'.

[109] Calvin, *Commentaire sur l'harmonie evangelique*, p. 748.

[110] Lavater, *Des apparitions*, pp. 153-56; T. de Bèze, *Sermons sur l'histoire de la resurrection de nostre Seigneur Jesus Christ* (Geneva: Jean le Preux, 1593), p. 327.

point esprit, et au contraire si elle est esprit elle n'est point corps.'[111] Couched in the language of the syllogism, the corporeal ghost stands outlawed as a logical impossibility.

Christ's instruction that his disciples should 'handle' him suggests not only that spirits lack bodies, but also that touch is a reliable guide to establishing the presence or absence of a body. And yet here many late sixteenth-century writers seem altogether less sure of their ground. This was doubtless partly because they were influenced by currents of philosophical scepticism, prompted not least by Henri Estienne's Latin translation of Sextus Empiricus, that had made it fashionable to question the reliability of the senses in general. But those writing on the topic also had to disentangle the evidence of everyday experience. Some tell of people who have indeed handled ghosts. A well-known passage in Cardano's *De subtilitate* recounts how a Milanese man had died having been attacked by a ghost; before he expired he told friends that, as he had grappled with his assailant, all he felt in his hands was something like cotton.[112] In similar vein, Lavater relates that those who have tried to strike apparitions report the sensation of thumping feather pillows. In another picturesque image Pierre Le Loyer describes how ghosts can feel soft and cold to the touch like 'une boulle de neige pressée sous la main de l'enfant'.[113] The numerous accounts of witches who had experienced physical pain during intercourse with the Devil also muddied the separation between spirits and body. Likewise Maldonado, who devotes considerable space to the passage in Luke, and states that tangibility alone cannot be trusted to discern spirits from bodies because sometimes even touch can be deceived, as madmen and those suffering from fever will attest. The Spanish Jesuit cautions too against concluding that spirits cannot eat, a proof that Taillepied, for instance, finds altogether more convincing.

Maldonado's reluctance to trust touch or other physical signs as a reliable means of separating out ghosts from physical phenomena is not untypical of late-century writing on the subject. But that does not mean that theologians in the period were any less steadfast in the ontological division between the spiritual and material. Spirits could certainly maintain a

---

[111] Michaëlis, *Pneumalogie*, sig. 19ᵛ: 'There is an antithesis between a body and a spirit such that the consequence is always that the one is necessarily the negative of the other: to the extent that if a thing is a body it immediately follows that it is not a spirit and, on the contrary, if it is a spirit it is not a body.'

[112] J. Cardan (= G. Cardano), *Les Livres de Hierosme Cardanus medecin milannois, intitulés de la Subtilité, et subtiles inventions, ensemble les causes occultes, et raisons d'icelles*, trans. by R. Le Blanc (Paris: C. l'Angelier, 1556), sigs. 374ʳ⁻ᵛ.

[113] P. Le Loyer, *Quatre livres des spectres ou apparitions et visions d'esprits, anges et demons se monstrans sensiblement aux hommes*, 2 vols. in 1 (Angers: G. Nepveu, 1586) I, p. 417: 'a snowball pressed in the hand of a child'.

physical presence in the world, able as they were to adopt aerial bodies or—as Nicole Obry found to her cost—take up cadavers from their graves. But none of these borrowed bodies, or *corpora peregrina* as Tertullian called them, with which spirits make themselves sensible to men actually belonged to those spirits' core nature. This would be to deny the authority of scripture. As Michaëlis concludes, reaching back to the firmer ground of scriptural authority in Luke 24: 'quand il n'y auroit autre texte, il seroit suffisant pour prouver qu'un esprit n'a point de corps'.[114]

And yet, returning to the episode of Jesus's appearance to the disciples, there remained a problem. How had Jesus—if he was so emphatically *not* a ghost—contrived to enter a room bolted shut on the inside? Discussions of this feat might be said to dramatize an enduring uncertainty over the nature of Christ's resurrected body. Christ's entry to the locked room also carried with it a number of doctrinological implications. Luke's account ('and as thus they spake, Jesus himself stood in the midst of them') already contains an obscure hint of Christ's impossible entrance. The fourth Gospel is more emphatic, stressing that 'the doors were shut' both on Christ's first appearance (John 20:19), and then again when Thomas joins them later (John 20:26). Even granted that Jesus was resurrected in a glorified body, how were palpable 'flesh and bones' able to pass through solid walls? Nor is the theme of the risen Christ's ambiguous materiality limited to this episode alone. Matthew's resurrection narrative suggests a similar ability to pass through solid objects when the angel removes the stone covering Christ's tomb, and reveals him to be missing (Matthew 28:6). John's narrative, by contrast, appears to imply that Christ himself 'rolled back' the stone (John 20:1). This gesture suggests a relationship between the risen body and its physical surroundings different from both Matthew's narrative and John's own story of the locked room. The question of Christ's tangibility is complicated further when, meeting Mary Magdalene in the garden, he commands her not to touch him (John 20:17). Again John's version contrasts with that in Matthew, where the holy women are said to have held on to Christ's feet (Matthew 28:9). Similar contradictions attend Luke's narrative of the supper at Emmaus, which immediately precedes the appearance in the locked room. There, Jesus was corporeal enough to eat with the two pilgrims and yet, Luke tells us, suddenly 'vanished out of their sight' (Luke 24:31).[115]

---

[114] Michaëlis, *Pneumalogie*, sig. 19^v: 'even if there were no other text, it would be sufficient to prove that a spirit has no body'.
[115] For more on the biblical inconsistencies in accounts of Christ's resurrected body, see P. Carnley, *The Structure of Resurrection Belief* (Oxford: Clarendon Press, 1987), pp. 16–19. On theological discussions of resurrection and the body more generally, see C. Walker

The dual nature of the resurrected body, at once seemingly ghostly and yet determinedly not so, has troubled Christological reflection from late antiquity to the present day. Sixteenth-century discussion of the topic is at times particularly involved, since it had important implications for the theology of the sacraments. For humanist biblical scholars, some aspects of the problem could be resolved philologically. Where the Vulgate employs the word 'evanuit' to describe how Christ's body 'vanished' at Emmaus, for instance, Erasmus contests this choice, arguing that the term is more appropriate to the action of smoke or ghosts.[116] Here the solution was simple enough: inaccurate translation had obscured the true nature of Christ's body. For Erasmus's implication here is clear, and heavily co-loured by Christ's words in Luke 24: the resurrected body is emphatically not a spirit.

For those (principally Catholic) theologians still working in the trad-itions of scholasticism, however, the philological niceties of Erasmus did not change the awkward fact that Christ's entrance to the locked room challenged a central tenet of Aristotle's *Physics*. This was the philosophical impossibility of *penetratio dimensionis*, or the penetration of dimensions. Jean de Champaignac, author of an early seventeenth-century vulgarisation of Aristotle, sums up the issue when he remarks that 'il estoit necessaire qu'en penetrant les corps des portes, ou des fenestres, ou de la muraille, son precieux corps et celuy des portes, ou des fenestres, ou de la muraille se rencontrassent ensemble en un mesme lieu'.[117] The problem for Champaignac was that scholastic commentators on the fourth book of Aristotle's *Physics*, dealing with definitions of place, had long proscribed the possibility of *penetratio dimensionis*, or the notion that any two bodies could occupy a single place at once.[118] How could this tradition, which endured in early modern

---

Bynum, *The Resurrection of the Body in Western Christianity, 200–1336* (New York: Columbia University Press, 1995).

[116] 'De fumo et spectris apte utimur evanescendi verbo; hic non de spectro, sed de vero corpore fit mentio'. See D. Erasmus, *Opera omnia* (Amsterdam: North Holland, 1969–), VI (pt. 5 = *Annotationes in Novum Testamentum*, ed. by P. F. Hovingh, 2000), p. 604.

[117] J. de Champaignac, *Sommaire des quatre parties de la philosophie, logique, ethique, phisique et metaphisique* (Paris: Fleury Bourriquant, 1606), p. 176: 'it was necessarily true that by penetrating the bodies of the doors, or of the windows, or of the wall, his precious body and that of the doors, windows, or wall must have come together in one and the same place'.

[118] The key passage was *Physics,*IV.1 209a2: 'Now a place, as such, has three dimensions of length, breadth, and depth, which determines the limits of all bodies; but it cannot itself be a body, for a "body" were in a "place" and the place itself were a body, two bodies would coincide'; see Aristotle, *The Physics*, ed. and trans. by P. H. Wicksteed and F. M. Cornford, Loeb Classical Library, 2 vols. (London: Heinemann, 1929), I, p. 283. See also St Thomas Aquinas, *In octo libros physicorum aristotelis expositio*, ed. by P. M. Maggiòlo (Rome: Marietti, 1954), p. 206.

physics, account for the interpenetration of Christ's risen body and the walls of the locked room?[119]

Catholic attempts to unscramble this mystery usually followed Aquinas. In a densely argued passage in the *Summa Theologica*, Aquinas had claimed that even glorified bodies, possessed though they were of extraordinary subtlety, could not contravene the proscription on *penetratio dimensionis*.[120] Instead he claims somewhat evasively that Christ's entrance could have only occurred through divine intervention (*ex virtute divinitatis*). Quoting Gregory the Great, he concludes that Christ's appearance in the midst of the disciples was a miracle comparable to the penetration of the locked womb of the Virgin. As for how it was achieved, he recalls Augustine's adage: 'si comprehendis modum, non est miraculum' ('if you understand the means, it is not a miracle'). Champaignac adopts this Thomist line when he redescribes Christ's body in Luke as a 'corps sans extension'. For reasons we need not seek to understand, such bodies could not only exist, with divine permission, in the same place as non-glorified bodies, but were also capable of occupying several places at once: 'Joint qu'il ne repugne non-plus qu'un lieu soit accomodé à plusieurs corps, qu'un corps soit accomodé à plusieurs lieux.'[121] In this way the episode of the locked room was able to serve, through its very contravention of Aristotle's physics, to found the theological basis for Christ's ubiquity.

Thanks to this extraordinary piece of exegetical chutzpah, the Counter-Reformation was able to transform the problem of the locked room into a polemical opportunity. For the idea of corporeal ubiquity not only solved the problem of Christ's walking through walls but also served apologists of Real Presence, whose central claim was that Christ could be present at God's right hand and—simultaneously—in the Eucharistic bread. This association was not lost on Jean Calvin, who counters the idea of the glorified body in a number of his works. Here he found himself opposed to both Catholic and Lutheran teaching. The former is ridiculed in his *Traicté sur la Cène*, where he attacks the doctrine of transubstantiation, according to which the substance of Christ's body replaces that of the bread: 'Pour soubstenir cela, il fault confesser, ou que le corps de Christ est

---

[119] For instance, see F. Toletus, *Societatus Iesu Commentaria una cum quaestionibus in octo libros aristotelis de physica auscultatione* (Venetiis: apud Iuntas, 1580), sig. 106ʳ; A. Scaino, *In octo Aristotelis libros de physica auscultatione accuratissima expositio* (Francofurti: apud Claudium Marnium, et heredes Ioannis Aubrii, 1607), p. 122.

[120] *Summa theologica*, IIIa, q. 54, a. 1. The same argument appears in St Thomas Aquinas, *Super evangelium S. Ioannis lectura*, ed. by P. Raphael Cai (Rome: Marietti, 1952), p. 468.

[121] Champaignac, *Sommaire*, p. 176: 'Just as it is possible that a place be accommodated to several bodies, a body might be accommodated to several places.'

sans mesure, ou qu'il poult estre en divers lieux. Et en disant cela, on vient en la fin à ce poinct, qu'il ne differe en rien d'un Phantasme.'[122] Calvin's recourse to the figure of the ghost ('phantasme') here suggests that, by propounding the theory of Real Presence, his Catholic opponents were effectively repeating, at every Mass, the disciples' error in the locked room: ignoring the essential physicality of the risen Christ's body, they had simply transformed him back into a ghost.

Luther's doctrine of consubstantiation drew a similar riposte, again framed in the opposition between bodies and ghosts. A passage in Calvin's *Institution* claims that those adhering to Luther's position, for whom Christ's glorified body is co-present with the bread, similarly 'despouillent Jesus Christ de son corps, et le transfigurent en un fantosme'.[123] Of course, in maintaining this position Calvin is thrown back painfully upon the puzzle of how Christ entered the locked room. Against both his Catholic and Lutheran opponents, Calvin advances in the *Institution* a radically different explanation for the appearance in the locked room: it was not Christ's body, but the nature of the walls, that was transformed in the miracle. Just as the water, when he walked on the lake, had been changed into a 'pavé ferme' for his feet, so 'on ne doit trouver estrange si la dureté de la pierre s'est amollie pour luy donner passage'.[124] Elsewhere Calvin concedes, with Augustine, that the miracle is itself locked against human understanding.[125] But his own conviction in Christ the body, as against Christ the 'fantosme', persists unmollified. Calvin's writing on Luke is as striking a demonstration as any how far ghosts intruded, albeit as a shadow or negative term, on the central battlegrounds of Reformation exegesis.

Communing with the Dead: Lazarus and Dives

If the story of Christ's appearance to the Apostles raised the question of scriptural justification for belief in ghosts, we have also seen how Christological discussion of the episode also carried far-reaching scientific implications:

[122] J. Calvin, *Three French Treatises*, ed. by F. M. Higman (London: Athlone, 1970), pp. 120–1: 'In order to support that thesis, one needs to confess either that the body of Christ is without measure, or that it can exist in several places. And by saying this, one ends up saying that he differs in no way from a ghost.'

[123] Calvin, *Institution*, IV, p. 381: '[They] strip Jesus Christ of his body, and transform him into a ghost.'

[124] Ibid., p. 417: 'one should not find it strange that the hardness of the stone softened to allow him through'. For a leading Jesuit's response to this argument, see J. Maldonat, *Commentarii in quattuor evangelistas* (Venice: G.-B. and G.-B. Sessa, 1597), p. 1108.

[125] J. Calvin, *Commentaires de Jehan Calvin sur le Nouveau Testament*, 4 vols. (Paris: C. Meyrueis, 1854–5), II, 397.

for the corporeality of spirits, and for the physical relationship between spirits, bodies, and place. The parable of Lazarus and Dives (Luke 16:19–31) posed similar questions for those who sought biblical support for the idea that the dead could return to the living, though its broader implications bore less on physics than morality. What should be the relationship between the souls of the deceased and their living relatives or friends? And what kind of restrictions does God place on contact between the two?

'If they hear not Moses and the prophets, neither will they be persuaded, though one rose from the dead' (Luke 16:31). These are the words spoken by Abraham to the rich man (Dives) who, languishing in hell, had begged that Lazarus might be permitted to return to and warn his surviving brothers of the fate awaiting them. Another instance of the New Testament's association of ghosts with impossibility or error, Abraham's refusal of Dives's request had served the case against ghosts since late antiquity. Most notable within this sceptical tradition was Augustine's view that, while the tale's central refusal was not proof that return from the dead was impossible, the story does suggest that God was generally unwilling to release ghosts from the world beyond.[126] In a moving aside in his short treatise *De cura pro mortuis gerenda* ('How to Help the Dead'), Augustine adds that if ghosts were indeed free to return to the living, 'me ipsum pia mater . . . nulla nocte desereret, quae terra marique secuta est, ut mecum viveret' ('my dear mother . . . who followed me over land and sea to be with me, would never leave me for a single night').[127] Like Lazarus, St Monica was a non-ghost—a would-be ghost who never was.

Early modern readers of Luke 16 and its great patristic commentator were forced to adopt one of two conclusions in response to Abraham's refusal. The first, found in Calvin and some others, was that it was clearly not God's will that the dead should return to the living. The second, favoured among Catholics, was that souls may come back from the dead, but that something in Dives's circumstances prevented it in this specific case. These two positions, which arise again and again in early modern debates of ghosts, are worth exploring in more detail.

The parable of Lazarus and Dives was particularly attractive to Protestant theologians. Not only did Abraham's refusal suggest the impossibility of return from the dead, but the terms in which that refusal is couched ('if they hear not Moses and the Prophets') also lent considerable force to

---

[126] See Schmitt, *Revenants*, p. 36.

[127] Augustine, *De fide et symbolo . . . De cura pro mortuis gerenda*, ed. by J. Zycha, Corpus Scriptorum Ecclesiasticorum Latinorum 41 (Section V, Part III) (Prague: F. Tempsky, 1900), p. 647. For the translation, see Augustine, *How to Help the Dead*, trans. by M. H. Allies (London: Burns & Oates, 1914), p. 42.

the great Reformist slogan, *sola scriptura* (through Scripture alone). In this spirit Calvin's commentary on Luke uses the story as an opportunity for a polemical sideswipe against all those who pass over the testimony of Scripture: 'Nous voyons que ceux ausquels toute l'Escriture vient à desgoust, se jettent volontairement et d'une affection ardente aux laqs de Satan. De là est venue la necromantie et semblables abus, lesquels le monde non-seulement receoit ardemment, ains aussi court après d'un appetit enragé.'[128] Calvin's implication here—that Dives was petitioning Abraham to engage in a form of necromancy—is a common refrain among writers sympathetic to the Protestant cause. Johann Weyer, for whom the desire to learn from the dead represents the worst kind of curiosity, also invokes Luke's words, 'ils ont Moyse, et les Prophetes', in condemning necromancy.[129] For this Weyer decries not only Saul's damnable attempt to raise the ghost of Samuel, but also several theological colleges where, he claims, the study of necromancy had only recently been removed from the schools' curriculum.[130] Such methods, he concluded, never brought true contact with the dead, but only with the Devil who appeared in their place.

It need hardly be said that Catholic apologists for ghosts encouraged very different readings of Christ's parable in Luke. The story served to overcome an important objection to ghosts issuing not from Protestant circles, but from scholastic tradition. The difficulty surrounded a passage in Aristotle's *De anima*, which suggested that dead souls retain no memory of, still less affection for, those they left behind. Although Aristotle does not deny that the soul was immortal, he stipulates quite clearly that 'memory and love' vanish when it perishes, since they were never part of the soul alone, but what he calls 'the whole entity'.[131] The negative implications of Aristotle's position, which found some support in the writings of Aquinas, were clear for those who wished to uphold that ghosts still returned to the living: if the living still cared for the dead, the dead no longer cared for the living.

---

[128] J. Calvin, *Commentaires... sur la concordance ou harmonie composee de trois evangelistes, asçavoir S. Matthieu, S. Marc et S. Luc* [1558] (Geneva: Joachin de Contrieres, 1564), p. 196: 'We see that those to whom Scripture is distasteful throw themselves willingly and with a burning desire into the snares of Satan. From that has arisen necromancy and similar abuses, the which the world not only fervently receives, but pursues with enraged appetite.'

[129] Weyer, *De l'imposture*, sig. 89ʳ.

[130] Ibid., sig. 95ᵛ. A similar accusation is made in C. Peucer, *Les Devins, ou commentaire des principales sortes de devinations*, trans. by S. Goulart (Lyon: B. Honorati, 1584), fo. Eiiʳ.

[131] Aristotle, *De anima* 408b ll. 19–32. English quotation from Aristotle, *On the Soul; Parva Naturalia; On Breath*, trans. by W. S. Hett, Loeb Classical Library (Cambridge, MA: Harvard University Press, 1957), p. 49.

Early modern arguments against that position are often set up as a debate between Aristotle and Plato, in whose philosophy the memory of the soul was, by contrast, a central tenet. For the sixteenth-century Platonist Cornelius Agrippa, the case against Aristotle and his follower Aquinas is clear. Demonstrating that his scepticism about stories like Montalembert's *Merveilleuse Hystoire* did not translate into a universal hostility towards ghosts, Agrippa cites a number of narratives in his *De occulta philosophia*, mainly drawn from classical sources, in which dead souls do indeed return to the living. He claims that ancient accounts in which the ghosts of slain men or abandoned women pursue those who wronged them prove beyond doubt that 'in anima seiuncta a corpore perturbationes et memoriae sensus remanent' ('when the soul is separated from the body, perturbations and memories of the sense remain').[132] Returning to the theme in his *De incertitudine et vanitate scientiarum*, Agrippa makes the still more telling observation that the Aristotelian position contravenes not only Platonist teaching and the literary evidence, but also that of Scripture. The rich man of Luke's parable undeniably retains some affection for his brothers, he adds, or he would not have petitioned Abraham to send Lazarus to warn them.[133] Though Counter-Reformation theologians viewed Agrippa with suspicion, his verdict against Aristotle, and especially his reading of the Lazarus story, was put to frequent use among apologists for ghosts.[134]

The arguments against Aristotle were usually confined to a Catholic theology in dialogue with its own scholastic heritage, so that to dispute his claims over the forgetfulness of souls was not a specifically anti-heretical manoeuvre. The challenge posed by Protestant readings of Luke 16 was rather, as we have seen, the contention that God was unwilling to let the dead return. Catholic theologians answered this proposition with a familiar strategy. Just as Christ, in showing the Apostles that he was not a ghost, did not deny the existence of ghosts in general, similarly Abraham's words to Dives cannot be used as proof that the dead are *never* permitted to visit the living. Rather, there must be something specific to Dives's circumstances that meant God saw fit to refuse his request. It is in answering the question of what this something might be that Catholic theology was able to engage moral objections to enquiring of the dead.

---

[132] H. Cornelius Agrippa von Nettesheim, *De occulta philosophia libri tres* (1531), ed. by V. Perrone Compagni (Leiden: Brill, 1992), p. 524.

[133] Agrippa, *De incertitudine*, sigs. 63ᵛ–4ʳ.

[134] See Crespet, *Discours catholiques*, sigs. 283ᵛ–4ʳ; Boaistuau, Belleforest, et al., *Histoires prodigieuses*, III, pp. 354–6.

Calvin had argued that commerce between the living and the dead is always diabolic. Catholic theologians too were far from unaware of such dangers. Noël Taillepied, in his analysis of Luke 16, looks back to the scholastics' gloss on an often-cited passage in Peter Lombard's *Sententiae*. According to the schoolbooks, any vain or curious attempt to seek an audience with ghosts is sinful. This disapprobation is not limited to those who have recourse to witches and wizards; it even extends to those who strive to meet the dead through outward shows of devotion or prayer: 'Mesmes qui invoqueroit Dieu afin qu'il fist apparoistre une ame, n'ayant autre intention que vanité ou curiosité, il offenceroit grievement.'[135] André Valladier, preaching his Advent sermons on demonology late in 1612, issues a similar warning against premeditated pacts between the living and the dead. Agreements made between friends, whereby a dying man would promise to visit the other and tell him the secrets of the afterlife, had become something of a ghost-narrative topos in the later Middle Ages, with Boccaccio's story of Meuccio and Tingoccio the most celebrated example.[136] Valladier's rhetorical question 'peut-on faire pacte, tu viendras à moy, et te monstreras à moy si tu meurs le premier?' is therefore not entirely idle.[137] He warns in response that he judges 'tels essays et tels pactes estre dangereux, temeraires et fort exposez aux illusions de Sathan'.[138] Here, as for Taillepied, curious intentions are invitations to the Devil.

Since Dives's desire to warn his brothers was in itself laudable, the question of motive alone cannot explain Abraham's refusal, however. The main obstacle was Dives's and his brothers' lack of piety. Taillepied writes that not only did 'la cruauté et l'inhumanité du mauvais riche envers le pauvre, ne meritoit pas d'estre exaucee', but his brothers' faithlessness was such that they did not merit an audience with the dead.[139] Unlike Calvin, Taillepied is not here making a point about the relative priority of ghostly messengers and Scripture. He is concerned rather to distinguish between different qualities of witness. Some will never give credence to revelation from the dead. This point is reinforced with an appeal to a second biblical Lazarus, the brother of Martha and Mary resurrected by Christ (John

[135] Taillepied, *Psichologie*, p. 224: 'Even he who would call on God to make a soul appear for motives of mere vanity or curiosity would be committing a serious offence.'

[136] G. Boccaccio, *Decameron*, trans. by G. H. McWilliam (London: Penguin, 2003), pp. 544–50 (seventh day, tenth story). On the iconography of this story, see Schmitt, *Les Revenants*, pp. 244–5 and plate 27.

[137] 'Can one make a pact? You will come to me, and show yourself to me if you die first.'

[138] A. Valladier, *La Saincte Philosophie de l'âme, sermons pour l'Advent preschez à Laris, à Saint Méderic, l'an 1612* (n.d., n.p.), pp. 742–3: 'such attempts and pacts to be dangerous, overbold and highly vulnerable to the illusions of Satan'.

[139] 'the cruelty and inhumanity of the wicked rich man towards the poor man was not deserving of pity'.

11:1–44). Taillepied here reads the extraordinary experience of this Lazarus as an historical instantiation of the parable in Luke. John's account is
cited as proof of Abraham's words that 'though one rose from the dead'
and revealed the truths of the beyond, there were still some among those
watching who would not lend him credence. Taillepied asks rhetorically:
'Les Juifs ont ils adjousté foy à ce qu'il [Lazarus] disoit, non plus qu'à
nostre Seigneur qui estoit descendu du sein de son Pere, et apparu icy
bas pour enseigner le peuple?'[140] As the reference to the Jews' denials of
Christ's own resurrection shows, too great a suspicion of the dead can be
just as disastrous as excessive curiosity. Between them, the two Lazaruses
serve to show how the living might, and occasionally must, profit from the
lessons of the dead.[141]

The apparition of ghosts is a real possibility, but they only appear to a
certain kind of witness. Where Protestants saw in Abraham's refusal a
categorical repudiation of ghosts, then, Catholic readings relativize the
motives and character of those who see them. This difference is crucial. If
Peter Lombard, Valladier, and Taillepied prohibit certain individuals from
seeking commerce with the dead, for others they prise open a space for
sanctified communion. As Taillepied is keen to stress, to request dialogue
with the departed is not always to be condemned as necromantic, especially if its purpose is to help those suffering in Purgatory: 'Si on le [i.e.
contact with the dead] demande à bonne intention, afin de sçavoir en quel
estat sont les amis, voisins, bienfaicteurs, peres, meres, et comment ils se
portent, et que s'ils sont en peine, on leur puissent aider et faire par
suffrages qu'ils soyent plustost delivrez, cela n'est point malfait.'[142] Desire
for communion with dead loved ones is here legitimized within the
context of familial and communitarian ('amis, voisins, bienfaicteurs,
peres, meres') obligations. Valladier makes a similar observation. However
unconscionable the prurient pact of Boccaccio's Meuccio and Tingoccio,
he insists the desire to relieve dead souls in Purgatory is not to be

---

[140] Taillepied, *Psichologie*, p. 225: 'Did the Jews believe what Lazarus said any more than
they did our Lord who had descended from his father's breast, and appeared here below in
order to teach the people?'

[141] A tradition conflating the Lazarus of Luke's parable with the risen Lazarus dates back
(at least) to Origen's commentary on John's Gospel. See Origen, *Opera omnia*, trans. by
C. and C. V. Delarue, Bibliotheca Patrum Graeca, 7 vols. in 9 (Paris: J.-P. Migne, 1862),
IV, p. 474. For a discussion of this tradition, see A. Marchadour, *Lazare: histoire d'un récit,
récits d'une histoire* (Paris: Cerf, 1988), pp. 163–6.

[142] Taillepied, *Psichologie*, pp. 224–5: 'If one asks for it [i.e. contact with the dead] well-
intentionedly, in order to find out about the state in which friends, neighbours, benefactors,
mothers, fathers, find themselves and how they are faring, and if they are in torment, and if
one can help them and ensure through indulgences that they be soon delivered, this is no
wicked deed.'

condemned: 'sçavoir si l'on peut ce qu'elles [les ames] veulent, et le faire avec discretion, et non autrement: irreprehensible'.[143] Provided those seeking out the dead proceed with good intentions, they might receive the privilege that God denied to Dives's sinful brothers.

'Faire avec discretion', Valladier's exceptionalism—that only the 'discreet' witness can have dealings with the dead—effectively brings this chapter full circle. The Catholic response to hostile Protestant readings of Luke 16 represents a fusion of the demonological and pastoral strands of sixteenth-century *discretio spirituum*. On the one hand, exegetical discussion in writers such as Taillepied and Valladier is embedded within a broader reflection on necromantic curiosity. To this extent, their readings of Luke's parable, like those of Calvin, intersect with the demonological preoccupations of Maldonado, Crespet, and (as we shall see in a later chapter) witchcraft prosecutors such as Henri Boguet and Pierre de Lancre. On the other hand, their concern is not to prohibit all contact with the dead, as Calvin did, but rather to set limits on how such contact is conducted. In this respect they differ both from their Protestant opponents and from the growing demonological tendency, increasingly influential in the last decades of the sixteenth century, to diabolize ghosts along with witchcraft and the pact. By placing the moral character of the witness at the centre of discernment, several late-century writers suggest that ghostly encounters presented not so much a doctrinal or juridical problem, as a pastoral opportunity. Those who claimed to see ghosts need not be denounced as superstitious, or condemned as witches or magicians. In the hands of Taillepied and Valladier, such visitations could validate and reinforce the pious habits of the witness. Nor was this optimism the preserve of Catholic theology alone. For while Protestants such as Calvin and Farel denied that the dead might appear to the living, they did not rule out the possibility that 'spirits' of other kinds might serve the cause of Reformation. A notable example of this was Ludwig Lavater's 1571 *Trois livres des apparitions des esprits*. This influential text and Noël Taillepied's reply, both instances of what might thus be termed 'pastoral demonology', are the subjects of the following chapter.

---

[143] Valladier, *Saincte philosophie*, p. 743: 'to know if one can do what they [the souls] desire, and do it with discretion, and not otherwise: irreproachable'.

2

Pastoral Demonology

In the previous chapter we saw how during the later Middle Ages expertise in visionary matters—characterized after St Paul as *discretio spirituum*—was secured as the privilege of learned clergymen. However, whereas medieval authorities such as Pierre d'Ailly and, principally, Jean Gerson concerned themselves primarily with the regulation of female mystical and visionary experience, the business of discernment in the sixteenth and early sevententh centuries began to shift in two directions. First, what I chose to term 'pastoral discernment', theorized by Loyola and François de Sales, and practised by spiritual directors such as Da Fermo, maintained a strong focus on female devotional experience, but largely emptied it of visionary content. The 'spirits' with which pastoral *discretio* contended were no longer dreams or mystical visitations, but benign or malign impulses that jostled for control of the laywoman's daily moral conduct. Second, 'demonological discernment'—still focused on women in the figure of the witch—displays a different emphasis again. Unlike its Gersonian ancestor and its pastoral variant, demonological discernment externalized the 'spirits' of *discretio spirituum*. Made newly urgent through the outbreak of the European witch craze, its task was to make legible the difference between apparitions apprehended through the senses: ghosts, angels, and demons.

In the latter half of the sixteenth century a third, hybrid, strand appeared in Europe. This form of expertise still involved the relationship between religious authority and lay spiritual experience. But here the ordinarily divergent foci of pastoral and demonological discernment came together. 'Pastoral demonology', as I propose to call it, viewed apparitions as an opportunity above all to influence the domain of daily lay devotion, fiercely contested as it was in the years following the Council of Trent. The texts that constitute this corpus remain largely unexplored.[1]

---

[1] A notable exception is B. Gordon, 'Malevolent Ghosts and Ministering Angels: Apparitions and Pastoral Care in the Swiss Reformation' in *The Place of the Dead: Death*

Preoccupied as modern historians have been with witchcraft, which is to say a relationship between a spirit and its witness that has already been determined as criminal, other—more morally problematic—forms of supernatural experience have tended to pass unnoticed. One such form is, precisely, the layperson's encounter with apparitions of the dead. What must the ordinary witness do when visited by ghosts?

Several European texts in the period, or portions of texts, attempted a careful definition of what was and was not devotionally permissible in lay transactions with spirits claiming to be the souls of the departed. Some of these were written in Latin and aimed mainly, one must suppose, at clergy of all three confessions: these include the German Protestant Johannes Rivius's relatively early *De spectris et apparitionibus umbrarum* (1541), several late-century works of the Jesuit Petrus Thyraeus, large portions of Delrio's *Disquisitiones magicarum* (1599), and Scherertzius's *Libellus consolatorius de spectris, hoc est apparitionibus et illusionibus Daemonum* (1621). In France, however, and in line with an effort to reach the lay reader himself, a small number of pastoral demonologies had begun to appear in the vernacular. Examples of this tendency include René Du Pont's *La Philosophie des esprits* (1602), André Valladier's remarkable Advent sermons on apparitions, printed as *La Saincte Philosophie de l'âme* (1612), and Jean de l'Espagnol's *Traicté des apparitions des esprits et fantosmes* (1617).

Any of these texts might have served as illustrations of pastorally oriented demonology in early modern France. For the purposes of this chapter, however, two other, slightly earlier works have been preferred. The first is the Protestant Ludwig Lavater's enormously influential *Von Gespaenstern*, translated into French in 1571; the second is Noël Taillepied's Catholic reply to Lavater, *Psichologie, ou traité de l'apparition des esprits*, printed in 1588. These two texts (Lavater's in particular) have already received some scholarly attention, though they have never been subjected to sustained analysis and comparison.[2] What follows here introduces each author and treatise, describes the circumstances of the texts' publication, and explores the two authors' handling of ghost narrative within the works. From that comparison of narrative method will emerge some important differences in the two authors' attitudes to gender, and to narrative setting. These distinctions are important, and allow us to

---

and Remembrance in Late Medieval and Early Modern Europe, ed. by B. Gordon and P. Marshall (Cambridge: Cambridge University Press, 2000), pp. 87–109.

[2] The fullest attempt to bring them together remains J. Newton, 'Reading Ghosts: Early Modern Interpretations of Apparitions' in *Early Modern Ghosts*, pp. 57–69; see also Clark, *Vanities of the Eye*, pp. 207–14 (on Lavater, Taillepied, and suspect visual phenomena).

make some more general observations about the ground on which Protestant and Catholic pastoral demonology conflicted—and sometimes surprisingly converged—in the period.

LUDWIG LAVATER, *TROIS LIVRES DES APPARITIONS DES ESPRITS* (1571)

Author and Text

Ludwig Lavater's life and career were those of a distinguished Protestant humanist.[3] Born in the German-speaking Kyburg in 1527, he travelled to Strasbourg at the age of eighteen, where he encountered the prominent humanist scholars Martin Bucer and Johann Sturm. From Strasbourg he moved on to Paris to study under a number of French luminaries, including Adrien Turnèbe, Denis Lambin and, most importantly, Petrus Ramus, with whom he would keep up a lengthy correspondence. Following a final excursion to Italy in the late 1540s, Lavater returned to Switzerland, where he was made archdeacon and canon at the Grossmünster in Zurich. In the years that followed, he became a leading Protestant controversialist, and in 1585 was consecrated chief pastor in Zurich. He died in July of the following year, leaving behind a number of Old Testament commentaries, a text on the institutes of the Church of Zurich, a treatise on the Eucharist, a biography of his father-in-law, Heinrich Bullinger, and a short history of comets. But most celebrated of all, both now and within the author's own lifetime, is the treatise on apparitions that is the subject of what follows.

Lavater's *Von Gespaenstern* was first published in German in 1569. Three translations followed in quick succession, into Latin, French, and English.[4] A brief look at this print history reveals an effort on the part of

---

[3] The following biographical information is drawn from M. Godet, V. Attinger, H. Türler et al., *Dictionnaire historique et biographique de la Suisse*, 7 vols. (Neuchâtel: Administration du dictionnaire biographique et historique de la Suisse, 1921–33), IV, p. 482. See also D. Langwehr, 'Gut und böse Engel contra Arme Seelen. Reformierte Dämonologie und die Folgen für die Kunst, gezeigt an Ludwig Lavaters Gespensterbuch von 1569' in *Bilderstreit, Kulturwandel in Zwinglis Reformation*, ed. by H.-D. Altendorf and P. Jezler (Zurich: Theologischer Verlag, 1984), pp. 125–34.

[4] *Von Gespaenstern, unghüren, faeln, und anderen wunderbaren dingen, so merteils wenn die menschen sterben soellend, oder wenn sunst grosse sachennd enderungen vorhanden sind, beschaehend, kurtzer und einfaltiger bericht* (Zurich: C. Froschauer, 1569); *De Spectris, lemuribus et magnis atque insolitis fragoribus, variisque praesagitionibus quae plerunque obitum hominum, magnas clades, mutationesque imperiorum praecedunt, liber unus* (Geneva: J. Crespin, 1570); *Trois livres des apparitions des esprits, fantosmes, prodiges et accidens merveilleux qui precedent souventesfois la mort de quelque personage renommé, ou un grand*

both the author and his publishers to reach a large, and intellectually diverse, international readership. In common with all of Lavater's previous works, the original German text was published in Zurich by Christoph Froschauer, nephew and successor of the great printer of the same name.[5] Though Froschauer had produced a number of luxury editions throughout his career, a small octavo format was deemed to suffice for *Von Gespaenstern*. The result was an inexpensive text that would have been affordable not only for the gentleman scholar, but also for a readership of more modest means. An attempt to reach the same readership appears to have prompted the author's choice of language. For the humanist-educated Lavater, all of whose previous works had been published in Latin, a treatise in German constituted a radical new departure. In his preface to the treatise the author explains, using a formula that remains constant throughout the German, Latin, French, and English editions, how he holds it to be vital that he and others like him write in the vernacular in order to 'teache, instructe, and confirme the rude and unlearned people'.[6] In this ambition Lavater reflects more than just the Protestant emphasis on the vernacular; he also upholds the educational ideals of his father-in-law, and Zwingli's successor in Zurich, Heinrich Bullinger.[7]

In the event, the German edition achieved only moderate popularity among subsequent printers and editors.[8] By contrast Lavater's own Latin

---

changement és choses de ce monde... traduits d'Aleman en françois, conferez, reveus et augmentez sur le Latin... Plus trois questions proposées et resolues par M. P. Martyr... lesquelles conviennent à cette matiere (Geneva: F. Perrin for J. Durand, 1571); *Of Ghostes and Spirites Walking by Nyght, and of Strange Noyses, Crackes, and Sundry Forewarnynges, which Commonly Happen before the Death of Menne, Great Slaughters, and Alterations of Kyngdomes*, trans. by R. H. [Robert Harrison?] (London: H. Benneyman for R. Watkyns, 1572). Gordon claims ('Apparitions and Pastoral Care', p. 95) that Lavater's work was also translated into Spanish and Italian, though he provides no references. I have found no trace of these translations.

[5] On the Froschauer family and their influence in Reformed Zurich, see G. M. Ella, *Henry Bullinger (1504–1575): Shepherd of the Churches* (Durham: Go, 2007), pp. 442–5.

[6] *Of Ghostes*, sig. Bi[v].

[7] On Bullinger's educational reforms in Zurich, see P. Biel, *Doorkeepers at the House of Righteousness: Heinrich Bullinger and the Zurich Clergy, 1535–1575* (Bern: Peter Lang, 1991), ch. 6 ('When Teaching isn't Preaching'); K. J. Rüetschi, 'Bullinger and the Schools' in *Architect of the Reformation: An Introduction to Heinrich Bullinger, 1504–1575*, ed. by B. Gordon and E. Campi (Michigan: Baker, 2004), pp. 215–29.

[8] *Von Gespaenstern* was reprinted once by Froschauer's workshop in 1578, and again in 1586, as part of a folio-volume compilation of demonological texts: see R. Lutz et al., *Theatrum de veneficis, das ist, Von teuffelsgespenst Zauberern und gifftbereitern Schwartzkunstlern Heren und Unholden, vieler fürnemmen Historien und Exempel... sehr nützlich und dienstlich zu wissen und keines Wegs zu verachten*, ed. by A. Saur (Frankfurt am Main: N. Basseum, 1586).

translation, printed one year later in 1570, made a far greater impact.[9] This text, entitled *De spectris*, marked another new departure. In charge of this Latin edition was the Genevan printer, Jean Crespin. This new collaboration appears to have been successful. Crespin himself published two editions in 1570; these were followed by two further editions, in 1575 and 1580, from the workshop of his son-in-law Eustache Vignon; after a long hiatus the Latin text continued to be re-edited, and indeed illustrated, well into the seventeenth century.[10] Lavater's choice of Crespin as publisher, himself the author of the celebrated Protestant martyrology, *Le Livre des martyrs*, may have been influenced by a combination of two factors. The first has to do with the material composition of the text. *De spectris*, like the original *Von Gespaenstern*, was published in a relatively small-format edition. Unlike Froschauer, however, Crespin was a specialist in what we would now call 'mass-media' publication, and would have been well suited to the task of printing a large number of such texts.[11] Second, and just as importantly, the Genevan publisher was well placed to introduce *De spectris* to a francophone readership. Indeed, it was probably thanks to Crespin's involvement that a French edition of the treatise was also printed at Geneva in 1571.

The French version, translated anonymously and entitled *Trois livres des apparitions des esprits*, was published in the workshops of François Perrin and Crespin's one-time associate, Jean Durand.[12] The title informs the reader that the *Trois livres* have been translated from the German and checked against ('conferez sur') the Latin. Appended to the text, once again a relatively inexpensive octavo, was a translation of Pietro Martire Vermigli's Latin commentary on the biblical episode of Samuel's apparition to Saul. Like *De spectris*, the French translation of Lavater's work appears to have been more successful than the original German text. In 1581, perhaps keen to capitalise on the impact of Bodin's *De la Demonomanie des sorciers*, published the year before, the Zurich printer Guillaume

---

[9] Gilmont suggests in his book on Crespin that the Latin edition was also published in 1569. I have found no convincing evidence for this earlier date. See J.-F. Gilmont, *Jean Crespin: un éditeur réformé du XVIe siècle* (Geneva: Droz, 1981) p. 162.

[10] The two 1570 imprints are marked 'apud Joannem Crispinum' and 'anchora Crispiniana'. Aside from Vignon's imprints of 1575 and 1580, further editions appeared in 1659, 1683 (illustrated), and 1687.

[11] According to A. Stegmann. See his 'Comment constituer une bibliothèque en France au début du XVIIe siècle: examen méthodologique', in *Le Livre dans l'Europe de la Renaissance: actes du XVIIIe colloque international d'études humanistes de Tours*, ed. by P. Aquilon and H.-J. Martin (Paris: Promodis, 1988), pp. 467–501 (p. 476).

[12] On Durand, see P. Chaix, *Recherches sur l'imprimerie à Genève de 1550–1564* (Geneva: Droz, 1954), pp. 180–1.

des Marecz printed a second, slightly different, edition.[13] Des Marecz follows Vermigli's commentary on I Samuel with *Un brief discours sur le fait de la magie*, a single-gathering 'abrégé' of ancient and modern writing on witchcraft and magic. The printer's decision suggests that, in the ten years since its first publication, Lavater's treatise had profited from an expanding interest in European vernacular demonology.[14]

There are a number of slight differences between the editions described above, and especially between *De spectris* and Durand's French text. Though the number and scale of these distinctions should not be overstated, they tend to confirm the natural assumption that the Latin and vernacular texts were destined for different kinds of reader. Despite the titular claim that the French *Des apparitions* had been 'conferez sur le latin', there are several moments in *De spectris* where the author has recourse to various kinds of technical vocabulary missing in Durand's French translation. Rhetorical terminology is one feature of the Latin edition absent in the French. For instance, *De spectris* contains a number of references to the terms *metaphora* and *metonymia*.[15] Since the recent publication of Ramus's *Rhetorica* of 1567, these terms had become the twin pillars of Ramist *elocutio*.[16] Lavater, who had not long since corresponded with Ramus on the proper division of the tropes and figures, here employs, for his Latin readers, the buzzwords of contemporary humanist fashion.[17] The absence of such terms in *Des apparitions* suggests that the

---

[13] L. Lavater, *Trois livres des apparitions des esprits, fantômes, prodiges et accidens merveilleux qui précèdent souventesfois la mort de quelque personnage renommé ou un grand changement ès choses de ce monde, composez par Loys Lavater... traduits d'aleman en françois, conferez... et augmentez sur le latin. Plus trois questions proposées et résolues par M. Pierre Martyr... lesquelles conviennent à ceste matière, traduites aussi de latin en françois; avecques lesquels nous avons de nouveau... ajouté un brief discours sur le fait de la magie... Le tout recueilli de la Demonomanie de M. Bodin et autres divers livres tant grecs que latins* (Zurich: G. des Marecz, 1581).

[14] While it is possible that Lavater, through Crespin and Des Marecz, had some involvement with the publication of the French editions, the same is unlikely to be true of the English translation that appeared in London in 1572. According to the title page of this text, published by Richard Watkyns and entitled *Of Ghostes and Spirites Walking by Nyght*, this translation was the work of one 'R. H.' usually considered to be Robert Harrison, later a Brownist separatist from the Church of England. For an introduction to Harrison and a selection of his works, see *The Writings of Robert Harrison and Robert Browne*, ed. by L. H. Carlson and A. Peel (= vol. 2 of *Elizabethan Non-Conformist Texts*), 6 vols. (London: Routledge, 2003), pp. 1–25 (introduction) and pp. 26–149 (selected works).

[15] *De spectris*, p. 122 (*metaphora*) and p. 165 (*metonymia*).

[16] On the categorization of the tropes and figures in Ramus's *Rhetorica*, see K. Meerhoff, *Rhétorique et poétique au XVIe siècle en France: Du Bellay, Ramus et les autres* (Leiden: Brill, 1986), p. 294.

[17] On Lavater's correspondence with Ramus, see ibid.

translator, the publishers—perhaps even Lavater himself—may have imagined a less erudite readership for the French vernacular edition.

A further, and more immediately striking, difference between *De spectris* and *Des apparitions* concerns the Latin edition's inaugural chapter on philology.[18] *De spectris* begins with a conspectus of around fifty classical terms—'spectrum', 'visum', 'phantasmata', 'phasmata', 'manes', 'incubi', 'succubi', and so on—with which the field of study might be delimited and defined. This lexicon, which shows the influence of Scaliger, made a considerable impression on later humanist readers, among them Le Loyer in his *Quatre livres des spectres*.[19] However, in *Des apparitions* the chapter disappears, now replaced with a translator's note explaining the difficulty of providing French renderings for Greek and Latin terms.[20] Here again, as with the removal of specialist rhetorical terminology, the French translator's bias downplays the humanist colouration of Lavater's Latin version.[21]

The French translator's hesitations over specialist terminology may be a function of a wider uncertainty over the kind of readers his publisher envisaged. By introducing ghosts into the language of his native France, Durand was entering uncharted territory. It is important to remember that the homeland of Bodin and Pierre de Lancre did not yet have a native, vernacular demonology when *Des apparitions* appeared in 1571. Not that francophone writers had lacked interest in ghosts and related subjects: Rabelais's *Tiers Livre* (1546), Ronsard's 'Hymne des Daimons' (1555), Boaistuau's *Histoires prodigieuses* (1560), and Robert du Triez's *Les Ruses, finesses et impostures des esprits malins* (1563) all pre-date Lavater.[22] But the vernacular prose treatise on demons had still to become sedimented as a distinct generic form. The Swiss francophone, Lambert Daneau, only had his dialogue on witchcraft printed in 1574; Jean Poupy's mini-compilation of demonological texts by Pierre Massé, René Benoist, and Pierre Nodé appeared in 1579; and it was not until 1580 that Jacques du Puy brought out Jean Bodin's landmark *De la demonomanie des sorciers*.[23]

---

[18] *De spectris*, Book 1, ch. 1.
[19] On the late Renaissance terminology of ghosts, see Introduction, pp. 2–4.
[20] *Des apparitions*, sig. *viii[v].
[21] By way of contrast, Benneyman and Watkyns's *Of Ghostes and Spirits*, whose format and layout appeals to a more scholarly readership, preserves both the opening chapter of *De spectris* and its Ramist lexicon.
[22] On Rabelais and Ronsard, see ch. 5 below; on Boaistuau, see pp. 116–28; on Du Triez's dialogue (Cambrai: N. Lombart, 1563), see Chesters, 'Demonology on the Margins'.
[23] Daneau, *Deux traités nouveaux*. The Poupy volume contains five texts, four printed by Poupy himself and one by Jean du Carroy: P. Massé, *De l'imposture et tromperie des diables, devins, enchanteurs, sorciers, noueurs d'esguillettes, chevilleurs, necromanciens, chiromanciens, et autres qui par telle invocation Diabolique, ars magiques et superstitions abusent le peuple* (Paris:

Durand may have been encouraged, it is true, by the recent success, in French translation, of other German-speaking authors writing in Latin on adjacent subjects. The late 1560s had seen the publication of Du Pinet's translation of Lemnius's *De miraculis occultis naturae*, as well as Grévin's French version of Weyer's *De praestigiis daemonum*.[24] The success of these works, on divination and witchcraft respectively, may have held out the promise of a similar reception for Lavater in France. In truth, however, *Des apparitions* was not so much entering a pre-existing discursive field, as helping to produce it.

One purpose of this book, and particularly this chapter, is to describe and delimit that territory. To begin with an obvious move, it is certainly tempting, in the light of later developments, to situate *Des apparitions* within the rapidly increasing number of texts on witchcraft in this period. This is certainly where the publisher of the second French edition, Guillaume des Marecz, seems to locate the treatise in 1581. His decision to append to it a *Brief discours sur le fait de la magie* suggests that Lavater's text was readily assimilable to the new and growing market for writing on witchcraft and the pact. And yet, however vulnerable it became to the realignments and appropriations of the Bodin generation, *Des apparitions* itself explores a set of concerns quite distinct from those of the *Demonomanie*. Unlike Massé, Bodin, Remigius, Delrio, Boguet, De Lancre, and so many others, Lavater is almost entirely indifferent to the subject of witchcraft. The preface to *Des apparitions* cites several learned men, notably Peucer, Weyer, and Milichius, 'qui ont escrit en general touchant les devinations, superstitions, adjurations, enchantemens, sorceleries et autres impostures et illusions du diable'.[25] Yet apart from a scattering of mentions, Lavater continually plays down the question of sorcery. The elision of these more strictly demonological concerns goes beyond

---

J. Poupy, 1579); R. Benoist, *Trois sermons de S. Augustin, ausquels il est enseigné que ceux qui adherent aux magies, sorceleries, superstitions et infestations diaboliques, pour neant sont Chrestiens et abusent de leur foy* (Paris: J. Poupy, 1579); idem, *Petit fragment catechistic d'une plus ample catechese de la magie reprehensible et des magiciens, pris de l'une des Catecheses et opuscules de M. René Benoist Angevin, Docteur en Theologie et Curé de S. Eustache à Paris* (Paris: J. Poupy, 1579); idem, *Traicté enseignant en bref les causes des malefices, sortileges et enchanteries, tant des Ligatures et neuds d'esguillettes pour empescher l'action et exercise du mariage qu'autres, et du remede qu'il faut avoir a l'encontre* (Paris: J. Poupy, 1579); P. Nodé, *Declamation contre l'erreur execrable des maleficiers, sorciers, enchanteurs, magiciens, devins, et semblables observateurs des superstitions: lesquelz pullulent maintenant couvertement en France* (Paris: J. du Carroy, 1578); J. Bodin, *De la Demonomanie des sorciers* (Paris: J. du Puys, 1580).

[24] L. Lemnius, *Les Secrets Miracles de nature, et divers enseignemens de plusieurs choses*, trans. by A. du Pinet (Lyon: J. Frellon, 1566); Weyer, *De l'imposture et tromperie des diables*.

[25] *Des apparitions*, sig. *iv[r].: 'touching divinations, blessings, jugglings, conjurings, and divers kinds of sorcerie, and generally of all other divelishe practises' (*Of Ghostes*, sig. bii[r]).

Lavater's markedly Weyerian caution, visible at several moments in the treatise, over the prosecution of witches.[26] What is being staked out here is a distinct discursive field whose true focus, we discover, is not the alliance of witches and demons but, rather, the independent operation of ghosts and apparitions.

Towards a Pastoral Demonology

Like the German, Latin, and English versions, the French *Trois livres des apparitions des esprits* comprises three books. Book One is a conspectus of ancient and modern wisdom on apparitions.[27] Lavater begins by describing the case against belief in spirits, arguing that many so-called 'apparitions' can be shown to be the work not of supernatural but of natural agencies operating in the sublunary world. Drawing on natural philosophical authorities, Cardano in particular, he argues that men and women who suffer infirmities of the imagination (brought on by drink, melancholy, or excessive timidity), or of the senses (such as scholars whose eyesight has been dimmed by too much study), often falsely believe that they have witnessed apparitions. Hoaxers, especially corrupt priests, are cited as another natural cause: Lavater reproduces a number of well-known anticlerical narratives, including Erasmus's letter to Bishop Longlond and the scandal at Orleans.[28] Occasionally the hoax is accidental, as in the famous case of Pericles whose servants, seeing him sleepwalking on the roof of his house, mistook him for a ghost. More commonly encountered are a number of non-human causes, among which are to be found naturally occurring phenomena such as cats' eyes, putrefied wood, glow-worms, brimstone, sulphur, mirrors, and echo. All are routinely mistaken for spirits, claims Lavater, even by those in full control of their faculties.

However, not all apparitions can be ascribed to natural causes, and the second half of Book One sets about arguing the case for belief in spirits. Lavater finds ample evidence for apparitions in ancient history, the Church fathers, a number of more recent sources, and, as we shall see in more detail later, in everyday experience. Underwriting all these instances is the authority of Scripture. Aside from extensive reference to Samuel's apparition to Saul, and the familiar arguments (reviewed in the previous chapter) from Luke's resurrection story, Lavater cites the mysterious writing on the wall at Belshazzar's feast (Daniel 5), and the phantom

---

[26] Hints at Lavater's opposition to the prosecution of witches can be found in *Des apparitions*, pp. 18, 93, 177 and especially 52–3 (on which see below, p. 79).
[27] Henceforth all references to *Des apparitions* are incorporated into the text.
[28] See above, pp. 43–8.

horse that appears to Heliodorus as he is poised to sack the temple (2 Maccabees 3). By the close of Book One, and despite good reasons for suspicion in particular cases, the scriptural evidence leaves no doubt that spirits truly do appear.

What are these spirits, and what is their purpose? Book Two, markedly more polemical in flavour than its predecessor, shifts the focus from apparitions in general to ghosts in particular. Can the souls of the dead truly return to the living? For Lavater, who shared his co-religionaries' suspicion of Catholic teaching on Purgatory, the answer to this question is firmly in the negative. All spirits must be either angelic or—more commonly—demonic in origin; apparitions of the dead are only ever illusions wrought by other spirits for good or evil ends. Polemically speaking, Lavater breaks little new ground in this rejection of ghosts. Whether he is discussing pagan, Jewish, Muslim, and Catholic attitudes to the dead, the absence of patristic or scriptural evidence for Purgatory, clerical exploitation of indulgences, or Satanic agency in the witch's raising of Samuel, there is little in these sections that cannot also be found in the writing of Protestant predecessors such as Calvin, Farel, Viret, or Peter Martyr.[29] It should also be remembered that, beyond the influence of individual theologians, Lavater inhabited an atmosphere characterized by thoroughgoing suspicion of images in general. As Lee Palmer Wandel has pointed out, Zurich (along with Strasbourg and Basel) was one of the earliest centres of Reformation in which iconoclasm was 'completed'.[30]

Much of the force of Lavater's arguments in this section derives less from their novelty, or their individual presentation, than from the tensions established between Books One and Two. If Book One had made an enthusiastic case for the existence of spirits in general, Book Two's denial of ghosts in particular constitutes an arresting narrative reversal. And, chillingly, if Book One established the seemingly all-pervasive presence of error—through melancholy, sensory infirmity, human deceit, or qualities in nature—Book Two reveals the influence of Satan in these ghostly misperceptions. Here the diabolical apparition of Samuel forms the main part of the discussion, though Lavater also revisits other episodes of necromancy, notably that of the slain soldier conjured by the terrible Erichtho in Lucan's *Pharsalia*. In Lucan the malign hand of the witch, as well as the pagan context, confirms that the soul of the soldier cannot have

---

[29] Calvin, *Institution chrestienne*, III, ch. 5; Farel, *Traicté de Purgatoire*; Viret, *Disputations chrestiennes*.

[30] L. P. Wandel, *Voracious Idols and Violent Hands: Iconoclasm in Reformation Zurich, Strasbourg, and Basel* (Cambridge: Cambridge University Press, 1995), p. 21; on iconoclasm in Zurich, see pp. 53–101.

truly been called back; instead Lavater argues that the corpse of the dead man had been raised up by a demon.[31] For the Protestant minister, the accumulation of such cases, whether culled from ancient history or Scripture, serves to diabolize all apparitions of the dead. Like Purgatory itself, ghosts must be dismissed as fictions of the Devil.

Book Three, finally, examines the consequences of apparitions in practical contexts. As Lavater puts it, 'que doyvent faire ceux à qui telles choses se presentent?' (p. 183). It is this section of *Des apparitions*, towards which the first two books have been building, that suggests most powerfully the pastoral thrust of Lavater's treatise. For the purpose of apparitions, as he makes clear at the outset of Book Three, is to guide men to the better life: 'Si Dieu ne nous mettoit quelque chose au devant, nous ne nous cognoistrions point, et ne cognoistrions nos nescesitez, ni ne prierions si ardamment le Seigneur qu'ils nous gardast de mal, augmentast nostre foy, et nous munist de patience.' (p. 184)[32] These virtues—of self-knowledge, prayer, faith, patience—dominate the pastoral demonology of Book Three, where the minister's chief purpose is to convey the resolutions, attitudes, and procedures that the lay reader must internalize if he is to rid himself and his family of spirits.

Invoking an Old Testament figure on which he would later preach at length as a minister, Lavater urges the reader haunted by spirits to follow the example of Job.[33] Like Job, he explains, 'il te faut porter patiemment la tyranie de Satan, puis que Dieu le veut' (p. 200). The subject of one chapter, for instance, is a warning against fear (Book Three, chapter 5). Good Christians should not fear spirits, 'mais faut qu'ils soyent fermes en foy' (p. 199). Addressing his reader directly, Lavater counsels as follows: 'Encore qu'un esprit face du mauvais, et renverse bancs et chaires, ne t'espouvante pas pourtant. S'il fait grand bruit et tintamarre, ne t'en soucie pas: laisse le faire jusqu'à ce qu'il soit las et se retire.' (p. 200)[34] The answer to fear, insists the minister, is patience. But he is careful to stress that this quality is not, as the term might suggest, a merely passive virtue; on the contrary, patience entails a programme of active self-improvement. He

---

[31] On the apparition of Samuel to Saul, see below, pp. 108–16; on the dead soldier raised by Erichtho, see below, pp. 114–16.

[32] 'Except God did shut up the waye before us with certaine stops and lets, we shold not know our selves, we shoulde not understand wherof we stand in needm we shold not so earnestly pray unto God, to deliver us from evill, to strengthen our fayth, and to give us pacience, and other necessarie things.' (*Of Ghostes*, p. 176).

[33] See L. Lavater, *Das Buch Job aussgelegt undd erkläret, in CXLI Predigen* (Zurich: C. Froschauer, 1582).

[34] 'Be not dismayde, although thou heare some spirit stir and make a noyse, for in case hee rumble onely to make thee afrayde, care not for him, but lette hym rumble so long as he wyll, for if hee see thee wythout feare, hee wyll soone depart from thee.' (*Of Ghostes*, p. 191).

who is visited by spirits must reject drunkenness, greed, or 'voluptez charnelles'; instead he must 'veiller, prier, jeusner' and, above all, 'amender sa vie' (p. 203). Whereas the natural philosophy of Lavater's early chapters had located the ghostly experience firmly within the seat of man's sensory or imaginative faculties, the example of Job serves to show how the appearance of ghosts, who usually visit the weak or the sinful, is often the symptom of a moral imperfection. As the gaze turns inward and the conscience is stirred, the apparition will just as surely disappear.

Lavater's new Protestant praxis is constructed in large part against existing models of response to ghosts. One of these is provided by the apotropaic superstitions of ancient Roman methods. He cites Suetonius's tale of Caligula, whose ghost was only assuaged when his palace was razed to the ground (p. 197), and also writes with distaste of the obsequies, burials, temple-building, sacrifices, and elaborate festivals—the *feralia* and *lemuria*—with which the Romans made peace with their dead (Book Three, chapter 4). The outward shows of ancient ceremonial could not stand further from Lavater's call for withdrawal and introspection.

While ancient apotropaic custom provides Lavater with an object lesson in how *not* to banish spirits, it is of course the modern avatars of the ancient practice, the ritual exorcisms of contemporary Rome, which constitute the most pressing opposition in the treatise. For Lavater, patience entails an obstinate refusal to speak to, or otherwise engage with, supposed apparitions of the dead: 'Ne te mesle gueres de vouloir curieusement interroguer tel esprit que ce soit, de ce que tu dois faire ou croire, ou des choses avenir: aussi ne luy demande pas qui il est, ni pourquoy et à quelle fin il se monstre et se laisse voir.' (p. 204)[35] In some of this advice, Lavater concurs implicitly with Catholic teaching on ghosts: learning from Luke's parable of Lazarus and the rich man (Luke 16), the School textbooks, among many others, had warned against excessive curiosity in enquiring of the dead.[36] But when Lavater enjoins those who see a spirit not to ask it 'qui il est, ni pourquoy et à quelle fin il se monstre et se laisse voir', he stands in direct opposition to clerical tradition. Lavater holds the main representative of that tradition to be the Carthusian author Jacobus of Clusa, whose *Tractatus de apparitionibus* first appeared towards the end of the fifteenth century.[37] Lavater reproduces large portions of that work, which provide a detailed description of

---

[35] 'Enter into no communication with suche spirites, neither aske them what thou must give, or what thou must doo, or what shal happen hereafter. Ask them not who they are, or why they have presented them selves to bee seene or hearde.' (*Of Ghostes*, p. 196).

[36] On Taillepied and curiosity, see below, p. 89; see also Bodin, *Demonomanie*, sig. 78ᵛ.

[37] Jacobus of Clusa, *Tractatus de apparitionibus* (n.p., n.d.).

the clerical *discretio spirituum*, the rigorous procedures by which spirits were tried (*probare*) or discerned (*discernere*).[38]

Against Jacobus, and the tradition of *discretio spirituum* he is called upon to represent, Lavater proposes what might be termed a therapy of introspection. Like much else in Protestant polemic, that therapy has the great advantage of eliding the mediations of a corrupt and scheming clergy. With the figure of the priest are dispatched, accordingly, a whole range of clerical commodities. The Ave Maria, the sign of the cross, prayers for the dead, holy water, candles, palms, bells, the smoke from burning grasses: none of these methods, according to Lavater, is of the slightest use against spirits (Book Three, chapters 9 and 10). Those who employ an Agnus Dei—the Gospel of Saint John hung around the neck in a purse or pouch—or rub their faces during the raising of the host, also act in error. 'Où est-ce que nostre Seigneur Jesus ou ses apostres nous enseignent,' Lavater asks, 'de chasser avec choses corporelles le diable qui est esprit, et pourtant n'a point de corps?' (p. 226).[39] These, argues Lavater, are no substitutes for faith, but only its outward, corporeal signs.

Lavater does not establish his pastoral programme uniquely in opposition to the rival traditions of the ancients or the Church of modern Rome, however. Indeed, if the final chapters of the treatise are oppositional, then it is above all the spontaneous, untutored reflexes of the layman towards ghosts that the minister seeks to bring under control rather than those of ancient holy men and contemporary priests. He includes a highly influential chapter on 'do's and 'don't's for those whose homes are haunted by spirits (Book Three, chapter 9). As with the section on fear, much of the chapter seeks to forestall a set of instinctive responses to ghosts. One common response, on encountering a spirit, is to fall to swearing and cursing. Such language, Lavater warns, is music to the Devil's ears: 'le diable s'esjouit fort d'ouir jurer et blasphemer: et s'il fait semblant de fuir, ce sera pour approcher plus pres' (p. 227).[40] A second prohibited response is physical violence. Lavater is forced to allow, in the light of his earlier remarks on fear, that 'c'est bien une chose à louer de ne s'espouvanter point' (ibid.).[41] But physical force is of no use against spirits. Some men draw their swords on seeing a ghost, but 'cuidant frapper quelque fantosme,

---

[38] On the medieval *discretio spirituum*, see above pp. 24–9.

[39] 'Where doth Christ and his disciples teache us to expell the Divell (which is a Spirit, and therefore without any body) by bodyly things?' (*Of Ghostes*, p. 213).

[40] 'Nothing can be more acceptable and pleasing to the Divel, than when any man useth cursing and banning. He feyneth that he is hereby driven away, but in the meane season he crepeth invisibly into their bosoms.' (*Of Ghostes*, p. 214).

[41] 'Surely it is praise worthy when a man meting with a spirite is not afrayd' (*Of Ghostes*, p. 215).

ont pensé proprement toucher un coussin bien mol' (p. 228).[42] Others have tried to throw ghosts out of windows, and yet hear only the sound of shingle falling through the trees. Like their clerical masters, these men and women misread the sense of the ghostly encounter. They must lay down material weapons, Lavater concludes with a rallying cry, and take up the 'espee spirituelle' (ibid.).

Job under Siege: Inventing the Haunted House

The foregoing summary of *Des apparitions* places especial emphasis on Book Three of the treatise. In doing so it remains faithful to the text's own rhetorical progression: having mined the reader's faith in his own senses (Book One) and in Church tradition (Book Two), Book Three comes to the rescue by offering what I have called Lavater's 'pastoral demonology'— a project that sought to extend, refine, and finally supplant the various modes of clerical discernment described in the first chapter of this book. Underpinning this move towards a pastoral demonology are three aspects of the treatise that deserve further attention: its narrative structures, its distinctive protagonist, and the very specific scenography of the narrative space we have now come to call 'the haunted house'.

Lavater's English translator, Robert Harrison, remarks on the pleasure to be derived from the narratives contained in his treatise on ghosts. But it is a pleasure mixed, according to the Horatian ideal, with considerable profit to the reader:

> For he so intreateth this serious and terrible matter of spirites, that he now and then insertying some strange story of Monkes, Priestes, Fryers and such like counterfeyts, doth both very lively display their falsehood, and also not a little recreate his reader: and yet in the ende he so aptly concludeth to the purpose, that his hystories seeme not idle tales, or impertinent vagaries, but very truethes, naturally falling under the compasse of his matter.[43]

Harrison's insistence on Lavater's seamless commingling of pleasure and profit is a commonplace topic of paratextual publicity. But in this case it masks what is for the most part a near-puritan restraint in the handling of ghost stories. We shall see in later chapters how a number of late Renaissance writers fail to resist the narrative temptations afforded by the ghost tale; the stories of *Des apparitions*, by contrast, are tightly marshalled within the homiletic scheme of the *exemplum*, whose inclusion is invariably placed

---

[42] 'when they would have striken a Spirit with their sword, have thought they have striken the fetherbed' (*Of Ghostes*, p. 215). On violence against ghosts and spirits, see ch. 5.
[43] Lavater, *Of Ghostes*, sigs. *i^v–*ii^r.

at the service of polemical and pastoral didacticism. Even in the chapters on clerical hoaxes (Book One, chapters 6–8), the accounts of which often resemble self-enclosed *contes*, narrative for Lavater is never an 'impertinent vagary'. Even in this, the most productive portion of *Des apparitions* in narrative terms, the ghost story naturally falls 'under the compasse' of Lavater's instructional matter. For Lavater, narrative always edifies.

Carefully accredited either within the body of the text or in marginal notes, Lavater's exemplary narratives are taken from a wide variety of written sources, both ancient and modern. His favourite ancient source is by some distance Plutarch, though he has frequent recourse to biblical and patristic texts, especially those of Augustine. If short, these borrowed narratives are imported wholesale; longer anecdotes are paraphrased for the sake of brevity. In either case, they are concatenated under chapter headings without intervening glosses. The more frequently cited modern sources include Cardano's *De subtilitate* and Olaus Magnus's cosmographies of northern Europe. In terms of their layout and presentation, both are treated similarly to the biblical and classical sources. Exceptions to this rule, as already noted, include the longer anticlerical narratives of Book One, drawn for the main part from the histories of Johannes Sleidanus, in which each clerical hoax is allocated its own chapter.

Lavater does not restrict himself, in his choice of sources, to the written word alone. Though he offers none of his own experiences in support of the existence of spirits, the treatise does include a small number of ghost narratives personally communicated to the minister himself. These are generally accredited to a local dignitary of Lavater's acquaintance. Whether the source is named or unnamed, his credentials as a witness are always underscored with recourse to the laudatory adjectives 'bon', 'sage', 'docte', etcetera. Such procedures achieve the additional effect of reinforcing Lavater's own authority, both politically, through reference to the circles in which he moves, and as a figure of expertise whose opinion others seek.

Though these, too, are sparse in the telling, Lavater's more personal narratives are revealing in the common ground they share. One striking feature is their protagonist. If a treatise on ghosts can have a hero, then the hero of Lavater's is unquestionably Job. We have already seen how Job is used in the treatise as an exemplar of patient introspection. And although he is only a fleeting presence in *Des apparitions* (it is not until Lavater's sermons of 1582 that he devotes sustained attention to the Old Testament father), we do encounter a number of what might be deemed his early modern avatars—Protestant *patres familias* whose home, and sometimes whose very identity, comes under threat from spirits.

Two instances stand out, both narrated in the final chapter of Book One ('A qui, en quel temps, en quel lieu les esprits apparoissent, et que c'est qu'ils font'). The first story Lavater has heard, typically, from a learned ('docte') but unnamed Zurich magistrate. As the magistrate and his servant were walking through his pasture land one early summer morning, he spotted his neighbour defiling a mare. The shocked magistrate called at the neighbour's house only to find that he had not set foot out of doors all morning. Here Lavater adds an unusual aside to the reader, and one that hints at Lavater's Weyerian caution over the issue of witchcraft and the sabbath. Had the magistrate not checked up on the matter, Lavater observes, an innocent man could have been imprisoned and tortured for his crime—a crime clearly committed by the Devil in his place. 'Je recite ceste histoire, afin que les juges soyent bien avisez en tels cas', he concludes (p. 93).[44]

The second narrative, which is the last to be recounted in Book One, is called upon to illustrate an extraordinary phenomenon: ghosts so terrifying that those who witness them are turned white-headed in one night. Again, the anecdote is given a learned provenance: 'J'ay memoire d'avoir entendu une histoire à ce propos, que racontait Jean Willing bon et docte personnage et mon ancien ami, d'un quidam demourant en la conté de Hannaw, lequel depuis quelques annees en çà, ayant rencontré de nuict un fantosme, fut tellement changé, que retournant en sa maison ses filles ne le recognoissoyent point.' (p. 98)[45] Unlike that of the neighbour and the mare, and more typical of the treatise as a whole, this brief narrative appears without any accompanying commentary: its final image—the terrified father unrecognized by his daughters—is left unresolved.

Aside from their male protagonist, the two narratives cited above also share a setting. Crucially, each makes ghosts a feature of what Lavater himself terms 'l'experience quotidienne'. Although, as we have seen, the bulk of Lavater's evidence for the existence of spirits is drawn from ancient sources, stories such as that of Johann Willing (literally) bring the phenomenon home. It is true that to speak of daily experience was not to name a new category in writing about spirits. Jacobus of Clusa, an author Lavater knows well, had also appealed to *experientia quotidiana* as evidence for ghosts at the end of the previous century.[46] In Lavater, however, the appeal to daily experience is more sustained and more far-reaching. It becomes clear from narratives such as those cited above that 'l'experience

---

[44] 'I reherse this history for this end, that Judges should be very circumspect in these cases.' (*Of Ghostes*, p. 91).

[45] 'I remember I have heard the like historie of my olde friend John Willing, a godly and learned man, of one in the Countie of Hannow, who not many yeares ago, meeting with a walking spirite in the night season, was so much altered, that at his returning home, his own Daughters knewe him not.' (*Of Ghostes*, p. 96).

[46] See Jacobus of Clusa, *De apparitionibus*, sig. B3ʳ.

quotidienne' is not only an evidential category in Lavater, but a theatre in which the ghost produces a continual and, even with the help of the Protestant minister, at times insoluble, domestic crisis.

By creating our likeness in other places or by frightening us beyond recognition, ghosts constitute a threat to the very idea of who we are. That threat cannot be imagined, for Lavater, without reference to the space of the early modern home. In the first narrative, that space constitutes a scene of resolution. The magistrate's neighbour is recognized as the neighbour, and thereby exonerated, precisely by dint of his appearance in the doorway to his house. However prone to usurpation out of doors, the friend's identity is secured through its location in domestic, private space. In Johann Willing's story, likewise staged in the entrance to the home, that security and the space that guarantees it are radically thrown into crisis. The setting for Willing's narrative corresponds, or should correspond, to an idealized tableau of everyday life—the homestead, family, refuge, warmth. But something has made this frightened Job a stranger to his daughters. The father's alteration is configured as an estrangement from his household: the homecoming scene, once a scene of daily recognition, is now one of rupture and dislocation.

Willing's tale in particular, and the more general menace ghosts pose to personal and social integrity, is the nightmare from which Lavater—the pastoral father—seeks to awaken his readers. In order to achieve this, however, they must be aware of the dangers. For, as he demonstrates throughout *Des apparitions*, 'l'experience quotidienne' is not only the space of other people's stories. It could be you: your kitchen, your bedroom, your parlour may find itself the theatre in which another ghost story is played out. Taken together, the two stories underscore the extent to which the theatre of Lavater's pastoral demonology is no longer the churchyard or the convent, as it so often was in medieval narratives or in Adrien de Montalembert's *Merveilleuse Hystoire*, but deep inside the early modern home.[47]

It is in this sense that we might speak of Lavater as the inventor of the haunted house. This bold claim requires two qualifications. First, it is notable that neither Lavater nor his French translator employ any such expression. In early modern French, it is not clear that the verb *hanter*—to frequent—had any special association with ghosts or apparitions, and the formula *maison hantée* does not appear regularly until the nineteenth century.[48] But this is not to claim that no such expression existed in

---

[47] On Montalembert, see above, pp. 35–41.
[48] Writing of those situations in which young men and women are most likely to 'contrefaire l'esprit', Pierre Le Loyer alludes in his *Quatre livres des spectres* to an angevin

early modern Europe. As the Jesuit demonologist Petrus Thyraeus shows in the titles of his works, it was not uncommon to speak in Latin of 'loci infesti'; some French authors of the period, such as André Valladier, took up the phrase and rendered it as 'maison infestée'. To this extent, then, Lavater's failure to settle on a term—while striking—in no way proves that the concept itself was unavailable to him. The second qualification involves ancient precedent. As with other forms of early modern *inventio*, Lavater's invention was as much a matter of finding (*invenio*: I come upon, or find) as creating afresh. We shall see in a later chapter how Pliny's *Epistles* or Plautus's *Mostellaria* had already imagined an analogous narrative space long before Lavater. These texts were widely read in the French Renaissance, and in Pierre de Larivey's *Les Esprits* (considered briefly in the Introduction to this book) the haunted house was even made the setting for a play.[49] But, as we shall see, the inflection of the theme in antiquity, and humanist treatments of the theme in early modern Europe, differed a great deal from Lavater's haunted homestead.

The primary difference, and what seems to have been the peculiar distinctiveness of Lavater's invention, resides in the extent to which his haunted house is experienced *from the inside*. Lavater's pastoral focus on 'l'experience quotidienne', unlike the comic exaggerations of a Plautus, revels in the homeliness of bumps in the night. As if anticipating Freud, *Des apparitions* places ghosts at the uncanny intersection of the strange and the familiar.

In a thoroughgoing and often bravura exploitation of domestic paranoia, Lavater constructs a vivid sense of life in a sixteenth-century 'maison infestée'. Whether he is discussing ghosts imagined or real, that house is a frightening place. Even when empty of ghosts, cats' eyes, precious stones, rotten wood, or glow-worms, mirrors and tricks of perspective lie in wait to terrify the home-owning lay reader. The ear, too, can play tricks on the listener: 'Le vent jettera quelque chose par terre en une maison, fermera ou ouvrira quelque fenestre: sur ce on trouvera des gens ausquels on ne sauroit oster de la fantasie que ce sont des esprits qu'ils ont ouy.'[50] (p. 49) 'Ghosts' have also been heard in the cries of rats, cats, weasels, martens, and bitterns, in the sound of a horse stamping its feet, or the noise of worms in the wainscot. The truly haunted house is more terrifying still. In one

---

proverb: 'Où sont fillettes et bon vin / C'est là où hante le lutin'. However, the ghostly context may be coincidental.

[49] On Larivey, see above pp. 4–5.

[50] 'The wind in the night, overthroweth some thing, or shaketh a casement or lid of a window: many by and by thinke they see a spirite, and can very hardly be brought fromt that vayne opinion.' (*Of Ghostes*, p. 50).

chapter, tellingly entitled 'L'experience nous enseigne tous les jours qu'il y a des esprits qui apparoissent' (Book One, chapter 15), Lavater mobilizes a wealth of images, sounds, and other sensations that are commonly experienced when ghosts are, to quote the title of the English translation, 'walking by nyght'. In the corridor, ghosts can be heard coughing, sighing, and dragging themselves along. In the bedroom, when you have settled down to sleep, 'quelqu'un viendra tirer ou emporter la couverture du lict, se mettra dessus ou dessous icelle, ou se pourmenera par la chambre' (p. 72).[51] Ghosts have been heard turning the leaves of a book, telling money, or playing dice. And not all such experiences can be blamed on priestly hoaxers, or 'autres gens pervers' (p. 73). Even those who lock and check their houses can find themselves the object of a ghostly visitation:

> On sait bien que beaucoup d'esprits sont apparus en chambres closes, lesquelles on avoit diligemment visitees avec la lumiere pour voir s'il y auroit point quelqu'un caché sous les licts, chose que plusieurs ont accoustumé faire avant que se coucher.[52]

Meanwhile, outside the locked room and down the stairs to the kitchen, strange noises can be heard:

> Il est advenu souvent que les domestiques pensoyent proprement ouir quelqu'un qui remuoit les chauderons, pots, plats, tranchoirs, tables, bancs, ou les jettast par les degrez: cependant le lendemain on trouvoit le tout agencé en sa place.[53]

Others ghosts are less inclined to clear up in their wake. They will rip doors from their hinges and throw them to the ground, knock over furniture and, leaving the house in ruins, 'tourmentent fort le monde' (p. 73). Here, as in much of the treatise, the domestic scenography of ghosts is described not in the preterite of narrative, but in the perfect, present, or even the frequentative future. These tenses only add credence to the feeling that ghosts are not a past but an imminent prospect, and one against which the reader must stand constantly on guard.

---

[51] 'Some man goeth to bed, and laieth him down to rest, and by and by there is some thing pinching him, or pulling off the clothes: sometimes it sitteth on him, or lyeth downe in the bed with him: and many times it walketh up and downe in the Chamber.' (*Of Ghostes*, pp. 71–2).

[52] 'Even in those mennes chambers when they have bene shut, there have appeared such things, when they have with a candle diligently searched before, whither any thing have lurked in som corner or no.' (*Of Ghostes*, p. 72).

[53] 'It hath many times chaunced, that those of the house have verily thought, that some body hath overthrowne the pots, platters, tables and trenchers, and tumbled them downe the stayres: but after it waxed day, they have found all things orderly set in their places againe.' (*Of Ghostes*, p. 73).

By making ghosts a matter of 'l'experience quotidienne', Lavater's Protestant minister succeeds in gaining admission to the early modern home. In doing so, his achievement is threefold. First of all it displaces the ghostly encounter from the clerical settings that dominate earlier ghost narrative traditions. The church, graveyard, or monastery had long been the setting for Catholic ghost tales; now, through a steady accumulation of narrative and generalized description, ghosts belong to the hallway, cellar, pantry, stables, kitchens, and bedrooms—the familiar territories through which Lavater constructs the scenography of daily experience. Second, such a displacement effectively removes the need for the clergy. As good Protestants check their houses 'pour voir s'il y auroit point quelqu'un caché sous les licts', the priest is locked out of the scene. In his place, albeit internalized as the promptings of Protestant 'conscience', is left a new figure of expertise: that of the Protestant minister. But there are losses as well as gains. Lavater's third, more ambivalent, message is that while we might lock the doors against clerical fraud, and chase priests out of the house, ghosts are left to fill our homes. Worse: the haunted house is one that we must tackle alone. If Lavater saw in this space an opportunity— the chance, through inward searching, to 'amender sa vie'—it was an opportunity bought at the price of an ever-present, and only imperfectly mastered, fear. It was from that fear that the Franciscan Noël Taillepied sought to rescue his readers in his polemical reply to Lavater, the 1588 *Psichologie, ou traité de l'apparition des esprits*.

NOËL TAILLEPIED, *PSICHOLOGIE, OU TRAITÉ DE L'APPARITION DES ESPRITS* (1588)

Taillepied was not the first Catholic writer to respond to Lavater. The most immediate rejoinder came from the celebrated Spanish Jesuit, Jean Maldonat (Juan Maldonado). Professor of theology at the Collège de Clermont in Paris, Maldonat delivered, in Latin, a series of lectures on demonology in 1571–2.[54] Against Protestants in general and Lavater in particular, his lectures restate the case for return from the dead; they also

---

[54] On Maldonat's demonology, see J.-M. Prat, *Maldonat et l'université de Paris au XVIe siècle* (Paris: Julien and Lanier, 1856), pp. 262–5; P. Schmitt, *La Réforme catholique, le combat de Maldonat, 1534–83* (Paris: Beauchesne, 1985), pp. 412–14; J. L. Pearl, *The Crime of Crimes: Demonology and Politics in France, 1560–1620* (Ontario: Wilfred Laurier University Press, 1999), pp. 59–75. On Montaigne's admiration for Maldonat, whom he met on his travels through France, Germany, and Italy in 1580–1, see P. de Lancre, *Tableau de l'inconstance des mauvais anges et demons* [1612] (Paris: N. Buon, 1613), p. 77.

reinstall the 'remedes de l'Eglise' (e.g. exorcism, almsgiving, fasting, and prayer) against which Lavater had written a year or two before.[55] In terms of substance, then, Maldonat's response rested less on learned innovation than on an appeal to Catholic listeners to retrench and conform. In matters of style, however, Lavater had forced more far-reaching concessions from his Catholic opponents. Maldonat's lectures are also evidence of how, faced with the vernacular sophistication of Reformation polemic, Catholic ghost-speak was forced to adapt to the new challenge.

Although Maldonat's addresses were delivered in Latin, he felt they should reach a wider spectrum of listeners than usually attended Clermont. In the prolegomenon to the series he announces that these will be the only lectures to take place on public holidays and that, when the weather is fine, the talks will be given outside. Furthermore, the less forbidding environment would be matched, in linguistic terms, by a lower, more accessible style: he promises that, although demonology was a subject that bred theological subtleties, he would offer a less recondite treatment, suitable for listeners versed in other disciplines. Finally, the Jesuit scholar expresses the wish that one day his lectures might be translated into French.[56] It appears that, even for learned theologians, ghosts were among a number of other theological topics that, under the pressure of the Protestant challenge, were beginning to move into the vernacular.[57] In the event, Maldonat's talks were extremely well attended. But it was not until 1605 that the lecturer's final wish was accomplished and a French version brought out. In the meantime, Lavater had begun to provoke other vernacular responses. Among these was Taillepied's *Psichologie, ou traité de l'apparition des esprits.*[58]

Author and Text

Taillepied was born in Pontoise, Normandy, around 1540. He joined the Franciscan order at a relatively young age, and was soon received doctor in theology at the faculty of divinity in Paris. His subsequent career was

---

[55] *Traicté des anges et demons*, sig. 182ʳ.

[56] Maldonat's prolegomenon is reproduced from the manuscript in Prat, *Maldonat et l'université de Paris*, pp. 567ff.

[57] For a concise analysis of the shift from Latin to French in the Counter-Reformation polemic of the late sixteenth century, see F. Higman, 'The Reformation and the French Language' in *The French Renaissance Mind: Studies Presented to W. G. Moore*, ed. by B. C. Bowen (= *L'Esprit Créateur*, 16 [1976]), pp. 20–36 (pp. 32–6).

[58] All references are to Jean Osmont's Rouen edition of 1602. Though Osmont removed the title word 'Psichologie', I have retained it throughout for the sake of clarity. Page references are incorporated into the text.

divided between Lyon, Rouen, and his native Pontoise.[59] The early part of his work, the large majority of which was composed in French, is devoted to anti-heretical polemic, including a defence of indulgences (1576), and lives of Luther, Karlstadt, and Peter Martyr (1577).[60] In the 1580s Taillepied's work shifted away from theology towards philosophical and historical subjects. From this period emerged an 'epitome', in French, of Aristotle's writings on physics, ethics, and dialectic (1583), and a treatise on the laws and customs of the ancient Gauls (1585).[61] Especially important, at least within the domain of urban topography, are his two *Recueils des antiquitez*, written in the tradition established by Gilles Corrozet, of Rouen and Pontoise (both 1587).[62] But it is for his treatise on ghosts, first published in 1588, that Taillepied is now best known. The *Psichologie* is dedicated to a layman, Claude Groulart, president of the Rouen parliament. As with his study of Aristotle, the treatise on ghosts can be considered an 'epitome' of sorts, designed to popularize Church teaching in the vernacular. Though Taillepied was not entirely averse to innovation or neologism—indeed, his 'psichologie' is the first recorded use of the term in French—he insists throughout on his role as mere compiler or collator. The preliminaries contain a comprehensive list of all the authors cited; in the dedication to Groulart he writes of his 'petit livre

[59] See E. Frère, *Manuel du bibliographe normand*, 2 vols. (Rouen, 1858–60), ii, p. 252; H. Le Charpentier, 'Notice sur Noël Taillepied' in N. Taillepied, *Les Antiquités et singularités de la ville de Pontoise*, ed. by A. François (Pontoise: A. Seyrès, and Paris: H. Champion, 1876), pp. 1–55. Montague Summers's introduction to his translation of Taillepied's treatise borders on the hagiographic, and is not to be trusted; see N. Taillepied, *A Treatise of Ghosts*, trans. and ed. by M. Summers (London: Fortune Press, 1933).

[60] N. Taillepied, *Brief traicté et declaration de l'an jubilé et efficace des pardons et indulgences données et octroyées par le souverain Evesque de Rome aux fidelles chrestiens, l'an 1576* (Paris: J. Parent, 1576); idem, *Histoire des vies, meurs, actes, doctrines et mort de Martin Luther et André Carlostad, hérétiques de nostre temps* (Paris: J. Parent, 1577). For fuller bibliographical details, see F. Grudé de La Croix du Maine, *Premier volume de la bibliothèque du sieur de La Croix du Maine, qui est un catalogue général de toutes sortes d'autheurs qui ont escrit en françois depuis cinq cents ans et plus* (Paris: A. l'Angelier, 1584), p. 362; A. Du Verdier, *La Bibliothèque d'Antoine du Verdier, seigneur de Vauprivas* (Lyon: B. Honorat, 1585), p. 926.

[61] N. Taillepied, *Oeuvres de philosophie, à sçavoir: dialectique, phisique et ethique d'Aristote* (Paris: J. Parent, 1583); idem, *Histoire de l'estat et republique des druides, eubages, saronides, bardes, vacies, anciens François, gouverneurs des païs de la Gaule, depuis le deluge universel, jusques à la venuë de Jesus-Christ en ce monde* (Paris: J. Parent, 1585).

[62] N. Taillepied, *Recueil des antiquitez et singularitez de la ville de Rouen, avec un progrez des choses memorables y advenues depuis sa fondation jusques à present* (Rouen: R. Petit, 1587); idem, *Recueil des antiquitez et singularitez de la ville de Pontoise* (Rouen: G. l'Oiselet, 1587). On Taillepied's history of Rouen, see L. de Duranville, *Essai sur l'histoire de la côte Sainte-Catherine et des fortifications de la ville de Rouen, suivi de mélanges relatifs à la Normandie* (Rouen: Lebrument, 1857), pp. 373–417. On Taillepied, Corrozet, and urban history in sixteenth-century France, see C. Liaroutzos, *Le Pays et la mémoire: pratique et représentation de l'espace chez Gilles Corrozet et Charles Estienne* (Paris: Champion, 1998), pp. 50–1.

([que j'ay] extrait des escrits de divers autheurs)' (sig. *ii^v); signing off the treatise, he claims to have communicated, in his words, 'ce qui *se dit* de l'apparition des Esprits' (p. 314; my emphasis). To insist in this way on the work as, in Montaigne's phrase, 'un travail en seconde main', is to situate ghosts within canonical tradition. Whereas Lavater's *Des apparitions* constitutes a new departure, Taillepied's response, like that of Maldonat, is best viewed as one of restatement and retrenchment.

The notion of Taillepied as popularizer or disseminator is reinforced by the technological and ideological context of the work's publication. It seems that the *Psichologie* was meant for distribution on the largest possible scale. The book's relatively inexpensive duodecimo format provides some clue as to the size and constitution of Taillepied's readership, as does its publisher, the Parisian bookseller and well-known *ligueur*, Guillaume Bichon.[63] Bichon placed most of his output in the service of Counter-Reformation propaganda, and specialized in the 'mass-media' dissemination of texts; in 1588 alone, his workshop produced 110 separate publications. But aside from Bichon's religious and political sympathies, and the mass-productivity he was able to place at Taillepied's disposal, there was a more specific motivation for the friar's choice of publisher. Bichon had recently begun to show a marked interest in demonological writing. In 1586 he had published Bénigne Poissenot's *Nouvelles Histoires tragiques*, to which the author had appended a short 'Discours confirmatif de l'authorité des anciens touchant l'apparition du mauvais démon ou génie'.[64] In the following year he brought out the more substantial *Pneumalogie, ou discours des esprits* by the theologian and inquisitor, Sébastien Michaëlis.[65] The publication of that text, along with those of Poissenot and Taillepied, place Bichon at the forefront of the growing vogue for demonological writing in the France of the mid 1580s.

As with Lavater, however, care should be taken to distinguish Taillepied's project from mainstream writing on witchcraft. Unlike Michaëlis's *Pneumalogie*, which was written, its full title claims, 'en tant qu'il est besoing pour entendre... la matiere difficile des sorciers', Taillepied, like Lavater, takes little interest in sorcery and the pact. Although the word he

---

[63] The work was printed for Bichon in Rouen by the little-known Michel Le Deutre. On this printer, see G. Lepreux, *Gallia Typographica ou répertoire biographique et chronologique de tous les imprimeurs de France*, 5 vols. (Paris: Champion, 1909–14), III (i), pp. 247–8. On Bichon's life and other publications, see P. Renouard, *Imprimeurs et libraires parisiens du XVIe siècle*, 5 vols. (Paris, 1964–), III, pp. 382–439.

[64] On this text, see below, pp. 136–41.

[65] This text, containing an influential chapter on ghostly bodies, was briefly discussed in ch. 1; see above, pp. 52–3.

coins in order to describe his own area of intellectual enquiry, 'psichologie', enjoyed no lasting success (at least in the sense Taillepied intended) and was dropped from subsequent editions after the death of the author in 1589, the recourse to fresh terms is in itself a strong indication that Taillepied considered himself to have broached a new discursive field. The extent of that territory, and the borders it shares with those adjacent to it, are mapped in Taillepied's preface to the work. There he writes of 'plusieurs personnages de qualité et d'eminente literature' who have written on the subject of spirits: 'entr'autres Peucer, Wier, Milichius, Rivius, Camerarius, P. Martyr, Lavater, Cardan, Bodin, Agrippa, [Sébastien] Michaelis, Melchior [Flavin], [Léonard] du Vair, et autres, des escrits desquels me suis aidé'. (sig. iv^r)[66] While Taillepied may have turned to these authors for assistance in composing his own treatise, he is careful to insist on two points of distinction. The first of these is sectarian: Taillepied urges suspicion of not only Lavater's work on spirits, but also of all those (Peucer, Weyer, Milichius, Rivius, Camerarius, and Petrus Martyr) who 'en ont opiné selon leur propre fantasie cauterisee de nouvelles opinions' (sig. *iiii^r).[67] Taillepied's second distinction concerns the rapidly expanding corpus of texts written on witchcraft and the pact. He here renders explicit Lavater's dissociation of spirits from judicial demonology. Unlike those (i.e. Agrippa, Weyer, Bodin, Michaëlis) who have 'seulement touché le poinct des Charmeurs et Sorciers, sans s'arrester à decider de l'apparition des esprits, sinon en passant' (sig. *iiii^r), Taillepied makes his focus the nature, power, and purpose of spirits in themselves.[68] This was to be a work of pastoral, not judicial, demonology.

Dialogues with the Dead: Memory and 'oubliance'

Taillepied's *Psichologie* is organized into twenty-six chapters. Though there is no division into books, as there is in Lavater, the first sixteen chapters correspond, with a few notable exceptions, to Book One of *Des apparitions*. Chapter 1, which derives largely from Michaëlis's *Pneumalogie*, concerns 'ceux qui ont douté s'il y avoit des esprits'. These include Epicureans, Saducees, and atheists (e.g. 'Lucianistes', 'Machiavelistes',

---

[66] 'Among others Peucer, Weyer, Milichius, Rivius, Camerarius, P. Martyr, Lavater, Cardan, Bodin, Agrippa, [Sébastien] Michaelis, Melchior [Flavin], [Léonard] du Vair, and others, whose writings have been of help to me.'

[67] 'have expressed views according to their own fantasy, branded as it is with new opinions'.

[68] 'only touched upon charmers and sorcerers, without stopping to decide the matter of apparitions of spirits, except in passing'.

and 'Rabletistes', p. 8), as well as 'mal devots' such as Lavater, Calvin, and Farel. Chapter 2 establishes a characteristically tripartite schema. Angels and ghosts appear, as in Lavater, but so too here do visions of the dead. From this last category Taillepied excludes the spirits of dead animals, 'ains seulement ceux des creatures intellectuelles'. Chapter 3–5 are based heavily on Lavater and discuss those who are most prone to seeing 'ghosts': these include melancholics (ch. 3), the timorous (ch. 4), and people suffering from various forms of sensory deprivation (ch. 5). Chapter 6, devoted to ghost hoaxes, is shorter than the equivalent in *Des apparitions*, since Lavater's anticlerical content has been deliberately suppressed. Chapter 7 repeats Lavater's exploration of various natural causes (echo, mirrors, etcetera) sometimes mistaken for ghosts. Chapters 8–13 are devoted to proof of the existence of spirits of all kinds. Taillepied, again following Lavater, draws his evidence from Scripture (ch. 8), ancient and modern history (chs. 9–10), the Church Fathers (ch. 11), and daily experience (ch. 13). Among these he interpolates a chapter on recent French cases (ch. 12). Chapters 14 and 15 return to Lavater with a section on ghostly apparitions as portents or prodigies (ch. 14), and on the times and places at which spirits are most likely to appear (ch. 15). Chapter 16, derived almost entirely from Michaëlis, takes up the demonological topic of spiritual bodies.

Following the model of *Des apparitions*, the next seven chapters (chs. 17–23) constitute the second section of Taillepied's treatise, while the remainder (chs. 24–6) parallel Lavater's Book Three. Chapters 17–23 mount a defence of Catholic belief in the return of the dead. In Chapter 17 Taillepied discusses the question of why the dead appear, arguing that they do so in order to instruct and console the living, and occasionally act as God's messengers on Earth. Chapter 18 is written predominantly against Bodin and Calvin, and argues for a rigorous discernment of dead souls from angels. The next two chapters address disputes of whether it is in God's will that the dead should appear (ch. 19), and the pagan notion that some dead souls, unable to enter Hades, are doomed to wander the Earth (ch. 20). Chapters 21 and 22, which are taken over directly from Melchior Flavin's *De l'estat des ames apres le trespas*, set out the Jewish, Muslim, and Catholic theologies of the afterlife. The question of Samuel's ghost is the subject of Chapter 23. It is the task of the final three chapters (chs. 24–6) to place ghosts under the ministry of the priest. Chapter 24 reinstates the *discretio spirituum*, supervised by a Catholic clergyman, as the proper response to apparitions. Chapter 25, entitled 'Moyen de conjurer les esprits', follows Lavater in prohibiting cursing and violence among those who witness ghosts. The final Chapter 26 is also indebted to

its counterpart in Lavater: here Taillepied prescribes the suitable reaction
to prodigious apparitions.

We shall dicuss in due course the—often striking and not only
structural—similarities between the *Psichologie* and Lavater's *Des apparitions*. First it is essential to acknowledge the very obvious divergences in
doctrine and, consequently, pastoral approach. What Taillepied attempts
to restore in his *Psichologie* is the desirability of a dialogue with the dead.
We have already seen in the previous chapter how he, like other Catholic
writers, were highly aware of the dangers of such a scheme. Actively to seek
an audience with the departed left the Catholic witness vulnerable to the
charge of necromancy, or raising the dead, an accusation all the more
likely to be made in an age so obsessed with witchcraft and the pact. The
Protestants Kasper Peucer and Johann Weyer, whose works Taillepied
knew, had levelled precisely that allegation: it was not so long ago, both
write, that divination by spirits was a favourite topic in the Schools.[69]
Nonetheless, Taillepied counters, and as Luke's parable of Lazarus and
Dives shows, it is possible to imagine that an encounter with the dead
might in some cases prove desirable.[70] After all, he asks, 'Si les ames
apparoissent, et requerroit aide, pourquoy ne requerroit on le mesme à
Dieu pour icelles?' Certainly, the Protestant alternative—tantamount to
turning away from the plight of dead souls—remained for Taillepied just
as grave a proposition.

The desirability of communing with the dead may have its origins in
Taillepied's own intellectual concerns. As he neared his own death in
1589, remembrance, and especially collective remembrance, seems to have
become a thematic preoccupation for the Franciscan friar. Three of his late
works are, in their different ways, archaeologies; all exhibit the same
concern to preserve the past from the neglect of the present. The first
words of his *Histoire de l'estat et republique des druides*, first published in
1585, decry 'la negligence de nos ancestres Gaulois'.[71] Meanwhile the
Recueils des antiquitez (of Rouen and Pontoise) bear witness to a similar
desire to rescue the past from under what he terms 'le rideau d'oubliance'.[72] To speak of a dialogue with the dead in such contexts is, of course,
to speak metaphorically. In the treatise on ghosts, however, that metaphor
turns literal. Here the urban topographer does not need to figure France's
ruins—for instance, the château de Vauvert, the château de Bicêtre, or
the Franciscan monastery in Nice—as symbols of a neglected past.

[69] Peucer, *Les Devins*, sig. E2^r; Weyer, *De l'imposture et tromperie des diables*, sigs. 95^v–6^r.
[70] On the parable of Lazarus and Dives in debates over ghosts, see above, pp. 57–63.
[71] Taillepied, *Histoire de l'estat et republique des druides*, sig. aii^r.
[72] Taillepied, *Recueil des antiquitez et singularitez de la ville de Pontoise*, p. 1.

These are haunted places: they speak out against forgetting in the accents of the dead.[73]

The *Psichologie* speaks of 'oubliance' as a vice of the Reformers. According to Taillepied, most forgetful of all are those, like Lavater, whose imagination has been 'cauterisee de nouvelles opinions' (sig. *iv^r). In the history of his native Pontoise, he had reminded his dedicatee, Nicolas Fournier, 'marchand et bourgeois', how Protestants had sacked the town during the last wars of religion; it was only thanks to Nicolas's father, a municipal governor, that the attack was repulsed and the town's monuments saved.[74] But worse still than these material 'pillages', which targeted only the bricks and mortar of communal memory, was the Reformers' contempt for the remembrance of dead spirits. Their 'negligence', Taillepied writes in the *Psichologie*, does not even spare their own. Because they are unwilling to credit belief in Purgatory, the Protestant dead lie forgotten and uncared for: 'Tous ceux qui ont esté abreuvez du fetide et bourbeux lac Genevois, tendent à ce but de nier l'apparition des ames quand elles sont separees du corps, non pour autre fin que de les sevrer des suffrages des survivans.' (p. 9)[75]

The language of severance underlines both the totality and the cruelty of the Protestant break with the community of the dead. Meanwhile, the reference to Geneva maps sectarian difference onto a difference of place. As we shall see, from Paris to Meulan-sur-Seine, Boulogne to Nice or Rodez, Taillepied's ghost narratives, like his histories, unfold for the most part on native French soil. Like the Rouen and Pontoise immortalized in his histories these are, to borrow a term of Pierre Nora, 'lieux de

---

[73] *Psichologie*, p. 169 (Vauvert and Vincestre); pp. 172–3 (Nice). The château de Vauvert, built in the tenth century by Robert II following his excommunication, had become proverbial as a haunted site during the Middle Ages; see F. Rabelais, *Pantagruel*, ed. by V. L. Saulnier (Geneva, Droz, 1965), p. 107: 'Ce diable de Pantagruel, qui a convaincu tous les Sorbonicoles, à cest heure aura son vin, car cest Angloys est un aultre diable de Vauvert.' Prior to its restoration as a military hospital under Louis XIII, the ruined château de Vincestre (or Bissestre, as it was commonly known) had developed a similar reputation. See *Histoire memorable et espouventable, arrivée au chasteau de Bissestre pres Paris, avec les apparitions des esprits et fantosmes qui ont esté veuz aux caves et chambres dudit chasteau* (Paris: N. Alexandre, 1623); *La Chasse donnée aux espouvantables esprits du château de Biscestre, près la ville de Paris, par la demolition qui en a esté faite, avec les estranges tintamarres et effroyables apparitions qui s'y sont toujours vus* (Paris: J. Brunet, 1634); F. Lavocat, 'Les Fantômes du Ballet de Cour' in *Dramaturgies de l'ombre*, pp. 177–200. On the early history of Bicêtre, see A. Du Chesne, *Les Antiquitez et recherche des villes, chasteaux et places plus remarquables de toute la France* [1609] (Paris: J. Boüillerot, 1648), p. 187.

[74] *Recueil des antiquitez et singularitez de la ville de Pontoise*, sig. Aii^r.

[75] 'All those who have drunk from the fetid and muddy Genevan lake, tend because of this to deny the apparition of souls separated from their bodies, for no other end than to sever them from the intercessions of the living.'

mémoire'.[76] Catholic France, unlike fetid Geneva, is a place where the dead will be remembered.

'Un bon personnage sage et discret': The Return of the Priest

Perhaps the principal achievement of Lavater's pastoral demonology is his dismissal of the priest as a figure of expertise. Presiding over the ghostly encounter in *Des apparitions* stands instead the minister, internalized as the stirrings of Protestant conscience. We have seen how this process of dismissal, supplantation, and internalization entailed a number of new strategies for Lavater: the move from Latin into the vernacular, the transition from clerical space to the haunted house, the establishment of the male *pater familias* as narrative hero, and the production of a persistent, and never quite negotiable, ambience of fear. The chief aim of Taillepied's treatise, by contrast, is to restore the banished priest. As we shall see, this project involves a markedly different attitude to narrative in the *Psichologie* and, within that narrative, divergences in Taillepied's treatment of setting, of gender, and of fear. To gain a full sense of what was at stake in religious disagreements over ghosts in early modern France, it will be necessary to examine these differences in some detail.

The clearest statement of Taillepied's intention to reinstall the priest as a mediating figure between the ghost and the lay witness is found late on in the treatise, in Chapter 24. As we shall see shortly, however, the role that Taillepied proposes for the priest is not simply a reversion to that which he enjoyed in the high Middle Ages. Less conspicuously interventionist than that of the medieval exorcist, and in what might be read as a concession to Protestant polemic, the priest here invites the lay reader to internalize the practice of *discretio spirituum* that was previously the preserve of the clerical classes. Indeed, the schema he proposes, reduced for clarity's sake to 'quatre marques, par lesquelles on peut discerner un bon esprit d'avec un mauvais' (p. 287), seems designed as a guide for confronting spirits alone, that is to say, in the absence of a priest. Though we have already encountered Taillepied's scheme in the previous chapter, it bears repeating here:

1) *Affect.* Fear that gives way to consolation or joy indicates the presence of a good spirit. The reverse should make us wary of an evil apparition.

2) *Appearance.* Good spirits usually take the shapes of doves, men, and lambs; these are often 'environné de clarté ou de couleur blanche'.

---

[76] P. Nora, *Les Lieux de mémoire* (Paris: Gallimard, 1984–92).

Lions, bears, dogs, toads, snakes, and cats usually indicate the presence of an evil spirit. The sound made by an apparition is a less reliable indication. Beware not only a voice that is 'espouventable, cruelle et terrible', but also one that is 'aimable, agreable, douce, basse', or 'plaintive'.

3) *Behaviour.* Exercise caution in dealing with spirits who adopt gestures of 'humilité, recognoissance de pechez, soupirs, pleurs, gemissemens', as well as 'orgueil, menaces, imprecations, et blasphemes'.

4) *Doctrine.* Beware any spirit that speaks out in such a way that is contrary to 'la parole de Dieu, aux traditions des Apostres, à la doctrine des Anciens' or 'la foy et les bonnes oeuvres'. (pp. 287–8)

However, things are not as simple as they might at first seem. Taillepied lays particular emphasis on the fact that the attitude adopted towards spirits by the newly empowered lay witness, armed though he now is with the gift of the discernment of spirits, will still need confirmation by an authority greater than his own. No wonder: as the tortuously ambiguous criteria of appearance and behaviour indicate, the process of *discretio spirituum* is so uncertain, at times, that even the most expert of readers is liable to error. In case of doubt, Taillepied recommends, 'aider se faut du conseil de quelque bon personnage sage et discret, et bien versé en la cognoissance de telles choses' (p. 279).[77] The identity of this 'bon personnage' is not in doubt: these lines can be read as an attempt to reinstate the priest, exiled as he was by Lavater in *Des apparitions*, as an authoritative presence within the lay ghostly encounter.

If the priest in Taillepied's *Psichologie* is secured as a figure of authority, it is in no small part due to his role not only as an agent in, but also as a narrator of, contemporary ghost narrative. This raises the important question of who is speaking through Taillepied, since it must be emphasized that the 'je' of the *Psichologie*, in line both with his self-appointed role as a compiler and collator, refers less specifically to the individual author himself than to the hypostasized authority of the figure of the priest. Indeed, almost all of Taillepied's recent narrative sources are derived from the work of other theologians, with Pierre Boaistuau the only non-theological contemporary writer named in the treatise, and cited only once (p. 161). The theological narratives are mainly to be found clustered in Chapter 12 ('Preuves que les esprits reviennent, par autheurs plus recens, du pays mesme de France'), where Taillepied includes a brief allusion to

----

[77] 'it is necessary to seek help from some good personage—wise, discreet, and well versed in the knowledge of such things'.

Montalembert's *Merveilleuse Hystoire* of 1528, which had recently been reprinted in Paris by Jean Pinart, along with a number of more developed ghost narratives gleaned from, and on this occasion accredited to, Melchior Flavin and Jean Lambert.[78] Taillepied's uncharacteristic willingness to confess his debts to both of these clergymen signals his intention to set up a rival to Lavater's strategy of self-authorization. Where Lavater names the sources of his anecdotes as local dignitaries or learned friends, Taillepied derives his authority from a network of Catholic theologians writing in French. Such accreditations help to consecrate the priest as the only legitimate narrator of the early modern ghost.

Two ghost anecdotes, both taken from Lambert's *Discours evangeliques et instructions chrestiennes et catholiques*, will serve to illustrate the priest's intervention, as a rival to the Protestant minister, in the spaces of everyday life. They will also allow a more detailed comparison between Taillepied's and Lavater's treatment of narrative. The first, characteristically brief, is worth citing in full:

> Environ l'an mil cinq cens cinquante neuf, un gentilhomme d'un village pres Meulan sur Seine, seigneur de Flins, avoit ordonné par testament qu'on ensevelist son corps avec ses ancestres, en la ville de Paris. Quand il fut trespassé, son fils heritier ne s'en souciant beaucoup d'executer la volonté de son pere, le fit inhumer en l'Eglise dudit village. Mais advint que l'esprit du pere fit tant grand bruit et tourmente dans la chambre du fils, qui couchoit en son lict à Paris, que le fils fut contraint d'envoyer des saquemans qu'il loüa à grand pris d'argent, pour aller deterrer le corps dudit trespassé, et le faire apporter au lieu où il avoit elue sa sepulture. Le lendemain matin, je fus à ce village, en un jour de Dimenche, où l'histoire me fut recitee tout au long: et y avoit dans l'Eglise une si grande puanteur de ce corps qui avoit esté levé le jour precedent, qu'on n'y pouvoit aucunement durer pour l'infection. (pp. 130–1)[79]

---

[78] Lambert, whom Taillepied introduces as 'religieux de Clugny et Prieur de saint Denis de Nogent au Perche' (p. 128), was the author of the *Discours evangeliques et instructions chrestiennes et catholiques* (Paris: J. Poupy, 1582). I have consulted the second edition (Paris: G. Bichon, 1586), which Taillepied may have encountered through his acquaintance with Guillaume Bichon.

[79] 'Around the year 1559, a gentleman from a village near Meulan sur Seine, the seigneur de Flins, had ordained in his will that his body should be buried with his ancestors, in the town of Paris. When he died his son and heir, none too concerned to execute his father's wishes, had him buried in the church of the aforesaid village. But it so happened that the father's spirit made such a great noise and tumult in the chamber of the son, who was lying in his bed in Paris, that the son was obliged, at great expense, to send hired hands to go and dig up the deceased's body, and have it brought to the place which he had chosen for his burial. The next morning, a Sunday, I was in that village, where I was told the story in all its detail: and there was in the church such a great stench made by the body, dug up the day before, that nobody could stay there for long, on account of the infection.'

Three stylistic or rhetorical features differentiate this story from Lavater's typical narrative. The first is Taillepied's precision concerning names ('seigneur de Flins'), dates ('environ l'an mil cinq cens cinquante neuf') and places ('un village pres Meulan sur Seine'). This level of detail, also present in a number of his other recent narratives, is characteristic of Taillepied's anecdotal style.[80] In Lavater such particulars were sacrificed in favour of a generalizable *exemplum*. Returning briefly to the two stories cited earlier from *Des apparitions*: the first, while specifying a Zurich magistrate, does not refer to him by name; nor, probably for reasons of discretion, does it name the neighbour he saw (or thought he saw) violating the horse in the pasture. Meanwhile, the hero of the second narrative is simply 'un quidam'; and although we are told that the events occurred 'en la conté de Hannaw', the date too remains vague ('depuis quelques années en ça'). In contrast, Taillepied's narrative brings such details back as a guarantee of veracity. To this extent, it might be said that the dates, times, and names serve as so many *effets de réel*.

If Taillepied's precision risks particularizing his narrative *exempla*, and thereby rendering them remote from the concerns of the average lay reader, the effect is mitigated by a second rhetorical feature. This involves the removal of anything resembling an affective dimension to the tale. Although mention is made of the ghost's 'grand bruit et tourment' as the son tries to sleep, Taillepied refuses to record the witness's emotional response. Instead the ghost represents little more than a pragmatic inconvenience: the son must have the body disinterred (at great expense) and brought to its rightful place in Paris. This pragmatism, which seems to appeal less to the soul than to the purse of the lay witness, stands out all the more when compared to the menace of Lavater's ghost stories. Unlike Taillepied, the minister's narratives placed repeated emphasis on the emotional response of the witness, whether that of the magistrate, dumbfounded ('esbahy') at seeing his neighbour violating a mare or, in Johann Willing's story, the transforming terror that engulfs the father in the night. The story of the Seigneur de Flins looks back rather to a medieval tradition that Jean-Claude Schmitt, in his history of apparitions in the Middle Ages, has described as the banalization of ghosts.[81] The dead are quickly tamed in Taillepied; they leave no lasting effects. To cite another prominent historian of the dead, then, it might be argued that the *Psichologie*,

---

[80] See for instance the story of the 'fille naturelle du sieur de la Meronniere', said to have unfolded 'à deux lieuës près de Boloigne sur la mer' (p. 173), or the tale of a Lyonnais playing-card manufacturer who pursued a ghost with his sword while Taillepied was staying with him in 1574 (p. 297). On this second example, see below, pp. 184–5.

[81] On Schmitt's concept of 'banalization', see above p. 22.

through stories such as this, continues to subscribe to the ideal of 'la mort apprivoisée'.[82] The third feature of Lambert's account concerns the denouement, which, as we shall see, involves a characteristic move in Taillepied's treatise: namely, the entrance of the priest himself ('je fus à ce village') and, correspondingly, the location of *discretio* in clerical, rather than domestic, space.

The priest's physical presence, at the end of the tale, in the church at Meulan-sur-Seine is evoked partly in order to explain how it was he came to know of the events ('l'histoire me fut recitee tout au long') and, more importantly, to lend the narrative further confirmation by remarking on the presence of the 'puanteur' and 'infection'. These are important functions, since they contribute to the status of the priest (to adopt Lacan's phrase) as 'he who is supposed to know'. Correspondingly, the priest's appearance also marks a significant transition, towards the end of the tale, from domestic to clerical space. Though Lambert is absent from the scene of the ghostly encounter, the conclusion of the story in the church, and 'en un jour de Dimenche', effectively clericalizes what would otherwise constitute a purely lay narrative. In a reversal of Lavater's trajectory, the question of burial, and the commemorative duties of the son towards his father, are ultimately restored to the dominion of the clergy.

The role of the priest as he who is supposed to know, and therefore as the ultimate provider of closure and confirmation, is similarly configured in Lambert's second tale. The heroine of that narrative is a local girl who, while he was composing his sermons, 'fut assez longuement travaillee de plusieurs visions et de jour et de nuict' (p. 129).[83] The girl determines to speak with the spirit and, 'ne sçachant quel remede employer pour s'en garantir, se disposa un jour de feste, et s'arme du sacrement de Penitence, et du sacrement de l'Autel' (p. 129).[84] Having readied herself in this way, she waits until midnight for the ghost to appear. This it duly does, whereupon she demands it reveal to her its purpose. The apparition replies that it is the soul of her dead brother who, having been killed on the road, 'n'auroit sçeut faire restitution de quelques petites choses qu'il avoit de l'autruy' (p. 129).[85] On hearing this, the girl restores the borrowed goods to their rightful owner, and the ghost is seen no more. The story ends as she enters the church the following day, and imparts her tale to Lambert, her spiritual director:

---

[82] On Ariès and 'la mort apprivoisée', see above, p. 22.

[83] 'was for quite a long time taxed with several visions both by day and by night'.

[84] 'not knowing what remedy to adopt to protect herself from it, prepared herself one feast day, and armed herself with the sacrament of penitence, and with the sacrament of the Eucharist'.

[85] 'could not make restitution of a few little things that he had of someone else's'.

Le lendemain ceste pauvre fille se retrouva en l'Eglise, où elle me fit tout le discours en propos de rendre graces à Dieu qu'elle estimoit l'avoir delivree de cet ennuy par ce colloque qu'elle avoit eu avec cest esprit, faisant offrir le sacrifice de l'autel à ceste intention, et mesme pour le remede de l'ame de son deffunct frere.[86] (p. 130)

As in the story from Meulan-sur-Seine, the tale ends in church, only this time as both priest and parishioner are giving thanks to God for revealing the truth of Catholic ghost praxis. Unlike the son of the Seigneur de Flins, however, whose laxity in following his father's wishes required correction from the ghost, Lambert's young girl has, by the time she met her brother's ghost, already internalized the devotional ideals of Catholic doctrine on spirits. Here the function of the priest's appearance is merely to confirm the procedures adopted by his young lay witness: her decision to fast, and her recourse to the sacraments of penitence and Mass. That neither her age nor her sex would habitually suggest, in the sixteenth century, 'un bon personnage sage et discret', shows the extent to which, at least for Taillepied, the Counter-Reformation had already succeeded in shaping popular devotion. However uncodified her knowledge of spirits ('ne sçachant quel remede employer pour s'en garantir'), the young girl embodies, if not through learning, then—perhaps all the more powerfully— through instinct and through faith, the pastoral ideals of Taillepied's *Psichologie*.

The heroine of Taillepied's second narrative is only one among a number of female witnesses in the *Psichologie*. This raises the question of gender more generally, not only in contradistinction to Lavater (whose witnesses to ghosts are unvaryingly male), but also via a return to the long discernment tradition described in the first chapter of this book. There we saw how, from Gerson to François de Sales and beyond, Catholic discernment was principally focussed on women as those most vulnerable to— and therefore the most exemplary victors over—the disturbance wrought by ghosts and apparitions. To this extent Taillepied's treatise suggests that, while Job stood as the patron of the haunted Protestant patriarch, the heroine of Catholic ghost stories continued to be Mary. This difference, and the consolidation of the female protagonist in the early years of the seventeenth century, will become significant in later chapters, where narrative interest in this figure will take a more prurient direction.

---

[86] 'The next day that poor girl turned up at the church, where she told me all about it in order that she might give thanks to God, who she considered to have delivered her from her troubles by means of the conversation she had had with this spirit, offering up to that end the sacrifice on the altar, and also in order to assist the soul of her dead brother.'

EPILOGUE: INVERSION AND SYMMETRY

This chapter has reproduced the conflictual flavour of much early modern religious discussion of ghosts by pitting, as it were, the Protestant Lavater against the Catholic Taillepied. But there is some evidence, developed more fully in the following chapter, that matters are not so simple. Before taking leave of the two adversaries, we must finally examine a feature unremarked on (perhaps intentionally) by Taillepied's twentieth-century English translator and editor, Montague Summers. That feature concerns the extent of his compilation of other writing on spirits, and especially of his debt to his Swiss Protestant opponent.

As little as 20 per cent of the *Psichologie* is the work of Taillepied and Taillepied alone. Of the authorities he cites in his preface, the works of Melchior Flavin and Sébastien Michaëlis furnish the material for a small proportion of the work. Remarkably, the rest—possibly as much as 60–70 per cent—is provided by none other than Lavater himself. It is important to be clear that this does not take that form of polemical riposte in which one cites one's opponent *in extenso* the better to refute him point by point later on.[87] For although Taillepied confesses his status as an epitomizer in the preface, the 'borrowings' from Lavater, often verbatim and spanning several pages, are almost entirely unacknowledged in the body of the treatise. To this extent the *Psichologie* is the work not only of a compiler but of a plagiarist.

To remark upon the scale of Taillepied's debt to this particular precursor is not to pass judgement on his treatise as a whole. The category of 'plagiarism' involves a set of moral, aesthetic, and now legal assumptions far from self-evident in an early modern culture with very different notions of imitation and 'invention'.[88] More interesting is the light that Taillepied's debt casts on the view, expressed by Summers and numerous other twentieth-century commentators, that Catholics and Protestants entertained entirely different conceptions of the early modern ghost. It seems, from Taillepied's plagiarism, that things are less straightforward. If Summers is right, how can it be possible that a text declaring itself implacably opposed to the Protestant opinion should silently rework so much of Lavater's treatise? The answer may lie in what Stuart Clark has deemed

---

[87] Cf. Le Loyer, who employs precisely that strategy in the *Quatre livres des spectres*, II, pp. 91–124.

[88] Although this did not prevent Antoine du Verdier accusing Claude de Tesserant, one of the contributors to the *Histoires prodigieuses*, of stealing his (illustrated) translation of a ghost story from Pliny. On this case of 'plagiarism', see below p. 153 n. 38.

to be a structural, or grammatical, imperative at work in all demonological writing: inversion.[89]

What Clark means by demonological inversion, which he takes to be a fundamental property of witchcraft as a concept (left-handed, backwards moving, upside-down, anally fixated, etcetera), can be illustrated with reference to a notorious case that we encountered in the previous chapter, namely that of Nicole Obry—the 'démoniaque de Laon'.[90] Obry was finally rid of her possessing spirit when, in a public ceremony attended by spectators from all over Europe, she was presented with the Eucharist in Laon town square. What Protestant and Catholic spectators observed was identical: a demon banished from a girl at the sight of bread and wine. But interpretations differed. While Catholics wondered at the apotropaic victory wrought by the holy sacraments, Protestants came to a directly inverse conclusion: Satan had indeed left Obry when confronted in the Mass, but only to mire the Catholic faithful more deeply in superstitious error.

Inversions of this kind are especially visible in Taillepied's plagiarism of Lavater. We might go further: it is only on account of invertibility that such plagiarism works at all. Take this example, in which first Lavater and then Taillepied are writing about the times at which ghosts are most likely to appear:

Lavater:
Les esprits sont apparus le temps passé, et apparoissent tant de jour et de nuict, mais le plus souvent environ la minuict quand on est esveillé du premier somne. Item ils apparoissent le plus souvent les vendredis et samedis et aux jours de jeusne, pour confermer d'autant plus les superstitieux.[91]

Taillepied:
Le temps passé les esprits sont apparus, et apparoissent encore tant de jour que de nuict, mais le plus souvent environ la minuict quand on est eveillé du premier somme, lors que les sens sont libres et en repos. Item ils apparoissent le plus souvent les vendredys et samedys et autres jours de jeusnes, d'autant qu'en tels jours on n'est point addonné aux mondanitez, ains se retire on à prieres et oraisons, et s'efforcent les gens de bien de se mettre en bon estat.[92]

---

[89] Clark, *Thinking with Demons*, ch. 5 ('Inversion').

[90] See above pp. 33–5.

[91] 'Time past spirits used to, and [still] do, appear by day and by night, but most often around midnight when we are aroused from our first slumber. Also they appear most frequently on Fridays and Saturdays and on days of fast, all the better to confirm the superstitious in their beliefs.' *Des apparitions*, p. 91.

[92] 'Time past spirits used to, and still do, appear by day and by night, but most often around midnight when we are aroused from our first slumber, and when the senses are free and at rest. Also they appear most frequently on Fridays and Saturdays and other days of

The first sentence of Taillepied's text makes minimal revisions to the source in Lavater: a reversal of word order ('le temps passé les esprits sont apparus'), the addition of a word ('encore') and of a brief explanatory gloss ('lors que les sens sont libres et en repos'). The inversion occurs in the second sentence. For Lavater, who is here writing only about demonic apparitions, spirits appear on holy days precisely in order to confirm Catholics in their superstition. Taillepied, who is writing about Purgatorial ghosts, agrees on the days of the week most propitious for seeing ghosts ('vendredys et samedys et autres jours de jeusnes') but inverses the polarity of Lavater's explanation: the timing of such apparitions arises not from superstition but, on the contrary, *confirms* the value of the Catholic devotional calendar.

It might be argued that this example (there are more) shows the extent to which plagiarism might be mobilized as a form of aggressive appropriation, with Taillepied taking up the words of his Protestant opponent only, and all the more forcefully, to turn them against him. A less conflictual interpretation might remark instead that while inversion implies difference, it also—and as importantly—implies symmetry, as when two shapes are reflected in a single axis that both share. This may well apply to Taillepied as an inversion of Lavater. The Franciscan is only able to articulate his distinction from the Zurich pastor on account of the commonality, rather than the difference, between the two writers' assumptions. Just as the Protestants and Catholics in Laon town square could not begin a polemic on the Eucharist without first agreeing on what they saw, so too Lavater and Taillepied inhabit what is essentially a homologous conception of the ghostly encounter. For all Taillepied's protestations of polemical intent, the Catholic's inversion of his Protestant opponent remains only the function, or surface structure, of what is otherwise a deep conceptual complicity.

This chapter has shown how that complicity rested on a common objective, namely pastoral intervention in the daily life of the lay reader. The purpose of the next will be to show how the threat to that objective came less from inside religious discourse, that is to say from a sectarian opponent, than from the growing body of writing that placed ghosts beyond theology.

---

fast, since on these days we are not given to worldly things, but retire to give prayers and orisons, and good people strive to put themselves in a good state.' *Psichologie*, p. 168.

PART II

GHOSTS BEYOND RELIGION

3

Beyond Purgatory

THE SHIBBOLETH

To many the story of Part I, concerning the place of ghosts within religious theory and practice, may already sound familiar. Social and intellectual historians have long been attentive to what ghosts reveal within the larger narrative of the Reformation and the changes it wrought in attitudes to death and remembrance. This is especially true of students of Reformed societies such as England or Geneva, where official condemnation of ghost belief and practice is commonly supposed to have driven a powerful wedge between the communities of the living and the dead.

Perhaps the most influential of these accounts has been that offered, in an English context, by Keith Thomas.[1] As a well-known passage in his *Religion and the Decline of Magic* puts it:

> Although it may be a relatively frivolous question today to ask whether or not one believes in ghosts, it was in the sixteenth century a shibboleth which distinguished Protestant from Catholic almost as effectively as belief in the Mass or Papal Supremacy.[2]

Placed in their proper context, ghosts might thus be considered a crux of confessional debate, and the progress of official attempts to abolish them a barometer of successful Reform. True enough, Thomas goes on, belief in ghosts did not entirely disappear in the wake of the English Reformation, a persistence he describes as a form of 'cultural lag'. But official doctrine had slammed the door shut on Purgatory, and associated beliefs in return from the dead, leaving the English to look to alternative forms of commemoration. These, he argues, ranged from elaborate epigraphs on tombstones, through the keeping of books of remembrance, to the immortality topoi of Shakespeare's sonnets.[3]

---

[1] Thomas, *Religion and the Decline of Magic*, ch. 19 ('Ghosts and Fairies').
[2] Ibid., p. 589.
[3] Natalie Zemon Davis reaches similar conclusions, though from a different theoretical standpoint, in 'Ghosts, Kin, and Progeny', pp. 92–6.

Thomas's notion of the 'shibboleth', and the thesis it supports, are cited in virtually every (anglophone) account of ghosts written since. Although subsequent scholars have sometimes challenged the top-down model of cultural and religious change implied by his idea of 'cultural lag'—according to which peasant laymen prove slow to catch on to the lessons of their betters—the broad thrust of his proposals is still repeated among historians and non-historians alike.[4] R. A. Bowyer writes that 'when the Reformation came to Northern Europe, the picture changed drastically: the Church formally severed diplomatic relations with the Other World.'[5] Likewise, 'one of the most profound effects of the protestant elimination of purgatory', argues David Cressy more recently in 1997, 'was to shrink the community of souls and to sever the relationship between the dead and the living'.[6] Another field that has helped to bolster this suggestion of traumatic severance has been Shakespeare studies. From Dover Wilson via Sister Myriam Joseph to Stephen Greenblatt, critics of *Hamlet* in particular have sought to ascribe the prince's famous inaction to his astonishment, on vacation from Luther's Wittemberg, at having encountered a ghost from a place—Purgatory—he had been taught did not exist.[7] For these readers, *Hamlet*'s paralyzing doubt emerges all the more powerfully against the backdrop of religious certainty implied in Thomas's shibboleth. For them, as for Thomas, the fate of ghosts, and beliefs in them, was fastened tight to a Europe-wide crisis in religious belief.

Even in France, where the story of Reformation is otherwise so different, there exists compelling support for Thomas's thesis. As we have seen in Part I of this study, French Catholics and Protestants disagreed vigorously about ghosts. In France as in England, apparitions of the dead buttressed devotional practices (fasting, almsgiving, requiem masses) that the Church had administered—Protestants would have said 'exploited'— for at least three hundred years. As discussed in Chapter 1, disagreement over ghosts sometimes surfaces in the form of narrative exchange, as in that between Montalembert's apologetic *Merveilleuse Hystoire* and Protestant counter-accusations of faked apparitions; on other occasions it emerges as part of exegetical debate over the parable of Lazarus and

---

[4] Zemon Davis takes issue with Thomas for viewing the uneducated laity as little more than passive receptacles for elite thought; see 'Some Tasks and Themes', p. 309.

[5] Bowyer, 'The Role of the Ghost-Story in Mediaeval Christianity', p. 190.

[6] D. Cressy, *Birth, Marriage, and Death: Ritual, Religion, and the Life-Cycle in Tudor and Stuart England* (Oxford: Oxford University Press, 1997), p. 396.

[7] J. Dover Wilson, *What Happens in Hamlet?* (Cambridge: Cambridge University Press, 1935), Ch. 3 ('Ghost or Devil?'); M. Joseph, 'Discerning the Ghost in *Hamlet*', *PMLA* 76 (1961), pp. 493–502; S. Greenblatt, *Hamlet in Purgatory* (Princeton: Princeton University Press, 2001).

Dives, or over differing views of Christ's resurrected body. Meanwhile the stakes within specialist monograph treatments of the subject, such as the popularizing vernacular works of Lavater and Taillepied explored in Chapter 2, could hardly have been higher. Their works show the extent to which belief in ghosts or its repudiation went right to the heart—or, more pointedly, right to the hearth—of how lay readers after Trent experienced their homes. For career theologians like Lavater and Taillepied, ghosts without doubt marked off the 'true faith' from the false, standing as a 'shibboleth' of old attitudes and new.

Good reasons remain, then, for viewing the early modern ghost through the prism of theological opinion. But there are also limitations. An unfortunate and doubtless unintended consequence of Thomas's thesis has been to privilege the evidence of theological and sectarian discourse (and lay reactions to it) to the exclusion of all others. We have come to expect that the apparition of an early modern ghost is always and unavoidably a *religious* experience. This expectation has fostered a version of what the economist Amartya Sen has called a 'solitarist' approach to human identity.[8] For Sen, who is writing in the different context of contemporary attitudes to Islam, 'solitarism' describes the deluded presumption that the allegiances of a given community are only or primarily defined by a single framework (in this case faith). This presumption, which Sen calls 'a good way of misunderstanding nearly everyone in the world', can be external and racist, as when a far-right political party brands all Arabs as 'fanatics'; it can also be internal and theocratic, as when a prominent Islamic faith group claims to represent all British Muslims. Either way, both versions of solitarism are deluded since, as Sen shows, the social, political, and intellectual interests of many Muslims in reality exist in several different planes—relating to class, profession, age, gender, sexuality, taste in music, etcetera—among which faith is only one. Of course, historians of the Reformation have long recognized that confessional allegiance may often have been trumped by other forms of association, as when Catholic members of the printing guilds rescued their Protestant colleagues from the Saint Bartholomew's Day mob. But even those cases are sometimes discussed as if they were only temporary suspensions, brought on by war or crisis, of the solitarist norm.

To return now to the context of this study, the sway that the grand narrative of Reformation has continued to hold over modern studies of ghosts is evident to varying degrees. Most explicit is the tendency among some scholars to privilege those figures, like Lavater and Taillepied, whose

[8] A. Sen, *Identity and Violence: The Illusion of Destiny* (London: Allen Lane, 2006), p. XII.

solitarist vision best justifies their own. This can sometimes lead to the spectacle of modern scholars appearing to restage the sectarian battles that are the object of their study. One extreme case is Montague Summers's extraordinarily partisan edition of Taillepied's treatise on ghosts. Making no mention of (indeed, perhaps deliberately concealing) Taillepied's considerable debt to Lavater, Summers, himself a Catholic priest, prefers instead to promote the originality of the *Psichologie* which, as he claims with some gusto, strikes Lavater 'grovelling into the dust'.[9] Such intellectual bad faith (or, at best, editorial incompetence) renders Summers's edition virtually unusable.

Less marked, though no less telling, is the extent to which early modern sectarian discourse, the main object of this study, has begun to contaminate our own descriptions of it. The widespread language of 'severance', for instance, might give us pause for thought. When Bowyer writes, in the passage quoted a moment ago, that 'when the Reformation came to Northern Europe...the Church formally *severed* diplomatic relations with the Other World', or when Cressy claims that an effect of this abolition of Purgatory was 'to *sever* the relationship between the dead and the living', one wonders whether they take early Catholic protests too much at their word. Their terms bear a striking resemblance to Counter-Reformation laments for the loss of faith in Purgatory, as when Taillepied (for instance) claims that the Protestants had denied that ghosts appeared 'non pour autre fin que de les *sevrer* des suffrages des survivans'.[10] Whether or not such 'severance' actually took place, such echoes should make us wary of merely replicating the polemic of the Counter-Reformation, as if what lay behind it were not a matter of value—contentious, polemical, uncertain—but of settled historical fact.

The continuing dominance of sectarian theological debate as the 'natural' context for ghosts in modern histories of the subject represents, four centuries on, an unwonted triumph for churchmen of all confessions. Their own solitarism has reproduced itself as ours. When considering that triumph one is struck not so much by what separates polemicists like Lavater and Taillepied as what places them resolutely on the same side. At

---

[9] Taillepied, *A Treatise of Ghosts*, p. xii: 'In one sense the *Traité de l'apparition des esprits* is an answer—and how crushing an answer!—to *De spectris* of Ludwig Lavater, whom he strikes grovelling into the dust. This mischievous book, with its blank materialism, has been recently proclaimed as possessed of a Shakespearean interest, but this, to me at least, appears very artificial. The mind of Shakespeare when he wrote *Hamlet* was far more attuned to the doctrine of Noël Taillepied than to the arid and ambiguous fantasies of the Zurich pastor.' Summers also cannot resist disparaging references to Dover Wilson's recent edition of this 'weak and wicked' book; see pp. 190 and 215–16.

[10] 'for no other end than to sever them from the intercessions of the living'.

the end of the previous chapter we saw how the very structure—inversion—usually supposed to divide the minister and the priest can in fact resemble tight symmetrical complicity. What Taillepied and Lavater, acting together, offer is a sealed and airtight system, impervious to any perspective that might issue from outside. If the stakes in theological disagreement over ghosts were indeed high, the stakes in consensus—that theology remain the only discourse within which resolution could be found—were perhaps even higher.

In reality, and as this chapter will show, theology had no monopoly on ghosts as a learned subject, however much religious controversialists such as Lavater or Taillepied might have wished that it had. Early modern attitudes to apparitions of the dead existed in more than just one plane. Perhaps weary of the kind of ideological stalemate reached by theologians such as Lavater and Taillepied, a number of sixteenth- and seventeenth-century writers take ghosts not only out of sectarian polemic, but bracket theology more generally out of their discussion. This so-called 'naturalist' body of writing, in which phenomena are investigated according to the principle 'de naturalibus naturaliter' ('natural things by natural means'), is very large indeed. Vernacular discussions of ghosts, whether in French or translated from other languages, appear in medical works on the interpretation of dreams; in natural magic after Cardano, especially in the tradition of 'subtilités' and 'plaisantes inventions'; in the moral philosophy of the *diverses leçons*; in legal wrangles over property and in the proceedings of criminal tribunals; in vulgarizations of Aristotelian philosophy; in chronicles and other historical works; in prosopography, or the description of illustrious personages; in the table-talk of writers such as Guillaume Bouchet; in personal reflections, such as the essays of Montaigne and the *Journal* of Pierre de L'Estoile; in medical and juridical demonology; in the series of *Histoires prodigieuses* inaugurated by Pierre Boaistuau; and in comparative ethnography.[11]

---

[11] For 'visions nocturnes' in medical works concerning dreams, see for instance A. Julian, *L'Art et jugement des songes et visions nocturnes, avec la physionomie des songes, et visions fantastiques des personnes, et l'exposition d'iceux selon le cours de la lune* [1558] (Paris: Nicolas Gay, 1645), pp. 149–51; this text, dated 3 January, 1551, exists in an earlier edition (Lyon: B. Rigaud, 1572). For discussions of ghosts in natural magic, see especially Cardano, *De la Subtilité*, Book Eighteen; Prévost, *La Premiere partie des subtiles et plaisantes inventions*, sig. 49ᵛ–50ᵛ; Della Porta, *La Magie naturelle*, pp. 148–9; J. J. Wecker, *Les Secrets et merveilles de nature, recueillis de divers autheurs et divisez en XVII livres*, trans. by G. Chappuys, ed. by P. Meyssonnier (Lyon: B. Honorat, 1586), pp. 992–9. For ghosts in moral philosophy, see P. Messie (P. Mexía), *Les Diverses Leçons de Pierre Messie, gentilhomme de Sevile, avec trois dialogues dudit auteur, contenans variables et memorables histoires*, trans. by C. Gruget (Lyon: B. Honorat, 1577), Book Four, ch. 14; J. des Caurres, *Oeuvres morales et diversifiées en histoires pleines de beaux exemples* (Paris: G. Chaudière, 1575), ch. 37; L. Guyon, *Les Diverses Leçons de Loys Guyon, sieur de La Nauche... suivans celles de Pierre Messie et du sieur de*

Detailed study of all these discursive contexts is beyond the scope of this book. Instead this chapter will focus, first, on early modern discussion of the one biblical ghost narrative not studied in Chapter 1, that of Samuel's apparition to Saul (I Samuel 28). There, despite the ostensibly theological context, we shall see a number of secular writers intervening from outside. In the rest of the chapter, devoted principally to the phenomenally popular *histoires prodigieuses* and *histoires tragiques*, we witness theological discussion of ghosts either substantially downplayed or bypassed altogether.

GHOSTS, WITCHES, KINGS, WAR: REREADING SAMUEL AND THE WOMAN OF ENDOR

One of the most contentious topics within early modern discussion of ghosts was the question of how to interpret the Old Testament story of Samuel's appearance to Saul (I Samuel 28). Responses to the episode often bear the stamp of confessional allegiance; but, as we shall see, that is far from the whole story.

Fearful of defeat the following day against the Philistine army, King Saul breaks his own ban on wizards and diviners ('magos et ariolos') and consults a wise woman in the village of Endor. Saul asks the woman to conjure the spirit of the prophet Samuel. To this she agrees, although what

---

Vauprivaz [1604], 2nd ed. (Lyon: C. Morillon, 1617), Book Three, chs. 26–7. For ghosts in legal cases, see *Recueil de plaidoyez notables de plusieurs anciens et fameux advocats de la cour de Parlement faicts en causes celebres, dont aucunes plaidées en presence des Roys. Et divers arrests intervenus tant sur lesdicts plaidoyez, qu'en autres affaires publiques et de consequence* (Paris: veuve J. du Brayet and N. Rousset, 1611), pp. 246–64; and Chapter Four below, pp. 148–54. For ghosts in vernacular *abrégés* of Aristotle, see F. de Gravelle, *Abbregé de philosophie, physique, metaphysique, morale, et divine: sur la cognoissance de l'homme et de sa fin* (Paris: J. Perier, 1601), sigs. 321^v–2^r. For ghosts in historical works, see Surius, *Histoire ou commentaires de toutes choses memorables*, sigs. 183^{r-v}; P. Camerarius, *Les Meditations historiques de M. Philippe Camerarius, docte Jurisconsulte, et Conseillier au Senat de Nuremberg ville Imperiale . . . Nouvelle edition, reveue sur le Latin, augmentée par l'auteur, et enrichie d'un tiers par le translateur*, trans. by S. Goulart, (Lyon: veuve A. Harsy, 1610), pp. 359–65; idem, *Les Heures desrobees ou meditations historiques du docte et fameux jurisconsulte M. Philippe Camerarius Conseiller du Senat de Nuremberg ville Imperiale*, trans. by F. de Rosset (Paris: J. Cottereau, 1610), pp. 109–18; S. Goulart, *Histoires admirables et memorables de nostre temps, recueillies de plusieurs autheurs*, 2 vols. (Paris: J. Houzé, 1606–7), I, sigs. 32^r–4^v, 380^v–94^v; idem, *Thresor d'histoires admirables et memorables de nostre temps* (Geneva: J. Crespin, 1628), pp. 59–65, 548–52. For ghosts in prosopography, see Du Verdier, *La Prosopographie, ou description des personnes insignes* (Lyon: A. Gryphius, 1573), pp. 297–306. On Bouchet's *Sérées*, see below, p. 167. On ghosts in Montaigne, see above, p. 7, and below, pp. 247–52; on ghosts in L'Estoile, see below, pp. 168–72. On ghosts in comparative ethnography, see especially C. Guichard, *Funerailles et diverses manieres d'ensevelir des Rommains, Grecs, et autres nations, tant anciennes que modernes* (Lyon: J. de Tournes, 1581), pp. 346, 395–6, 440, 448, and Ch. 4 below, pp. 154–63.

happens next is unclear from the text. Given Saul's next question to her ('What did you see?'), some have assumed that she retires into some form of inner chamber, though it is clear, a few lines further on, that Saul too sees the ghost directly. The woman's reply is 'vir senex ascendit et ipse amictus est pallio' ('an old man cometh up; and he is covered with a mantle.')[12] Then appearing directly to Saul, the dead prophet (or a figure resembling him) angrily condemns him for disturbing his rest, before confirming the king's worst fears. 'Cras mecum... eris' ('Tomorrow shalt thou... be with me'), the apparition tells him.[13] The prediction is fulfilled the next day when Saul perishes in battle.

Samuel is not the only dead prophet in the Bible who returns to speak with the living: Moses and Elias appear in Christ's transfiguration on the mount (Matthew 17:1–4; Luke 9:28–33). But whereas Moses and Elias are manifestly divine in their origin and purpose, the ghost of Samuel is shrouded in doubt. Is the figure conjured by the woman truly a soul returned from the dead? Or is it, as many suspected, a diabolical illusion wrought to plunge Saul—long plagued by demons—into despair? These questions were already of long vintage by the late sixteenth century, reaching back as they did to Augustine and beyond. Augustine himself was inconsistent in his answer, wavering between the thesis of demonic interference and that of a true ghost. Since then discussions of the topic had grown in complexity.[14] Early modern commentators pondered a number of difficulties. Would Samuel really have been buried in the 'mantle' worn by the spirit? What must we imagine the 'mecum' of 'cras mecum eris' to imply—Abraham's bosom or *Sheol*, the Jewish under-world? And what credence should be given to the apocryphal book of Ecclesiasticus, which states unequivocally that Samuel's soul indeed appeared?[15]

For some, the answer to such questions was determined by matters of principle. To admit that the true Samuel returned would be to concede power over dead souls to witches and black magic, thereby seeming to suppose Satan capable of miracles. Since this possibility ran directly counter to orthodox demonological thinking, the diabolic thesis grew in

[12] I Samuel 28:14.

[13] I Samuel 28:19.

[14] For detailed studies, see J.-Cl. Schmitt, 'Le Spectre de Samuel et la sorcière d'En Dor. Avatars historiques d'un récit biblique: I Rois 28', *Études rurales*, 105–6 (1987), pp. 37–64; T. Chesters, 'Jean de La Taille et la scénographie du "creux": *Saül le furieux* (1572)' in *Dramaturgies de l'ombre: spectres et fantômes au théâtre*, ed. by F. Lecercle and F. Lavocat (Rennes: Presses Universitaires de Rennes, 2005), pp. 101–18; Lecercle, 'Les Bénéfices de la trahison'; Clark, *Vanities of the Eye*, pp. 240–6.

[15] Ecclesiasticus 46. The deuterocanonical or apocryphal book of Ecclesiasticus, attributed to Jesus of Sirach, is not to be confused with the Old Testament Ecclesiastes.

its appeal: a demon must have appeared in the guise of the dead prophet. But that line of thinking was also not without its problems. To propose that a demon took on Samuel's shape would be to grant Satan the gift of prophecy (since the spirit correctly predicts Saul's downfall in the field)— this, too, an aptitude that orthodox opinion normally forbade him. Much was at stake in such conundrums, not least the basic question—especially vexed in the Reformation context—of whether dead souls indeed *ever* visited those they left behind.

   Given these stakes, we should not be surprised to find much theological opinion on Samuel divided along predictable sectarian fault-lines. Keen as they were to strike a blow against ghosts in general, and against Purgatory in particular, Protestant interpreters tended overwhelmingly to diabolize the apparition. Peter Martyr Vermigli's extended analysis of the episode, whose French translation was appended to Lavater's *Des apparitions*, is one prominent example: he concludes with the view that 'ç'a esté un fantosme'.[16] As is frequently the case in early modern French, 'fantosme' here implies the presence of illusion, here an illusion over which the Devil himself presided. The similar findings of Lavater himself ('que ce ne fut point le vray Samuel qui apparut à la sorcière en Endor') and of Lambert Daneau ('c'est bien le diable qui parle lors, mais sous le nom d'un autre') are other instances.[17] Ranged against this Protestant position stood a number of prominent European Catholic theologians, including Peltanus and Delrio, as well as, in France, lesser known controversialists such as Jacques d'Illaire, Taillepied, Claude Durand, Valladier, François Feu-Ardent, and Guillaume Baile.[18] D'Illaire's highly orthodox treatise on Purgatory, *Le Purgatoire des ames catholiques*, is typical in placing Samuel at the heart of a fierce attack on Calvin, whose diabolic reading of Samuel he condemns as a broader Protestant attempt to cut traditional bonds between the living and the dead.

   And yet it was not simply a matter of new religion versus old. As soon as we set aside career theologians such as Peltanus or d'Illaire, the Catholic consensus on I Samuel 28 begins to splinter and divide. One area in which Catholic writers tend to diabolize the apparition, as it were against their

---

[16] P. Martyr Vermigli, *Sommaire des trois questions proposees et resolues par M. Pierre Martyr* in Lavater, *Trois livres des apparitions des esprits*, p. 250.
   [17] Lavater, *Trois livres des apparitions*, p. 131; Daneau, *Deux traitez nouveaux*, p. 20.
   [18] Peltanus, *De Purgatorio*, sig. Aiii^r; Delrio, *Les controverses magiques*, sig. Riii^r; J. d'Illaire, *Le Purgatoire des ames catholiques . . . où est monstré le soin que nous devons avoir des morts* (Paris: C. Rigaud, 1612), pp. 72–3; Taillepied, *Psichologie*, ch. 23; Durand, *Purgatoire des fideles defuncts*, pp. 246–8; Valladier, *Saincte Philosophie*, p. 700; Feu-Ardent, *Semaine des dialogues*, II, pp. 86–7; Baile's position, along with the response of the Protestant André Rivet, can be found in A. Rivet, *Sommaire et abbregé des controverses de nostre temps touchant la religion* (La Rochelle: H. Haultin, 1608), pp. 536–41.

co-religionaries, is judicial demonology. A number of Catholic lawyers such as Pierre Massé and Pierre Le Loyer, and witch-finders, such as Nicolas Rémy and Henri Boguet, view Samuel's appearance as Satanically inspired.[19] Writing in his *Quatre livres des spectres*, Le Loyer devotes over a hundred pages to the topic in which, instead of countering Lavater (elsewhere cast as his opponent), he cites *Des apparitions* extensively in favour of his diabolic thesis. Boguet, for his part, explicitly condemns Delrio's findings on the subject, despite the high esteem in which the Jesuit was held. Perhaps this is not so surprising. Judicial demonology had its own esteemed traditions: one of its foundational textbooks, the *Malleus maleficarum*, claimed that a demon deceived Saul.[20]

One reason for this division in Catholic opinion, noted by Schmitt, has to do with the involvement of the character described in the Vulgate as 'mulier habens pythonem' ('a woman having a familiar spirit').[21] The connotations of illicit magic already present in the biblical narrative (as the 'magos et ariolos' prohibited by Saul) received ever greater emphasis during the witchcraft persecutions. Something of this evolution is evident in the terminology used. In the sixteenth-century French discussions of the episode the woman has become variously 'enchanteresse', 'divineresse', and—increasingly assimilated to the historical witches of the persecutions— most often 'sorcière'. For many judicial demonologists, the mere presence of this figure was enough to condemn the apparition as a diabolical illusion. As Boguet puts it, there are strong reasons for believing the demonic thesis 'quand bien l'on n'auroit autre raison, sinon que la femme Pythonique et devineresse entrevint en cet acte'.[22] Less concerned with defending the doctrine of Purgatory than highlighting the scope— and the dangers—of magic practised in the pact, Catholic witch-hunters such as Boguet had little cause to back the orthodox position favoured by the clergy.

The witch's intervention even led prominent Catholic theologians to favour the diabolic thesis. Among demonological writers these included Leonardo Vairo, whose treatise on charms was translated into French in

[19] Massé, *De l'imposture et tromperie des diables*, p. 37; Le Loyer, *Quatre livres des spectres*, Book Four, Ch. 1; N. Remigius, *Daemonolatreiae libri tres ex judiciis capitalibus nongentorum plus minus hominum, qui sortilegii crimen intra annos quindecim in Lotharingia capite luerunt* (Lyon: ex off. Vicentii, 1595), p. 186; H. Boguet, *Discours des sorciers, avec six advis en faict de sorcelerie, et une instruction pour un juge en semblable matière* [1602] (Lyon: P. Rigaud, 1608), p. 34.

[20] J. Sprenger, *Malleus maleficarum*, ed. and trans. by C. S. Mackay, 2 vols. (Cambridge: CUP, 2006), I, pp. 359–60.

[21] I Samuel 28:7.

[22] 'even when there is no other reason but that the Pythonic woman and enchantress intervened in this act'. Boguet, *Discours des sorciers*, p. 34.

1583, and Maldonat (in his enormously influential lectures on demonology of 1570–1), though the opinion was shared much more widely, especially among clergy sympathetic to the Catholic League.[23] The political parallels were there for all to see: the story of a monarch who, losing his grip on power and reality, had desperate recourse to sorcery, held a particular attraction for ultra-Montane opponents of the last Valois kings. Ever since Catherine de' Medici invited Nostradamus to court in the 1550s, accusations of magic had hung over the Valois dynasty; into the late 1570s and 1580s, a number of *ligueur* pamphlets accuse Henri III of consorting with witches in the woods around Paris.[24] It is in this spirit, for instance, that the minim Pierre Nodé opens his *Declamation contre l'erreur execrable des maleficiers* with a plea to Henri not to follow Saul in his tolerance of witchcraft. Saul was deceived, Nodé insists, by a demon at Endor; France must not fall into a similar error.[25]

Meanwhile, other theologians, less convinced than Nodé or Maldonat, preferred to follow Augustine and not declare their hand. René du Pont, writing in his *La Philosophie des esprits*, suspends judgement on the question.[26] Others still switched between positions depending on the context. The example of the Celestine Pierre Crespet is instructive. When writing his theological polemic, the *Discours catholiques, de l'origine, de l'essence, excellence, fin, et immortalité de l'ame*, Crespet is keen to defend the possibility that ghosts appear from Purgatory and argues, albeit tentatively, that a true Samuel appeared to Saul.[27] In his more demonologically oriented *Deux livres de la hayne de Sathan*, by contrast, he concludes in favour of a demonic Samuel.[28] Crespet's (perhaps strategic) indecision on the matter shows just how malleable, and contextually determined, Catholic opinion on ghosts could sometimes be.

Given the political context of anti-Valois propaganda, the presence of the witch was perhaps compelling enough reason for the late sixteenth century to view Samuel's ghost with suspicion. But there was also a second, more complex, reason for the progressive diabolization of Samuel's ghost. This relates to the discursive contexts within which the episode was read. We saw in Chapter 1 how, after Trent, the interpretation of the

[23] L. Vair (= L. Vairo), *Trois livres de charmes, sorcelages, ou enchantemens*, trans. by J. Baudon (Paris: N. Chesneau, 1583), pp. 321–2; Maldonat, *Traicté des anges et demons*, sigs. 179^r–81^r.

[24] See, for instance, *Les Sorceleries de Henry de Valois, et les oblations qu'il faisait au diable dans le bois de Vincennes* (Lyon: P. Chastain, 1589).

[25] Nodé, *Declamation contre l'erreur execrable des maleficiers*, sig. Aiii^v.

[26] Du Pont, *Philosophie des esprits*, sig. Aiv^r.

[27] Crespet, *Discours catholiques*, sig. 279^v.

[28] P. Crespet, *Deux Livres de la hayne de Sathan*, sigs. 108^r–9^v.

Gospels became the unique prerogative of clergy. As a result discussion of key episodes within the ghost debate, such as the parable of Lazarus and Dives or the narrative of Christ's appearance in the locked room, were effectively barred from magistrates such as a Rémy or a Boguet. No such restriction applied to the Old Testament. This made I Samuel 28 fertile hermeneutic ground for judicial demonology. So it is that we find Hebraists, such as Bodin or Le Loyer, delving deep into Rabbinical tradition. For other writers, with a less esoteric humanist training, the discursive availability of Samuel's ghost prompted more mainstream classical associations, in which Samuel was to be read alongside not Lazarus or Moses and Elias, but the risen dead of pagan—and therefore diabolized—antiquity.

Examples of this discursive realignment are frequent in early modern France. One such occurs in Rabelais's *Tiers Livre*. Panurge, wishing to know whether he should take a wife, consults Herr Trippa, a dubious old magician. Having proposed a whole range of divinatory methods by which Panurge might examine his own future, Trippa finally offers to raise him up a corpse:

> Ou bien par Necromantie? Je vous feray soubdain resusciter quelqu'un, peu cy devant mort, comme feist Apollonius de Tyane envers Achilles, comme feist la Phitonisse en praesence de Saül, lequel nous en dira le totage, ne plus ne moins que à l'invocation de Erictho un deffunct praedist à Pompée tout le progrès et issue de la bataille Pharsalicque. Ou si avez paour des mors, comme ont naturellement tous coquz, je useray seulement de Sciomantie. [29]

Here Samuel's ghost rubs shoulders with the pagan dead. Herr Trippa's necromantic triad—Apollonius of Tyana, the witch of Endor, Erichtho—is often to be found in judicial demonology.[30] In almost all cases, the outer exemplars of pagan superstition lent a decidedly suspicious air to the woman who raised the prophet in I Samuel 28.

Apollonius, known to Renaissance readers through Flavius Philostratus's *Life of Apollonius of Tyana*, was widely condemned in this period as a pseudo-mystic whose many 'miracles', including resurrections of the dead,

[29] F. Rabelais, *Le Tiers Livre*, ed. by J. Céard (Paris: 1995), p. 247: 'Or else by necromancy? I'll suddenly bring back to life for you someone who died not long ago, as did Apollonius of Tyana for Achilles, as did the witch of Endor in the presence of Saul, and this former dead man will tell us the total, no more nor less than at Erichtho's invocation a deceased man told Pompey the whole outcome of the battle of Pharsalia. Or if you're afraid of the dead, as all cuckolds naturally are, I'll just use Sciomancy.' (*Complete Works*, p. 330)
[30] Remigius, *Daemonolatreiae libri tres*, Book Two, ch. 1; Boguet, *Discours des sorciers*, pp. 113–14.

were wrought to set their maker on the same footing as Christ.[31] After 1599, readers unversed in Latin enjoyed access to Vigenère's French translation of the *Life*, with a rich demonological commentary by the humanist scholar Artus Thomas.[32] Thomas's treatment of the episode referenced by Herr Trippa, the 'resurrection' of Achilles, is characteristic of late Renaissance attitudes towards the raising of the dead. Like Herr Trippa, Thomas is careful to distinguish between necromancy (where body and soul are raised) and the somewhat less reprehensible sciomancy (where the soul is raised alone), and decides that, in his raising of Achilles, Apollonius is guilty only of the latter. Either way, such illusions are damnable, since they are only made possible through the intervention of the Devil.[33] Apollonius's crime is viewed as doubly heinous in those moments where, as in many other episodes in the *Life*, the raising of Achilles seems to parody the holy resurrection. One redolent phrase, describing how the stone of the Greek warrior's tomb was rolled back ('sa sepulture commence à crouler') draws especial condemnation. Such instances make clear that Apollonius, or rather the demon he serves, acts as the *simia dei*, or ape of God. It is hardly surprising that once Samuel was placed in company like this, suspicions only grew around the ghost raised at Endor.

The third member of Herr Trippa's necromantic coven, Lucan's Erichtho, appears to have cast a similarly demonic shadow over the Endor narrative.[34] The episode was much admired in late Renaissance France, and this for a number of reasons.[35] Politically speaking, and like the story of Saul and Samuel, Lucan's story shared with that period a context of bitter civil war. As in the biblical narrative, Lucan tells of a powerful ruler—or in this case the ruler's son, Sextus Pompeius—visiting a witch in order that he might know the outcome of a battle. The horrifying portrait of Erichtho also registered an impact. In a set piece of rhetorical *descriptio* much admired by baroque writers of the later sixteenth and early seventeenth centuries, the poet tells of her hair festooned with

[31] On the reputation of Apollonius in Rabelais, and in Renaissance France more generally, see G. Demerson, 'Apollonios de Tyane chez Rabelais: Christ dans un miroir déformant?' in *Cité des hommes, cité de Dieu*, ed. by A. Meyer (Geneva: Droz, 2003), pp. 503–12 (esp. p. 509).
[32] F. Philostratus, *De la Vie d'Apollonius Thyaneen en* VIII *livres* [1599], trans. by B. de Vigenère, ed. by F. Morel and A. Thomas, and with a commentary by T. Artus, 2 vols. [1599] (Paris: veuve M. Guillemot, 1611).
[33] Philostratus, *Vie d'Apollonius*, I, 774.
[34] Erichtho's raising of a dead soldier is narrated in *Pharsalia*, VI, pp. 413–830. See Lucan, *The Civil War (Pharsalia)*, trans. by J. D. Duff, Loeb Classical Library (London: Heinemann, 1977), pp. 334–65.
[35] For a fuller discussion, see J.-C. Ternaux, *Lucain et la littérature de l'âge baroque en France: citation, imitation et création* (Paris: H. Champion, 2000).

snakes, her breath that can kill flowers, and her power to bring down the stars from their spheres. Finally, the episode served as a repository of Roman wisdom on the operation of witches and their familiars. It is not unusual to find early modern learned commentators on the *Pharsalia* reading this portion of Lucan's narrative as a source of demonological expertise, and using his poem as a pretext for expounding on the difference between necromancy and sciomancy, and between licit and illicit magic.[36]

The political, rhetorical, and demonological colouration of Lucan's Erichtho made her ripe for updating to the late Renaissance context, and an unavoidable companion to the woman of Endor. Among the most notorious of her early modern avatars is Agrippa D'Aubigné's depiction of Catherine de' Medici in *Les Tragiques*, whose lexis and rhetoric is strongly redolent of Lucan's. There Erichtho bequeathes to the Queen Mother a whole range of diabolical paraphernalia, as well as the power to raise up the dead from their graves:

> La nuict elle se veautre aux hideux cimetieres,
> Elle trouble le ciel, elle arreste les eaux,
> Ayant sacrifié tourtres et pigonneaux
> Et desrobé le temps que la lune obscurcie
> Souffre de son murmur'; elle attir' et convie
> Les serpens en un rond sur les fosses des morts,
> Desterre sans effroi les effroyables corps,
> Puis, remplissant les os de la force des diables,
> Les fait saillir en pieds, terreux, espouvantables[37]

Although the level of detail both here and in Catherine's Latin original seems a far cry from the concision of I Samuel's 'mulier habens pythonem', this did not prevent a strong association between Erichtho and the woman at Endor. It is telling that, in another Protestant reflection on civil war, Jean de La Taille's stage version of I Samuel, *Saül le furieux*, the invocations of the 'pythonisse' resemble those of Lucan's terrifying witch.[38]

---

[36] See, for example, Lucan, *M. Annei Lucani Cordubensis... Pharsalia libri*, x, ed. by L. Hortensius (Basilae: ex off. Henric Petrina, 1578), p. 754.

[37] *Les Misères*, II, pp. 902–10, in A. d'Aubigné, *Oeuvres*, ed. by H. Weber (Paris: Gallimard, 1969), p. 42: 'At night she wallows in the hideous graveyards, she disturbs the heavens, she stops the flowing waters, having sacrificed doves and pigeons and stolen the time that the hidden moon suffers her murmuring; she attracts and calls on the snakes to circle round the graves of the dead, calmly disinters the awful cadavers, and then, filling their bones with the force of the demons, stands them up on their feet, smeared in earth, terrifying.'

[38] J. de La Taille, *Tragédies*, ed. by E. Forsyth (Paris: Société des Textes Français Modernes, 1998), pp. 50–2 (Act III, ll. 619–76).

In his preface to the play La Taille is at pains, in spite of his religious allegiance, to stress his belief that the soul of Samuel truly appeared at Endor.[39] On seeing his witch, however, spectators of his play may have reached the more sinister conclusion that was gaining ground elsewhere: that the woman, like Erichtho and Catherine, was a witch working in league with the devil to trick a desperate ruler.

The increasing diabolization of Samuel's ghost in early modern France does not of itself invalidate Thomas's 'shibboleth'. And yet, as the foregoing discussion has suggested, those who privilege the confessional significance of ghosts risk viewing in monochrome a picture cast in many different shades. As so often, context is everything. Where the context was that of theological polemic, opinion on Samuel does indeed appear to split along sectarian divides. In the context of witchcraft persecutions, *ligueur* propaganda, or the classical legacy of Philostratus and Lucan, however, the dictates of orthodoxy grow ever more faint. On reflection, this is perhaps unsurprising. Early modern readings of I Samuel 28 provide a good demonstration of how religion for many writers—theologians included—was only one among multiple allegiances. If theology remained a privileged framework within which to interpret the figure of the ghost, it was only one framework. Other contexts, too, had begun to stake their claim.

PRODIGIOUS HISTORIES: PIERRE BOAISTUAU

A further indication that ghosts were moving into new areas is the emergence, from around 1560 onwards, of the secular ghost-tale anthology. Here the object of secular writers was not to intervene on the previously exclusive terrain of theological debate, as they did with Samuel, but to skirt around the framework of theology altogether. The assembling of ghost narratives into collections was nothing new in itself. We remarked in Chapter 1 how compilations of ghost stories, along with other *mirabilia*, were already common in the Middle Ages; in Chapter 2 we saw how Lavater and Taillepied, likewise, mobilized the demonological anecdote in support of their respective sectarian positions. In each of these cases, however, the short narrative form tended towards the sparse and formulaic, almost always placed at the service of a broader homiletic or polemical purpose. In contrast, the secular ghost-tale anthology that began to appear in the later sixteenth century was all but shorn of its didactic function.

---

[39] La Taille, 'De l'art de la tragedie' in *Saül le furieux*, pp. 12–14.

Now dispensed from the need to convince or convert, the ghost story begins to enjoy a certain narrative autonomy.

Influential in this development was the growing prestige of vernacular humanist miscellanies or *sylvae*, already popular in Spain, such as the *Diverses leçons* of Pierre Messie (Mexía) and of the Gascon physician Louis Guyon. These writers compiled materials across a huge range of subjects, including ghosts.[40] Especially popular, also Spanish in origin, and more exclusively concerned with supernatural subjects, was Antonio de Torquemada's *Jardín de flores curiosas* of 1570, a dialogue translated into French by Gabriel Chappuys in 1579.[41] Torquemada's concern to establish a new, non-theological space for discussing apparitions of the dead is characteristic of the genre, and exhibits a meticulous awareness of where discursive boundaries begin and end.

In the third book of the dialogue Torquemada's characters narrate a large number of demonological anecdotes, including tales of ghosts. One in particular stands out, above all for the care with which it treads the narrow line between the sacred and profane. One character, Louys, tells the story of a Spanish knight who, having been separated from his hunt and lost deep in woodland, is visited by his dead father from Purgatory. The father leads him deep into the forest to a cavern with a ladder descending into it; lower down on the ladder stands the ghost of the knight's grandfather. The father's ghost explains that both are being purged for having usurped monastic property during their lifetime; if the son does not return it, a place in the cavern awaits him too. Hearing this, and having rejoined the hunting party, the knight returns home, restores the property, gives up all his possessions, and spends the rest of his days as a monk.

[40] Messie, *Les Diverses Leçons*, Book IV, ch. 14; L. Guyon, *Diverses Leçons*, Book III, chs. 26–7. On Mexía, see F. Pues, 'La "Silva de varia lección" de Pero Mexía', *Lettres Romanes* 13 (1959), pp. 119–43; on Mexía's reception in Europe, see idem, 'Les sources et la fortune de la "Silva" de Mexía', *Lettres Romanes* 13 (1959), pp. 279–92; on the fortunes of Mexía in France, and the growth of the French vernacular miscellany, see idem, 'Du Verdier et Guyon: deux imitateurs français de Mexía', *Lettres Romanes* 14 (1960), pp. 15–40.
[41] A. de Torquemade (= A. de Torquemada), *Hexameron, ou six journees, contenans plusieurs doctes discours sur aucuns poincts difficiles en diverses sciences, avec maintes histoires notables et non encore ouyes* [1573], trans. by G. Chappuys (Rouen: R. de Beauvais, 1610). Chappuys's translation went through five editions between its first publication and 1625. For an introduction to Torquemada, see G. D. Crow, 'Antonio de Torquemada: Spanish Dialogue Writer of the Sixteenth Century' in *Hispania: A Journal Devoted to the Teaching of Spanish and Portuguese* 38 (3) (September 1955), pp. 265–71; on the *Jardín de flores curiosas*, see J. Ferreras Savoye, 'Doutes et ruptures dans le dialogue humaniste: le *Jardín de flores curiosas* de Antonio de Torquemada' in Arnould, Demarolle, and Roig-Miranda (eds.), *Tourments, doutes et ruptures*, pp. 81–91.

For all its edifying potential, Louys's story leads on not to a moral lesson about the usurpation of land belonging to the Church, but to a more general discussion of whether the dead can truly return. This discussion is barely begun, however, when Louys cuts it short in favour of a formula we will see repeated several times throughout this chapter: 'laissons en la determination à autres meilleurs Theologiens'.[42] Here we find that the theme of usurpation, far from disappearing altogether, has instead simply been raised to the meta-discursive level. Unlike the knight's grandfather and father who took over Church terrain to which they had no rightful claim, Louys knows the danger of transgressing sacred boundaries. And in contrast to the knight himself, who loses his way in the woods, the speaker knows the limits of the *sylva*—or literary forest—as a genre, and cautions against an imprudent incursion into the theological territory beyond it.[43] In this way both the story itself and the ensuing discussion stage the production of their own discursive space: the unthreatening 'garden' ('*jardín*') of Torquemada's ghostly flowers.

More important still within this emergence of the ghost-tale anthology, and more distinctively French, were the *histoires prodigieuses*—a series of volumes on wonders and marvels, which began with Pierre Boaistuau's volume of 1560 and ran until the close of the sixteenth century. Here, too, the anecdotal form is established from the outset as the dominant mode. Perhaps this dominance is unsurprising, given the genre's inaugurator: Boaistuau was not only an editor (with Claude Gruget) of Marguerite de Navarre's *Heptameron*, but his translations from Bandello, along with those of François de Belleforest, produced what was to prove another literary craze for the short narrative form: the *histoires tragiques*.[44] The extraordinary success of these sister genres—the *histoires prodigieuses* and *histoires tragiques*—is well known to historians of the period. Published in numerous editions and translated into several European languages, both series must count among the bestselling texts of the late sixteenth and early

---

[42] *Hexameron*, p. 278: 'let us leave others, better theologians, to determine its meaning'.
[43] Ferreras Savoye (in 'Doutes et ruptures dans le dialogue humaniste', p. 88) also remarks on the speakers' refusal to provide interpretations of the demonological anecdotes of the third dialogue, but attributes this to the author's desire for a diverting, open-ended text ('comme si l'auteur était désireux de divertir son public en même temps qu'il souhaitait le faire réfléchir en lui laissant le soin de l'interprétation à donner').
[44] On the life and career of Boaistuau, see M. Simonin, 'Notes sur Pierre Boaistuau', *Bibliothèque d'humanisme et Renaissance* 38 (1976), pp. 323–33. On the *histoires tragiques*, see (among others) R. A. Carr, *Pierre Boaistuau's 'Histoires tragiques': A Study of Narrative Form and Tragic Vision* (Chapel Hill: University of North Carolina Press, 1974). On the *histoires prodigieuses*, see M. R. Schenda, *Die Französische Prodigienliteratur in der 2. Hälfte des 16 Jh.* (Munich: Max Hueber Verlag, 1961), pp. 26–61; Y. Florenne, 'Un quêteur de prodiges' in *Mercure de France* 342 (1961), pp. 657–68; the classic account is in Céard, *La Nature et les prodiges*, pp. 252–335.

seventeen centuries. In them we see not only a shift towards the kind of narrative autonomy characteristic of the *Diverses leçons* and Torquemada's *Hexameron* but also, with the shift in discursive terrain, a corresponding transformation in the shapes and purpose of ghosts.

Boaistuau's first volume of the *Histoires prodigieuses* was published in Paris in 1560.[45] The succeeding volumes were written by Claude de Tesserant, François de Belleforest, Rodéric Hoyer, Arnauld Sorbin (translated from the Latin by Belleforest), a sixth author named 'I.D.M', and an anonymous seventh contribution published in 1597–8 by the widow of Gabriel Buon.[46] The structural principle of each volume is the same. Each chapter tackles either a single event (e.g. a recent monstrous birth) or a category of events (floods, tempests, comets) that appears to run against the ordinary course of nature. All the texts proceed mainly by narrative example, interspersed to varying degrees with learned commentary. Of the six volumes in total that make up the series, four devote significant space to the subject of ghosts and apparitions: Boaistuau, Tesserant, Belleforest, and the anonymous late sequel published by veuve Buon. This section will focus only on Boaistuau and Belleforest; the others will receive brief attention elsewhere.

Although Boaistuau's volume has until now been chiefly of interest to historians of monsters, it is notable nonetheless that of its forty chapters, the one devoted to apparitions, entitled 'Visions prodigieuses, avec plusieurs histoires memorables des spectres, fantosmes, figures, et illusions qui apparoissent de nuict, de jour, en veillant et en dormant' (Chapter 26), is by some distance the longest.[47] Like the speakers of Torquemada's dialogue on ghosts, Boaistuau is scrupulous, in the very opening lines, in distancing his own investigation from the current theological debate over

[45] P. Boaistuau, *Histoires prodigieuses, les plus memorables qui ayent esté observées, depuis la Nativité de Jesus Christ, jusques à nostre siecle: extraictes de plusieurs fameux autheurs, Grecz, et Latins* (Paris: Vincent Sertenas, 1560).

[46] Not included among these texts, though clearly influenced by Boaistuau's model, is Jean de Marconville's *Recueil memorable d'aucuns cas merveilleux advenuz de nos ans, et d'aucunes choses estranges et monstrueuses advenües es siecles passez* (Paris: J. Dallier, 1564). Marconville's text, mainly concerned with monstrous births, includes no mention of ghosts and so is not discussed here. Marconville may also be the author of the sixth volume, signed I.D.M, though this has also been attributed to Jean de Montylard. That continuation was reproduced in the volume of *Histoires prodigieuses* published by Guillaume Cavellat's widow in 1597–8. In Gabriel Buon's rival version, published in the same year, I.D.M's text is replaced with that of the anonymous seventh continuation. For more on the publishing history of the *Histoires prodigieuses*, see Céard, *La Nature et les prodiges*, p. 462, n. 12.

[47] On Boaistuau's monsters see especially Céard, *La Nature et les prodiges*, pp. 252–65; L. Daston and K. Park, *Wonders and the Order of Nature (1150–1750)* (New York: Zone, 1998), pp. 189–90.

apparitions of the dead. Here the ruling image is not that of a forest but of
a tortuous labyrinth:

> Je ne me veux point icy plonger en ce labyrinthe doubteux de rechercher si
> les ombres des mortz retournent, ou si les espritz ayans eschappé le naufrage
> de ceste vie mortelle, nous visitent quelquefois.[48]

Like many other lay writers on apparitions in this period, Boaistuau goes
on to legitimate this gesture of refusal by referring to the intractability of
the question of Samuel's apparition. When Augustine, Jerome, and 'pre-
sque tous les Ecclesiastiques se sont tourmentez à dissoudre le doubte de
Samuel', he asks, what chance does he—a curious amateur—have of
escaping the 'labyrinthe doubteux'?[49]

Boaistuau's preferred strategy consists in a discursive reinscription of
ghosts. Rather than treat apparitions of the dead as a theological conundrum, his chapter will read such figures, as he puts it, 'en termes de
philosophie'.[50] As so often in early modern Europe, this appeal to 'philosophie' does not herald a positively circumscribed expertise, or set of
intellectual concerns, but rather the fact that the discursive sovereignty
of theology has been momentarily suspended. Diplomatic reasons may
have played some part in this strategy. The *histoires prodigieuses* were first
presented, in an elaborate manuscript copy, to a Protestant queen, Elizabeth I of England. Given those circumstances, a Catholic defence of
Purgatory is unlikely to have been well received.[51] Whatever the political
expedients of bracketing theology, Boaistuau's self-description as a philosopher grants him a degree of discursive latitude that, as we shall see, he is
not slow to exploit.

Boaistuau's shift of discursive territory brings with it a dramatic transformation in the character of his ghosts. In the large majority of cases
these, like his strange births and battles in the sky, are given the status of
presages or 'prodiges'. Unlike the Purgatorial spirits of the Catholic
devotional tradition, these figures do not seek moral absolution for past
deeds; Boaistuau's apparitions are rather agents of God's vengeance, whose
future fulfilment the dead presage to the living. Though such figures do
appear in the more theologically oriented works of Lavater and Taillepied,

---

[48] Boaistuau, *Histoires prodigieuses*, sig. 105ʳ: 'I do not want to plunge here into that
dubious labyrinth that consists in asking whether the shades of the dead return, or if the
spirits who have escaped the shipwreck of this mortal life, sometimes visit us.'
[49] Ibid., sig. 105ᵛ.
[50] Ibid.
[51] This manuscript recently surfaced as the property of the Wellcome Institute in
London; see P. Boaistuau, *Histoires prodigieuses: MS 136 Wellcome Library*, ed. by
S. Bamforth (Milan: Franco Maria Ricci Spa, 2000).

their relative importance is accentuated here. Their status as 'prodiges' is made especially visible in the woodcut engravings accompanying the text: there each ghost, its hand outstretched, directs others' gaze (including the reader's) to dangers lying await in the near or distant future.

Boaistuau's conception of the ghost as 'prodige', which persists in later volumes of the *Histoires prodigieuses*, might best be explained with reference to two representative examples. Boaistuau has taken both from the *Dies geniales* of the late fifteenth-century legal authority Alessandro Alessandrini (Alexander ab Alexandro), a storehouse of anecdotes on a variety of subjects to which late-century French writers on apparitions frequently return. One of Boaistuau's woodcut images serves to illustrate Alessandrini's story of Catalde, Bishop of Tarente.[52] It shows the bishop's ghost standing before a child, his arm outstretched and pointing. The text explains how the bishop, who has been dead for over a thousand years, appears to the child in a dream and tells him of a book in which is written the future of the House of Naples. At first the child does not believe the vision, but when the bishop reappears to him as a ghost as he prays in church, the boy alerts his elders to the whereabouts of this mysterious text; the book is then read and its dread prophecies prove true.

The character of the child witness is especially noteworthy here, since such figures are uncommon in early modern French writing. Most writers, including Lavater and Taillepied, placed children in the category of the timorous and therefore unreliable witness, and it is rare that a child should—as here—stand witness to a true ghost. Though some writers, including Valladier, accept the widely held view that children born with hair ('les enfants nés coiffés') are privileged with special access to the world of the dead, these are the exceptions that prove the general rule.[53] But Boaistuau's child represents a further exception. In his narrative the reliability of the boy's statement is not once placed in doubt; indeed, the boy himself shows not credulity, but commendable caution in his dealing with the ghost. Instead Boaistuau's emphasis bears not so much on the credibility of his testimony as on the child as representative of futurity itself. He will live, after all, to see its prophecies come true. Though not himself a prodigy, the boy joins the thousand-year-old ghost as a sign— here a metonymic sign—of what is still to come.

The second story tells of a vision experienced by another young witness, Alessandrini's own servant. Fast asleep one night, the boy begins to sigh and lament at such a volume that the rest of the house is awoken. When asked what troubles him the servant replies that he has seen the dead body

---

[52] Boaistuau, *Histoires prodigieuses*, sig. 109ʳ.
[53] Valladier, *La Saincte Philosophie de l'ame*, pp. 734–5.

of his mother pass before his eyes as she is taken for burial. In what happens next we see, first of all, a regard for forensic precision entirely in keeping with Alessandrini's profession as a lawyer:

> J'observay (dict Alexandre) l'heure, le jour et la saison, en laquelle cecy estoit advenu, pour sçavoir si ceste vision annonceroit point quelque desastre au garçon. Et je fuz, dict il, estonné que quelques jours apres je veis venir à ma maison un serviteur de sa defuncte mere, qui nous annonça sa mort, combien qu'aucun de nous n'eust encores entendu nouvelles de sa maladie, et m'estant enquesté du jour et heure de sa mort, et l'ayant conferé avec ce que j'en avois écrit, je trouvay infailliblement qu'elle estoit morte le mesme jour, et la mesme heure qu'elle s'estoit representée morte à son filz.[54]

Here the ghost's annunciative function bears not on the future but rather on the present. In a narrative model that Boaistuau's successor, Belleforest, would develop in his second volume of the *Histoires prodigieuses*, dead figures often appear to announce their own passing to relatives or friends. The announcement is uncertain at first (hence the conditional of supposition in 'ceste vision *annonceroit*') but infallible at last, having been confirmed by a more trustworthy messenger ('un serviteur de sa defuncte mere, qui nous *annonça* sa mort').

Boaistuau's two stories suggest the extent to which ghosts, once abstracted from the traditional contexts of theological debate, take their place within a quite different regime of signs from that of the clerical ghost narratives discussed so far. In the discernment tradition of Gerson and its early modern variants, the main stake in reading ghosts was—broadly speaking—the fate of the dead in the afterlife: there the ghost's outstretched hand pointed to the soul's torment in Purgatory. In Boaistuau, the ghost's emphasis shifts instead onto the destinies of the living: the future of the House of Naples, or the revelation to a son of his mother's sudden death. In the discernment tradition, the dead urge their survivors towards a programme of intercession. Purgatorial ghosts are to this extent illocutionary signs, their appearance always read as some form of command: pray for me, fast for me, right the wrongs I have done to others, and so on. In Boaistuau, by contrast, there is no command, only an indexical sign of an unavoidable future.

---

[54] Boaistuau, *Histoires prodigieuses*, sig. 107^{r-v}: 'I observed (says Alexander) the hour, the day, and the season in which this had happened, in order to know whether this vision might not announce some disaster for the boy. And I was, he says, surprised, that a few days later I saw a servant of his dead mother coming to my house, announcing her death, even though none of us had yet heard news of her illness; and enquiring of the day and hour of her death, and having checked it against what I had written, I found that she had died on exactly the same day, and at the same hour, that she had showed herself as a dead woman to her son.'

This distinction between the illocutionary and indexical sign entails a further contrast, namely that between the *active* witness of Purgatorial ghost stories and the *passive* witnesses of Boaistuau's narratives. One of the most striking features of Boaistuau's characters is that, unlike the busy intercessors of clerical ghost tales, their function is limited to that of registering a fact divinely inscribed in advance. Alessandrini appears powerfully insistent as the first-person narrator of the foregoing narrative, and yet his ultimate function is that of passive registration: 'j'observay l'heure, le jour et la saison', 'l'ayant conferé avec ce que j'en avois écrit, je trouvay infailliblement qu'elle estoit morte le mesme jour...'. If the adverb 'infailliblement' allows the lawyer-narrator to claim for himself a measure of authority ('je trouvay infailliblement'), and perhaps agency, as a witness to the ghost, the reality is in fact rather different. For true infallibility here resides not in any human agency, but in the providentialist framework of the *histoires prodigieuses*, where ghosts come back to tell of that which—present or future—permits of no undoing. It is perhaps, above all, this inexorability that places these ghosts so firmly within what Richard A. Carr has called, with reference to the *Histoires tragiques* and the *Theatrum mundi*, Boaistuau's 'tragic vision'.[55]

That vision might also be considered tragic (in the strict sense of genre) in its focus on the fate of high-born families. The notion that ghosts held the secret of dynastic futures was not new, of course, and was shared by a number of Boaistuau's contemporaries. Particularly famous in this period was the story recorded by Cardano (among many others) of an old woman who appeared in the fireplace whenever a member of the Parma nobility was about to fall ill and die.[56] Similar was the tale of Galeas Sforza, recounted in (among other places) Simon Goulart's early seventeenth-century compilation of prodigious apparitions. Shortly after he died, Sforza's ghost appeared on the road to two servants of his brother Ludovico, Duke of Milan, instructing them to deliver a letter warning of his imminent ruin. Upon opening it, Ludovico saw that the letter bore a signature: simply 'l'esprit de ton frere'.

Both in the sheer unalterability of what they foretell, and the political magnitude of the news they report, these apparitions are as close as sixteenth-century prose comes to the protatic ghosts of the neo-Senecan stage.[57] All that changes, in the theatre of Jodelle, Garnier, and their

[55] Carr, *Pierre Boaistuau's 'Histoires tragiques'*.

[56] G. Cardano, *De rerum varietate libri xvii* (Basel: per Henricum Petri, 1557), Bk. 16, ch. 93 ('Daemones et mortui'), pp. 644–5.

[57] For a more developed study of ghosts on the sixteenth-century stage, see Millet, 'L'Ombre dans la tragédie française (1550–1640)'; idem, 'Faire parler les morts'; see also Martinez, 'Fantômes, oracles et malédictions'.

contemporaries, is the agent of registration. When the ghost of Égée appears on stage at the beginning of Garnier's *Hippolyte*, for instance, to foretell the destruction we will shortly see visited upon the House of Theseus, it now falls to the audience—or the chorus on the audience's behalf—to register the truth of what he says as it unfolds before their eyes. Neither the apparition nor those who hear its message can alter a future already determined in advance. One recent critic has remarked that this passive relation between ghost and witness, all the more marked in its distinction from the active collaboration implied in clerical *discretio spirituum*, contributes in no small part to the peculiarly static atmosphere of humanist tragedy.[58]

Away from the stage, the themes of providence and the fate of houses or nations took on a markedly political resonance in the years that followed the publication of Boaistuau's *Histoires prodigieuses*. We have already seen how the episode of Saul's raising of Samuel, and Pompey's of Erichtho, became freighted with contemporary significance—specifically anti-Valois propaganda—in the context of the French civil wars. Ghosts as prodigies were, likewise, to become urgently contemporary. The most notorious example of this kind occurred on the night that Charles de Guise, Cardinal de Lorraine, died in mysterious circumstances (some supposed poisoned on the orders of Catherine de' Medici, the queen mother). The episode, said to have occurred as Henri III held court at Avignon on the night of 23 December 1574, is related by Goulart and, in a later and slightly different version, by the Catholic *politique* Pierre de L'Estoile.[59] But again it is D'Aubigné, reporting the event both in his *Histoire universelle* and in *Les Tragiques*, who provides the richest account.[60] There, too, we see the ghost as prodigy and—crucially—the passive witness of Boaistuau's tales re-energized in the theatre of France's dynastic struggle.

In the *Histoire universelle* D'Aubigné writes that, according to Henri de Navarre, at that time still a prisoner at court following the Saint Bartholomew's Day massacre two years before, two prodigies accompanied the death of the Cardinal de Lorraine. D'Aubigné adds that the memory of

---

[58] On the relationship between protatic ghosts and stasis in humanist drama, see especially A. Howe, 'La Taille's *Saül*: A Play of Two Halves', *French Studies Bulletin* 19 (Summer 1986), pp. 3–5.

[59] Goulart, *Thresor d'histoires admirables et memorables de nostre temps*, pp. 548–9; P. de L'Estoile, *Registre-Journal du règne de Henri III*, ed. by M. Lazard and G. Schrenck (Geneva: Droz, 1992–), I (1574–5), pp. 100–3.

[60] For a broader discussion of D'Aubigné's attitude towards the Guises, see A. Thierry, 'La Maison de Guise dans l'oeuvre d'Agrippa d'Aubigné: exécration et estime' in *Le Mécénat et l'influence des Guises*, ed. by Y. Bellenger (Paris: Champion, 1997), pp. 81–94.

both still makes Henri's hair stand on end. The first prodigy, which occurred the night before, was the most powerful storm in living memory. This 'fulguration' shook the whole of Avignon, but especially the cardinal's own residence where, according to D'Aubigné's mysterious phrase, 'quelque chose de plus violent que le vent arracha et emporta en l'air les grilles et fenestres'.[61] The second prodigy occurred at the very moment of the cardinal's passing, as another 'quelque chose'—his ghost—appeared to Catherine, the Queen Mother, in her bed:

> La Roine s'estoit mise au lict au meilleure heure que de coustume, ayant à son coucher, entr'autres personnes de marque, le Roi de Navarre, l'Archevesque de Lyon, les Dames de Rets, de Lignerolles et de Sauves, deux desquelles ont confirmé ce discours. Comme elle estoit pressee de donner le bon soir, elle se jetta d'un tressaut sur son chevet, met les mains devant son visage, et avec un cri violent appella à son secours ceux qui l'assistoyent, leur voulant monstrer au pied du lict le Cardinal, qui lui tendoit le main, elle s'ecriant plusieurs fois, *Monsieur le Cardinal, je n'ai que faire de vous.* Le Roi de Navarre envoye au meme temps un de ses Gentilshommes au logis du Cardinal, qui rapporta comment il avoit expiré au mesme point.[62]

The dynamics of this scene, in particular the question of who sees what, are complex. The episode as a whole is straightforwardly witnessed and validated ('confirmé') by three people: Henri de Navarre and two of the noblewomen present. But who among the company saw the ghost itself? 'Leur *voulant* monstrer' appears to suggest that only Catherine witnessed it: she wants or means to show those present something no longer there. That said, 'qui lui tendoit la main' (a pose consistent with the iconography of Boaistuau's *Histoires prodigieuses*) remains ambiguous: do those present see this gesture, or is this detail only reported by the terrified queen mother?

The verse text of *Les Tragiques*, which recounts the same event, may clarify the question of exactly who saw what. It opens with an address to

[61] D'Aubigné develops his account of this storm in *Vengeances*, ll. 1035–66: 'something even more violent than the wind tore off and tossed into the air the window bars and windows'; A. d'Aubigné, *Oeuvres*, ed. by H. Weber (Paris: Gallimard, 1969), pp. 212–13.

[62] A. d'Aubigné, *Histoire universelle*, ed. by A. Thierry, 11 vols. (Geneva: Droz, 1981–2000), IV, pp. 257–60: 'The queen had gone to bed earlier than usual, and present at her bedside were (among other persons of note) the King of Navarre, the Archbishop of Lyon, the ladies of Retz, Lignerolles, and Sauves, two of whom confirmed this report. As she was hurrying to bid everybody goodnight, she suddenly jumped up on the side of the bed, placed her hands in front of her face, and cried out violently that those present might help her, trying to point to the cardinal who stood at the foot of the bed, holding out his hand to her. She cried out several time, "My lord cardinal, I want nothing to do with you." At the same time the King of Navarre sends one of his gentlemen to the cardinal's lodgings, who comes back with the news that he had expired at that very moment.'

Henri who, like the Jews of Jeremiah's lament, endured the bitter taste of
captivity:[63]

> Prince choisi de Dieu, qui sous ta belle-mere
> Savourais l'aconit et la ciguë amere,
> Ta voix a tesmoigné qu'au poinct que cet esprit
> S'enfuyoit en son lieu, tu vis saillir du lict
> Cette Royne en frayeur qui te monstroit la place
> Où le cardinal mort l'acostoit face à face
> Pour prendre son congé: elle bouschoit ses yeux,
> Et sa frayeur te fit herisser les cheveux.[64]

These lines strengthen the suggestion that only Catherine saw the ghost.
The phrase '. . . te monstroit la place / Où le cardinal mort l'acostoit face à
face' implies that though the ghost was apparent to Catherine (note the
imperfect of 'l'acostoit'), others present saw only an empty space. It is
further to be noted that in 'Et sa frayeur te fit herisser les cheveux', Henri's
fear is produced not as a reaction to seeing the ghost itself, but rather in
response to Catherine's own terror.

It makes sense, for Catherine's enemies, that it was only she who saw
the ghost. For what this means, and as the outstretched hand makes clear,
is that the queen mother has been made an unwilling object of a unique
election. The cardinal has visited her and her alone, and for a specific,
accusatory purpose: a purpose that Catherine rebuts frantically with her 'je
n'ai que faire de vous' and that D'Aubigné interprets, in the introduction
to his narrative, as linked to the rumours circulating ever since that, first,
the cardinal was Catherine's lover and, second, that she may have played a
role in his untimely death. Just as important for D'Aubigné, however, is
the very different kind of election bestowed upon Henri de Navarre,
'Prince choisi de Dieu'. This sense of election is underscored in part by
the pronouns of the verse text: Catherine herself singles him out as special
witness to the event ('*te* monstroit la place' as opposed to '*leur* voulant
monstrer' of the prose version), a singling echoed in D'Aubigné's insistent
second person ('ta vois', 'tu vis', 'te fit hérisser les cheveux'). The reference
to Jeremiah, in which Henri's captivity is compared to the fate of God's
chosen people, also contributes to the sense of his divine election.

---

[63] Jeremiah 23:15; Lamentations 3:15.
[64] *Misères*, ll. 1201–28; *Oeuvres*, p. 45: 'Prince chosen by God, who under your mother-
in-law tasted the bitterness of wormwood and gall, your voice bore witness that at the very
moment that that spirit fled, you saw that Queen leap out of bed in fright, showing you the
place where the dead cardinal accosted her face to face to bid farewell: she covered her eyes,
and her fear made your hair stand on end.'

Most emphatic of all, however, is Henri's own role as the ghost's interpreter. After the pattern of Boaistuau's tale from Alessandrini, the prose text insists on Henri's function as the agent of expert registration. Alessandrini, we remember, checked the details of the servant's mother's death and found that she had passed away 'le mesme jour' as her son's prodigious dream. Likewise:

Le Roi de Navarre envoye au meme temps un de ses Gentilshommes au logis du Cardinal, qui rapporta comment il avoit expiré au mesme point.

But there is a difference here, and the difference is what marks Henri out—in the words of *Les Tragiques*—as a 'prince choisi de Dieu'. The difference is that just as Catherine's dream coincides with the death of Charles de Guise ('il avoit expiré *au mesme point*'), so, crucially, does the instant of Henri's understanding ('[il] envoye *au mesme temps*'). Here the King of Navarre is not merely a passive recorder, who checks the date and time of one event against another. His knowledge—of the rise and fall of dynasties, the fortunes of his enemies, in short, of history—is itself inscribed within the magic of simultaneity within which the ghost appears. In the very moment that the demonic cardinal points his hand towards Catherine, his fellow ravager of France, so God designates, in Henri, the person of its saviour. Here, finally, we have something very different from the 'tragic vision' of Boaistuau's *Histoires prodigieuses*. Whereas the inexorability of history, for Boaistuau, meant invariably bad news, within the broader Protestant narrative of God's elected people, the very same inexorability becomes a cause for celebration.

The apparition of the Cardinal de Lorraine to the Queen Mother is only one example of the ghost as prodigy. But it does illustrate several features of the apparitions considered in this section. We saw in Boaistuau how, as distinct from the clerical tradition, the ghost as prodigy is concerned not so much with its own fate in the afterlife as with the future of those individuals or, more commonly, families or dynasties, it leaves behind. Sometimes it appears in order merely to announce its own death (as in Boaistuau's story of Alessandrini's servant); at other times, and more commonly in Boaistuau, it announces the future fall or death of others (Boaistuau's tale of the Bishop of Catalde, Cardano's of the woman in the fireplace, or Goulart's on the fall of the Sforzas); occasionally, as in D'Aubigné, it seems to hint at both. In each case inter-confessional debate around the question of Purgatory dramatically recedes. As the example of D'Aubigné's Protestant ghost narrative indicates, the ghost as prodigy is here imagined outside theology—as Boaistuau puts it, 'en termes de philosophie'. Instead of taking its place within a discussion of death, the afterlife and the power of the clergy, the ghost as prodigy joins Samuel in providing a means by which early modern subjects might imagine—whether to lament or celebrate—the future of their troubled body politic.

GHOSTS AND FRIENDSHIP: FRANÇOIS DE BELLEFOREST

François de Belleforest's continuation of Boaistuau's *Histoires prodigieuses* was first published in Paris in 1571, though a number of chapters, including that on apparitions, were not added until 1575.[65] The chapter devoted to ghosts concludes the volume. At first sight, Belleforest's attitude towards the return of the dead appears to differ slightly from that of his predecessor in his relative willingness to confront sectarian controversy. Though he concedes that to demonstrate the apparition of dead souls is not to insist on an article of faith, 'ains seulement sur chose indifferente', he reminds readers that the consequence of such a belief nonetheless 'traine apres soy une queue qui n'est pas de petite importance'.[66] Something of that 'queue' protrudes into the early part of the chapter, where Belleforest includes a number of references to prayers for the departed and the question of Purgatory, and at the end, when he attacks English Protestants for neglecting their dead.

At times the flavour of Belleforest's discussion indeed seems resolutely theological. The discussion of the return of the dead from Purgatory occurs in the context of a broader reflection on the love retained by dead souls for those they leave behind. Here Belleforest interrogates Aristotle's claim in *De anima* that (in Belleforest's paraphrase) 'le corps de l'homme allant en corruption et pourriture, l'ame sortie d'iceluy perd souvenance et amour, et n'est plus sujecte aux affections du sens'.[67] This contention, supported by no less a theologian than Thomas Aquinas, effectively denied dead souls what Belleforest, in his vulgarization of scholastic terminology, calls 'patibles qualités'—or the ability to suffer passions.[68] Against

---

[65] References will be to F. de Belleforest, *Histoires prodigieuses* in P. Boaistuau, F. de Belleforest, et al., *Histoires prodigieuses, extraictes de plusieurs fameux autheurs, Grecs et Latins, sacrez et prophanes . . . augmentees outre les precedentes impressions, de six histoires advenues de nostre temps, adjoustées par F. de Belleforest Comingeois, avec les portaicts et figures* [1575] (Paris: C. Macé, 1576), ch. 46 ('Diverses apparitions d'espritz aux hommes et si l'on doibt croire que il soit possible que les hommes voyent les espris').

[66] Belleforest, *Histoires prodigieuses*, sig. 169ʳ: 'Draws behind it a tail of no little importance'.

[67] Belleforest, *Histoires prodigieuses*, sig. 167ʳ: 'man's body descending into corruption and putrefaction, the soul having left it loses any memory of it or love towards it, and is no longer subject to sensible affection'.

[68] Ibid.

Aristotle and Aquinas, Belleforest sets Plato, and after him Augustine, for whom, he claims, the souls of the dead still preserve 'quelque sentiment et affection et quelque soucy du monde'.[69] Siding with this second position, in which the dead still hold to a memory of the living, Belleforest has recourse, like so many of his theologically trained contemporaries, to the parable of Lazarus and Dives (Luke 16), in which the rich man remembers the sinful brothers who survived him.[70]

The final paragraphs of Belleforest's volume return to the question of remembrance, albeit in the form of its negative counterpart, when he condemns heretics' disregard for the fate of the departed. Drawing a parallel with Heliodorus, who was punished by a spirit for profaning the holy Temple in Jerusalem, he tells the story of a certain English lord who, having built his castle on the ruins of an abbey dissolved by the king, is hounded out of his new home by 'une infinité d'apparitions de moynes . . . Dieu par là luy voulant donner à entendre, tout ainsi que jadis à Heliodore, que les lieux sacrez ne doivent ainsi estre mis en usages profanes'.[71] Here Belleforest's emphasis would seem closer to Taillepied's condemnation of Protestant 'oubliance' than to the concerns of secular anthologists like Torquemada or Boaistuau.[72]

It would be easy to conclude from the foregoing description that the chapter on ghosts in Belleforest's *Histoires prodigieuses*, published in 1575, had been coloured by the worsening religious conflict in France. After all, Belleforest's attitude to the Saint Bartholomew's Day massacre three years earlier had been far from neutral, as is evident from his two contributions to Jean Le Masle's verse celebration of the death of Gaspar de Coligny.[73] However, in reality, and for all the polemical posturing that frames Belleforest's chapter, the majority of his discussion fights shy of a full-bloodied intervention in the religious controversy of the period. As in Boaistuau and Torquemada, 'naturalist' slogans expressing discursive embarrassment, or an unwillingness to stray onto theological terrain, are common:

---

[69] Belleforest, *Histoires prodigieuses*, sig. 167^v: 'some sentiment and affection and some care for the world'.

[70] On theological readings of Luke 16, see above, pp. 57–63.

[71] Belleforest, *Histoires prodigieuses*, sig. 174^v: 'an infinite number of apparitions of monks . . . God wishing by virtue of those apparitions to make known to him, just as he once did to Heliodorus, that sacred places must not be put to profane uses'.

[72] On Taillepied and 'oubliance', see above, pp. 87–91.

[73] J. Le Masle, *Chant d'allegresse sur la mort de Gaspar de Colligny, jadis Admiral de France* (Paris: N. Chesneau, 1572), sig. Aiv^r. On Belleforest's reaction to the massacre, see M. Simonin, *Vivre de sa plume au XVIe siècle, ou la carrière de François de Belleforest* (Geneva: Droz, 1992), pp. 147–50.

> Or ces choses estant de grande consequence et difficiles à vuider, nous en laisserons aussi le vuidange, et resolution aux Theologiens.[74]

or:

> Je laisse (comme j'ay dit) le secret de l'apparition des morts à la saincte escole de Theologie.[75]

or again:

> Je laisse à discourir aux Theologiens (les lettres desquels je n'ay si avant penetrées que ie voudroy) ce que les ennemys de l'Eglise concluroyent contre ses traditions.[76]

and yet again:

> De tels secretz je me raporte à la sainte escole de Theologie.[77]

Of course not all such formulae should be taken at face value. Indeed on occasion one might suspect Belleforest of protesting too much. In some lay writers on ghosts and apparitions, as we shall see in the case of Pierre Le Loyer, theology is subject only to a mock evacuation, where the declaration of omission, or passing over, becomes a form of praeterition so that later interventions are made less vulnerable to censure. In Belleforest's chapter, however, the sectarian debate proves genuinely peripheral. His ghosts are part of a different narrative. In that story, the themes of 'amour et souvenance' are not subordinated to a theological discussion over the fate of the dead in the afterlife, but form the intellectual backdrop to a prolonged, and at times touchingly personal, reflection on friendship between the living.

Dominating Belleforest's chapter is a category of ghosts who, in his own phrase, 'se rapportent à l'amitié d'entre les hommes'.[78] Like Boaistuau before him, Belleforest reserves an important place for Alessandro Alessandrini; just as prominent, and very different from Boaistuau, is the inclusion of additional evidence from the author's own experience. Three stories stand out. The first, taken from Alessandrini, is one of the most

[74] Belleforest, *Histoires prodigieuses*, sig. 168[r]: 'Now these things being of great consequence and difficult to fathom, we shall leave their working out and resolution to the theologians.'

[75] Belleforest, *Histoires prodigieuses*, sig. 169[r]: 'I leave (as I've said) the secret of the apparition of the dead to the sacred school of Theology.'

[76] Belleforest, *Histoires prodigieuses*, sig. 169[r–v]: 'I leave to the Theologians (whose letters I have not mastered as deeply as I would like) discussion of all that the enemies of the Church would conclude against its traditions.'

[77] Belleforest, *Histoires prodigieuses*, sig. 172[v]: 'In regard to such secrets I throw myself back on the sacred school of Theology.'

[78] Belleforest, *Histoires prodigieuses*, sig. 171[v]: 'have to do with friendship between men.'

frequently cited ghost narratives in the early modern period, though it is rarely discussed in the context of friendship we find here. Two of Alessandrini's friends are travelling from Rome to the baths at Cuma. One suddenly falls ill and dies; the other, having overseen his companion's burial, returns home. Some nights later the ghost of the dead friend appears to him in his room, 'avec la mesme contenance et pasle couleur qu'il avoit lors qu'il mourut'.[79] The man speaks to the apparition who, without replying, undresses and climbs into bed beside him. The witness is filled with horror and withdraws to a corner of the bed, 'ce fantosme s'approchant de luy pour l'embrasser'.[80] Seeing his friend trying to push him away, the ghost angrily withdraws, takes up his clothes, and disappears. Terrified, the man is stricken with illness and almost dies himself.

For Belleforest, what prompts this ghost's appearance is the occult force of friendship. Freudian readers might wish to take this further, and make explicit the sexual tensions in play throughout the narrative. It would certainly appear that the episode stages repressed, if deeply ambivalent, homosexual desire. The bedroom encounter between the two men fulfils, albeit in far more explicit and terrifying form, a prospect that may well have awaited them at the baths they failed to reach: of homosocial—perhaps homosexual—intimacy between friends. This reading is lent added force by a detail of Alessandrini's story not included by Belleforest. In the original version, as the friend struggles to resist the ghost's advances, he feels the ice-cold touch of the apparition's feet—a sensation that greatly contributes to his near-fatal terror. This detail would appear to place the ghost in a category of Purgatorial apparitions, especially popular within medieval ghost narratives, whose burning or (less frequently) freezing touch confirms the manner of their purgation in the afterlife. But it also, and according to the Freudian reading, supports the suspicion of deep sexual disgust as the friend recoils in horror from the dead man's roving body.

Perhaps Belleforest's decision to omit the roving foot springs from an attempt, at the very outset of his discussion, to suppress any taint of sexual deviance from his—largely idealized—male 'amitié'. In any event, and whether the ghost represents homosexual, or merely homosocial, desire, Belleforest's reading of Alessandrini seemed to have gained some currency in the period. D'Aubigné again proves himself a keen reader of prodigy literature when, in his *Histoire universelle*, he includes a version of the narrative that, in its emphasis on friendship, is heavily redolent of Belleforest's.[81] There the friends of Alessandrini's narrative become two soldiers at

---

[79] Ibid.: 'with the same expression and pale complexion as he had when he died'.
[80] Ibid.: 'this phantom approaching him in order to embrace him'.
[81] D'Aubigné, *Histoire universelle*, vi, p. 60.

the siege of La Fere (June 1580). One of the men, Capitaine Atis, dies
in the battle and, that night, visits the other, Du Temps, 'fort bon ami
et compagnon de lict'. In D'Aubigné's account of what happens next,
Atis 'se jette entre les linceuls' alongside his friend. Du Temps, amazed,
feels the touch of the ghost's leg, 'plus asprement froide qu'un glaçon',
and leaps from the bed crying 'Capitaine Atis, que vous estes froid!'
On this the ghost takes his leave, through the window, complaining that
'on lui reprochoit son coucher'. 'Voilà comment nous l'a raconté Du
Temps, plein de vie et d'honneur', concludes D'Aubigné, adding only
that the two men's valets confirmed that Atis entered and left, and that
some claimed the ghost had returned more than once. Again, by leaving
the last word to the valets (whose account adds a detail lacking in
Du Temps's), and so placing the tale in the realm of servant gossip,
D'Aubigné may hint at a scabrous intimacy between the two 'compagnon
[s] de lict'.[82] Not wishing to enlarge upon this, or indeed upon the
controversial possibility that perhaps Protestant soldiers, too, might return
from the dead, D'Aubigné signs off with a formula familiar to us now:
'J'en laisse dire l'advis aux Theologiens.'

The theme of secret intimacy, or occult sympathy, only hinted at in
Belleforest's treatment of Alessandrini's narrative, emerges with far greater
force in the second, more personal, account. There Belleforest, best
known to anglophone scholars as a source for Shakespeare's *Hamlet*, tells
how once, as a child, he came face to face with the ghost of his own
father.[83] The passage, unusual (for the *Histoires prodigieuses*) in its insistent
first person, is worth quoting in full:

> Les amys morts loing de leurs affectionnez sont venus leur dire à Dieu sortans
> de ce monde: ce que je peux dire comme tesmoin oculaire qui en ay eu, et
> veu l'experience non couché, ny en sommeillant, ains estant debout et aussi
> bien esveillé que je suis à present que je descris ceste histoire. Car le propre
> jour que feu nostre pere mourut, comme je ne sçeusse rien de sa maladie, et
> moins de sa mort, le propre jour de la feste de nostre Dame de septembre, la
> nuit estant en un jardin sur les onze heures de nuit avec mes compagnons,
> j'allay pour esbranler un poirier, où je ne fus pas si tost escarté seul, que je voy
> devant moy la propre figure de mon pere tout blanc en couleur, mais d'une
> grandeur excedant la proportion naturelle laquelle representation s'approchant

---

[82] Homosexual undertones can also be found in a short comic ghost tale by Antoine
Tyron, 'De deux Merciers qui voulurent prendre leur passetemps d'un esprit nocturne, et
comme il les en paya'; see Tyron, *Recueil de plusieurs plaisantes nouvelles,* sig. 2ʳ.
[83] On Belleforest and the ghost in *Hamlet* (but with reference only to the *Histoires
tragiques*), see A. P. Stabler, 'King Hamlet's Ghost in Belleforest?', *PMLA* 77, no. 1 (March,
1962), pp. 18–20. For a reading of this story in a biographical context, see M. Simonin,
Vivre de sa plume, p. 24. Simonin dates the episode to 8 September, 1536.

de moy pour m'embrasser, je mescriay si hault, que mes compagnons soudain y accoururent, et la vision s'esvanouissant, je leur racomptay ce qui m'estoit advenu, et leur dis que pour vray c'estoit mon pere.

Nostre pedagogue adverty de ce fait s'asseura de la mort, laquelle pour vray advint sur l'heure mesme que ceste figure m'apparut: qui me fait penser que celle secrete liaison d'amitié qui est és coeurs des vrays amis peut donner quelque espece de leur similitude à telles apparitions.[84]

Belleforest's story features a number of recognizable ghost-narrative motifs: the use of the ecclesiastical calendar ('la feste de nostre Dame de septembre'), the suddenness of the appearance (evoked in 'si tost ... que'), the apparition's excessive size ('d'une grandeur excedant la proportion naturelle'), and the attempted embrace ('s'approchant de moy pour m'embrasser'). The figure of the pedagogue who checks the time of the father's death is also familiar from Alessandrini's story of the servant and his mother, to which Belleforest's tale bears a passing resemblance. Other details stand out as more particular. The orchard setting ('j'allay pour esbranler un poirier'), which offers another—almost certainly coincidental—parallel with *Hamlet*, may or may not be a discreet reference to Augustine's *Confessions*, whose author becomes aware of his own sinful nature—and by extension his own mortality—while out stealing pears as a boy.[85]

And then there are the slightly uncertain terms, resolved only at the end of the account, in which the ghost appears. This uncertainty does not proceed from the witness himself; this child, unlike Alessandrini's servant, is fully awake when he sees the apparition. It stems rather from the awareness of the ghost as a 'representation', a 'figure', or, to use another of Belleforest's terms, a 'similitude'. The adjacency of these terms to the more straightforwardly demonological 'illusion' prompts Belleforest, in

---

[84] Belleforest, *Histoires prodigieuses*, sig. 172ʳ: 'Dead friends, far from their loved ones, have come to say goodbye as they leave this world: the which I can confirm as a first-hand witness who has had direct experience of it not lying in bed, or sleeping, but standing upright and as awake as I am now, telling this story. For the very day that my late father died, with my knowing nothing of his illness, and still less of his death, on the very day of the feast of our Lady of September, being at night in a garden at eleven o'clock with some of my companions, I went to shake a pear tree. No sooner had I withdrawn from them alone than I saw the very figure of my father, all white in colour, but of a size exceeding his natural proportions. As this representation drew near in order to embrace me, I cried out so loudly that my companions suddenly came running and, the vision disappearing, I told them what had happened to me, and that truly this was my father. Our teacher, once informed of this fact, was certain of my father's death, the which truly occurred at the very moment that figure appeared to me. This makes me think that that secret liaison of friendship which ties the hearts of true friends can give some measure of their likeness to such apparitions.'
[85] Augustine, *Confessions*, trans. by F. J. Sheed and ed. by M. P. Foley (Indianapolis: Hackett, 2006), pp. 29–34.

the lines following the passage, to wonder what or who might lie behind such visions: the souls of the dead, or—on a more sinister interpretation— the machinations of the Devil? No sooner is the demonic thesis raised, however, than it is immediately dispelled: 'je ne me sçauroy persuader que ce soient des malins esprits'.[86] And yet this refusal to countenance the Devil's involvement does not entail any countervailing argument for a Purgatorial apparition: such things Belleforest leaves, in the customary phrase, 'à la saincte escole de Theologie'. Instead, he resolves the truth of the ghost's identity with reference to what he calls 'secrette liaison d'ami- tié' that he once shared with his father. The vision appeared '*pour vray*' at the very moment of my father's death; my love for him was that which dwells 'és coeurs des *vrays* amis'; to this extent, I know, '*pour vray* c'estoit mon pere'.

For Belleforest, the story of his father's ghost clearly demonstrates the extent to which, contrary to Aristotle's teaching, the dead retain both 'soing' and 'souvenance' of those they leave behind. So, too, the third and last of his narratives, this time concerning the ghost of the humanist publisher, Maurice de La Porte.[87] Belleforest claims he has the story on good authority from men who 'ne croient legerement telles visions'. One 'honorable citoyen', he adds, was even prepared to recount the following events 'en bonne compagnie':

Lors que feu M. Maurice de la Porte mourut en sa maison des Faubourgs saint Marcel, sur l'heure mesme de son trespas, il vint à luy ne sçay quelle figure, qu'il ne veit point, seulement ne sçay quel remuëment autour de sa couche et une voix rapportant à celle du susdit de la Porte, qui luy dit, il est mort: dequoy il demeura effroyé au possible: et autant en advint à un autre auquel la mesme parolle fut dicte plus ouvertement que Maurice de la Porte estoit mort. On marque l'heure que cela estoit advenu et trouve l'on que fut lors que le susdit rendit l'ame, et que sortant du monde il fut dire à Dieu à ses meilleurs amys. Que si on vouloit rapporter cecy à la vigueur, et effort de la fantaisie, et imagination, il n'auroit lieu en cest endroit, veu qu'on ne se persuadoit point encore que cest homme fut pour mourir de ceste maladie ou que s'il en devoit mourir on estimoit que la maladie en seroit plus longue: et d'avantage, quand l'imagination auroit lieu, encor ne sçauroit on deffendre

---

[86] Belleforest, *Histoires prodigieuses*, sig. 172[r–v]: 'I just cannot just persuade myself that they were evil spirits'.

[87] Maurice de La Porte II (son of Maurice de La Porte I), born 1531 and died 23 April 1571. One-time publisher (under 'les heritiers de Maurice de La Porte') of Denisot, Thevet, and Baïf, he is best known now as the author of *Epithètes françoises*, posthumously published by Gabriel Buon in late 1571. See P. Renouard, *Répertoire des imprimeurs, libraires, fondeurs de caractères et correcteurs d'imprimerie depuis l'introduction de l'imprimerie à Paris (1470) jusqu'à la fin du seizième siècle* (Paris: M. J. Minard, 1965), p. 240.

ceste voix entenduë, qui donnoit la signifiance, et portoit la nouvelle de la mort de ce gentil personnage.[88]

Like the apparition of Belleforest's father, this ghost is an effect of what the author terms 'la simpathie des coeurs'. The spirit's nebulous form ('ne sçay quelle figure', 'ne sçay quel remuëment') provides a perfect narrative realization of the mysterious power of friendship. Variations on the '*je-ne-sais-quoi*', here in its adjectival forms, often appeared in the context of occult qualities, and not least in that of friendship: that mysterious sympathy that renders two hearts one.[89] As we have seen, that 'simpathie' or 'secrete liaison des coeurs' can exist privately between father and son or, as in Alessandrini, between long-established friends. The La Porte narrative shows how it is also a force within humanist sociability. His ghost itself 'appeared' not to one friend, but to several. Their experience, and its subsequent retelling 'en bonne compagnie', helps to constitute this happy few as something like a circle. This friendship, it seems, is even more than friendship: it is the idealized bond of humanist *amicitia*.

Belleforest's preoccupation with *amicitia* might lead us to expect a widespread association between ghosts and friendship in the period. Certainly, there is plenty of evidence for such a connection. The narrative model according to which one friend promises to visit another as a ghost with news of the afterlife was well known at this time: as we saw in Chapter 1, such pacts, of which there were famous instances in Ficino and Boccaccio, were widely condemned in commentaries on Luke's parable of Lazarus. Further, more positive, connections between ghosts and friendship were made in readings of ancient epic. For instance, the apparition of Patroclus to Achilles lent considerable prestige to the figure

---

[88] Belleforest, *Histoires prodigieuses*, sig. 172ᵛ–3ʳ: 'When the late M. Maurice de la Porte died in his house in the district of Saint Marcel, at the very moment of his passing there came to him I know not what figure, which he saw not, only I know not what movement around his bed and a voice similar to that of the said de la Porte, which told him, he is dead, the which left him extremely frightened. The same thing happened to another man, to whom the same message was addressed more explicitly that Maurice de la Porte was dead. The time at which this had happened was noted and it was found that that was the moment the said de la Porte gave up his soul and that, leaving the world, he had come to bid farewell to his best friends. Some might want to attribute this to the force and vigour of the fantasy and imagination, but that would not apply in this case, since nobody yet thought that he would die of his illness, or that, if he was to die of it, that the illness would finish him so quickly. Furthermore, even if the imagination did play its part, there is no gainsaying that voice which was heard, and which bore the news of the death of this noble personage.'

[89] On the 'je-ne-sais-quoi', occult qualities, and friendship, see R. Scholar, *The Je-Ne-Sais-Quoi in Early Modern Europe: Encounters with a Certain Something* (Oxford: Oxford University Press, 2005), pp. 125–6, 132–3. On Renaissance ideals of friendship more generally, see U. Langer, *Perfect Friendship: Studies in Literature and Moral Philosophy from Boccaccio to Corneille* (Geneva: Droz, 1994).

of the ghost as friend: it provided the model for, among many others, Du Bellay's apparition to Ronsard in the 'Élégie à Louis des Masures'.

Yet it is rare that writers, whether on ghosts or friendship, theorize the connection as explicitly as Belleforest. Though this can only be a matter of conjecture, it is possible that the peculiar intensity of Belleforest's concern with friendship, loss, and the humanist circle, may stem from the author's personal circumstances at the time of writing. Another of the 'gentils personnages' and 'honorables citoyens' that once made up Maurice de La Porte's intellectual community was the cosmographer, André Thevet. In 1557 Thevet had entrusted to La Porte the publication of his *Singularitez de la France Antarctique*; the paratexts include an ode by Belleforest in praise of the author, then his friend and protégé. Eighteen years later the two men were to fall out spectacularly.[90] Belleforest was supposed to be providing scribal assistance to Thévet in the preparation of his vast *Cosmographie universelle*. But when in 1575 Belleforest published his own *Cosmographie*, an expanded translation of Sebastian Munster's *Cosmographica*, Thevet accused him of stealing his material.[91] The subsequent so-called 'guerre des cosmographes' was a sour and very public affair. According to Belleforest's biographer Michel Simonin, 1575—the year of Belleforest's chapter on ghosts—was probably the lowest point of the crisis. While Belleforest continued to protest his innocence, Thevet poured scorn on his one-time friend, reserving especial disdain for both the *histoires tragiques* and the *histoires prodigieuses* as 'contes pour faire peur aux enfans'.[92] Belleforest's chapter on ghosts, only added that year, might be understood in part as a poignant meditation on the loss of a soulmate, and on the noble—if brittle—ideals of humanist friendship.

GHOSTS AND THE STOIC: BÉNIGNE POISSENOT

The narrative anthologies for which Boaistuau and Belleforest are best known, both now and in the early modern period, are not the *histoires prodigieuses* but the *histoires tragiques*, written after the model of the Italian author, Bandello. Unlike the *histoires prodigieuses*, this parallel literary adventure found no place for preternatural or supernatural phenomena in the sixteenth century, either in the early volumes by Boaistuau and

---

[90] On the dispute between Thevet and Belleforest, see Simonin, *Vivre de sa plume*, pp. 180–6; F. Lestringant, *André Thevet* (Geneva: Droz, 1991), ch. 7 ('Le duel des cosmographes').

[91] Lestringant identifies the first hints of the 'brouille' as early as 1568. See his *André Thevet*, p. 167.

[92] Quoted in Simonin, *Vivre de sa plume*, p. 183, n. 52.

Belleforest or the later collections of writers such as Vérité Habanc and Jacques Yver.[93] This situation would not last long, however. Perhaps spurred on by the success of the bloodcurdling *canards*, the single-gathering octavo accounts of demons, monsters, floods, and crime in circulation since the 1570s, the seventeenth-century inheritors of the *histoires tragiques*, especially François de Rosset and Jean-Pierre Camus, reincorporate supernatural themes with great enthusiasm. Rosset's collection in particular, already known to historians of popular narrative genres, will be considered at some length in Chapter 6. Less well known, and more pertinent here, is the contribution of another writer of *histoires tragiques*, Bénigne Poissenot.

As might be expected from their early date (1586), the narratives of Poissenot's collection, entitled the *Nouvelles histoires tragiques*, follow Boaistuau, Belleforest, Habanc, and Hyver in excluding the supernatural as a theme.[94] However, the exclusion in this case is not absolute: appended to the collection is a short text devoted entirely to apparitions. This 'Discours confirmatif de l'authorité des anciens touchant l'apparition du mauvais demon ou genie' (pp. 267–73) is just long enough to fill what would otherwise have been blank leaves in the final octavo gathering; it was probably commissioned for this purpose by the printer, Guillaume Bichon, who would shortly signal his growing commercial faith in the subject by publishing Michaëlis's *Pneumalogie, ou discours des esprits* (1587) and, a year later, Taillepied's *Psichologie*. While not fully integrated into the principal matter, then, Poissenot's filler shows a supernatural subject knocking at the door of the *histoires tragiques* as a genre, some years before Rosset and Camus would grant it full admission.

The 'Discours' begins and ends with a theoretical discussion of apparitions; in between appears a brief narrative account of an extraordinary series of events that had recently befallen an unnamed acquaintance.[95] Like all the writers considered in this chapter, Poissenot is exercised by the question of 'autorité', and calls upon that word both in his title and in order to designate the text's addressee: a certain 'personnage d'autorité et d'honneur' (p. 267). The reference to 'l'autorité des anciens' immediately effects a reorientation of discursive authority away from the religious framework of a Lavater or a Taillepied. This does not exclude the customary

[93] See L. Sozzi, ed., *La Nouvelle française de la Renaissance* (Geneva: Slatkine, 1981); S. Poli, *Histoire(s) tragiques(s): Anthologie/Typologie d'un genre littéraire* (Paris: Nizet, 1992).

[94] B. Poissenot, *Nouvelles histoires tragiques* [1586], ed. by J.-C. Arnould and R. A. Carr (Geneva: Droz, 1996). References are to this edition and incorporated into the text.

[95] Poissenot's text has already received some attention in M. Simonin, 'Benigne Poissenot: Discours confirmatif de l'authorité des anciens touchant l'apparition du mauvais daemon ou génie', *Anagrom*, 7–8 (1976), pp. 37–44.

apology for the author's orthodox credentials. In particular, Poissenot
is careful to deny that he seeks to intervene on the specific question of
the return of the dead, 'attendu que je croy ce que l'Eglise Apostolique et
Romaine me commande de tenir sur ce poinct' (p. 268).[96] Nonetheless, it
becomes clear from what follows that this now familiar gesture is little
more than an instance of strategic praeterition. Poissenot's discussion
involves not only the specific apparition of the 'mauvais demon ou
genie' but a whole range of spirits, including apparitions of the dead.
The cast of authorities he cites confirms the humanist colouration of his
incursion in the field. From among the 'anciens' he alludes to Plutarch's
lives of Brutus and Dion Cassius and the works of Valerius Maximus, and
a number of more recent secular authorities, such as Alessandrini and
Bodin, who draw upon the ancients for evidence of spirits. Most notable
of all, and (unlike these) almost entirely absent from the pastoral demonologies of Lavater and Taillepied, are a number of contemporaries.
These include Jacques-Davy Du Perron who, in his recent funeral oration
for Ronsard, reports the dying poet's visions; Torquemada's *Jardín de
flores curiosas*; recent cosmographical reports of ghosts on Iceland's
Mount Hecla; Erasmus's *Colloquia*; and, as if to underline his own
place within a recently born and fast-growing generic tradition, Belleforest's *Histoires prodigieuses*.

Poissenot's text is a 'discours confirmatif': his authorities, ancient and
modern, are summoned in little more than a roll call of those who have
attested to—and thus confirm—the existence of spirits. Slightly more
expansive is the short narrative that forms the text's centrepiece. The
text's hero (introduced simply with 'je sçay un homme qui . . .') belongs
to a class of persons long associated with ghostly visitations: the love-sick
melancholic. This character is the recipient of three separate ghostly
visitations. The first occurs when the hero 'se retira des environs de la
rivière de Loire, à Paris' (p. 269). Lying awake one night, 'sentant son ame
allumée par l'ardeur d'une fureur amoureuse', he spies a dwarf or pygmy
'portant une grande barbe noire pendant jusques en terre et une trongne
fort affreuse' approaching his bed and making threatening gestures
(p. 269). Although this visitation rouses in him 'quelque frayeur', he
decides not to awaken his companion, who is sleeping in the same
room. The second apparition, which occurs soon afterwards, follows
another 'voyage malencontreux' undertaken by the hero. Returning
from his travels with a number of companions, the hero takes lodgings
in a hostel. That night 'il veit, sans s'effrayer aucunement . . . un grand

---

[96] 'given that I believe that which the Apostolic and Roman Church commands me to
believe on this point'.

paisan se pormenant, un gros baton en la main' (pp. 269–70). The figure takes one turn around the room, and disappears. At this point in the narrative Poissenot assures his readers that while the first two apparitions, being nocturnal and both occurring at times of anxiety or depression, may be open to some doubt, 'la tierce effacera tout le doubte qui pourroit demeurer' (p. 270). Two days later the gentleman is out walking early one morning, 'en la compagnie d'un jeune homme parmy un jardin, plein d'une humeur gaye', when he sees 'l'ombre d'un homme noir' standing on the turrets of the house and seeming to shake its fist in his direction (p. 270). The narrator describes the hero's response in the following terms:

> Ne se troublant aucunement, voire ne revelant à celuy avec qui il se pourmenoit ce qu'il avoit veu, il dict entre ses dents ces deux mots: *victus recedes*, voulant dire, plustost tu seras las de me tourmenter que je ne le seray d'endurer. (p. 270)[97]

Thus exorcized, the spirit disappears and Poissenot's story comes to an abrupt end.

How should we read Poissenot's curious narrative? It contains a number of elements already encountered in this chapter. For instance, the ghost's variable scale (first a dwarf, then a 'grand paisan'), the garden setting of the final apparition, and the proximate companion(s) recall Belleforest's encounter with his dead father as a child. More striking still is the hero's response to the apparition, which seems to combine elements of Taillepied's and Lavater's pastoral demonology. The words '*victus recedes*' evokes the clerical practice of exorcism, whose first rite often included the imperative form 'victus et prostratus abscede' (i.e. '[you must] withdraw defeated and prostrate').[98] The subsequent gloss ('plustost tu seras las etc.'), for its part, seems to take up Lavater's call for patience in *Des apparitions*: 'laisse le faire jusqu'à ce qu'il soit las et se retire'. Although the tale contains no reference to a priest or minister, its hero does appear to have absorbed their fundamental lessons. The threefold structure of the story gestures further to an origin in medieval homiletics.[99]

And yet to recuperate the hero's response, or the narrative architecture, to the models discussed in Part I of this book would be to ignore the author's own, and very different, framework for the tale. For Poissenot locates the protagonist's sangfroid (indicated throughout in phrases such as 'quelque frayeur', 'ne s'effrayant aucunement', and 'ne se troublant

---

[97] 'Not growing the least bit anxious, nor even revealing to his companion what he had seen, he said between his teeth these two words: *victus recedes*, meaning, you will sooner grow tired of tormenting me than I of enduring it.'

[98] See Poissenot, *Nouvelles histoires tragiques*, p. 270 n. 29.

[99] On the tripartite structure of the medieval ghost story, see above, p. 22.

aucunement') with reference not to penitential patience but to the classical tradition of stoic—and specifically Senecan— forebearance. The very first line of the 'Discours' reads as follows:

> Les prodigieux effects de la nature et puissance divine paroissent beaucoup plustost aux segnalez et courageux personnages qu'aux morfundus et contemptibles plebeians . . . tellement que pouvons à bon droict estimer ceux-là du tout malheureux qui n'ont, durant le cours de leur aage, esté assaillis d'aucune affliction. (p. 267)[100]

The attitude of stoic pride expressed in these lines, an expansion of a passage in Seneca's *De providentia*, produces what might be termed an aristocracy of witness, something that we could hardly expect to find in pastoral demonology's calls for humility. Lavater had complained in *Des apparitions* that 'il y a des gens qui s'estiment quelque chose, quand beaucoup de telles choses leur apparoissent'.[101] Poissenot's hero seems to embody precisely the view of which Lavater so strongly disapproved: that to be visited by ghosts is a mark of social or ethical *distinction*.

That this distinction was stoic, indeed Roman, in flavour is confirmed when we consider the role of another character in the 'discours confirmatif', a character who, in many respects, might be thought the hero of this chapter. This figure makes only a brief appearance in the story, as the man asleep on the occasion of the first, dwarf-like, apparition. He nonetheless occupies a special place in the narrative as a whole: for unlike the fellow travellers at the 'hostellerie', or the 'jeune homme' in the garden, he is the only companion to be informed of the hero's visitations. Unwilling to wake his friend at night, the protagonist had waited until morning to tell him of the spirit:

> Auquel, racontant le matin ce qu'il avoit veu, l'autre, qui a bonne cognoissance de toute sorte de lettres, luy respondit ces mots latins: *malus tuus Genius*. (p. 269)[102]

'I am your/It is your evil genius': the hero's learned room-mate here gestures, from within the story, to the most prestigious 'authorité' of Poissenot's surrounding frame: namely Plutarch, in whose *Lives* a mysterious apparition speaks these words to Brutus on the eve of his battle

---

[100] 'The prodigious effects of nature and divine power appear much more readily to notable and brave personages than to glum and contemptible plebeians . . . so much so that we might rightly account as quite wretched those who have not, over the course of their life, been assailed with any affliction.' On the Senecan sources, Poissenot, *Nouvelles histoires tragiques*, p. 267 n. 22.

[101] Lavater, *Des apparitions*, p. 90.

[102] 'To whom, recounting the next morning what he had seen, the other, who had good knowledge of all kinds of letters, replied to him with these Latin words: *malus tuus Genius*.'

against Mark Antony. A more leisurely reading of the 'Discours' might explore further the parallels and discrepancies between this morning-after and that of Plutarch's *Lives*, where Cassius persuades Brutus, celebrated for his melancholic disposition, that he had only imagined the dark figure in his tent. For the purposes of this chapter, however, it will suffice to note that the companion figures as an intradiegetic counterpart both for Poissenot himself and his learned addressee. His reading in Plutarch prompts him not to the Church Latin of the priestly exorcist, but instead to that of a very different expert: the man 'qui a bonne cognoissance de toute sorte de lettres', the secular humanist who is ready with an answer.

A man of many allegiances—not just that owed to his faith—the late Renaissance secular humanist has been the hero of this chapter. Alert to the labyrinthine knottiness of theological debates around the subject—typified by the discussion of Samuel's apparition—men like Boaistuau, Belleforest, and Poissenot took up ghosts in full cognizance of their disputed theological status, and took pains not to trespass on a fight that was not theirs. But they also offered new ways, and reinvigorated some old ways, of imagining the return of the dead. Boaistuau's prodigious ghosts show the historical and political fatalism of an age obsessed with providential signs. For the protagonists of his stories, reading those signs is no longer a matter of *discretio spirituum*, but an exercise in registering the tragic destiny of man. Belleforest, in a more private narrative of tragedy and loss, imagined ghosts as representing the occult force of friendship. Though he pays lip service to the traditional theological frame for this question, which is the parable of Lazarus and Dives recounted in Luke's Gospel, that frame soon dissolves to leave behind a far more personal reflection. That D'Aubigné—the fanatical Protestant—felt able to borrow from both writers, and weave ghosts into the warp of his *Tragiques* and *Histoire universelle*, should by now surprise only the solitarists among us.

4

Spectrology

'Beyond Purgatory': the previous chapter showed how a growing number of writers in late Renaissance France sought to find new ways of reflecting upon ghosts, and telling ghost stories, beyond the increasingly sterile confines of sectarian debate. This chapter continues in similar vein, though with more exclusive focus on one central text: Pierre Le Loyer's *Quatre livres des spectres*. How might the secular writer move beyond the anthologies of the *histoires prodigieuses* and make ghosts the subject of a sustained spectrology or (to use Le Loyer's own phrase) a 'science des spectres'? Le Loyer meant his treatise as an answer to this question though, as we shall see towards the end of this chapter, some early readers viewed his achievement in a rather different light.

The *Quatre livres des spectres* was first published in 1586, and then again, in two much revised and expanded editions, in 1605 and 1608.[1] The first version of the treatise has sometimes been considered the definitive Catholic answer to Ludwig Lavater. This is certainly how one contemporary theologian and fellow demonologist, Jude Serclier, heralded the work. Writing in his *Antidemon historial* of 1609, Serclier recalls his dismay at Lavater's assault on belief in ghosts—an attack launched, he complains, with 'toutes les pointes qu'un esprit aceré de malice peut darder contre ceste verité'.[2] Having later read Le Loyer's rebuttal, he

---

[1] All references to the *Quatre livres des spectres* are incorporated into the text. For a detailed summary of the treatise, see especially P. Demougin, 'Étude sur l'oeuvre démonologique de Pierre Le Loyer, 1550–1634' (unpublished doctoral thesis, Université de Paris I, 1994). See also C.-G. Dubois, '*Imaginatio phantastica*: le discours des spectres et apparitions d'esprits de Pierre Le Loyer (1586)' in *La Littérature fantastique: colloque de Cérisy* (Paris: Albin Michel, 1991), pp. 73–89; M. Yardley, 'The Catholic Position in the Ghost Controversy of the Sixteenth Century' in L. Lavater, *Of Ghostes and Spirites Walking by Nyght*, ed. by J. Dover Wilson (Oxford: Oxford University Press, 1929), pp. 220–51.

[2] J. Serclier, *L'Antidemon historial, où les sacrileges, larcins, ruses, et fraudes du Prince des tenebres, pour usurper la Divinité, sont amplement traictez, tant par le tesmoignage des S. Escritures, Peres et Docteurs de l'Eglise, qu'aussi par le rapport des Histoiriens sacrez et profanes* (Lyon: P. Rigaud, 1609), p. 491.

confesses to having felt 'fort soulagé'.[3] The *Quatre livres des spectres* also appears to have consoled other Counter-Reformation thinkers. Thomas Stapleton, the English Catholic controversialist and teacher at the English college in Douai, read it in detail; his heavily annotated copy is now held in the Bibliothèque Nationale.[4] So, too, did the owner of the Bodleian copy, in which Le Loyer's point-by-point refutation of Lavater's *Des apparitions* has been adorned with copious marginal notes.[5] The view of these readers of Le Loyer as a champion of Catholic dogma has persisted among more recent historians and critics. May Yardley's essay on his work is entitled 'The Catholic Position in the Ghost Controversy of the Sixteenth Century'. Her summary and reading of the work, appended to Dover Wilson's edition of Lavater, set the pattern for every study since.[6]

There is something to be said for thinking of Le Loyer as a religious polemicist. The *Quatre livres des spectres* shows strong structural affinities with the works of Lavater and Taillepied, texts that had their roots, as we have seen, in contemporary sectarian controversy. In spite of its title, Le Loyer's treatise is broadly tripartite in construction. Books One and Two affirm the existence of spirits; Book Three mounts a—sometimes aggressive—defence of ghosts; various procedures for dealing with ghosts are reviewed, more or less favourably, in Book Four. And yet to approach Le Loyer's work as a primarily Catholic manifesto is to ignore, in classic 'solitarist' fashion, the large number of its author's other—and sometimes—conflicting affiliations. As we shall see in this chapter, these affiliations were to a secular humanist community of poets and translators far closer to the worlds of Boaistuau and Belleforest than to those of Taillepied and Lavater. Whatever uses Serclier or Stapleton found for the treatise, or its structural similarities with *Des apparitions* and the *Psichologie*, reading Le Loyer's *Quatre livres des spectres* remains a fundamentally different kind of experience than that offered by the Franciscan friar and the Zurich pastor. To understand the scale of Le Loyer's distinctiveness, it is necessary to consider his early career, the context of the work's publication, and the polemical context that gave rise to his neologism: 'spectre'.

---

[3] Ibid.

[4] Bibliothèque Nationale de France [R-7829].

[5] Bodleian Library, Oxford [Douce L 214].

[6] For a similar emphasis on 'the Catholic Le Loyer', see (among many other examples), Dover Wilson, *What Happens in Hamlet*, pp. 63, 67; J. L. Pearl, 'French Catholic Demonologists and their Enemies in the Late Sixteenth and Early Seventeenth Centuries' in *Church History*, 52 (1983), pp. 457–67; Greenblatt, *Hamlet in Purgatory*, p. 212.

THE BIRTH OF THE *SPECTRE*

Before his treatise on ghosts appeared in 1586, Le Loyer was known as a playwright and poet.[7] Born in Huillé near Angers in 1550, he began his literary activities first as a student in Paris, where he was educated in the classics, and then at the faculty of law in Toulouse. In 1572 he was awarded the 'prix de l'églantine' by the Compagnie des Jeux Floraux for his *Idylle sur le Loir*, a pastoral work written in imitation of his fellow Angevin, Joachim du Bellay. In the years that followed, Le Loyer published a translation of Ovid's *Ars Amatoria*[8] and three comedies: *La Néphélococugie* (a version of Aristophanes's *The Clouds*), *L'Eritopegnie* and *Le Muet insensé*.[9] The last of these, inspired by a local case of village sorcery, anticipates some of the themes of the treatise on ghosts. An edition of his collected works appeared in 1579, with laudatory epigrams by Belleforest and Ronsard.[10] By the mid 1580s, Le Loyer was a writer of some repute. The bibliographer La Croix du Maine calls him a 'grand poète', and gives notice in his *Bibliothèque françoise* of a new work in the offing, *Thierry d'Anjou*, modelled on the epics of Ronsard and Pascal Robin.[11]

In the event, Le Loyer's regional epic never made it into print. Now settled back in Angers, and an adviser on the presidial council, the author chose to move away from poetry and devote his energies to a new project, a treatise on ghosts. Completed by the mid 1580s, the *Quatre livres des spectres* was first printed for sale in Angers and Paris. The publication was evidently a costly and complex undertaking. George Nepveu, who had just been made *maître libraire-juré* to the University of Angers, oversaw

---

[7] The following biographical detail is based on A. Menagius (= Gilles Ménage), *Vitae Petri Aerodii quaesitoris andegavensis et Guillelmi Menagii advocati regii andegavensis* (Paris: C. Journel, 1675), pp. 166–8; J.-P. Nicéron, *Mémoires pour servir à l'histoire des hommes illustres dans la république des lettres*, 43 vols. (Paris: 1727–45), XXVI, p. 323.

[8] On this text, see P. Le Loyer, *Pierre Le Loyer's Version of the 'Ars Amatoria'*, ed. by W. L. Wiley (Chapel Hill: University of North Carolina Press, 1941).

[9] Though the last two of these plays are among the first original comedies to be composed, in French, according to the principles of classical dramaturgy, only the first has attracted serious critical attention. See P. Le Loyer, *La Néphélococugie, ou la nuée des cocus* [1579], ed. by M. Doe and K. Cameron (Geneva: Droz, 2004); D. Perret, 'An Avine Cosmography: *La Nephelococugie*, or Aristophanes Gone Cuckoo in the French Renaissance', *The Comparatist: Journal of the Southern Comparative Literature Association*, 18 (1994), pp. 23–38. On the connections between Le Loyer's theatre and writing on ghosts, see M. Closson, 'Le "Théâtre des spectres" de Pierre Le Loyer' in *Dramaturgies de l'ombre*, pp. 119–39.

[10] P. Le Loyer, *Les Oeuvres et meslanges poetiques de Pierre Le Loyer, angevin* (Paris: J. Poupy, 1579), sigs. *v*ᵛ–*vi*ʳ.

[11] La Croix du Maine, *Premier volume de la bibliothèque du sieur de La Croix du Maine*, p. 403; see also Du Verdier, *Bibliothèque d'Antoine du Verdier*, pp. 1018–24.

the publication, which had to be financed at Le Loyer's own expense.[12] Too much for a single workshop, the task was shared between Antoine Hernault (in Angers) and Blaise Pétrail (in Nantes), who printed the text in two separate volumes.[13] These were then bound together and sold by Nepveu in Angers and (on the evidence of a variant title page) the man who had until recently been Ronsard's publisher, Gabriel Buon, in Paris.

Unlike Lavater's *Des apparitions* and Taillepied's *Psichologie*, then, both of which were published cheaply and intended for mass distribution, the result—a quarto of over a thousand pages—was an *objet de luxe*, marked out for the gentleman's library.[14]

As Le Loyer's title suggests, and in common with many other texts considered in this thesis, the *Quatre livres des spectres* is less concerned with the subject of witchcraft than a variety of spirits—demons, of course, but also angels and ghosts—conceived as the various species of one single genre. That genre he designates using the term 'spectre', a word he defines according to the following formula:

> Spectre est une apparition d'une substance sans corps qui se monstre sensible-ment aux hommes contre l'ordre de nature, et leur donne frayeur. (I, p. 1)[15]

This unpacking is not Le Loyer's own, but translated from Scaliger's definition of *spectrum*. It comprises several features of the conventional ghost wisdom encountered in earlier chapters of this study.[16] 'Substance sans corps' remains faithful to the orthodox view that spirits lack bodies; 'se monstre sensiblement aux hommes' specifies the spectre further to Augustine's category of *visio corporalis*, and so distinguishes it from those figures appearing in dreams (*visio spiritualis*) or ecstasies (*visio intellectua-lis*); and 'contre l'ordre de nature' translates the standard conception of marvels (*mirabilia*) as events occurring against the course of nature (*contra naturam*), as opposed to miracles or events above nature (*supra*

---

[12] On Nepveu, see E. Pasquier and V. Dauphin, *Imprimeurs et libraires de l'Anjou* (Angers: Éditions de l'ouest, 1932), pp. 191–2.

[13] On Hernault, see Pasquier and Dauphin, *Imprimeurs et libraires de l'Anjou*, pp. 125–6; on Pétrail, see *Répertoire bibliographique des livres imprimés en France au seizième siècle*, Bibliotheca Bibliographica Aureliana, 19: 'Nantes', ed. by J. Betz (Baden-Baden: V. Koerner, 1975), p. 22.

[14] On two such early buyers of Le Loyer's treatise, see P. Aquilon, 'Quatre avocats angevins dans leurs librairies (1586–1592)' in *Le Livre dans l'Europe de la Renaissance: actes du XVIIIe colloque international d'études humanistes de Tours*, ed. By P. Aquilon and H.-J. Martin (Paris: Promodis, 1988), pp. 502–49.

[15] 'Spectre is an apparition without a body that appears sensibly to men against the order of nature, and makes them afraid.'

[16] The same definition, along with the attribution to Scaliger, is also found in Lavater, *De spectris*, p. 1.

naturam).[17] The last four words ('et leur donne frayeur') remind us that, as in the traditional technology of the *discretio spirituum*, the affective dimension of witnessing apparitions is not an ancillary, but central, component in coming to terms with exactly what they are.

Le Loyer was not the first to write of 'spectres' in the vernacular; the term can be found as early as 1560. But it is only after the publication of his treatise that the word begins to bed down in common usage.[18] His neologism offers two powerful advantages. First of all, it provides an answer to a well-known humanist conundrum, and one that had even troubled his friend and fellow poet Ronsard: the lack of a native French term to describe apparitions.[19] Marc-Antoine Muret had framed the problem succinctly in his 1553 commentary on Ronsard's *Amours*. Glossing the line 'Ô nuict, ô jour, ô Manes Stygieux', Muret observes:

> *Manes* se nomment en Latin les ames sorties des corps. Il faut naturaliser, et faire François ce mot là, veu que nous n'en avons point d'autre.[20]

The want of a French term meant that much of the terminology of sixteenth-century French writing on apparitions—not only 'manes', but also 'incubes', 'succubes', 'genies', 'lares', 'larves', 'penates', 'lemures'— had to be derived from the literary legacy of ancient Greece and Rome. This was a perfectly satisfactory solution for poets like Ronsard. Le Loyer had to be more careful. The difficulty with 'manes', as he comments elsewhere in the *Quatre livres des spectres*, is that the pagan spirits described by the term are 'reprouvez et exilez de toute la Chrestienté' (i, pp. 428–9). By contrast, his own 'spectre', a theologically neutral designation, takes none of the risks of a pagan lexicon: in employing that term Le Loyer need not be hidebound by the fear of Church censure. With its etymological emphasis on sensory perception—and particularly sight—the 'spectre', unlike the 'diable' or the 'ange', is anterior to any moral or theological determination. This anteriority offers Le Loyer a second advantage,

---

[17] On these distinctions in medicine, theology, and law, see I. Maclean, *Logic, Signs, and Nature in the Renaissance: The Case of Learned Medicine* (Cambridge: Cambridge University Press, 2002), pp. 271–3.

[18] For two earlier instances of 'spectre', see P. Boaistuau, *Histoires prodigieuses*, sig. 105ʳ; Vair, *Trois livres de charmes*, p. 321. Le Loyer was also responsible, via Zachary Jones's 1605 translation of the *Quatre livres des spectres*, for the introduction of the 'spectre' into English. Jones only translated Book One of the original treatise (principally concerned with natural philosophy), probably for fear of offending his Protestant readership. See P. Le Loyer, *A Treatise of Spectres or Straunge Sights* (London: V. Simmes for M. Lownes, 1605).

[19] On the terminology of ghosts in the French Renaissance, see above pp. 2–4, 70.

[20] M.-A. Muret, *Commentaires au premier livre des 'Amours' de Ronsard* [1553], ed. by J. Chomarat, M.-M. Fragonard, and G. Matthieu-Castellani (Geneva: Droz, 1985), p. 92: '*Manes* is the Latin name for souls gone out of their bodies. We need to naturalise that word, and make it French, given that we have no other.'

that of being able to situate apparitions in a space within which the authority of churchmen is dramatically reduced. In this way the 'spectre' becomes instrumental in establishing a new heuristic field for ghosts and apparitions—linked, but no longer confined, to the domain of theology. 'Spectres', then, did not necessarily imply a religious experience, nor were those who refused to credit them inevitably Protestants. A further indication of this appears in Le Loyer's dedicatory epistle to Catherine de' Medici, a puzzling document that may not always have been fully understood. In it the author describes several categories of people who do not believe in 'spectres'. He claims first of all that he has composed his treatise in order to combat those he calls 'les nouveaux Dogmatistes' (sig. *ii^r). This incredulous faction, he continues, 'pour insinuer secretement, comme je croy, ez esprits des hommes une erreur Epicurienne, qu'il ne demeuroit rien des ames apres le deces, ont nié l'apparition d'icelles' (sig. *ii^r). Who are these 'dogmatistes'? The term is often taken to apply simply to Protestants such as Lavater, on account of their unbending—or dogmatic—insistence on the letter of Scripture. This is indeed sometimes the case, and Le Loyer has occasion to describe Lavater in this way. But as becomes clear at several other points in the treatise, 'dogmatiste' can also refer to natural philosophers like Pomponazzi and Cardano (e.g. I, pp. 252–310, and II, pp. 124–34). These were the modern-day (that is, 'nouveaux') avatars of the ancient *dogmatistae*, who for their part accept nothing not inscribed in their own hallowed book: Aristotle's book of Nature. It is just as much their dogmatism in rejecting those events that seem to run 'contre l'ordre de nature', as Lavater's in denying a scriptural foundation for Purgatory, that exercises Le Loyer in the *Quatre livres des spectres*.

Nor does Le Loyer's list of opponents end there. The letter to Catherine also promises to refute another category of unbelievers. This group Le Loyer describes, somewhat obscurely, as 'quelques esprits et cerveaux mal bastiz de nostre temps, inventeurs d'estranges et bigerres opinions' (sig. *ii^r). While the identity of these 'esprits' remains— perhaps intentionally—imprecise, the early chapters of the treatise may provide something of a clue. Towards the beginning of Book One, the author devotes a whole chapter to refuting those he terms 'les sectateurs de Pyrrhon'.[21] Interest in pyrrhonian scepticism had increased markedly following Henri Estienne's Latin translation of Sextus Empiricus in 1562, and the recent publication of Montaigne's *Essais*—a work that openly confesses its own 'bigarrure'—had done much to reinforce it as a fashionable philosophical trend.[22] Unlike the 'dogmatiste' (in this period a term

---

[21] Book One, ch. 5.
[22] See Cave, *Pré-histoires*, pp. 71–3; Clark, *Vanities of the Eye*, pp. 266–99.

that often denotes, precisely, one who is *not* a sceptic), the pyrrhonist refuses any notion of philosophical precept, instead preferring the suspension of judgement ('*epochè*'). Yet in spite of their differences, the sceptical philosopher joins the 'dogmatiste' in his rejection of spirits: for the same refusal to subscribe to the dogmatic *a priori* of a Pomponazzi or Cardano also challenges the empirical foundation of Le Loyer's 'spectre'. To return to the terms of Le Loyer's definition, a being that 'se monstre *sensiblement* aux hommes' communicates in a medium—the senses—fundamentally prone to error and misjudgement. One might say that a sceptic refuses to believe in ghosts precisely *because* he sees them.[23]

So often interpreted as an anti-heretical diatribe, the polemical epistle to Catherine in fact gestures to a far wider set of concerns than those of sectarian polemic alone. Many of these come powerfully to the fore in Book One of the treatise, and have to do with man's relationship to visual phenomena. When Le Loyer challenges Cardano's theory that Icelanders only see 'ghosts' on account of a poor diet of apples, root plants and fish-flour, or Pomponazzi's that graves exhale vapours in the shape of their dead occupant, he is attempting to preserve a space for preternatural phenomena that are inexplicable in terms of 'dogmatist' natural philosophy. Since the question of apparitions and sensory perception has received detailed treatment in Clark's recent work, what follows here will concentrate on two non-theological concerns in the *Quatre livres des spectres*. Representing Le Loyer's most important contribution to the ghost literature of late Renaissance France, these were law and cosmography.

GHOSTS ON TRIAL: LAW AND THE COURTROOM

Whether Le Loyer is writing against the Protestant reformers, natural philosophy, or the current vogue for scepticism, his polemical strategy remains the same: the mass accumulation of narrative examples. Weighing in at over one and a half thousand quarto pages, the *Quatre livres des spectres* constitutes by far the longest single work of French vernacular

---

[23] Given this stance, Le Loyer's own Greek epigraph from Sextus Empiricus in the preliminaries to the 1605 and 1608 editions of his treatise is mischievous. The passage quoted (from *Against the Mathematicians*) cites Democritus in order to criticize the superstitions of the ancients but, taken out of context, might be taken as support for the existence of ghosts: 'Democritus says that certain images impinge on men, and of these some are beneficent, others maleficent (whence also he prayed that he might have "propitious images")'. See Le Loyer, *Discours et histoires des spectres*, sig. Aiii^r; I have taken the translation from Sextus Empiricus, *Works*, trans. by R. G. Bury, Loeb Classical Library, 4 vols. (London: Heinemann, 1933), III, p. 11.

writing on apparitions. And with good reason, since there is nothing so likely to persuade the unbeliever, claims Le Loyer, as the abundance and variety of ghost-narrative *exempla*. The dedication to Catherine invokes not only 'la venerable antiquité', but also 'tous les livres du monde' against those who seek to deny the apparition of spirits (sig. *ii^r).

The sheer number, not to mention the range, of Le Loyer's sources are indeed impressive. So extensive is his reading in the Church Fathers and medieval theology, despite his lack of formal training, that Serclier was led to describe him as 'un grand jurisconsulte et theologien tout ensemble'.[24] Over and above his Patristic sources, which he shared with a number of other writers on ghosts, Le Loyer's *inventio* also included a number of hitherto unknown stories and examples. Already celebrated as a poet and a playwright, Le Loyer was also well known as an 'homme docte és langues'.[25] His knowledge not only of Latin and Greek, but of Hebrew, Arabic, and Chaldaean, is clear in the numerous French translations— from Homer, Virgil, Propertius, Martial, and Lucan, from the Koran and Rabbinical exegesis—incorporated into the body of his text. Ranging in length from the single line or stanza through to several pages of interpolated narrative, some of these texts were appearing in French for the first time. For instance, Le Loyer's most developed and, as we shall see in a later chapter, influential translation is that of the recently rediscovered Greek paradoxographer Phlegon of Tralles.[26] That author's *Book of Marvels*, first edited and translated into Latin by Xylander in 1568, includes the story of 'Machates and Philinnion', a ghost narrative that would later become a commonplace of demonological writing in the late sixteenth and early seventeenth centuries. Le Loyer's translations were also responsible for disseminating a number of East European ghost narratives. The interpolations from the Latin histories of Martin Cromer and Antonius Bonifinius, on Poland and Hungary respectively, both fall into this category; these may have prepared the ground for the later, and more decisive, reception of Slavic vampire legends in mid eighteenth-century France.[27] The popularization of writers like Phlegon, Cromer, and Bonifinius makes the *Quatre livres des spectres* the leading vernacular digest of ancient and modern ghostlore to have been published in the sixteenth century.

Aside from his ancient sources, Le Loyer also sought out and found numerous instances of ghosts in the legal record. He was evidently proud

---

[24] Serclier, *L'Antidemon historial*, p. 491.

[25] La Croix du Maine, *Premier volume de la bibliothèque du sieur de La Croix du Maine*, p. 403.

[26] On Le Loyer's translation from Phlegon, and its subsequent influence, see below, pp. 216–34.

[27] On Pierre de L'Estoile's reading of these translations, see below, pp. 168–72.

of his legal training, and the work's title page advertises his position as 'conseiller au siege presidial d'Angers'; and whereas the epigraph to Taillepied's treatise on ghosts had been John's 'Try the spirits', Le Loyer takes his from the *Edicts*, and Ulpian's definition of the Greek word φασματα ('phasmata').[28] The canonical record also provides an important source of ghost narratives in the body of the treatise. However, most are first-hand accounts reported to the author by his colleagues in the parliaments of Rouen, Brittany, and Paris. Whereas in the theological works of his co-religionists, Taillepied and Jean Lambert, the primary locus of ghost narrative exchange is the clerical space of the church, Le Loyer transfers the setting to the law court or tribunal. The edition of 1605 makes explicit this change, described in the passage below as a displacement of ghosts from 'les escoles de Theologie' to the 'barreaux des Advocats':

> Qui croiroit que la question du retour des Ames, laissant les escoles de Theologie eust esté en son rang ventilee és barreaux des Advocats pour estre plaidee, franchy le pas, et venuë és sieges des Cours inferieures et des Parlemens où la Justice s'exerce, et decidee des Juges?[29]

Le Loyer's shift in the scenography of ghost narrative exchange effectively elevates the lawyer to a position of considerable authority—not only an ally of, but perhaps even a rival to, the figure of the priest.

Le Loyer's appeal to the juridical tradition is not made without a measure of discursive embarrassment. In Book Three of the treatise, dealing specifically with apparitions of the dead, Le Loyer devotes a long section to a recent civil case in which the tenant of a property he claimed to be haunted had sought to have his contract annulled (II, pp. 47–66).[30] The author had a special interest in this suit—not the only case of its kind in sixteenth-century France—since his old teacher, René Chopin, had

---

[28] 'Ulpianus Libro vicensimo quinto, ad Edictum. Ostentum cum quid prodigiosum videtur, quae Graeci φασματα vocant'; Le Loyer, *Quatre livres des spectres*, sig. *i'.

[29] P. Le Loyer, *Discours et histoires des spectres, visions et apparitions des esprits, anges, demons, et ames, se monstrans visibles aux hommes* (Paris: N. Buon, 1605), p. 659: 'Who would have believed that the question of the return of the dead, leaving the schools of Theology, would have been taken up at the lawyers' bar for pleading, stepped forth, and come before the lower Courts and the Parliaments where Justice is dispensed, and decided by judges?'

[30] Valladier (*La Saincte Philosophie*, p. 699) mentions a similar case heard in Bordeaux, 1596, and presided over by 'monsieur le President de Chessac, grand personnage, si aucun y en a eu long temps y a, portant mortier en ce Royaume'; this is likely to be the same case reported by Antoine de Morry as having been heard in Bordeaux on 29 March 1595. This time the case was decided in favour of the tenant (who is refunded his advance rent in full). See A. de Morry, *Discours d'un miracle, avenu en la Basse Normandie, avec un Traité des Miracles, du pouvoir des Demons, et de leurs prestiges, et le moyen de les recognoistre d'avec les vrays miracles* (Paris: F. du Chesne, 1598).

been assigned the landlord's brief.[31] However, having debated the precedents at length, the civil court eventually suspended judgement on the
case, declaring it a matter for a clerical tribunal. Writing years later and
echoing Chopin's own satisfaction at the outcome, Le Loyer approves of
his colleagues' reluctance, as he puts it, to 'enjamber sur l'estat ecclesiastique, et nomméement la Theologie' (ii, 66).

To an extent, Le Loyer's discursive unease is unsurprising, given
the suspicion with which law was viewed in some theological quarters.
According to some in the Church, the juridical tradition was actively
hostile to belief in ghosts. Lecturing towards the beginning of the
1570s, Maldonat had observed that 'l'opinion des Jurisconsultes est que
ce sont purs fantomes': here 'fantomes' clearly stands for 'vain imaginings'.
Another Jesuit demonologist, Martin Delrio, will complain some years
later that even Catholic lawyers, such as André Tiraqueau or Girolamo
Maggi, credit stories of ghosts as nothing more than 'songes'.[32] A trained
lawyer himself, Delrio is particularly well placed to make the accusation.
If Le Loyer was finally able to establish the jurist as a figure of authority,
he would have to tread carefully.

Le Loyer's efforts to mobilize legal expertise in ghostly matters can be
seen in his report of two notorious recent cases. Both hinge on the
question of whether evidence furnished by the ghosts of murder victims
was admissible in the trials of their killers. This was not an entirely new
question, and was in some respects related to age-old debates over the legal
implications of post-mortem 'cruentation' (corpses that bleed in the
presence of their murderers). As might be expected, Lavater had scoffed
at the notion that the dead might return to give legal testimony. If God
did not permit Lazarus to appear to Dives's brothers to give evidence for
Hell, 'certes celuy là se rendroit ridicule,' Lavater claims, 'qui voudroit
prouver quelque chose devant la justice par le tesmoignage des morts'.[33]
Le Loyer endorses the opposite view. He cites first of all a recent episode
involving the celebrated jurist, Barnabé Brisson.[34] Prosecuting the men
accused of murdering the daughter of another prominent lawyer, Du
Moulin, Brisson 'ne craignit point de dire en plain Senat, ouy d'une

[31] For Chopin's original report of the trial, concluded on 6 March 1576, see R. Chopin,
De Sacra politia forensi libri III (Paris: N. Chesneau and J. Poupy, 1577), pp. 784–92.

[32] Maldonat, *Traicté des anges et demons*, sig. 182ᵛ; Delrio, *Les controverses magiques*,
sig. Qiiᵛ.

[33] Lavater, *Des apparitions*, p. 207: 'there is no doubt that anyone wishing to prove
something before the courts by the testimony of dead men would be deemed ridiciulous'.
On the parable of Lazarus and Dives (Luke 16:19–31), see above, pp. 57–63.

[34] For the official report of the trial, concluded on 22 March 1572, see *Recueil de
plaidoyez notables*, pp. 246–64.

infinité de personnes, que la fille du Moulin s'estoit apparue de nuict à son mary non dormant ains veillant, et luy auroit declaré et specifié par nom ceux qui l'avoient tuee elle et ses petits enfans, le suppliant d'en poursuyvre la vengeance' (II, 46). The daughter's calls for vengeance, rather than intercession for her soul, situate her ghost within a tradition more pagan and antique than devotional and Christian. Nonetheless, '[Brisson] ne craignit point de dire en plain Senat': if Brisson shared Le Loyer's anxiety at moving ghosts from the 'escoles de Theologie' to the courtroom, he does not show it here.

A more developed treatment of the same question emerges through a comparable case, communicated to Le Loyer by another friend, Launay Gaultier, a councillor in the Breton parliament. It concerns a domestic murder committed by a Breton woman, Marie de Sornin. Following an argument over dinner one evening, she had stabbed her husband to death as he slept. The body was taken down to the cellar, and concealed beneath a pile of salted meat. For a time, nobody missed the victim, whose trade as a merchant often entailed lengthy absences from home. But, as Le Loyer takes care to point out, in a passage whose emphasis on providential agency recalls Boaistuau's *Histoires prodigieuses*:

> Ce neantmoins Dieu, qui ne permet que les crimes (et nommément les homicides, lesquels il abhorre sur toutes choses) demeurent impunis, voulut que le crime homicidiaire de ceste femme fust decouvert en ceste façon. (II, p. 46)[35]

One day, Sornin's brother paid his sister-in-law an unexpected visit. As he was about to enter the house, something extraordinary happened:

> Comme il mettoit le pied sur le seuil de l'huis de la maison où avoit esté occis son frere, voicy merveille que luy apparoist l'ombre et spectre de son frere occis environné d'une lumiere ce luy sembloit. (ibid.)[36]

First afraid, then strangely reassured and emboldened, the brother followed the ghost down to the cellar, whereupon the apparition vanished 'justement où estoit le charnier' (ibid.). He informed Mme de Sornin of what had happened and, despite her attempts to dissuade him, demanded that the meat store be dug up. The body was found, half-decomposed, and

---

[35] 'Despite this, God, who does not permit crimes to remain unpunished (and especially murders, which he abhors above all things), desired that the murderous crime of this woman be discovered in this way.'

[36] 'As he placed his foot on the threshold of the doorway to the house where his brother had been killed, behold if not by some marvel there appeared to him the shade and spectre of his murdered brother surrounded by light, it seemed to him.'

the wife arrested. After a period of torture, she confessed to the crime and was sentenced to death.

A number of narrative precedents exist for the Sornin case, two of the most notable from the classical tradition. Le Loyer himself tells the famous story of Athenodorus the philosopher, first narrated in Pliny the Younger's epistle to Sura.[37] In that narrative, Athenodorus rents a haunted house in Athens, abandoned by the previous tenants and unoccupied for months. A ghost appears to him as he writes the following evening and beckons him into the garden, where the apparition vanishes. Athenodorus demands that the city magistrates dig at the spot where the spirit disappeared, whereupon human remains are found. Pliny's tale was probably the most often-cited ghost narrative in the period, variously translated, illustrated, and, in one version by Antonio de Torquemada, even relocated to contemporary Bologna.[38] The Sornin murder also bears a striking resemblance to a narrative first recounted in Cicero's *De divinatione* and popular with medieval storytellers, which had later come to be known in France as 'l'histoire des deux Arcades'.[39] In it an Arcadian traveller is murdered by an innkeeper. His ghost appears to his companion, who is lying awake (or, in some versions, dreaming) in a hostel on the other side of the city. The dead man instructs his friend to intercept a dung-cart leaving town the next morning. When the city magistrates stop the wagon, the friend's corpse is discovered at the bottom of its load. The man driving, the innkeeper, is arrested and punished for the crime.

Viewed through the prism of these venerable precedents, it is easy to see the attraction of Sornin's story for Le Loyer. Both Pliny's and Cicero's narratives lend considerable prestige to the unnamed magistrate who, at the end of each story, unearths the body and confirms the ghost's testimony. Part lawyer, part archaeologist, this figure combines the two salient

[37] Pliny the Younger, *Letters*, trans. by W. Melmoth, Loeb Classical Library, 2 vols. (London: Heinemann, 1915), II, pp. 67–77 (Book Seven, Letter XXVII).

[38] Examples include Du Triez, *Ruses, finesses et impostures*, sigs. 81^v–2^r; Des Caurres, *Oeuvres morales*, sigs. 126^v–7^r; Gravelle, *Abbregé de philosophie*, sig. 322^r. The fullest treatment can be found in Antoine du Verdier's *Prosopographie*, where on the basis of this story Athenodorus is granted his own entry; see Du Verdier, *La Prosopographie*, pp. 277–99. According to Du Verdier, Claude de Tesserant copied his work for his chapter on ghosts in the *Histoires prodigieuses*; see Boaistuau, Belleforest, et al., *Histoires prodigieuses*, II, pp. 117–20; Du Verdier's accusation is levelled in *Bibliothèque d'Antoine Verdier*, p. 200. For Torquemada's contemporary version of the story (in Chappuy's French translation), see Torquemade, *Hexameron*, pp. 243–8.

[39] *De Divinatione*, I, pp. xxvii; see Cicero, *De Divinatione*, trans. by W. A. Falconer, Loeb Classical Library (Cambridge, MA: Harvard University Press, 1996), p. 287. The same tale appears in Chaucer, *The Nun's Priest's Tale*, ll. 2984–3062. The 'histoire des deux Arcades' was made famous in early modern France by Boaistuau; see *Histoires prodigieuses*, sigs. 106^r–7^r.

features of Le Loyer's own claims to expertise as a legally trained antiquarian humanist. That attraction notwithstanding, Le Loyer insists on some notable differences between the Sornin case and its classical precedents. He is especially anxious to place the apparition within a Christian, rather than pagan, framework. While the pagan 'ghost' in Pliny is interpreted as a demonic presence in the *Quatre livres des spectres*, in the Sornin episode, by contrast, the avenging demon is sacralized as the return of a dead soul. Rereading the story, we see how its status as a Christian ghost is carefully encoded in a number of visual and narrative motifs: the providential framework ('Dieu voulut... que'); the halo of light surrounding the spectre's head; and the affective response of the witness, who is frightened at first, then mysteriously becalmed. Not that there is any mention of Purgatory, or indeed any discussion of whence, in theological terms, the ghost of Sornin's husband could have possible returned. Doubtless Le Loyer was concerned, as he would put it, not to 'enjamber sur l'estat ecclesiastique', though his silence might equally stem from another, more discursively aggressive, attempt to wrest ghosts away from the clerical monopoly. Once Christianized in this way, the avenging ghosts of pagan antiquity become, in partnership with lawyers like Le Loyer, legitimate agents of divine retribution.

GHOSTS ABROAD: NEW WORLD/OTHER WORLD

Le Loyer's expertise as a linguist and a lawyer allowed him access to an unprecedented range of spectral narratives. His treatise is also notable for being the first work of French demonology to draw extensively upon— and subsequently influence—contemporary European cosmography.[40] Before coming directly to Le Loyer's contribution, it will be useful to take leave of his treatise for a moment, and briefly review the place of Christian apologetics in general, and ghosts in particular, in the cosmographical writing of the decades that preceded him.

By the time Le Loyer published his treatise in 1586, the discovery of the New World was already a well-established topic within Christian apologetics. One reason for this was that the Americas provided a powerful spatial analogue for that other as yet 'undiscovered country' (to use Hamlet's phrase) awaiting us in death. The celebrated Spanish humanist

---

[40] See T. Chesters, 'Pierre Le Loyer et la cosmographie du spectre' in *Voyager avec le diable: voyages réels, voyages imaginaires et discours démonologiques (XVe–XVIIe siècles)*, ed. by G. Holtz and T. Maus de Rolley (Paris: Presses universitaires de Paris-Sorbonne, 2008), pp. 183–92.

Juan Luis Vives was probably the first to draw on this comparison—
between New World and Other World—in his chapter on the immortality
of the soul in his 1544 *De veritate fidei Christianae.*[41] Pierre Crespet,
a demonologist like Le Loyer, extends and develops Vives's idea in his
non-demonological work of Christian apology, the *Discours catholiques de
l'origine, de l'essence, excellence, fin, et immortalité de l'ame.* Crespet, adver-
tised on the title page of his book as a 'prieur des célestins de Paris', is
writing against atheists who are persuaded that the soul is mortal because we
never receive news of any other world:

> Pour respondre donc à ce qu'ils objectent, qu'on n'a point ouy parler de
> l'estat où sont les Ames apres la mort, et qu'on ne sçait ce qu'elles font en
> l'autre monde, d'où personne n'en est revenu. Je pourrois dire, qu'il suffit en
> croire au recit qu'ont fait les Saincts peres, comme dit David. *Auribus nostris
> audivimus, patres nostri annunciaverunt nobis.* Mais je demanderois volon-
> tiers, si auparavant qu'on eust descouvert les Isles neufves, il n'y avoit point
> de gens en icelles, jaçoit que nous n'en eussions eu revelation ne certitude,
> sinon que depuis un peu de temps, qu'on en a fait la preuve et l'experience.
> Eux aussi qui n'avoient jamais ouy parler de nous, assavoir si pour cela il
> n'estoit pas vray que nous estions? . . . On voit donc maintenant, que quelque
> distance de lieux qu'il y eut entre eux et nous, on a eu moyen avec le temps
> de les cognoistre, et eux nous, et frequenter ensemble. Et ce qui est encore
> notable, c'est que la distance des lieux, qui nous les rendoit incogneuz, n'est
> pas telle, que celle qui est de la terre au ciel, parquoy ne se faut esmerveiller, si
> nous avons si peu de cognoissance de l'estat des ames qui y sont.[42]

The 'Isles neufves', discovered a century before by European travellers
across the Atlantic, are here compared to that other New World: the as yet
unknown country that we go to when we die. Crespet makes Vives's
analogy sound tortuous here, and not just because of the pile-up of

[41] L. Vives, *De veritate fidei Christianae libri vi* [1543] (Basel: J. Oporinus, 1544),
pp. 147–8.
[42] Crespet, *Discours catholiques*, sig. 276ʳ⁻ᵛ. 'Let us respond to their objection that we
have not heard tell of the state souls are in after death, and that we do not know what they
do in the other world, from which nobody has returned. I could say that it is enough to
believe the account of the holy fathers, as David does: *Auribus nostris audivimus, patres nostri
annunciaverunt nobis.* But I would go further and ask whether, before the New Islands had
been discovered, there were for all that no people there, since the fact remains that we had
had no revelation or certainty that they existed, except since that short time ago when we
gained proof and experience of them. Neither did they have any knowledge of us: is it true
then that we did not exist? . . . We now see therefore that whatever the distance separating
them from us, it has been possible with time for us to know them, and they us, and each to
frequent the other. And what is also to be noted: that the distance between places, which
made us ignorant of them, is not as great as that between the earth and the sky. For this
reason it is not surprising that we have so little knowledge of the state of the souls who reside
there.'

if-clauses, multiple negatives, and subjunctives that clutter the middle section of the passage. Part of the reason is Crespet's desire to entertain a relativistic perspective in which his reader is invited to imagine the view from the other shore: not only had we not heard of the New World natives, he insists, but they had never heard of us. More importantly still, the analogy is asymmetrical. While travellers frequently return with news of the New World, death is a land 'd'où personne n'en est revenu'. Crespet acknowledges this asymmetry when he speaks of how great a distance separates the living and the dead ('la distance des lieux, qui nous les rendoit incogneuz, n'est pas telle, que celle qui est de la terre au ciel'). And yet, that acknowledgement notwithstanding, the logical extension of the comparison prompts a question explored further in Crespet's demonological writing. It is the same question that faces Hamlet: what if dead travellers sometimes really do return?

Crespet's interest in the view from the Other World, and the tacit possibility that its dead might reach the living, leads us to a second – and more developed – role for New World discovery in Christian apologetics. This entailed what Frank Lestringant has called 'le dogme de l'unité du genre humain'.[43] Numerous accounts of expeditions to the New World express obvious satisfaction at the discovery of peoples who appear to believe, despite the lack of Christian revelation, in a world beyond our own. The possibility that this belief might be consecrated as an anthropological universal, that is as a value separating the human believer from his bestial Other—the atheist—proves seductive for a number of early modern apologists.

As Lestringant has shown, this appeal to the universality of religious belief is almost always made with reference to a celebrated formula in Cicero. Sixteenth-century authors commonly refer to a passage in *De legibus* where Cicero claims that there is 'no race either so highly civilized or so savage as not to know that it must believe in a god'.[44] For instance, André Thevet writes in his *Singularitez de la France Antarctique* that 'il 'n'y a nation tant barbare, que par l'instinct naturelle n'aye quelque religion, et quelque cogitation d'un Dieu'.[45] Similarly, Jean des Caurres's *Oeuvres morales et diversifiées en histoires*, published in 1575, contains the claim that 'jamais il n'y a eut nation au monde tant ignorante, cruelle et barbare,

---

[43] F. Lestringant, *Jean de Léry, ou l'invention du sauvage: essai sur l'Histoire d'un voyage faict en la terre du Brésil* (Paris: Champion, 1999), pp. 107–8.
[44] Cicero, *De legibus*, I, pp. 8, 24; the translation is taken from *De re publica; De legibus*, trans. by C. W. Keyes, Loeb Classical Library (London: Heinemann, 1966), p. 325.
[45] A. Thevet, *Les Singularitez de la France Antarctique, autrement nommée Amerique: et de plusieurs terres et isles descouvertes de notre temps* (Paris: Maurice de La Porte, 1558), sig. 52ᵛ.

qui n'ait eu, et n'ait quelque forme de religion'.[46] Even if these two works are characterized above all by their taste for difference (whether this is set under the sign of 'diversité' or 'singularité'), each nonetheless acknowledges a religious prompting that appears to unite all the planet's people. Faced with the ethnographical phenomena of the New World, the negative locutions of Cicero and his imitators ('jamais il n'y a eut nation . . . qui n'ait eu', etcetera) carry all the more force in that they challenge that other series of negations, equally abundant in cosmographical writing of the period, so central to the writing of Utopia. To cite a famous example, Montaigne's 'Des Cannibales' (1.31) includes the claim that in the land of the cannibals 'il n'y a aucune espece de trafique; nul cognoissance de lettres; nulle science des nombres; nul nom de magistrat ' nuls contrats, nulles successions; nuls partages, nulles occupations qu'oysives';[47] the famous 'quoy! ils ne portent pas de haut de chausses' with which the essay ends is only another, ironic, instance of the same negative formula.[48] And yet none of these negations are extended to deny the existence of the Brazilians' religious fervour. A few pages on, Montaigne tells us that the same cannibals 'croyent les ames éternelles, et celles qui ont bien merité des dieux estre logées à l'endroit du ciel où le soleil se leve; les maudites, du costé de l'Occident'.[49] The same exception is made for religion in the passage from Jean des Caurres cited earlier:

> Ceux qui ont navigué pardelà [aux terres 'nouvellement découvertes'], ont trouvé plusieurs gens vivans sans lettres, sans loix, sans Roys, sans Republiques, sans arts: non toutefois sans Religion, qui croyent les ames aller en autres lieux, dignes des choses par eux faites en ceste vie.[50]

'Sans . . . sans . . . sans . . . non toutefois sans': Des Caurres's line clearly reveals the breach opened in Utopian discourse by the universal belief in the survival of the soul. Through that breach it becomes possible to glimpse a topos dominant within Christian apologetics of the period: that which holds

---

[46] Des Caurres, *Oeuvres morales*, sig. 120[v].

[47] Montaigne, *Essais*, p. 206: 'there is no sort of traffic; no knowledge of letters; no science of numbers; no name for a magistrate . . . no contracts, no successions; no partitions, no occupations but leisure ones' (*Complete Works*, p. 186).

[48] Montaigne, *Essais*, p. 214: 'But what's the use? They don't wear breeches.' (*Complete Works*, p. 193).

[49] Montaigne, *Essais*, p. 208: 'They believe that souls are immortal, and that those who deserved well of the gods are lodged in that part of heaven where the sun rises, and the damned in the west.' (*Complete Works*, p. 187).

[50] Des Caurres, *Oeuvres morales*, sig. 120[v]: 'Those who have navigated in those parts have found many people living without letters, without laws, without republics, without arts. Not, however, without religion: they believe that souls proceed to other places, worthy of the deeds performed in life.'

belief in immortality to be a ground of common understanding—rather
than conflict—between Christian and savage.

But what, specifically, of beliefs in apparitions of the dead? As a short
passage on this topic from Jean de Léry's *Histoire d'un voyage faict en la
terre du Brésil* makes clear, the place of ghosts within ethnography is a good
deal more complex. Lestringant has already shown how Léry refuses to
subscribe to the optimist's belief in the universality of religious conviction.
That refusal appears all the more marked when he begins to describe the
beliefs of the Tupinambas in the return of dead souls. In the eleventh
chapter of his book Léry describes a bird not much bigger than a pigeon,
and of greyish feathers, whose nocturnal song announces, according to
'nos povres *Toüoupinambaoults*', news of their dead. There then follows a
short account of Léry's own personal experience of this funereal song, an
experience that reminds him of certain superstitions closer to home:

> Je couchay une fois en un village, appelé *Upec* par les François, où sur le soir
> oyant chanter ainsi piteusement ces oyseaux, et voyant ces pauvres sauvages si
> attentifs à les escouter, et sachant aussi la raison pourquoy, je leur voulu
> remonstrer leur folie: mais ainsi qu'en parlant à eulx, je me prins un peu à rire
> contre un François qui estoit avec moy, il y eut un vieillard qui assez
> rudement me dit: Tais-toy, et ne nous empesche point d'ouir les bonnes
> nouvelles que nos grans peres nous annoncent à present: car quand nous
> entendons ces oyseaux, nous sommes tous resjouis, et recevons nouvelle
> force. Partant sans rien repliquer (car c'eust esté peine perdue) me ressouve-
> nant de ceux qui tiennent et enseignent que les ames des trespassez retour-
> nans de Purgatoire les viennent aussi advertir de leur devoir, je pensay que ce
> que font nos pauvres aveugles Americains est encor plus supportable en cest
> endroit: car comme je diray parlant de leur religion, combien qu'ils con-
> fessent l'immortalité des ames, tant y a neantmoins qu'ils n'en sont pas là
> logez, de croire qu'après qu'elles sont separées des corps elles reviennent, ains
> seulement disent que ces oyseaux sont leurs messagers.[51]

[51] J. de Léry, *Histoire d'un voyage faict en la terre du Brésil*, ed. by F. Lestringant (Paris: Livre de Poche, 1994), pp. 287–8: 'I once spent the night in a village which the French call *Upec*; toward evening, hearing these birds sing so piteously, and seeing these poor savages so attentive in listening to them, and also knowing the reason why, I tried to point out to them their foolishness. But while I was speaking to them, I began to laugh at a Frenchman who was with me, and an old man said to me rather brusquely, "Be quiet, and do not prevent us from hearing the good news that our grandfathers are even now announcing to us; for when we hear these birds, we all rejoice, and receive renewed strength." So without replying (for it would have been of no use), and remembering those who believe and teach that the souls of the deceased return from purgatory to warn them of their duty, it occurred to me that what our poor blind Americans do in this respect is more tolerable: for as I shall describe when I speak of their religion, although they confess a belief in the immortality of souls, they do not go so far as to believe that souls return after being separated from their bodies, but say only that these birds are their messengers.' J. de Léry, *History of a Voyage to the Land of*

The Calvinist traveller's derision disturbs the Tupinambas's ritual of listening to their dead. Directed against his French companion first, and then against those of his compatriots who still adhere to the doctrine of Purgatory and, by extension, to the return of the dead, his laughter belongs squarely to the tradition of Protestant satire described earlier in this study. A note printed in the margin leaves little room for doubt on this score. Summing up Léry's remark that at least the natives did not believe the dead themselves appeared, it reads: 'Ameriquains plus advisez que ceux qui croyent que les ames apparoissent apres la mort des corps'.[52] Whereas the Christian apologetics of Crespet, Thevet, or Des Caurres targeted the atheist or the Epicurean, the Huguenot traveller here addresses his Catholic enemies. Far from supporting the thesis of universal human religiosity, Léry's 'ghost' narrative here serves, on the contrary, as a pretext for underscoring the violent disagreements that split his native France.

Before 1580 the protagonists of that debate—on both sides of the confessional divide—paid little attention to the ethnographical findings of travellers in the New World. Virtually no reference to Amerindian superstitions are to be found in the work of Du Triez, Maldonado, Daneau, or Taillepied, and only scattered mentions in that of Weyer, Lavater, Amboise Paré's *Des monstres et prodiges*, and Bodin's *Demonomanie*. It is only upon the publication of Le Loyer's *Quatre livres des spectres* that New World cosmography acquires the status of an evidential category within early modern discussion of ghosts.

In the first edition of the treatise of 1586, ghosts abroad make only a tentative appearance. Le Loyer's uncertainty over their evidential value can be felt on a number of levels: the little space they are accorded and the poverty of the sources consulted, as well as the fundamentally hesitant tone of his arguments concerning them. Only three pages are given over to the demonological beliefs of the New World Indians, and these inserted at the very end of a chapter entitled 'L'opinion des Sectateurs de la Loy de Mahommet, Turcs, Mussulmans, et Arabes, ensembles les Caldeans, et ceux des terres menües sur les Ames sorties de leurs corps, et si elles reviennent'.[53] As yet no special place is granted to the beliefs of the savage, which appear only on the same footing as those of that second great Other within the European imagination: the Turk. Nor is Le Loyer's storehouse

---

Brazil, otherwise called America, trans. by J. Whatly (Berkeley: University of California Press, 1990), p. 91.

[52] Ibid: 'Americans possessed of more sense than those who believe that souls appear after the death of the body'.

[53] Le Loyer, *Quatre livres des spectres*, ii, pp. 88–91.

of doxographical evidence as copiously stocked as in other parts of the
treatise. Indeed he draws on only one named source in this section,
Levinus Apollonius, even if he relies discreetly on Thevet, whom he
does not name.

As for what Le Loyer makes of his sources, the tone of the argument
remains, as he himself admits, broadly conjectural. In the most developed
of his reflections on the New World, he begins by discussing the religious
beliefs of the inhabitants of Cusco, Peru's first city. The passage, notable
for its equivocations, is worth quoting in full:

> Et ce qui me fait conjecturer que les Cusquiens ont opinion que les Ames
> errent et se monstrent apres le trespas de leurs corps, c'est qu'ils honorent
> encore aujourd'huy un de leurs Roys deffunct qui avoit nom Guainacaba, et
> avec l'honneur qu'ils luy portent, aussi le craignent ils et le redoutent comme
> s'il estoit encores vivant. Et vrayement c'est une chose ridicule de craindre un
> mort, voire selon le tesmoignage de Theudotus Rheteur, et Sophiste, ce
> mauvais Conseiller qui conseillant à Ptolomee le jeune dont il estoit pre-
> cepteur, de faire mourir ce Grand Capitaine et Empereur Pompee, luy dist
> que les morts ne mordoient point. Que dirons nous donc de ceste folie des
> Cusquiens de craindre ainsi un mort? Nous ne pouvons dire que ce soit à
> cause de la cruauté de Guainacaba envers ses subjets pendant qu'il vivoit et
> regnoit sur eux, laquelle les auroit non moins effrayez apres sa mort, que
> Neron auroit espouvanté quelques uns des Romains qui le regardoient, non
> sans trembler ayant les yeux entr'ouvers et rouillez en la paupiere apres qu'il
> se fut donné du poignard dans la gorge, ainsi que rapporte Suetonius
> Tranquille. Il est certain selon le recit des Cusquiens que Guainacaba estoit
> le Prince autant aymé de ses subjets lors qu'il estoit en vie qu'autre qui ait
> regne en Cusco, et qui a plus deffendu le païs des assaux et courses des
> Caraibes ou Canibales, et plus conquesté de terres: tellement qu'il faut
> conclurre qu'ils ont opinion que son Ame et ses Manes logent avec son
> corps dessous le tombeau, et se vengent de ceux qui passent sans celebrer
> annuellement avec solemnité ses *Anniversaires* et funerailles.[54]

---

[54] Le Loyer, *Quatre livres des spectres*, II, pp. 89–90: 'And what makes me conjecture that
the people of Cusco believe that souls wander and appear after the death of the body is that
they still honour today one of their dead kings who was called Guainacaba, and with the
respect that they pay him, they also fear him and hold him in dread as if he were yet living.
For truly it is a ridiculous thing to fear the dead: Theodotus the rhetoritician and sophist,
that bad advisor and tutor to Ptolemy the younger, urging him to kill that great captain and
Emperor Pompey, even went as far as to assure him that the dead men do not bite. What
should we say of the Cuscans mad fear of a dead man? We cannot say that it is because of
Guainacaba's cruelty towards his subjects while he lived and reigned over them, the which
would have affrighted them after his death no less than Nero did certain generals who
trembled even as they looked upon him with his eyes half-closed and rolled back under the
lids, after he had plunged a dagger into his heart (so reports Suetonius). According to the
story the Cuscans tell, it is certain while he was alive Guinacaba was the best loved by his
subjects of all the kings of Cusco, and the one who had best preserved the country from the

Aware that he lacks any direct evidence to suggest a firm belief in ghosts ('ce qui me fait *conjecturer*'), Le Loyer is reduced in this passage to a piece of purely inductive reasoning. The Peruvians fear their dead king, Guainacaba. Even bad counsellors like Theudotus assert that 'les morts ne mordent pas', especially a dead man who—unlike Nero—was not feared while still alive: *ergo* the Peruvians believe that 'son Ame et ses Manes' continues to wonder near his tomb, ready to avenge itself on all those who pass without paying their respects. Incapable, except by antiphrasis, of finding any point of connection between the Peruvians' behaviour and the antique models so dear to him, Le Loyer seems at a loss faced with Amerindian beliefs. The final uncertain doublet—'son Ame' and 'ses Manes' (singular or plural? Christian or pagan?)—only appears to confirm the author's confusion.

The 1605 edition of Le Loyer's treatise (which will be introduced more fully in the following section) is testimony to a marked evolution in the importance of cosmography within demonological thinking. Whereas in 1586 the appropriation of cosmographical discourse seemed reticent and provisional, the place accorded to New World ghosts is far more extensive, and the tone more decisive, twenty years later. Three pages in 1586 become eight in 1605. The arrangement of the chapters is also significant: where, in the first edition, Amerindian ghost belief was ranged alongside that of the Turk, in the second it is granted a chapter of its own. This new chapter, now entitled 'Ce que les Barbares et Indiens ont creu et croyent des Ames apres la mort du corps', indicates a breadth of reading far greater than that of 1586: included are references to Jacques Cartier, Giovanni da Verrazzano, Agustín de Zárate, Léry, and the English mathematician and traveller, Thomas Harriot. Naturally, these are not all given the same treatment. Le Loyer produces a lively critique of Cartier and Verrazzano's travel narratives for having cared 'fort peu de rapporter ce qui estoit spirituel, et ne traitans que de ce qui les chatouïlloit le plus, qui est la paillardise laquelle à bon droit les fait haïr de toutes nations'.[55] Léry's account of his Brazilian adventure is more useful to him, despite the religious convictions of its author: Le Loyer reproduces the description of the ghost-bird, even if he does remove the Calvinist's satirical asides.[56] Harriot, for his part,

---

assaults of the Caraibs and Canibals, and conquered the most lands. For these reasons one must conclude that they believe his soul and his *manes* to lodge with his body in the grave, and wreak vengeance on those who pass by without solemnly celebrating, every year, his *Anniversary* and obsequies.'

[55] Le Loyer, *Discours et histoires des spectres*, p. 555: 'little to report back on spiritual matters, only discussing that which aroused them the most, namely that lustfulness which makes them justly hated by all nations'.

[56] Ibid., p. 554.

furnishes two 'histoires' ('si telles se doivent nommer et non plustost fables')
illustrating the beliefs of the people of Virginia.[57]
    The first of Harriot's stories involves a 'meschant garnement du pays'
who, following his death and burial, climbs up out of his tomb 'tout vif'
in order to tell of how he would have fallen into 'la fosse de Popogusso'
(that is to say, Hell) had it not been for the intervention of one of their
gods, who instructed him to return to his family and warn them against
succumbing to a similar fate. The second story reverses the moral polarity
of the first, describing a man of good character who comes back to
proclaim the wonders of Paradise ('chemins couverts d'arbres', 'fruits',
'palais où il trouve l'âme de son père', etcetera). That Le Loyer places these
two accounts under the sign of fable does little to diminish their polemical
value. They are followed by a lengthy comparison with similar cases in
Homer, Sappho (some of whose verses Le Loyer translates), and Herodo-
tus. Whereas in 1586 the humanist reader had proved reticent in deci-
phering native American belief, 1605 sees a new-found confidence:
antique myth and ethnographical fable finally converge to bear witness
to, and so reinforce, the same primordial beliefs.
    The same aura of interpretive confidence surrounds Guainacaba, the
King of Peru, as he appears once more—revised and updated—in the
edition of 1605. In the years between the first and second editions, it
seems that the popular fear of his dead spirit has hardened into proof of his
subjects' beliefs in the return of the dead. It is no longer a question, as it
was twenty years earlier, of 'conjecture simple':

> Est une chose assez estrange, que ceux de la ville de Cusco Capitale du Peru,
> craignent un de leurs Inges deffuncts, qui est Guyanacape, comme s'il estoit
> vivant. Ils pensent, comme je croy, que ses Manes logent encores soubs la
> tombe. Et ne dis point cecy tant pour conjecture simple, qu'il n'y ait encores
> de la verissimilitude en mon dire. Car j'ay leu és Relations des Espagnols que
> les Peruviens se vantoient qu'ils voyoient quelquesfois les Spectres de leurs
> Rois et Inges morts qui se presentoient à eux en pompe et magnificence
> Royale, leur disoient qu'ils vivoient Royalement en l'autre monde habillez de
> vestemens Royaux, heureux, pleins d'aise et de contentement, sans soin, sans
> ennuy, sans affaires.[58]

---

[57] Ibid., p. 554–55.
[58] Le Loyer, *Discours et histoires des spectres*, p. 553: 'It is a strange thing that those living
in town of Cusco, capital of Peru, fear one of their deceased rulers, named Guinacaba, as if
he were alive. They think, as I see it, that his *manes* lie beneath his tomb. And I do not
venture this as simple conjecture, as what I say is likely. For I have read in the Spanish
accounts that the Peruvians boasted of sometimes seeing the spectres of their dead kings and
rulers who presented themselves to them in pomp and royal magnificence, told them that
they were living royally in the other world, dressed in royal clothes, happy, full of wellbeing
and contentment, without cares, without troubles, without business.'

The ghosts of Peruvian kings retain the attributes they possessed when still alive. They continue to enjoy their 'vestemens Royaux' and their 'magnificence Royale': in short, 'ils vivoient Royalement'. But this triad 'Royale-Royalement-Royaux' is doubled by another, where it is less a question of worldly possession than of happy privation. For the ghost, unlike the living king, finds himself in the world beyond, 'sans soin, sans ennuy, sans affaires'. These 'sans' lend themselves to a further conjecture. It is commonplace in the Renaissance to speak of the dead as freed from the worries of the living. Shakespeare's Duncan, as imagined by Macbeth, is a case in point: 'Treason has done his worst: nor steel, nor poison / Malice domestic, foreign levy, nothing / Can touch him further'.[59] And yet even if Macbeth is visibly haunted by the spectres of his crime, the Duncan described here is not quite a literal ghost. Indeed, among the hundreds of ghost narratives consulted in the preparation of this study, these Peruvian kings remain the only example of this fortunate privation. 'Sans soin, sans ennuys, sans affaires': these are the 'withouts' of both Utopia and Death or—to return to the equivalence with which this section began—of both the New World and the Other.

To explain the growing importance, after 1586, of Amerindian belief as an evidential class in French demonology, it would be necessary to invoke a whole range of possible factors: the re-edition of Léry's works, the increasing number of new travelogues (especially those emerging from the Jesuit mission), or the development of comparative ethnography (such as that found in Claude Guichard's *Funerailles et diverses manieres d'ensevelir des Rommains, Grecs, et autres nations, tant anciennes que modernes*, 1581, or in certain essays of Montaigne). But the role of Le Loyer should not be neglected. Much of his evidence, and his reasoning, is repeated in the works of demonologists such as Crespet, Martin Delrio, and Pierre de Lancre. It is thanks to Le Loyer that André Valladier, in his sermon on the return of the dead preached for Advent in 1612, appeals not only to 'toute l'antiquité, tous les Theologiens . . . et à l'Écriture saincte', but also 'à toutes les nations, à l'Afrique, Asie, Europe, Amerique' in mockery of his Protestant opponents.[60] Le Loyer was not the first to write of ghosts in different parts of the globe; but he was the earliest writer to draw them together as a category of demonological enquiry.

---

[59] *Macbeth*, III, II.
[60] Valladier, *Saincte Philosophie*, p. 712.

'SCIENCE DES SPECTRES' OR 'CONTE À PLAISIR'?

The second, much revised and enlarged, edition of Le Loyer's treatise was printed in 1605 in Paris by Nicholas Buon.[61] The title of the new edition bears witness to the same polemical strategy as that of the first:

> Discours et histoires des spectres ... divisez en huit livres, esquels par les visions merveilleuses, et prodigieuses apparitions avenuës en tous siecles, tirees et recueillies des plus celebres autheurs tant sacrez que prophanes, est manifestee la certitude des spectres et visions des esprits.[62]

The new text too is a 'recueil', though the eight books of the second edition add a large quantity of new material to the four books of the first. In spite of Le Loyer's continuing fondness for the massive accumulation of anecdotal *exempla*, that narrative prolixity is accompanied in the later edition by an unmistakeable sense of anxiety.

The preface begins by acknowledging the pleasure so many take in the subject of ghosts and apparitions:

> En tous les propos communs et familiers qu'en compagnie l'on entame de choses qui semblent esloignées de la nature, et sont escartées de nos sens, il n'y a rien de si prompt, rien de si ordinaire, que faire marcher en place les visions d'esprits, qu'on appelle spectres, et si ce qu'on dit d'eux est veritable. C'est une matiere que volontiers on entremesle, et où plus longuement on s'arreste pour estre abondante en exemples, le sujet beau et plaisant, et le discours moins ennuyeux qui se puisse trouver. (p. 1)[63]

Such is the fascination exerted by the 'spectre', Le Loyer continues, one would have thought that 'cela auroit invité de sçavans hommes d'en faire des livres entiers' (ibid.). This is indeed the case, and yet:

> Ils m'excuseront si je leur dy franchement en quoy leurs escrits peuvent pecher: ils ne different en rien des propos familiers que je disoy se tenir en compagnie touchant les spectres, comme s'il estoit permis à ceux qui mettent

---

[61] References are incorporated into the text.

[62] 'Discourses and histories of spectres ... divided into eight books, in which by means of marvellous visions, and prodigious apparitions that have occurred in every age, drawn and gathered from the most famous authors both sacred and prophane, is proved the certainty of spectres and visions of spirits.'

[63] 'In all common and familiar conversations that are struck up about those things that seem far removed from nature, and distant from our senses, nothing is brought so readily or ordinarily to bear as those visions of spirits we call spectres, and if what is said of them is true. It is a topic that we entertain gladly, and that we are especially apt to pore over because it is rich in examples, the subject attractive and enjoyable, and discussion of it the least boring imaginable.'

la main à la plume, d'escrire aussi negligemment comme ils se pourroient
licentier de parler et deviser privément. (ibid.)[64]

If the 'spectre' constitutes 'en compagnie' a narrative being, its nature
must change when it enters written discourse. Other writers relegate the
'spectre' to the lower discursive realm of 'des propos communs et familiers', a fate from which Le Loyer proposes to rescue it:

> La matiere des spectres est-ce quelque chose de laquelle on puisse faire tant
> de cas, et qui doive estre traittée serieusement, et tout autrement qu'on ne
> fait les choses qui dependent du discours du vulgaire? Je pense qu'oüy... Mais
> on peut doncques à mon dire bastir une science des spectres? C'est ce que
> j'entends ici monstrer. (p. 2)[65]

The sophistication of the lawyer's rhetoric, whose questions suggest (the
better to set aside) the incredulity of others, enacts the very principle it sets
out to establish: that to extract the subject of ghosts from polemical debate
is not necessarily to deliver it into the untutored mouths of the 'vulgaire'.
On the contrary, it is to constitute the ghost as an object of knowledge and
expertise, to establish what Le Loyer calls a 'science des spectres'.

The third edition of Le Loyer's treatise, which Buon published in 1608,
restages the same conflict between 'science' and mere 'propos familiers'.[66]
The text of this edition is virtually identical to that published in 1605, the
only substantive changes being a shortening of the title and a new,
expanded, prolegomenon to the reader. The new title, *Discours des spectres*,
deliberately downplays the role allotted to narrative by removing a key
word—'histoires'—from the previous edition. The same sense of narrative
embarrassment is prolonged and intensified in the additions to the preface, where the anxious questioning of the previous edition has, clearly, not
quite been put aside. 'Qu'est-ce rien que les spectres qu'un amas et
collection d'histoires,' Le Loyer asks, 'advenuës à diverses personnes et
en divers temps, que le moindre du peuple qui aura quelque mediocre
erudition peut autant bien digerer, escrire et rapporter, que feroit le plus
sçavant qu'on sçauroit dire?' (p. 2).[67] After all, he continues, 'les exemples

---

[64] 'They will forgive me if I tell them candidly where their writings go astray: they do not
differ in the slightest from those familiar conversations on the subject of spectres that I was
describing as taking place in company, as if those who put pen to paper were free to write as
negligently as they might permit themselves to speak and debate privately.'

[65] 'Is the subject of spectres really something of such great value, and that deserves to be
treated seriously, and in a different manner from those things that depend on the talk of the
common people? I think it is... But am I saying that it is possible to establish a science of
spectres? That is what I intend to show here.'

[66] References are incorporated into the text.

[67] 'What are spectres but a piled-up collection of stories, befalling different people at
different times, and that the very commonest of men, gifted with some moderate erudition,

sont en la bouche de tous', and, as the rhetorical question gives way to the balder, reductive statement, 'ce n'est qu'une narration nüe que les spectres dont le vulgaire est capable, et qui semble n'avoir esté reservee que pour le vulgaire' (ibid.).[68] Here, then, is an author still haunted by the spectre of narrativity or, more precisely, the narrativity of the 'spectre'. Hence a new attempt at discursive exorcism, banishing narrative, like pleasure, to the realm of the 'oral' or the 'vulgar', in order to take refuge in the space of written expertise:

> Je ne suis pour tout cela d'accord qu'on doive traicter par escrit ceste matiere, comme si c'estoit quelque conte à plaisir où se plairoit le vulgaire.[69] (ibid.)

Le Loyer's treatment of the 'spectre' will be based, he goes on, 'non d'exemples seules, ains d'autres considerations meilleures et bien plus fortes que les exemples et les contes' (ibid.).[70] For the ghost, he concludes:

> aime et demande qu'on face exacte recherche de ses principes, de ses causes, de ses raisons et arguments qui sont ses fondemens qui n'entrent en l'esprit du vulgaire comme les histoires et exemples. Et d'où peuvent venir ces raisons que de la science? (ibid.)[71]

This final rhetorical question, no longer incredulous but triumphant in tone, brings Le Loyer's prefatory argument—with others, no doubt, but also and perhaps primarily with himself—to a close.

The roots of Le Loyer's anxiety over the role and status of the ghost narrative, powerfully clear in the prefaces of 1605 and 1608, may be ascribed to a number of causes, beginning with the growing vogue for tales of the strange or the aberrant. The rising popularity of such narratives is evident from, among other things, the phenomenal success of the *Histoires prodigieuses*. These diverting narrative *recueils*, begun by Boaistuau and

---

would be just as capable of digesting, writing down and relaying as the most learned one could name?' Behind the phraseology here may lie a veiled attack on Montaigne, who writes in 1.21 ('De la force de l'imagination') that 'Advenu ou non advenu, à Paris ou à Rome, à Jean ou à Pierre, c'est tousjours un tour de l'humaine capacité'; Montaigne, *Essais*, p. 105: 'Whether they have happened or no, in Paris or in Rome, to John or to Peter, they exemplify, at all events, some human potentiality.' (*Complete Works*, p. 91).

[68] 'Examples are in everybody's mouths...Spectres are a matter for nothing but bald narrative, of which the common people are capable, and that seems to have been confined only to the common people.'

[69] 'For all that I do not agree that this topic should be treated in writing as if it were some amusing tale to please the common people.'

[70] 'not on examples alone, but on other better and much more powerful considerations than examples and stories'.

[71] 'wishes and requires us to look precisely into its principles, its causes, reasons and arguments—all that is fundamental to it and does not enter the head of the common people as examples and stories do. And from where do those reasons proceed except from science?'

continued well into the 1590s, may well be one target of Le Loyer's prefatory critique; the *Essais* of Montaigne may be another.[72] More specifically, however, Le Loyer's concern over narrative may also have arisen from the early reception of his own *Quatre livres des spectres.* Certainly, to judge by the response of a number of contemporary authors, writing in a variety of different genres, it seems that Le Loyer's treatise could itself be—and indeed was—read as an elaborate narrative *recueil.*

Among the most prominent of Le Loyer's early readers was Jean Bodin, a writer whose debt to the *Quatre livres des spectres*, for chronological reasons, has so far been overlooked. The first edition of Bodin's *Demonomanie* appeared in 1580, six years before Le Loyer's treatise on spectres. But it is clear from the second edition of Bodin's work, published in 1587, that he had read parts of his fellow Angevin's treatise. This is not to claim a wide-ranging influence, however. It is notable that rather than adopt Le Loyer's 'principes', 'raisons et argumens'—doubtless too orthodox for Bodin's maverick theology—the author of the *Demonomanie* has simply mined the *Quatre livres des spectres* for 'histoires et exemples'. In Book Two, Chapter 3 ('Des invocations expresses des malins esprits'), for example, Bodin includes a story from Phlegon of Tralles that he has clearly taken from Le Loyer; a little further on, in the context of a discussion of vengeful apparitions, he interpolates the story of the murdered Sornin's ghost.[73] In each case the debt to the *Quatre livres des spectres* is entirely beyond doubt; both borrowings, however, remain wholly unacknowledged, and each is made without regard for its context in Le Loyer.

The same two stories are also taken up and repeated, now shorn of their learned context in Le Loyer, outside specialist demonology. It seems, first of all, that the 'spectre' had quickly become a topic within the genre of polite conversation, at least as transcribed by authors such as Bouchet. The *devisants* of Bouchet's *Sérées* make ample reference to the Sornin case, as well as several others from the *Quatre livres des spectres.*[74] Both that episode and the Phlegon translation also find their way, in the decades that followed the publication of Le Loyer's treatise, into the related discursive

---

[72] For two more general studies on the tension between learned demonology and the *Histoires prodigieuses*, see M. Simonin, 'La Vérité de l'estrange: pédagogie et poétique du fantastique à la Renaissance', *Studi di Letteratura francese*, 212 (1987), pp. 30–44; H. Campagne, 'Démonologie ou 'Histoires prodigieuses'?: au carrefour de la science et de la littérature', *Studi Francese*, 43 (1999), pp. 496–503.

[73] Bodin, *Demonomanie*, sigs. 78ᵛ, 79ᵛ.

[74] G. Bouchet, *Les Sérées de Guillaume Bouchet, sieur de Brocourt*, ed. by C. E. Roybet, 6 vols. (Paris: A. Lemerre, 1873–82), III, pp. 73–4. On Bouchet's sources for *Les Sérées*, see A. Janier, 'Les Sources des *Sérées* de Guillaume Bouchet' in *La Nouvelle française de la Renaissance*, ed. by L. Sozzi (Geneva: Slatkine, 1981), pp. 557–86.

contexts of the *histoires prodigieuses, histoires tragiques*, and the sensation-alist *canards*. A short pamphlet appearing in 1633, for instance, entitled *Arrest de mort donné au Parlement de Bretagne, contre Damoiselle Marie de Sornin, accusée et convaincue d'homicide par l'estrange apparition de l'esprit de son feu mari*, is a verbatim transcription of Le Loyer's own account.[75] Meanwhile, Phlegon's narrative of Philinnion and Machates was perhaps especially successful in capturing the imagination of Le Loyer's contem-poraries. A variant sixth continuation of the *Histoires prodigieuses*, pub-lished in 1598, reproduces that narrative in full, accredited to 'le docte Loyer', under the title *Merveilleuse Histoire d'un cadavre d'une fille duquel le diable se servit pour exercer luxure avec un jeune homme*.[76] As we shall see in the next chapter, Rosset includes a similar story in his *Histoires memor-ables et tragiques* of 1614, in which a nightwatchman is seduced in identical fashion. Finally, Le Loyer's translation of Phlegon, to which Rosset alludes in the conclusion to his own narrative, was also the inspir-ation for an early seventeenth-century *canard*, entitled *Histoire prodigieuse d'un gentilhomme auquel le Diable s'est apparu, et avec lequel il a conversé, sous le corps d'une femme morte*.[77] As with the Sornin affair, the moralizing potential of the Phlegon narrative, combining as it does a sensationalist blend of misogyny and violence, made it perfectly adaptable to the *canard* as a genre. While it is true that many of these re-contextualizations post-date the *Discours des spectres*, they suggest nonetheless that, alongside Jude Serclier's praise for Le Loyer as a 'grand jurisconsulte et theologien tout ensemble', there also existed another mode of reading: one that construed the *Quatre livres des spectres*, as its author feared, as little more than 'un amas et collection d'histoires'.

Is Le Loyer's 'spectre', then, primarily a creature of narrative or an object of knowledge? Do the later editions of the treatise constitute a 'science des spectres'? Or does it remain, despite its author's best inten-tions, nothing more than a 'conte à plaisir'? One response to these questions is provided by the early seventeenth-century Parisian chronicler and bibliophile, Pierre de L'Estoile. L'Estoile's celebrated *Journal* provides ample evidence of its author's fascination—L'Estoile himself describes it as an obsession—with contemporary reports of witchcraft, monsters, and demons. Scattered throughout the text are references to *canards* he has purchased. His response to these 'balivernes', as he calls them, is (with very

---

[75] Paris: P. Mettayer, 1633.

[76] P. Boaistuau, F. de Belleforest et al., *Histoires prodigieuses et memorables, extraictes de plusieurs fameux autheurs, grecs et latins, sacrez et prophanes, divisées en six livres*, 6 vols. in 2 (Paris: veuve G. Buon, 1598), sigs. Aaaaii^r–Bbbbviii^r. On this edition of the *Histoires prodigieuses*, see above p. 000.

[77] Paris: F. de Carroy, 1613.

few exceptions) one of incredulous amusement. In June 1608 his *Journal*, which he terms more than once the 'magasin de mes curiosités', announces the arrival of a new acquisition:

> Le vendredi 13e, M. Chrestien m'a presté un livre *des Spectres*, imprimé à Paris, in-4°, relié en veau noir. Livre curieux, et duquel on m'a fait cas.[78]

Eleven days later, we find the following entry:

> Le 24e de ce mois, j'ay renvoyé à M. Chrestien son livre *des Spectres*, après l'avoir leu d'un bout à l'autre: qui n'est pas ce que je pensois et qu'on m'avoit donné à entendre; car, encores qu'il y ait beaucoup de choses curieuses audit livre, ramassées de divers aucteurs sur ce subject, se sont-elles entremeslées de tant de fadèzes, qu'à peine me suis-je peu donner la patience de les lire.[79]
> (II, p. 345)

Two 'fadèzes' in particular appear to have exhausted L'Estoile's patience. He goes on:

> Il y en a deux, entre autres, l'une, pour le Purgatoire, et l'autre, pour la Confession, qu'il allègue de Martin Cromer, qui a escrit l'Histoire de Polongne, et d'Antoine Bonifinius, qui a redigé par escrit l'Histoire de Hongrie, lesquels deux passages, pour me sembler peu croyables et ridicules, ne pouvois croire estre de la façon qu'il les met dans son livre, en ces bons aucteurs, jusques à ce que, les aians vérifiés, Chrestien et moy, sur l'un et sur l'autre, ils sont tels, et qui ne les voudra croire ne doit estre réputé Huguenot pour cela. (ibid.)[80]

For all his impatience, L'Estoile does trouble to copy out the offending narratives by hand and insert them into the body of his journal. The first story, by Cromer, unfolds in the kind of legal framework familiar throughout

---

[78] P. de L'Estoile, *Journal pour le règne de Henri IV*, ed. by L.-R. Lefèvre and A. Martin, 3 vols. (Paris: Gallimard, 1948–60), II, p. 343. All references are to this edition and are incorporated into the text: 'On Friday 13th, M. Chrestien lent me a book, *des Spectres*, printed in Paris, in quarto, bound in black calf. A curious book, of which I have heard good things said.'

[79] 'The 24th of this month I sent back to M. Chrestien his book, *des Spectres*, having read it from cover to cover. It was not what I had thought it would be or what I had been given to expect; for, although there are many curious things in this book, gathered from various authors on the subject, they are mixed up with so many trifles that I could hardly find the patience to read them.'

[80] 'Among others there are two of these—one supporting Purgatory, the other Confession—that he cites from Martin Cromer's History of Poland and Antonius Bonifinius' History of Hungary that, seeming to me so little believable and so ridiculous, made me think that there must be some difference between the way in which they appear in his book, and in the two good authors' originals. But indeed, Chrestien and I having checked each version against the other, found that there is indeed no difference, and whosoever might wish to disbelieve them should not be thought a Huguenot on that account.'

Le Loyer's *Discours des spectres*. It concerns a certain Bishop of Cracow, Stanislas, who resuscitates a man dead for over two years. Stanislas was at that time embroiled in a land dispute with the King of Poland; the support of the dead man's testimony proved the decisive factor in winning the case. In the second narrative, from Bonifinius, the skull of a dead man killed in battle demands that a priest be sent for in order to hear his confession.

L'Estoile's review of the stories from Cromer and Bonifinius is significant in at least two respects. First, it is clear that, in common with readers of the first edition, the *journaliste*'s view of the *Discours des spectres* centres primarily on the isolated narrative. Indeed, the insertion of the tales into the body of L'Estoile's *Journal* indicates the degree to which Le Loyer's 'histoires', far from being confined to a merely exemplary function, always risk escaping the master discourse of his 'science'. In his preface, Le Loyer himself writes disapprovingly of 'une matiere que volontiers on entremesle'. Here 'entremeslés' within L'Estoile's 'magasin des curiosités', however, his ghosts have become creatures of narrative stripped bare, for the most part, of their scientific value: these are 'conte[s] à plaisir'. It is true that L'Estoile concedes, as a good Catholic, the didactic function fulfilled by each of the two stories: one, he claims, Le Loyer evidently intends 'pour le Purgatoire', the other 'pour la Confession'. And yet, he goes on, 'qui ne les voudra croire ne doit estre réputé Huguenot pour cela'. This last *boutade* raises a second important feature of L'Estoile's response to the treatise, namely the opening of a space for private, secular readings of the 'spectre'. That space here takes the form of the gentleman's library in which L'Estoile and his friend, M. Chrestien, compare Le Loyer's French translations with their originals in Latin.

In his diary entries for September of the same year, 1608, it is clear that L'Estoile's interest in Le Loyer remains undiminished. The third edition has just left Buon's presses; L'Estoile buys his own copy, bound in parchment, for a total price of sixty-two *sous*. The *journaliste* explains that he has returned to this 'livre curieux' because he has had it recommended to him by 'beaucoup d'hommes de sçavoir' (II, p. 372). He continues:

> Qui a esté cause de me le faire acheter et y escrire au commencement ung sonnet gaillard, sur ceste matiere, fait par Passerat, il y a longtemps, qui le donna à un mien ami. (ibid.)[81]

---

[81] 'Because of this I bought it and wrote at the beginning an amusing sonnet on this topic, composed by Passerat long ago and given by him to a friend of mine.'

Another textual 'entremêlement', then, only this time the direction is reversed: here Le Loyer's text is embellished with additions from another, on this occasion the poet Jean Passerat. Like L'Estoile, Passerat was a prominent member of the 'politique' faction during the *ligue*; it is no surprise that, 'il y a longtemps' (Passerat died in 1602), the two men had friends in common. The identity of the poem inscribed in L'Estoile's copy of Le Loyer is not certain. But one poem included in the *Recueil des oeuvres poetiques de Jean Passerat*, published by Claude Morel in 1606, answers particularly well to L'Estoile's description. It is simply entitled 'Les esprits qui reviennent':

> Tu te ris des esprits, qu'un autre craint et fuit,
> C'est monstrer que tu es de bien dure creance:
> Quelque Moine Bourré en fera la vengeance,
> Si jamais à Paris tu vas rauder de nuit.
> L'esprit sans corps (dis-tu) au corps vivant ne nuit:
> As-tu en ce seul poinct fondé ton asseurance?
> Veu qu'un corps sans esprit a bien tant de puissance
> Que d'aller, de se plaindre, et de faire du bruit.
> Contemple un amoureus: c'est un corps sans son ame:
> Toutesfois il chemine, et se plainct de sa dame
> Trop fiere en sa beauté, qui luy tient mille torts.
> Escoute d'autre-part tant de gens qui soustiennent
> Avoir veu et ouy les esprits qui reviennent,
> Tu orras sans esprit parler autant de corps.[82]

It is easy to see how L'Estoile might have been attracted to Passerat's 'sonnet gaillard'. Like Le Loyer's own preface, the sonnet opens with an address to the figure of the 'incrédule', and so begins as a defence of ghosts and apparitions. In the end, however, the final tercet stages an abrupt *volte-face* with respect to those who 'entremeslent en compagnie la matière des spectres'. Here the scene of narrative exchange is no longer Le Loyer's law court, nor even L'Estoile's private library. Ghost stories circulate here as idle Parisian chatter, 'les propos communs et familiers' that Le Loyer decried in his preface. In this way the poem serves as an ironic riposte both

---

[82] J. Passerat, *Recueil des oeuvres poetiques de Jean Passerat... augmenté de plus de la moitié, outre les precedentes impressions* (Paris: C. Morel, 1606), pp. 238–9: 'You laught at spirits that others fear and flee. That shows that you are not quick to believe. Some bogeyman will take revenge upon your incredulity, if ever you go wandering through Paris at night. Spirits without bodies, you say, cannot harm a living body: is that the only basis for your confidence, given that bodies without spirit are quite able to move around, groan, and make a racket? Consider a lovesick man: he's a body without its soul: but that does not stop him wandering about, complaining to his lady who, too proud in her beauty, does him many wrongs. Or listen to all those people who claimed to have seen and heard returning spirits: then you will hear so many bodies speaking without spirit ['esprit' = wit].'

to the 'fadaises' assembled on the subsequent pages and, by extension, to
the 'hommes de sçavoir' (or here, 'esprit') who rush to recommend the
treatise. The central pun turns on the idea that in speaking of 'esprits'
(ghosts), such figures show themselves to be lacking in 'esprit' (wit).
A little further on in the same entry (19 September 1608), L'Estoile
appears to increase the ironic distance that, with Passerat's help, the
journaliste had already begun to place between himself and Le Loyer's
treatise on spectres. Quoting a famous line from Terence, he remarks that
the *Discours des spectres* contains little more than 'nugae', or trifles:

> De moy, pour le regard du plus plaisant et curieux qui s'y peult remarquer,
> je diray tousjours avec l'autre: *Nae ille magno conatu magnas nugas dixerit.*
> (p. 373)[83]

Despite his scorn for Le Loyer's laborious attempts to establish the
'spectre' as an object of learning, something in L'Estoile has brought
him back to the *Discours des spectres*, so that perhaps he himself becomes
the butt of Passerat's sonnet. The key term in this passage is the word
'plaisant'. For nobody is better qualified than L'Estoile to speak of the
pleasure to be gained from the early modern 'spectre'. He too speaks, both
with his friend Chrestien and in the pages of his journal, of 'les esprits qui
reviennent', and does not try to hide his fascination for stories of ghosts
and other wonders. Indeed, L'Estoile remains perhaps the fullest and most
self-conscious example of a figure dominant throughout the texts considered in this chapter: that of the learned lay reader in whom the ghost
produces not—or not only—a theological dilemma but also, and more
simply, a taste for ghost stories.

---

[83] 'For my part, when it comes to the most amusing and curious things to be observed in
the book, I will always agree with he who said: *Nae ille magno conatu magnas nugas dixerit.*'
The Latin is taken from Terence's *Heautontimoroumenos*. L'Estoile may have remembered it
from the beginning of Montaigne's chapter, 'De l'utile et de l'honneste' (III.1). See
Montaigne, *Essais*, p. 790.

PART III

STORIES

5

The Show of Violence

Parts I and II of this book have sought to explain how ghosts became a recurring topic of late Renaissance vernacular writing in France, both as part of a religious debate about Purgatory and beyond that debate in a range of secular contexts. The object of Part III is to explore the extent to which certain developments within both these domains began to inflect other, more literary, treatments of ghosts and apparitions in the period. One topic around which these inflections became particularly visible is that of the body. This could involve both the problematic physicality of ghosts themselves, and the response—whether aggressive or desiring—that they produce in the bodies of those who see them. Chapter 6 will focus on the increasing number of stories that frame ghostly bodies as a site of sexual possibility. This chapter concentrates on violence towards ghosts.

The nature and constitution of ghostly bodies was a topic afforded ever-increasing importance in late sixteenth-century demonology. How, wondered a number of early modern writers, might it be possible to account for witches' confessions of sexual congress with demons? Were demons and their adepts able to reproduce?[1] The subject was also of interest to writers like Lavater and Taillepied who, while little concerned with the experiences of witches, were keen to regulate their readers' everyday experience of spirits. One prominent aspect of that regulation was the proscription of violence towards spirits.

A common point of reference for Renaissance discussion of this theme was the most prominent medieval theorist of ghostly corporeality, the eleventh-century Byzantine polymath, Michael Psellus. Psellus was the author of a highly influential dialogue on demons, the *Peri energeias daimonon dialogos*. Brought to prominence through its inclusion in Ficino's *Corpus Platonicorum*

---

[1] For instance, Remigius, *Daemonolatreiae*, Book One, Ch. 6; Du Pont, *La Philosophie des esprits*, sig. Ev^v; De Lancre, *Tableau de l'inconstance*, pp. 214–34; Valladier, *La Saincte Philosophie*, pp. 614–16; F. M. Guazzo, *Compendium maleficarum* [1698], trans. by E. A. Ashwin, ed. by M. Summers (New York: Dover, 1988), pp. 30–3.

at the end of the fifteenth century, the dialogue is frequently cited in French writing on ghosts at the close of the sixteenth. And yet the recourse to writers from older intellectual traditions entailed certain disadvantages, since the philosophical positions adopted were not necessarily consonant with the ideals of late-century pastoral demonology. Indeed, as the case of Psellus in particular shows, the vernacularization of ghosts in the period often constituted difficult, and far from ideologically innocent, intellectual appropriations. Taking the subject of ghostly bodies as its focus, the first section of this chapter tells the story of the changing reception of Psellus in late Renaissance France.

An alternative method of engaging with ghostly bodies was to place them at the centre of a narrative. This chapter contains a number of stories, occurring both inside and outside theoretical writing on ghosts, that feature what might be termed, in Shakespeare's phrase, a 'show of violence' against ghosts. Taken together, these appear to constitute something close to an archetypal scene of sixteenth-century ghost narrative. Following the introduction to Psellus and his reception in late Renaissance France, the rest of the chapter presents a close reading of two such moments, both drawn from well-known literary works of the period. The first takes us to the battles with spirits imagined and theorized by Panurge in Rabelais's *Tiers Livre*. Then, in the light of Rabelais's story, and of the grander narrative of changing attitudes to the ghostly encounter charted in the opening section, the last section examines a constellation of similar moments in Ronsard, centred around the poet's celebrated verse translation of Psellus, the 'Hymne des daimons'.

SUFFERING GHOSTS: PSELLUS AFTER TRENT

Towards the end of the first scene of *Hamlet*, Horatio and the watch attack the ghost of Hamlet's father. The cock has crowed; the shape has 'started like a guilty thing / Upon a fearful summons':[2]

HORATIO:	Stop it, Marcellus.
MARCELLUS:	Shall I strike at it with my partisan?
HORATIO:	Do if it will not stand.[3]

Marcellus, Horatio, and a third character, Barnardo, each try to land a blow. But all to no avail: the spirit vanishes away. The ghost's exit provides Shakespeare with the chance to stage a theatrical *tour de force* much

---

[2] *Hamlet*, i, i, 153–4.   [3] Ibid., 142–4.

enjoyed in the period. As the watchmen pursue the figure, it fades and reappears in different corners of the stage:[4]

BARNARDO: 'Tis here.
HORATIO: 'Tis here. [Exit Ghost.]
MARCELLUS: 'Tis gone.[5]

Chastened by their failure, Marcellus muses:

> We do it wrong, being so majestical,
> To offer it the show of violence,
> For it is as the air, invulnerable,
> And our vain blows malicious mockery.[6]

The threefold attempt to strike, or more often embrace, an apparition is a commonplace of Renaissance poetry inherited from epic.[7] But the moment of contrition ('we do it wrong') expressed by Marcellus is new. It is motivated by two factors in particular. First of all it arises from the ghost's 'majestical' bearing. This reminder that, in death as in life, the figure of the king should lie beyond violence, at once prepares and worsens the dreadful revelation of his brother's regicide. Marcellus's subsequent talk of 'vain blows' and 'malicious mockery' (i.e. only a mockery of malice) springs from a second, demonological, objection. Shakespeare's guardsman is here summing up a conviction, increasingly entrenched towards the end of the sixteenth century, as to the fundamental invulnerability of ghosts to physical aggression. We saw briefly in the previous chapter how, for all the differences between Protestant and Catholic devotional responses, Lavater and Taillepied were as one in their proscription of violence towards ghosts. Marcellus, who may or may not be a reader of pastoral demonology, here repeats their standard lesson.

So why then does Horatio—'a scholar'—initially approve the guardsman's rash suggestion? He is not merely caught up, as we suspect Marcellus may be, in the heat of the moment. What is more likely is that Horatio has in mind a different, and much older, learned tradition. A certain strain of Neoplatonist philosophy held that ghosts were corporeal in nature and that, far from 'invulnerable', apparitions often fled when faced with swords and other weapons. The most developed theorization of

---

[4] For an early modern guide to the mechanics of this trick, see N. Sabbatini, *Pratique pour fabriquer scènes et machines de théâtre*, trans. by M. Canavaggia, R. Canavaggia, and L. Jouvet (Neuchâtel, 1942), ch. 56 ('Comment faire paraître et disparaître avec prestesse une ombre ou fantôme en divers endroits du plancher de la scène').
[5] *Hamlet*, I, i, 144–6.
[6] *Hamlet*, I, i, 147–51.
[7] On the same motif in Ronsard's 'Elegie à Louis des Masures', see Introduction, p. 12.

this position available to the period was the *Peri energeias daimonon dialogos*, originally composed in Greek by the medieval Byzantine chronicler, poet, and philosopher, Michael Psellus.[8] Thanks to Ficino's Latin paraphrase of 1497, Psellus's treatise on demons was well known throughout the Europe of the early sixteenth century.[9] Reprinted on numerous occasions, Ficino's Psellus, entitled *De daemonibus*, circulated alongside his translations of a number of earlier Platonizing philosophers, including Iamblichus, Proclus, Porphyry, and Synesius. As we shall see, the latter half of the sixteenth century saw a gradual disintegration of this Neoplatonic anthology, and Psellus begin to emerge as a figure in his own right. In the middle years of the century, however, it was as part of the Ficinian corpus that the two authors considered later in this chapter, Rabelais and Ronsard, came to know his work.

Ficino's selective résumé opens with Psellus's contention that 'daemones propria cum corporibus praesentia sibi apparuisse' (sig. Ni^r), and that if Scripture appears, conversely, to insist on the incorporeality of spirits, it is only because demonic bodies are of a different, more subtle, order than our own. Ficino then proceeds to explain Psellus's famous, and often-repeated, division of spirits into six categories. Five of these are organized hierarchically according to habitat: ethereal, aerial, terrestrial, aquatic, subterranean. The sixth type, the 'lucifugus' (i.e. 'light-fleeing'), is the basest demon of them all, and most closely resembles, in its hatred of God and men, the devils as imagined by the Christian Church. In a later section entitled 'Cur daemones timeant minas' (sig. Nv^r), Psellus/Ficino explains that all demons, however, are susceptible to pain ('patiuntur'), and therefore likely to flee threats of physical aggression.

Psellus was by no means the first to argue that demons possessed bodies capable of feeling pain.[10] Nor was he alone in promoting the apotropaic virtues of swords and other weapons.[11] In the Judeo-Christian tradition, the glint of iron weapons was often considered to be a reflection of God's light. According to Rabelais, one basis for this notion was God's decision, at Genesis 3:24, to place a flaming sword at Eden's Eastern Gate: fearful of

---

[8] For the only detailed studies of this work, and of Psellus's demonology more generally, see C. Zervos, *Un philosophe néoplatonicien du XIe siècle: Michel Psellos, sa vie, son oeuvre, ses luttes philosophiques* (Paris: E. Leroux, 1920); K. Svoboda, *La Démonologie de Michel Psellos* (Brno: Vydává filosofická fakulta, 1927).

[9] Psellus's *De Daemonibus* is contained in Iamblichus et al., *De Mysteriis Aegyptiorum, Chaldaeorum, Assyriorum* etc., trans. and ed. by M. Ficino (Venice: A. Manutio, 1497). References are to this edition and are incorporated into the text.

[10] On Psellus's precedents, see Svoboda, *Démonologie de Michel Psellos*, pp. 25–6.

[11] See ibid., pp. 41–2.

this weapon, 'les Diables n'entrent jamais en paradis terrestre'.[12] The use
of physical violence against ghosts and apparitions is also a topic of pagan
history and epic. Plutarch tells the well-known story of a Spartan soldier
who, brandishing a spear, chased a ghost down the street crying 'Come
back, or you shall die a second time!'[13] The motif appears in Homer's
Odyssey. There Circe instructs Odysseus, poised on the threshold of
Hades, to use his sword to ward off the shades of the dead.[14] And Circe's
words were reprised more famously still by Virgil's Cumean sybil. As
Aeneas embarks on his journey into the underworld, she advises, 'Vagina
[que] eripe ferrum' ('Unsheath your sword').[15]

None of these parallels is made explicit in Psellus; it was left to his early
sixteenth-century humanist readers to locate the classical precedents.
Caelius Rhodiginus, in his *Lectionum antiquarum libri xxx*, was among
the first to connect the Psellian thesis with the words of the Cumean
sybil.[16] Cornelius Agrippa echoes Rhodiginus in his *De occulta philosophia*
of 1531. The chapter entitled 'De corporibus daemonum' reviews the
opinions of Augustine, Saint Basil, Aquinas, Gregory Nazianzen, and
Apuleius on the nature and constitution of spiritual bodies. But it is
'Psellus platonicus et christianus' who is given pride of place:

> Licet spirituale corpus sit, maxime tamen sensibile est et tactum patitur; et
> licet resectum, coit rursum recreatque sicut aër et aqua, interim tamen
> maxime dolet: hinc timent aciem ferri et tela et enses. Hinc apud Vergilium
> Sibylla ait Aeneae:
>
> Tuque invade viam vaginaque eripe ferrum.[17]

Rhodiginus and Agrippa, enthusiastic supporters of Florentine Neoplatonism, both illustrate the degree of prestige accorded to the early, Ficinian,
Psellus. In so doing, they also granted intellectual credibility to the
tradition of showing violence to ghosts that he can be said to represent.

---

[12] F. Rabelais, *Le Tiers Livre*, ed. by J. Céard (Paris: Livre de Poche, 1995), ch. 23,
ll. 119–23. For more on this episode, see 2.2.
[13] Cited, for instance, in Le Loyer, *Discours et histoires des spectres*, p. 827.
[14] Homer, *The Odyssey*, trans. by A. T. Murray, Loeb Classical Library (Cambridge,
MA: Harvard University Press, 1975), x, ll. 535–7.
[15] *Aeneid* vi, p. 260 in Virgil, *Works*, trans. by H. Rushton Fairclough, Loeb Classical
Library, 2 vols. (London: Heinemann, 1950).
[16] Basel: A. and A. Froben, 1566; first edn. 1516, p. 43.
[17] Agrippa, *De occulta philosophia*, pp. 457–8: 'Although it is a spiritual body, it is
extremely sensitive and suffers when touched. And if it is severed, it is reunited in the
manner of air or water, though during that moment afflicted with the greatest pain. For this
reason they [spirits] fear swords and other weapons. That is why Virgil's sibyl tells Aeneas:
Go on your way and unsheath your sword.'

Towards the end of the sixteenth century, Psellus's French readers begin to take a very different view. In 1576–7 the Parisian publisher Guillaume Chaudière brought out a French and Latin translation of the *Peri energeias daimonon dialogos*.[18] Translated by Pierre Moreau, both were prefaced with a lengthy introduction by the Franciscan friar and polemicist, François Feu-Ardent. Moreau's Psellus, unlike Ficino's abridged selections, returns to the dialogic form of the original Greek text. Two characters appear: the inexpert 'Timothée', who asks the questions, and his more authoritative friend, 'Le Capitaine'. The captain himself often invokes an absent third figure, 'Frère Marc', to whose learned opinion he usually defers.

Towards the end of their interview Timothée asks the captain whether demons feel the pain of hellfire. If so, is it therefore possible to strike or wound demonic bodies, or threaten them with violence? The captain replies that it is. He reminds Timothée of an earlier point in their discussion where he had explained that, in addition to the angels and higher demons, there exists a class of more terrestrial spirits that are both 'materiels et patibles' (sig. 18ᵛ). As a result, he goes on, 'on les peult frapper jusqu'à leur faire grand' douleur, si on les atteint vivement en la peau' (sig. 49ᵛ). It is true that, on being struck in this way, the demonic body reform 'comme font les parcelles de l'air, ou de l'eau, qui auroient ahurté à quelque corps solide' (fols. 50ʳ⁻ᵛ). But while this occurs at incredible speed, 'si est ce qu'il endure grand douleur au mesme instant qu'on luy baille taloche, et pour ceste cause craint il fort les pointes de cousteaux, espees, et autres ferrements' (sig. 50ᵛ). Knowing this, those who wish to rid themselves of spirits thrust knives or swords up towards them, 'là part où ne veulent qu'ils approchent' (sig. 50ᵛ).

Feu-Ardent's prologemenon to the dialogue finds much to recommend in Psellus, often praising him as a scourge of heresy.[19] But he is also at pains to iron out some of the Byzantine's more heterodox edges. One of the more conspicuous alterations made to Ficino's version appears in the French (though not, interestingly, the Latin) title, where the translator has

---

[18] M. Psellus, *Traicté par dialogue de l'energie ou operation des diables... avec les chapitres xxxiii et xxxv du quatriesme livre du Tresor de la foy catholique du venerable Nicetas de Colosses*, trans. by P. Moreau and ed. by F. Feu-Ardent (Paris: G. Chaudière, 1576). For an early twentieth-century edition of Moreau's French translation, minus the preface, see E. Renauld, 'Une traduction française du *Peri energeias daimonon dialogues* de Michel Psellos', *Revue des études grecques*, 151 (1920), pp. 56–95. All references are to Chaudière's original edition and are incorporated into the text. M. Psellus, *Dialogus de energia, seu operatione daemonum*, trans. by P. Moreau and ed. by F. Feu-Ardent (Paris: G. Chaudière, 1577).
[19] Psellus was engaged in the suppression of the Euchite heresy. See Svoboda, *Démonologie de Michel Psellos*, p. 57.

replaced the Neoplatonic 'daemones' with the more orthodox Christian 'diables'. The change reflects the growing intolerance of Neoplatonist spiritual vocabulary in the Counter-Reformation where, against the syncretistic grain of earlier Christian humanism, we see increasing concern to restate Augustine's classic condemnation of pagan superstition in Books VI–VIII of *De civitate dei*.[20] Another concerns Psellus's attachment to the idea of ghostly bodies. Feu-Ardent rejects the long philosophical traditions—both Aristotelian and, in particular, Platonic—in which demons are thought to be possessed of a material form. As a consequence, he adds, 'ce qu'escrit Psellus est digne de grande admiration, disant les Demons craindre les tranchans des espees' (sig. evi[r]). Spirits, he claims, cannot be 'combatus ou empoignez, ny vraiment picquez, blessez par les pointes des haches, ny bruslez par les ardeurs des flambes' (sig. Ii[v]). The important word here is 'vraiment'. What distinguishes the 'diables' of the French text from Ficinian 'daemones' is the penchant of the former for illusion and deceit. Although devils do not in fact experience bodily sensation, Feu-Ardent explains, they are able to 'malicieusement simuler et ... faindre toutes les choses que dessus' (sig. Ii[v]). Psellus is here shown to have been duped by an illusion. Whereas he had claimed that spirits suffer genuine pain on being struck by material weapons, Feu-Ardent is led to a more sinister conclusion: 'toute la douleur', he writes, 'en est au visaige' (ibid.).

Feu-Ardent's repackaging of Psellus is entirely in keeping with a late-century theological orthodoxy, operative on both sides of the sectarian divide, that steadfastly disembodied the early modern ghost. Whether based on the corporeal revenants of popular folklore or on the Neoplatonic *daemones*, belief in embodied spirits found itself firmly situated on the side of pagan superstition. Sébastien Michaëlis devotes an entire chapter in his *Pneumalogie ou discours des esprits* to the question of whether 'les esprits ont corps'.[21] Writing against Psellus, Michaëlis invokes a powerful intellectual basis for the new orthodoxy of spiritual disembodiment, namely Luke's account of the risen Christ's appearance to the disciples in the locked room.[22] Awestruck by their master's sudden presence in their midst, the eleven suppose the figure before them to be the apparition of a spirit. Michaëlis remarks that Christ's rebuke to his followers ('handle me and see; for a spirit hath not flesh and bones as ye see me have') set

---

[20] See for instance René Du Pont's disapproval of the Neoplatonic formula 'bon demon', a contradiction in terms in Christian theology; *La Philosophie des esprits*, sigs. Cciii[r–v]. For a more developed diabolization of the Neoplatonic *daemones*, see Gravelle, *Abbregé de philosophie*, sigs. 321[v]–2[r].

[21] *Pneumalogie*, ch. 2.

[22] On exegetical discussion of this episode, see above, pp. 51–7.

ghosts and bodies in an intractable antithesis.[23] And yet such theories of
ghostly incorporeality nonetheless raised a difficult problem: if spirits by
their nature lack any kind of body, how do they become available to
sensory perception?

This paradox had been identified in earlier periods, and the terms of late
Renaissance discussion often remain those of Bonaventure, of Dionysius
the Pseudo-Areopagite, of Peter Lombard's *Sententiae*, and, especially, of
Thomas Aquinas.[24] As the age of the witch craze developed, however, the
question is shot through with new urgency. Many trials featured reports of
intercourse with demons; Pierre de Lancre, among others, gives graphic
details of the pain suffered by witches in their couplings at the sabbath.[25]
The problem did not only concern touch, but all the senses. Martin Delrio
asks of demons, for instance, 'comment peut le demon se monstrer
visiblement aux yeux corporels, veu qu'il est incorporel?'[26] The same
question arises in respect to apparitions of the dead. In the *Dies caniculares*
of the Italian theologian Simon Maiolus, translated into French by François de Rosset in 1609, one character, a philosopher, wonders out loud:

> Seroit-il bien possible, que les corps des trespassez, desja reduits en poudre,
> peussent se representer sans resurrection? Les seules ames, puis qu'elles sont
> incorporelles, ne sçauroient rendre par quelque couleur, leurs faces visibles.[27]

Michaëlis himself observes that, being corporeal ourselves, we can only
apprehend a spirit—or a spirit can only represent itself ('se representer')
to us—through its material effects.

> Il nous est impossible de les [les esprits] voir et comprendre si ce n'est par les
> effects seulement, comme on cognoist par la vestige du pied laissé sur le
> sablon qu'un homme est passé sans pouvoir pourtant imaginer de la vertu,
> science, force, beauté, ou couleur d'iceluy.[28]

---

[23] Luke 24:39.
[24] For the most detailed conspectus of the relevant authorities, see Maldonat, *Traicté
des anges et demons*, sigs. 19ʳ–29ʳ.
[25] De Lancre, *Tableau de l'inconstance*, pp. 214–34.
[26] Delrio, *Les Controverses magiques*, sig. Tviiiʳ.
[27] S. Maiolus, *Les Jours caniculaires, c'est à dire vingt et trois excellents discours des choses
natureles et surnaturels*, trans. by F. de Rosset (Paris: R. Foüet, 1609), p. 76: 'Could it really
be that the bodies of the dead, already reduced to dust, have it in their power to represent
themselves without resurrection? Souls alone, since they are incorporeal, have no colour to
render their face visible.' A similar point is made in Valladier, *La Saincte Philosophie*, p. 678.
[28] *Pneumalogie*, sig. 11ʳ: 'It is impossible for us to see and understand them [spirits]
unless by their effects alone, just as we know from a footprint in the sand that a man has
passed by, without for all that being able to picture his virtue, learning, strength, beauty, or
colour.'

The corporeal effects of the ghostly encounter obscure, by dint of their very immediacy, the disembodied nature of ghosts and apparitions. Michaëlis further explains that examples of such material traces can be found in Scripture itself. Writing of the spirits of the Old Testament, he cites the stories of Abraham, 'qui leur lava les pieds'; of Lot, whom they threw to the ground; and of Jacob, who 'luicta toute une matinée avec eux'.[29] The resolution of the paradox of spiritual incorporeality is usually invoked with reference to a passage from Tertullian's *Liber de carne christi*. According to Tertullian, ghosts do not have bodies; they borrow them. This is the theory of the *corpus peregrinum*, which Michaëlis explains as follows:

> Il est vray qu'ils [les esprits] apportent un corps autrement ils ne pourroient estre veuz, car ils sont (comme dit Saint Paul) invisibles, ce pendant il ne faut pourtant nier la saincte escriture laquelle nous enseigne clairement qu'ils n'ont point de corps. Pourquoy il faut dire avec Tertulien, *Habere corpora sed peregrina non sua*. Ce sont corps, dit-il, empruntez et non pas de leur propre nature.[30]

The type of body borrowed depends, according to most, on the nature of the spirit. Demons can take up and manipulate corpses and sustain the illusion, at least for a time, that the body is alive.[31] By contrast dead souls, like angels, are thought to avoid the filth of putrefaction, and prefer to take on bodies of air and thicker vapours. Henri Boguet, employing a commonplace analogy, explains in his *Discours des sorciers* that since the watery vapours that form clouds often look to us like human shapes, or beasts, why should it be thought strange that spirits can do the same?[32] Bodies formed in this way could be touched as well as seen. Glossing a passage in Caeitanus, Le Loyer explains:

> Et vrayement que les demons se forment leurs corps des vapeurs terrestres par la froideur de l'air il appert par l'attouchement d'iceux corps qui sont froids desmesurément, et neantmoins mollissent et cedent sous la main, comme feroit du cotton ou une boulle de neige pressée sous la main de l'enfant.[33]

---

[29] *Pneumalogie*, sig. 20ʳ. These examples, derived from Tertullian, are commonplaces of sixteenth-century demonology: see also Feu-Ardent's preface in Psellus, *De l'Energie ou operation des diables*, sig. eviiiᵛ; Boguet, *Discours des sorciers*, p. 34.

[30] *Pneumalogie*, sig. 20ʳ: 'It is true that spirits carry a body: otherwise they could not be seen, since they are (as Saint Paul tells us) invisible. Nonetheless, we cannot for that reason deny holy scripture which teaches us quite clearly that spirits have no bodies. For this reason we should follow Tertullian in saying *Habere corpora sed peregrina non sua*. These are borrowed bodies and not of their own nature.'.

[31] On the demonic manipulation of corpses, see pp. 216–34.

[32] Boguet, *Discours des sorciers*, p. 33.

[33] Le Loyer, *Quatre livres des spectres*, i, p. 417: 'And truly that demons create their bodies from earthy vapours in the cold air it is clear from touching those bodies, which are

For all the picturesqueness of the closing simile, a snowball compressed in the hand of a small child, the experiential field from which it is derived is considerably more sinister. The vaporous constitution of ghostly bodies explains the many reports, heard in witches' confessions, that the semen of Satan felt colder than ice.[34]

The notion of the *corpus peregrinum*, invoked against Psellus in a number of demonological texts of the late sixteenth and early seventeenth century, thus placed a kind of ontological asymmetry at the heart of the ghostly encounter. While the ghost was able, by taking on a borrowed body, to make itself available to the body of the witness, the body of the witness could not be forced back upon the figure of the ghost. It is with reference to precisely that disjunction that, in the chapter entitled 'Il ne faut pas entreprendre de chasser les esprits et fantosmes, par iuremens, blasphemes ou armes corporelles' (Book Three, ch. 11), Lavater describes the futility of violence towards ghosts:

> C'est bien une chose à louer de ne s'espouvanter point: mais aussi il ne faut pas passer mesure ni estre outrecuidé. Aucuns, cuidant frapper quelque fantosme, ont pensé proprement toucher un coussin bien mol: les autres pensans le jetter par les fenestres, avoyent cest avis que c'estoyent des buschettes qui tomboyent en un buisson... En tel affaire il n'y a rien à gagner avec l'espee charnelle, mais avec la spirituelle. Ceux qui entreprennent de frapper ces esprits, battent l'air.[35]

Moving across the sectarian divide, a similar passage appears in Taillepied's *Psichologie*. Derivative as ever, Taillepied repeats Lavater's warning against cursing, blaspheming, and physical violence, adding a brief exemplary tale, taken from his own experience as an itinerant preacher:

> Il y en a d'autres qui desgainent l'espee s'ils voyent quelque fantosme, et vont à l'encontre, où taschent de le faire sauter par la fenestre, comme en l'an mil cinq cens soixante et quatorze advint en la ville de Lyon sur le Rhosne, qu'un soldat de la citadelle, cartier de son estat, se leva de nuict par plusieurs fois pour chasser l'esprit qui empeschoit sa maison par tintamarre, et le faisoit

---

extremely cold and yet soften and yield in the hand, as would cotton or a snowball pressed in a child's hand.'

[34] See for instance Remigius, *Daemonolatreiae*, Book One, ch. 6.

[35] Lavater, *Des apparitions*, pp. 227–8: 'Surely it is praise worthy when a man meting with a spirite is not afrayde, but yet boldnesse and rashnesse can not be commended... There have bin some who when they would have striken a Spirit with their sword, have thought they have striken the fetherbed, the Divel so mocked them. Others supposing they had throwen a spirit out of the window, by and by thought they heard shingles falling and ratling amongst the trees... We must not use a materiall sword against spirits and vayne shewes (for it profyteth nothing) but must use the sword of the Spirit.' (*Of Ghostes*, p. 215).

cesser de tarabuster, en le chassant de son espee. Toutesfois il falut à la fin user d'autre moyen, comme luy mesme me dit estant chez luy pour lors.[36]

This short story stages a characteristic intervention on the part of the priest, whose appearance serves, as in so many of Taillepied's narratives, to confirm the moral of the tale: that physical aggression must yield to an 'autre moyen'. That 'moyen' may be the Protestant practice of withdrawal and introspection or, as it was for Taillepied, Catholic recourse to the 'remedes de l'Eglise'. Either way, it is only once the lay reader has suppressed his instinctive 'show of violence' that he can reshape his body into postures of devotion. To this extent the late-century correction of the Psellian position in Feu-Ardent and Moreau, coupled with the increasingly vehement insistence on the notion of *corpus peregrinum*, is entirely complicit with the ideals of pastoral demonology.

This grander historical narrative of correction or revision is lent vivid local realization not only in Taillepied's story, in the figure of the penitent soldier, but also (to return to the introduction to this chapter) in the shape of Shakespeare's Marcellus:

> We do it wrong, being so majestical,
> To offer it the show of violence,
> For it is as the air, invulnerable,
> And our vain blows malicious mockery.

It is unlikely that Shakespeare was conscious of the shift in readings of the *Peri energeias daimonon dialogos*, even if we are tempted to hear in 'Marcellus' the combinative echo of its hero and its author ('Mark-Psellus'). That Shakespeare had read Lavater's *Of Ghostes and Spirits Walking by Nyght* is more probable, and the soldier's gesture of self-correction is certainly an indication that some early modern readers had begun to internalize the lessons of pastoral demonology. Similar 'shows of violence', followed by a gesture of revision, reform, or correction, are also present in two celebrated mid sixteenth-century French narratives: Rabelais's *Tiers Livre* and a long passage included towards the end of Ronsard's philosophical poem, the 'Hymne des daimons'.

---

[36] Taillepied, *Psichologie*, p. 297: 'There are others who unsheath their swords if they see some ghost, and go after it, or try to throw it out of the window, as happened in the year 1574 in Lyon on the Rhône, when a soldier of the citadel, a maker of playing cards by profession, got up several times in the night to chase away the spirit who was keeping the house awake with its racket, and made it stop its din, by pursuing it with his sword. However, in the end other means were needed, as he himself told me, who was staying with him at the time.'

'LE ULEMENT DES DIABLES': PANURGE THE DIABOLIST

The place of Psellus in the *Tiers livre* provides a striking example of how Rabelais is able to take a bewilderingly complex intellectual tradition— here involving the embodiedness of spirits—and mobilize its tensions to his own narrative ends. Here the Psellian thesis of demonic corporeality highlights a crucial distinction not only within the *Tiers livre* but within Rabelais's work as a whole: that between the spiritual and fallen demonologies of Pantagruel and Panurge.

Alban Krailsheimer observed long ago that the construction of Rabelais's demonology is essentially dialogic, adopting the form of a fragmented conversation between Pantagruel on the one hand and Panurge on the other.[37] That conversation ebbs and flows throughout the course of Rabelais's chronicles, but reaches a new level of intensity in the *Tiers Livre*, especially when Pantagruel recommends to his friend—anxious to know whether he should take a wife—that he should consult the dying poet, Raminagrobis.[38]

Before Panurge and his companions set out to meet the old man, the giant makes a speech on divination by the dying. The intellectual flavour of Pantagruel's speech is broadly Neoplatonic.[39] He tells how great men are visited by visions when they die, and privileged with secrets of the future. These are the numinous *daemones* of Ficino and his followers: intermediary, and theologically neutral, beings who translate between the realms of the human and divine. Following brief references to Aristophanes, the Apolline fury, and the prestigious motif of the 'cygnea

---

[37] On Rabelais's demonology in general, see P. Imbs, 'Le Diable dans l'oeuvre de Rabelais' in *Mélanges de linguistique française offerts à M. Charles Bruneau, professeur à la Sorbonne*, Société de publications romanes et françaises, 45 (Geneva: Droz, 1954), pp. 241–61; A. J. Krailsheimer, *Rabelais and the Franciscans* (Oxford: Clarendon Press, 1963), pp. 107–24; S. M. Gauna, '*De Genio Pantagruelis*: An Examination of Rabelaisian Demonology', *Bibliothèque d'Humanisme et Renaissance*, 33 (1971), pp. 557–70; R. C. La Charité, 'Devildom and Rabelais's *Pantagruel*', *The French Review*, 49 (1975), pp. 42–50; Céard, *La Nature et les prodiges*, pp. 87–158; Desrosiers-Bonin, *Rabelais et l'humanisme civil*, pp. 169–212.

[38] *Tiers Livre*, XXIII. On the Raminagrobis episode in general, see P. Sharratt, 'Rabelais, Ramus et Raminagrobis', *Revue d'Histoire Littéraire de la France*, 82 (1982), pp. 263–9; C. Raffini, 'Rabelais, Raminagrobis, and the Problem of Censorship, *Tiers Livre*, 21–23', *Romance Notes*, 36 (1996), pp. 35–46; E. M. Duval, *The Design of Rabelais's 'Tiers Livre de Pantagruel'* (Geneva: Droz, 1997), pp. 107–9.

[39] On Rabelais and Platonic influences, see G. Mallary Masters, *Rabelaisian Dialectic and the Platonic-Hermetic Tradition* (Albany: State University of New York Press, 1969), ch. 1 ('Rabelais Platonicus'); A. H. T. Levi, 'Rabelais and Ficino', in *Rabelais in Glasgow*, ed. by J. A. Coleman and C. M. Scollen-Jimack (Glasgow: Glasgow University, 1984), pp. 71–85.

cantio', or dying swan whose song prophesies the future, he calls upon the notion (common to both Platonic and more orthodox Christian thought) of the soul's exile in the body (xxi, ll. 1–16). In a well-known Ficinian conceit, he tells of the ship which, nearing its journey's end, finally approaches the peaceful welcome of the harbour. Just as those waiting on the shore stand and watch in silence while the ship is still far away, and begin to cry out as it finally draws near:

> Aussi les Anges, les Heroes, les bons Daemons (scelon la doctrine des Platonicques) voyans les humains prochains de mort . . . les saluent, les consolent parlent avecques eulx, et ja commencent leurs communiquer art de divination (xxi, ll. 29–36).[40]

Later on, once the friends arrive at the house, Raminagrobis will represent himself in similar terms: 'contemplant, et voyant et ja touchant et goustant le bien et félicité, que le bon Dieu a praeparé à ses fideles et esleuz en l'aultre vie et estat de immortalité' (xxi, ll. 106–08).[41] For all the episode's farcical or satirical elements, the evangelical tenor, and high seriousness, of Pantagruel's earlier speech is prolonged and confirmed in the poet's ecstatic vision.[42]

Terence Cave has pointed out how, as much as it owes to the topoi of Ficinian syncretism, Pantagruel's speech on the art of divination by the dying is not merely the expression of a fashionable philosophy. What emerges from under those topoi, investing them with unusual emotional force, is a personal catastrophe suffered by the author himself: the death of his patron, Guillaume du Bellay:

> Seulement vous veulx ramentevoir le docte et preux chevallier Guillaume du Bellay, seigneur jadis de Langey, lequel on mont de Tarare mourut le 10. de Janvier l'an de son aage le climatere et de nostre supputation l'an 1543 en compte Romanicque. Les troys et quatre heures avant son decès il employa en parolles vigoureuses, en sens tranquil et serain: nous praedisant ce que depuys part avons veu, part attendons advenir. Combien que pour lors nous semblassent ces propheties aulcunement abhorrentes et estranges, par ne nous apparoistre cause ne signe aulcun praesent pronostic de ce qu'il praedisoit.[43] (xxi, ll. 42–53)

---

[40] 'So the angels, heroes, and good demons (according to the doctrine of the Platonists) seeing humans close to death . . . greet them, console them, talk with them, and already begin to pass on to them the art of divination.' (*Complete Works*, p. 317).

[41] 'As I contemplated and saw, and already touched and tasted, the bliss and felicity that the good God has prepared for His faithful and elect in the other life and the state of immortality.' (*Complete Works*, p. 319).

[42] On the episode as a satire of Ramus, see Sharratt, 'Rabelais, Ramus et Raminagrobis'; on Raminagrobis as a farcical figure, see Duval, *Design of Rabelais's 'Tiers Livre'*, p. 102.

[43] 'I want only to recall to your memory the learned and valiant knight Guillaume du Bellay, formerly Lord of Langey, who died on Mount Tarare on the tenth of January, in the

According to Cave, in this account of the death of Rabelais's protector, and in the more developed retelling of the same episode midway through the *Quart Livre*, Du Bellay stands at the centre of what might be termed a 'démonologie à la première personne'.[44] As Pantagruel's 'nous' here attests, these are acts of personal remembrance. The event is hallowed with the date, the time and, in the *Quart Livre*, even a list of those present including—exceptionally—Rabelais's own name. Such is the intensity of the author's experience that it not only intrudes upon, but even over-shadows, the intellectual context in which it is framed. Pantagrueline demonology here appears less the articulation of a philosophical common-place, than the trace of past trauma. It is a therapeutic method of exorciz-ing grief.

Pantagruel's speech on divination by the dying is counterpoised with another demonological disquisition, this time from Panurge, shortly after he has left the dying poet's home.[45] In this way the encounter with Raminagrobis forms a kind of fulcrum, with the demonological dialogue between the two friends balanced on each side. In Panurge's speech, too, the inspiration is Neoplatonic and owes much, like Pantagruel's vision, to Ficino or (to be more precise) to Ficino's translation of Psellus. And yet, as we shall see, what Panurge imagines to inhabit the old man's home could hardly stand further from Pantagruel's idealizing visions. Panurge is convinced that Raminagrobis faces damnation for having, earlier that afternoon, chased off a party of monks who had come to perform the last rites. In a parody of the Catholic ideals of good works and repentance, he recommends that the party return to his side where, he suggests, 'nous le induirons à contrition de son peché' (xxiii, l. 5). However, suddenly fearful that 'la chambre est desja pleine de Diables', he changes his mind (xxiii, ll. 19–21). Having heard Panurge expound the dangers that await them, Frère Jean offers a note of reassurance. There is no need to worry, he says, since he himself will accompany Panurge with his 'bragmard on poing' (xxiii, ll. 99–101). The monk's remark prompts Panurge to embark on another extended speech in which, he claims, 'les Diables

---

climacteric year of his life, and by our count in Roman reckoning the year 1543. The three or four hours before his death, tranquil and serene in sense, he employed in vigorous words predicting for us what we have in part seen, in part are awaiting as coming; although for that time these prophecies seemed to us somewhat preposterous and strange, because at the time there appeared to us no sign heralding what he was predicting.' (*Complete Works*, p. 318).

[44] F. Rabelais, *Le Quart Livre* [1548–52], ed. by G. Defaux (Paris: Livre de Poche, 1994), ch. 27. On this episode, see Cave, *Pré-histoires*, pp. 87–93.

[45] *Tiers Livre*, ch. 23: 'Comment Panurge faict discours pour retourner à Raminagrobis'.

craignent la splendeur des espees aussi bien que la lueur du Soleil' (xxiii, ll. 102–59).

Panurge's speech to Frère Jean turns out to be a theme and variations on the Psellian thesis of ghostly bodies, and on the influential glosses in Rhodiginus and Agrippa.[46] He recalls the classic examples of Hercules and Aeneas wielding their swords in the underworld, as well as a more recent military hero, 'Jan-Jacques Trivolse'—an old soldier who died 'l'espee nue on point' while fending away the demons lying in wait for his soul (xxiii, ll. 113–19). In a comic exaggeration of the same idea, Panurge then urges Frère Jean to consider the sounds of early modern battle, where demons in attendance have been known to suffer what, in the euphemistic parlance of modern warfare, we might call 'collateral damage':

Quand tu voyds le hourt de deux armées, pense tu Couillasse, que le bruyt si grand et horrible que l'on y oyt, proviene des voix humaines, du hurtis des harnois? du clicquetis des bardes? du chaplis des masses? du froissis des picques? du bris des lances? du cris des navrez? du son des tabours et trompettes? du hannissement des chevaulx? du tonnoire des escoupettes et canons? Il en est veritablement quelque chose, force est que le confesse. Mais le grand effroy, et vacarme principal provient du deuil et ulement des Diables: que là, guestans pelle melle les paouvres ames des blessez, reçoivent coups d'espée à l'improviste.[47] (xxiii, ll. 131–42)

Panurge's description of battle is itself an unruly mêlée, with its abrupt shifts in focus from the infantry to the cavalry, from the drummers to the artillery. What connects these things is a noise conveyed not only in the clamour of the battle itself, but also the phonetic insistence of Panurge's own speech. As he accumulates the 'hurt*is* des harnois', 'clicquet*is* des bardes', 'chapl*is* des masses', 'froiss*is* des *pi*cques', 'br*is* des lances', and 'cr*is* des navrez', the vocalic phoneme [i]—the 'ulement des Diables'—begins to sound above the fray. In the end Panurge nearly convinces himself (Frère Jean needs no convincing) to return to the 'logis poëtique'. But noting, with an obvious measure of *double entendre*, that Frère Jean's

---

[46] For a brief study of Panurge's speech in lines 102–59, see D. Desrosiers-Bonin, *Rabelais et l'humanisme civil* (Geneva: Droz, 1992), p. 211.

[47] 'When you see the clash of two armies, do you think, billyballock, that such a great horrible noise as you hear comes from human voices? from the crashing of harnesses? from the clatter of horse armour? from the banging of maces? from the clanging of pikes? from the shattering of lances? from the screaming of the wounded? from the sound of drums and trumpets? from the neighing of the horses? from the thunder of pistols and cannons? True, there is some of that, I must confess. But the great turmoil and principal racket comes from the anguish and ululation of the devils, who, lying there pell-mell in wait for the poor souls of the wounded, unexpectedly receive sword-strokes.' (*Complete Works*, p. 325).

'bragmard' has grown rusty, and so useless 'par faulte de operer' (xxiii, ll. 150–8), Panurge reasserts his initial reticence. 'Le Diable m'emporte si je y voys' (xxiii, l. 159), he concludes, and the friends continue on their way.

Relative to Pantagruel's exalted demonology—the intellectual tradition to which it belongs, its privileged *topoi*, its figures of authority, and its roots in personal experience—the Panurgian version, or what he calls his 'diabolologie', is cast in the role of debased or fallen Other. Indeed, the notion of the Fall is central to Panurge's conception of the spirit-world. Scattered among the many weapons that Panurge brings to bear in his argument from Psellus (the 'lances' and 'picques' of his imaginary battle, the swords of Aeneas and Hercules, Frère Jean's 'bragmard') can be found the 'espee flambante' that God, after the Fall, placed at Eden's Eastern Gate. According to the 'Massorethz et Caballistes', Panurge explains, that sword excludes both Man and the demons from the terrestrial paradise (xxiii, ll. 119–23). While Pantagruel's Platonic schema can still envision, through the *daemones*, a communion with God under certain privileged conditions, for Panurge the worlds of man and God remain unbridgeably asunder. That remoteness is expressed through a number of parallel contrasts, both internal to Rabelais's chronicles and, generated by them, in adjacent intertexts. The first of these parallels, between the prophetic Guillaume du Bellay and the desperate Jean-Jacques de Trivulse, is staged as a contrast between two arts of dying.

The rise and fall of Jean-Jacques de Trivulse, who was, like Du Bellay, a prominent figure in the court of François I, would have been familiar to Rabelais's first readers. Milanese by birth, Gian-Jacopo Trivulzio had moved to France in 1495 and been a faithful servant in the court of Louis XII. His fortunes began to change with the accession of François I. In 1513 Trivulzio famously failed in the prosecution of the siege of Brescia, and never recovered his former standing at court. Brantôme, writing in *La Vie des grands capitaines estrangers*, views his final disgrace as the result of a political intrigue.[48] Knowing himself to be out of favour with François, Trivulzio had made approaches to the Swiss. Two of his enemies, M. de Lautrecq and his sister, Mme de Chateaubriand, had managed to persuade the king that Trivulzio was plotting to win back his native duchy of Milan. Brantôme paints a vivid picture of the old maréchal's despair, now despised and ignored by François:

---

[48] For Brantôme's life of Trivulzio, see Brantôme, *Oeuvres complètes de Pierre de Bourdeille, Seigneur de Brantôme*, ed. by L. Lalanne, 11 vols. (Paris: veuve J. Renouard, 1864–82), ii, pp. 221–6.

Ledict roy estant un jour à Chartres, et par un matin tournant de la messe, s'estant faict porter ledict Jehan-Jacques dans une chaire (estant fort boiteux, gouteux et attainct de quatre-vinctz ans, et fort cassé des grandes courvées de guerre qu'il avoit faict et souffert en sa vie), ainsi que le roy vint à passer sans faire semblant de l'avoir veu, ledict Jehan-Jacques s'escriant, luy dist: 'Sire, ah! Sire, au moins un mot d'audience!' Le roy, tournant la teste de l'autre costé, ne le voulut ouyr. Dont ce bon homme conceut un si grand despit, que de là il s'alla jetter dans le lict et n'en releva jamais jusques à ce qu'il fut mort.[49]

Brantôme's account ends with an embroidered version of the scene in Rabelais's *Tiers Livre*. In what is probably a buried reference to Psellus/ Ficino, he describes how Trivulzio, having 'ouy dire à quelques philo-sophes que les diables hayssoient fort les espées et en avoient grand frayeur', takes hold of his sword in readiness for his struggle with the demons.[50] But Brantôme is more sceptical than Panurge about the success of such a scheme. Making explicit what is only tacit in Rabelais's account, he cannot help but exclaim in conclusion, 'Quel abus et superstition de ce grand personnage!'[51]

The contrast with the death of Guillaume du Bellay could hardly be more stark, and Trivulzio's deathbed antics are made to seem all the more desperate when set against the 'parolles vigoureuses, en sens tranquil et serain' (xxi, 48–9) of Rabelais's dying patron. Rabelais describes the death of Du Bellay not only as a personal, but also a national, disaster. In the *Quart Livre*, the political significance of Langey's passing is recorded in the 'pro-diges, portentes, monstres, et aultres precedens signes formez contre tout ordre de nature' that prefigured his death. No such significance attends the death of Trivulzio. Ignored by the king, and so reassigned his original status as Italian and outsider, his passing, unlike Du Bellay's, was irrecu-perable to any such narrative of French national loss. Instead the tone of Panurge's description, strengthened further in Brantôme, is one of lightly comic pathos. That pathos emerges all the more powerfully in the context of military disgrace. While Langey is introduced, both in the *Tiers* and *Quart Livre*, as a 'docte et preux chevalier', Trivulzio is described as

---

[49] Brantôme, *Oeuvres*, II, p. 222: 'When the aforementioned king was in Chartres once, this Jean-Jacques, having had himself carried back from Mass one morning in a chair (being as he was extremely lame, gout-ridden and eighty years old, and completely broken from the exhausting military campaigns that he had suffered during his life), spied the king as he passed by pretending not to have noticed him. Jean-Jacques cried out, saying "Ah, my lord! My lord, at least grant me one word with you!" The king, turning his head away, would not hear him. The good man was so upset at this that from there he went and flung himself in bed, never to emerge until his death.'
[50] Ibid., p. 224 (var.).
[51] Ibid.

's'escrimant... comme vaillant et chevalereux' (XXIII, ll. 116–17). The difference, and the pathos, resides in the 'comme'. As he lies fighting with the shades, he is himself only a parody of valour—a shadow of the soldier, and the hero, he had been before his fall.

The elevation of Pantagrueline demonology, and the debasement of its Panurgian counterpart, is also a function of their respective intellectual traditions. The philosophical context for Panurge's demonology, as with its counterpart in that of Pantagruel, is broadly Neoplatonic. But the two Platonic strains run in opposite directions. In Panurge's mouth, 'Psellus platonicus' speaks for a bastardized Plato. Frère Jean's claim that, with his 'bragmard' in his hand, he has nothing to fear from demons, takes Panurge back to his old student days. It was then, studying under a Spanish magician, Picatrix, at the 'faculté diabolologique' in Toledo, that he had first heard of devils' fear of swords (XXIII, ll. 103–7), and he teases Frère Jean by comparing him to a college pedant, a 'docteur subtil en lard' (XXIII, ll. 102–3).[52] It is true that the subsequent discussion also contains, in more humanist fashion, a number of classical *loci*. These include the underworld journeys of Hercules and Aeneas and, later on in the passage, the wounding of Mars in the battle for Troy (XXIII, ll. 107–13, 147–50). For the most part, however, the authorities cited by Panurge, and the language he employs, are scholastic in origin. Panurge speaks, indeed boasts of speaking, 'en vraye diabolologie de Tolète' (XXIII, ll. 123–4). He tells, for instance, of how devils, when struck with a sword or other weapon, 'peuvent patir solution de continuité' (XXIII, ll. 126–7). They cry out at this 'sentiment de solution, laquelle', he adds in another phrase borrowed straight from the textbooks, 'leurs est doloreuse en diable' (XXIII, ll. 130–1). The cumulative effect of these formulae stands in sharp contrast with the prestigious humanist topoi of Pantagruel's evangelical demonology. Panurge's 'diabolologie' is little more than a relic of the Schools.

Finally, Panurge's fallen demonology is confirmed as such by the constant metaphorical slippage thanks to which Panurge's demons are always imagined through the language of the flesh. The reference to Panurge's Toledan education completes the critique of scholastic learning begun in Rabelais's more famous account of Gargantua's education. One recurrent feature of that critique, both here and in *Gargantua* and *Pantagruel*, is the imbrication of Schools learning with the motif of corporeal excess. The language of Panurge's 'diabolologie', like that of Rabelais's

---

[52] As Céard points out in his critical edition, 'Picatrix' was not in fact the name of a magician but of an Arabic manual of Hellenistic magic, the *Ghâyat al-hâkim*. A Latin translation of that text was dedicated to King Alfonso in 1256. See *Tiers Livre*, p. 226 n. 24.

earlier sophists—Janotus de Bragmardo in particular—always returns him to the body and to food.[53] It is a language, as he puts it, 'subtil en lard' (XXIII, l. 103). Screech has indicated that the pun here (Panurge also intends a 'docteur subtil en l'art') is a reference to Duns Scotus, often nicknamed *doctor subtilis*, and the archetypal college pedant for humanist reformers.[54] But there is also more to this than punning, more even than the obvious sexual play on the old and, as we discover later, underused 'bragmard' that Frère Jean holds in his fist. For the body—or, more particularly, meat—lies at the metaphorical centre of Panurge's speech to his friend. The language of the schoolroom is never far away from the kitchen or the pantry:

> Le grand effroy, et vacarme principal provient du deuil et ulement des Diables: qui là, guestans pelle melle les paovres ames des blessez, reçoivent coups d'espée à l'improviste, et patissent solution en la continuité de leurs substances aërées et invisibles: comme si à quelque lacquais crocquant les lardons de la broche maistre Hordoux donnoit un coup de baston sus les doigtz.[55] (XXIII, ll. 139–46)

The lexis here veers abruptly from 'l'art' towards 'lard': from scholastic talk of 'solution en la continuité', Panurge passes to the servant who steals scraps ('lardons') under the nose of 'maistre Hordoux'. Another carnal metaphor closes Panurge's set-piece. It is there that, in a further pedantic turn of phrase, Panurge notes that 'par discontinuation de officier et par faulte de operer', his friend's weapon has been robbed of its once-subtle power. Or, as he explains in more prosaic terms, it is rustier than the lock on a 'vieil charnier'.

The images of the 'lardons' and the meat store fulfil a comic function here, and the contrast of registers—on the one hand arcane, on the other, prosaic—is exploited for its bathos. But the play on 'l'art' and 'lard' also relates to a more serious purpose. Rabelaisian demonology is, as we have said, dialogic in its structure. It is also reflexive. The giant, on the one hand, imagines demons in his own spiritual likeness. Described both in terms of personal experience, through the privileged figure of Guillaume du Bellay and, further, through the prestigious topoi of Florentine Neoplatonism,

---

[53] F. Rabelais, *Gargantua*, ed. by M. A. Screech and R. Calder (Geneva: Droz, 1970), chs. 18–19.

[54] F. Rabelais, *Le Tiers Livre*, ed. by M. A. Screech (Geneva, Droz, 1964), p. 166 n.

[55] 'But the great turmoil and principal racket comes from the anguish and ululation of the Devils, who, lying there pell-mell in wait for the poor souls of the wounded, unexpectedly receive sword-strokes and suffer dissolution of continuity of their airy and invisible substances: as if, to some lackey swiping bacon strips from the spit, Master Slobby [the cook] gives a hard bang on the fingers with his stick.' (*Complete Works*, p. 325).

Pantagrueline *daemones* meet the soul as it takes flight from the confines of the body. They answer, despite Pantagruel's own corporeal bulk, to the spiritual lightness of his governing philosophy. What Panurge's carnal fixation makes clear is that he, too, figures spirits in his own image. But here the image is more salted than exalted. For Panurge, whom Rabelais's readers had first encountered basted and kebabbed in a Turkish prison camp, the numinous *daemones* are diabolized creatures—imprisoned, as Panurge himself was and still is, within the baleful lock-up of the meat-store, of the flesh.[56]

Fallen creature that he is, Panurge has misread the spirits who gather in Raminagrobis's 'logis poëtique'. For Pantagruel, that misreading is a product of Panurge's famous 'philautie'. It may have robbed him of the best advice so far: having read the old poet's prognostication, the giant will claim on Panurge's return that 'encore n'ay je veu response que plus me plaise' (xxix, l. 4). But instead of turning him back towards the wisdom of the dying Raminagrobis, Panurge's blindness spurs him onwards, and spiritually downwards, to his next consultation with the hoary wizard, Herr Trippa. There, in what turns out to be the most unambiguously diabolical encounter in the *Tiers Livre*, Panurge nearly gets to meet the devils his demonology deserves. Once again the attitude he adopts—surely wise on this occasion—is that of the hasty retreat: 'Le Diable le puisse emporter!', he exclaims of the magician, 'Dictez *amen*, et allons boyre.' (xxv, ll. 179–80).

VIOLENCE 'OUTRE LE LOIR': GHOSTLY RONSARD

The reception of Psellus in early sixteenth-century demonology was largely uncritical in Ficino, Rhodiginus, and Cornelius Agrippa. Once transposed into the fleshy, vernacular mouth of Rabelais's Panurge, the Psellian thesis of ghostly bodies becomes, as we have seen, more problematic. To this extent, Rabelais anticipates a gradual hardening of sixteenth-century attitudes towards postures of aggression in the ghostly encounter. The poetry of the next author considered in this chapter, Ronsard, is also part of this story. His poems of the 1550s and 1560s contain a number of

---

[56] F. Rabelais, *Pantagruel*, ch. 10 ('Comment Panurge racompte la manière qu'il eschappa de la main des Turcqs'). On this episode, see T. Hampton, *Literature and Nation in the Sixteenth Century: Inventing Renaissance France* (Ithica NY: Cornell University Press, 2001), pp. 47–65; W. Williams, 'Out of the frying pan...': Curiosity, Danger, and the Poetics of Witness in the Renaissance Traveller's Tale', in *Curiosity and Wonder from the Renaissance to the Enlightenment*, ed. by R. J. W. Evans and A. J. Marr (Aldershot: Ashgate, 2006), pp. 21–41.

Psellian moments, the best known and most widely discussed of which occurs at the end of the 'Hymne des daimons'. All subscribe, like Panurge, to the idea of meeting ghosts with violence. Towards the end of Ronsard's life, however, his view of that thesis appears to undergo a shift. In late editions of his work, especially those published after 1580, Ronsard's Psellian moments would begin to disappear. Critics of 'Les Daimons' have disagreed on the reason for this change. Some, such as Albert-Marie Schmidt, cite the poet's fear of ecclesiastical censure.[57] That thesis effectively locates Ronsard's show of violence as a version of the grand narrative traced in this chapter: no longer deemed appropriate in an age increasingly demanding of religious orthodoxy, the ghostly encounter in Ronsard is subjected to correction or revision. Others, such as Germaine Lafeuille, have argued that the changes to 'Les Daimons' were made for chiefly poetic reasons: perhaps Ronsard was dissatisfied at the sudden introduction, so late on in the poem, of a first-person account into a scientific poem.[58] The reading that follows below effectively steers a course between these two paths. Ronsard's Psellian moments, and the dialogue they construct between his early and late selves, can certainly be read as the expression of a changing philosophical or theological position. But they might be something more. Through the same reflexive dynamic that governs Rabelais's ghostly bodies, they also offer a new vision of the poet's own body as he dwindles, in the late sonnets, to a 'fantaume sans os' (XVII, 266, l. 9).

First published in the 'Hymnes' of 1555, 'Les Daimons' is an encyclopaedic verse compendium of demonology through the ages. But of all the authors cited in the poem as a whole, the most ubiquitous of all is Ficino's Latin Psellus.[59] Psellus' six-fold division of spirits according to habitat—ether, air, fire, water, earth, and subterranean—stratifies the poem. Towards the end of the hymn, having described the higher *daemones*, Ronsard moves on to write of those spirits who 'chargez d'un corps plus

---

[57] P. de Ronsard, *Hymne des daimons*, ed. by A.-M. Schmidt (Paris: A. Michel, 1939), pp. 76–7.

[58] G. Lafeuille, *Cinq hymnes de Ronsard* (Geneva: Droz, 1973), Ch. 5. The disagreement between Lafeuille and Schmidt is part of a broader debate over whether the Ronsard of the *Hymnes* should be considered a philosopher (in the broadest sense) or a poet. For Jean Céard's attempt to reconcile these (not necessarily contrary) positions, see J. Céard, 'Dieu, les hommes et le poète' in *Autour des 'Hymnes' de Ronsard*, ed. by M. Lazard (Paris: Champion, 1984), pp. 83–101.

[59] For the precise textual parallels, see Schmidt's commentary in Ronsard, *Hymne des daimons*; Lafeuille, *Cinq hymnes de Ronsard*, pp. 127–99; Céard's notes to the poem in P. de Ronsard, *Oeuvres complètes*, ed. by J. Céard, D. Ménager, and M. Simonin, 2 vols. (Paris: Gallimard, 1993–4), I, ll. 1444–7.

gras, / Et plus materiel, habitent les lieux bas'.[60] All these beings, he
attests:

> craingnent les cousteaux
> Et s'enfuient bien tost s'ils voyent un espée,
> De peur de ne sentir leur liaison coupée.
> Ce que souventefois j'ay de nuict esprouvé,
> Et rien de si certain, contre eux, je n'ay trouvé.[61]
>   (VIII, 134, ll. 342–6)

In the versions of the poem published before 1584, the poet now relates,
by way of an example, what befell him one night on his way to a lover's
assignation. The beginning is well known:

> Un soir, vers la minuict, guidé de la jeunesse
> Qui commande aux amans, j'allois voir ma maistresse
> Tout seul, outre le Loir, et passant un destour
> Joignant une grand croix, dedans un carrefour,
> J'oüy, ce me sembloit, une aboyante chasse
> De chiens qui me suyvoit pas-à-pas à la trace.[62]
>   (viii, 134, ll. 347–52)

The 'chasse' turns out to be Hellequin's hunt—a pack of demons pursuing, in this case, the shade of a moneylender not long dead, and assumed
by local people to be suffering in Hell. The young poet's first response is
one of fear. Suddenly, however, God intervenes and, the poet explains:

> me meit en la pensée
> De tirer mon espée, et de couper menu
> L'air tout-au-tour de moy, avecques le fer nu.[63]
>   (viii, 135, ll. 368–70)

The poet heeds God's counsel and brandishes his sword. Sure enough the
demons, 'craignant paoureusement de se sentir hacher' (viii, 135, l. 374),
disperse into the night.

---

[60] P. de Ronsard, *Oeuvres complètes*, ed. by P. Laumonier, 20 vols. (Paris: Hachette,
1914–75), viii, p. 131, ll. 297–8. All subsequent references are incorporated into the text.

[61] 'They are afraid of knives, and take fright as soon as they see a sword, for fear they may
feel their sinews severed. I have myself experienced this many times at night, and have found
no means to be so powerful against them.'

[62] 'One night, around midnight, guided by the youth who presides over lovers, I was
going to see my mistress all alone, beyong the Loire, when passing by a detour and coming
to a great cross, at a crossroads, I heard, it seemed to me, a hunting pack of barking dogs
who followed fast on my heels.'

[63] 'Gave me the idea of drawing my sword, and to slice into bits the air all around me,
with the naked weapon.'

In the 1584 edition of Ronsard's complete works, the last to be prepared during the author's own lifetime, the poet's struggle with the demons entirely disappears. Modern critics have fought shy of explanations for this dramatic self-revision. Few, nonetheless, have failed to notice the curious, liminal, status of the encounter 'outre le Loir'.[64] The tale is ushered in straightforwardly enough. As the encyclopaedic present ('[ils] craignent les couteaux / Et s'enfuient bien tost s'ils voyent une espee') gives way to the frequentative past ('Ce que souventesfois j'ay de nuict esprouvé'), the reader feels the onset of an exemplary narrative. That expectation is confirmed in the lines that follow, where 'souventesfois' duly narrows to talk of 'un soir' and the verbs make the switch to the preterite of narrative ('j'oüy...je vy'). But another kind of shift subtends the movement of these lines and disrupts the story's place within a rhetoric of exemplarity. Not temporal, or aspectual, but spatial in dimension, that shift is mapped out in terms of a precise topography. Three coordinates, in particular, dominate this topography. First, though Ronsard's midnight journey appears to claim the status of *exemplum*, the tale is also configured as a momentary 'detour'. Second, the story is set up as an instance of transgression, as the poet, driven by the youthfulness of passion, travels outwards on a voyage 'outre le Loir'. Third, the ghostly encounter unfolds at the site of the 'carrefour'. Taken in their turn, these three coordinates—of digression, transgression, and intersection—combine to form the structure of a reading.

The 'detour' is marked, above all, through the voice of the narrator. 'J'oüy', 'je vis', 'j'advisay', 'si fussé-je étouffé d'une crainte pressée': here the 'je' of the poem is no longer the 'je' that compiles and collates; it is the hero of a story who sees, hears, and feels. To this extent, Ronsard's Psellian moment is offered in sharp distinction to its cousin in Rabelais's *Tiers Livre*. In that work, Panurge conveyed the Psellian thesis through the dubious mediations of others' expertise; in contrast, Ronsard's 'show of violence', and its philosophical underpinnings, is enacted in the person of the poem's own narrator. It is not merely, then, that expertise has given way to a narrative of experience. Ronsard here offers something not promised until now: to return to a phrase of Terence Cave's, cited earlier in the section on Rabelais, these lines constitute 'une démonologie à la première personne'.[65]

For some early readers of 'Les Daimons', this ostentatious 'je' marked not only a 'detour'; it also deserved censure as a moment of transgression.

---

[64] See especially H. Moreau, 'Les Daimons, ou de la fantaisie' in *Autour des 'Hymnes' de Ronsard*, pp. 215–42 (p. 215); Cave, *Pré-histoires*, pp. 93–8.
[65] See above, p. 188.

In the Calvinist pamphlets of the 1560s, in particular, this first-person demonology recurs as a target of polemic. Jacques Grévin, citing 'Les Daimons' as a prominent example, mocks Ronsard's addiction to ghosts and apparitions. Either, Grévin supposes, he had taken to the practice of black arts, or—and this may have stung him more keenly than the first— the poet's invention had been reduced to a facile reliance on the device of *prosopopeia*.[66] Even among friends, however, there is another sense still in which the journey 'outre le Loir' might seem to overstep the mark. Theologically speaking, the story in 'Les Daimons' is recklessly committal. Here the terms of that poem should be compared with another of Ronsard's Psellian moments. This occurs in a work of the same period, and from the same collection: the 'Hymne de la Philosophie' of 1555. Like 'Les Daimons', the 'Hymne de la Philosophie' is typical of the speculative character of mid-century demonology. Unlike that poem, however, the first-person is missing; in its stead there appears the impersonal 'on'. In one passage, the poet describes how Philosophy grants us ('on') our knowledge of the spirits. Such is its authority that the whole sequence hangs on the opening words, 'elle sçait':

> elle sçait les bons et les mauvais,
> Leurs qualitez, leur forme, et leurs effectz,
> Et leur mystere, et ce qu'on leur doit faire
> Pour les facher, ou bien pour leur complaire:
> Et pourquoy c'est qu'ilz sont tant desireux
> De la matiere, et couhards, et poureux,
> Craignant le coup d'une transchante espée.[67]
>   (VIII, 88, ll. 41–7)

Though these lines, too, were suppressed in 1584, they are less theologically committal than their cognates in 'Les Daimons'. As the speaker of that poem describes his first thoughts on seeing the spirits, it is not

---

[66] 'On diroit proprement, depuis que tu es Prestre, / Qu'un million d'esprits te viennent apparoistre: / Ou que tu es sans cesse aux sepulchres des morts, / Mettant, comm'un charmeur, des esprits dans leurs corps, / Pour les faire parler, et des choses futures, / Par eux, de point en point, scavoir les avantures.'; A. Zamariel [A. de Chandieu] and B. de Mont-Dieu [J. Grévin], *Response aux calumnies continues au discours et suyte du discours sur les miseres de ce temps, faits par Messire Pierre Ronsard, jadis poëte, et maintenant Prebstre* (n.p., 1563), sig. Giii^v: 'It really could be said that, since you became a priest, a million spirits appear to you, or that you are always hanging around the graves of the dead, putting spirits into their bodies, like an enchanter, to make them speak and tell of future events, to learn from them the detail of human affairs.'

[67] ['She [Philosophy] knows the good ones and the evil, their qualities, their forms, their effects, and their mystery, and what one must do to thwart them, or else to satisfy them: and why it is that they are so desiring of matter, and cowardly and fearful, frightened by the blow of a cleaving sword.']

Philosophy, but divine wisdom, that calls forth the 'transchante espee': '*Dieu* me meit en la pensée / De tirer mon espée' (my italics). Here Ronsard, who presumes to grant Psellus the authority of God, has strayed beyond the 'hymne' as philosophical genre: he has trespassed on the province of the minister or the priest.

In terms of its first-person voice, and the theological authority that it arrogates to itself, Ronsard's Psellian moment in 'Les Daimons' appears both as 'detour' and passage 'outre'. But neither of these movements should be read without reference to the 'carrefour' in which the story unfolds. Mapped in terms of a cultural topography, the crossroads, which often played host to a gallows or a gibbet, is deeply inscribed as a *locus* of ghosts and apparitions. The theologian, René Du Pont, explains that ghosts are particularly apt to appear at the crossroads 'par ce que ce sont des lieux où se commettent le plus de volleries et d'assassinats': hence the Christian tradition of erecting crosses in such places.[68] Read figuratively, however, the 'carrefour' also suggests a site of generic intersection. At least three genres converge in the encounter at the crossroads. In one direction, the story looks back to the folkloric tradition of the 'Mesnie Hellequin'.[69] Hellequin's hunt was a late medieval motif, closely linked to the *danse macabre* and, according to De Thou, especially popular in Ronsard's native Tourangeau.[70] As in 'Les Daimons', the 'Mesnie Hellequin' or 'Chasse sauvage' was normally encountered in remote or lonely places. The hunt is always in pursuit of the souls of damned men, a role usually filled, as in 'Les Daimons', by usurers and misers. The tale reminds the young man at its centre of the price of his attachment to the things of this world.

A second branch of the generic 'carrefour' is the path that leads back to Ronsard's epic sources. 'Tirer ton espée': these are not only the words of 'la Philosophie', or God, but also those offered to Aeneas by the Cumean sibyl ('Vagina[que] eripe ferrum'). In another of Ronsard's Psellian moments, in his later *Franciade*, the classical connection is especially clear. At one point in the fourth book of that poem Hyante, the enchantress, readies Francus for his descent into Hades. She instructs the hero that he will offer the shades a sacrifice. Then:

> Quand tu verras que les esprits voudront
> Boire le sang, et qu'espais se tiendront

[68] *Philosophie des esprits*, sig. Ff^v.
[69] On the 'Mesnie Hellequin', see Schmitt, *Les Revenants*, Ch. 5. On Ronsard's debt to the 'Mesnie Hellequin' tradition, see H. Guy, 'Les Sources françaises de Ronsard', *Revue d'Histoire Littéraire de la France*, 9 (1902), pp. 217–56 (pp. 227–8); G. Cohen, *Ronsard: sa vie et son oeuvre* (Paris: Boivin, 1946), pp. 167–8.
[70] Cited in Ronsard, *Hymne des daimons*, pp. 64–5.

> Pres de la fosse au sang toute trempée,
> Hors du fourreau tire ta large espée,
> Les menaceant, et ne souffre hardy
> Boire un esprit, si je ne te le dy.[71]
>
>   (xvi, 269, ll. 575–80)

This text clearly owes more to its precedent in Homer than to Ficino's Latin Psellus.[72] Hyante's words are not meant to convey a philosophical position. Rather, drawing swords before such journeys is a signature of epic: it finds its motivation in the dictates of the genre. It is possibly for this reason that this promised 'show of violence', unlike that at the end of 'Les Daimons', remains in the editions after 1584. Indeed, it is notable that in later versions of the poem, Ronsard's nod towards Psellus—dimly present in 'espais se tiendront'—is not tempered, but strengthened in these lines:

> Hors du fourreau tire ta large espée,
> Et fais semblant de les vouloir trancher,
> Car ils ont peur qu'on ne coupe leur chair.[73]
>
>   (xvi, 269, ll. 578–80 [variant])

The example of *La Franciade* serves to show how the topic can still flourish within the generic space of epic, whilst escaping the kinds of censure to which philosophy was prone.

'Guidé de la jeunesse / Qui commande aux amans': Ronsard's Psellian detour also leads to the space of love lyric. There is a cluster of such moments in the poems of the 1550s. Take the example of a piece in the *Meslanges*: the 'Élégie à Jean Brinon' of 1555. Drawing its inspiration from a passage in Plato's *Symposium*, that poem begins:

> Aus fait d'amour Diotime certaine
> Dit à bon droit qu'Amour est capitaine
> De noz Daimons…[74]
>
>   (vi, 149, ll. 1–3)

The poet goes on to describe to his friend how, before he fell in love, he was 'honteux et poureux'. He tells of his fear when out walking at night:

---

[71] 'The moment you see that the spirits wish to drink the blood, and are gathering thick by the blood-soaked ditch, unsheath your broad sword, threatening them, and do not suffer to let a spirit drink, unless I so instruct you.'

[72] These and the preceding lines are an imitation of *Odyssey*, X. 516ff.

[73] 'Unsheath your broad sword, and make as if you wanted to slice them, since they are afraid of having their flesh cut up.'

[74] 'When it comes to love resolute, Diotima is right to say that Love is the captain of our Daemons…'.

> Si j'entendoi quelque chose en la rue
> Grouler de nuit, j'avoi l'ame éperdue.[75]
>
> (VI, 150, ll. 13–14)

His problem was even more acute in lonely, isolated places:

> Mais par sur tout je perdoi le courage
> Quand je passoi de nuit, par un bocage
> Ou près d'un antre, et me sembloit avis
> Que par derriere un esprit m'avoit pris.[76]
>
> (VI, 150, ll. 25–8)

Now, however, Love has made him manly. No longer does he fear 'les Daimons des antres soliteres':

> Ni les espris des ombreus cemeteres,
> Car le Daimon qui leur peut commander
> Me tient escorte, et me fait hazarder
> De mettre à fin tout ce que je propose.[77]
>
> (VI, 150, ll. 33–7)

Of course, Love has brought with it a new set of concerns. The subsequent lines describe the poet's fear of gossip, jealous husbands, or that another— 'plus riche'—might come to steal his place (VI, 151, ll. 38–50). But Ronsard ends the poem on an upbeat, as he returns to Love's bracing its adepts against the spirits on the road:

> Doncque, Brinon, si tu te plais d'avoir
> L'estomac plein de force et de pouvoir,
> Sois amoureux, et tu auras l'audace
> Plus forte au coeur, que si une cuirasse
> Vestoit ton cors, ou si un camp armé
> Pour ton secours t'enserroit enfermé.[78]
>
> (VI, 151, ll. 51–6)

In a sonnet included in the first book of *Amours*, the lover's 'force et pouvoir' is put to the test. As in the 'Élégie à Brinon', the focus of the ghostly encounter is not the corporeality of the spirit but a renewed and vivid sense of the poet's own—passionate—body. Here, as if concluding

---

[75] 'If I heard something in the street growling at night, my soul was in panic.'

[76] 'But above all I lost heart when I passed through a wood by night, or close to a cave, and it seemed to me that a spirit had seized me from behind.'

[77] 'Not the spirits of shady cemeteries, since the Daemon that might command them now escorts me, and gives me courage to undertake whatever I wish.'

[78] 'So, Brinon, if you want your stomach full of strength and power, fall in love, and your heart will be emboldened as if you were wearing a breastplate, or an army were camped around you for your protection.'

the tale from 'Les Daimons', the poet goes on to reach the home of his 'maistresse':

> En escrimant un Démon m'eslança
> Le mousse fil d'une arme rabatue,
> Qui de sa pointe aux aultres non pointue,
> Jusques à l'os le coulde m'offença.
> Ja tout le bras à seigner commença,
> Quand par pitié la beaulté qui me tuë,
> De l'estancher soigneuse s'evertuë,
> Et de ses doigtz ma playe elle pança.[79]
>
> (IV, 133, ll. 1–8)

Here the encounter with the spirit belongs to a rhetoric of passion. Others may not sense 'le mousse fil d'une arme rabatue'; but, already injured by his love for his mistress, the poet is made to suffer his wound 'jusques à l'os'. The cut received at the hands of the demon signs the sensual materiality of the Petrarchan lover's body: like the demons of Psellus' treatise, it is a body that is fully 'materiel et patible'. In this restricted sense, the speaker of the poem is a relative of his contemporary, Panurge. Though less cowardly than Pantagruel's friend, and apt to frame his courtship in more elevated terms, the speaker of the sonnet has visited his mistress, 'la puce à l'oreille'. Like Panurge, and as in 'Les Daimons', the poet of this sonnet fashions ghosts in his own sensual image.

Generically speaking, Ronsard's midnight excursion is staged, then, in the interstices of at least three distinct genres. In one direction, the 'carrefour' heads off towards the moral fables of 'la Mesnie Hellequin'; in another it glances back to epic precedents in Homer and Virgil, or forward to Ronsard's imitations in his own *La Franciade*. Finally, and most explicitly, the path the poem travels leads away to the world of the *Amours*. By the mid 1580s, however, that world too had changed. As the century had grown old, so Ronsard had aged with it, and the late amorous persona bears no resemblance to that of the earlier love lyric. In the 'Élégie à Brinon' the poet spoke of the full, or potent, body: love gave him 'l'estomac plein de force et de pouvoir'. By the time Ronsard revised 'Les Daimons' in 1584, however, the speaker has hollowed out to little more than a disembodied voice. This corporeal dimunition is often expressed, in Ronsard's late verse, through the figure of the ghost. Where, in 'Les Daimons', the body of the speaker was the focus of

---

[79] 'During a bout of fencing a Demon thrust towards me the blunt edge of a well-worn weapon which, with its point—pointed only to me—wounded my elbow right to the bone. Already my whole arm was beginning to bleed when, out of pity, the beauty who is fatal to me strove to stem the flow and, with careful fingers, bandaged my wound.'

sensation ('j'oüy', 'je vis', 'je sentis'), the older lyric subject tells a very different story: 'Je ne puis ny toucher gouster n'ouir ny voir: / J'ai perdu tous mes Sens, je suis une ombre blesme' (xvii, 329, ll. 5–6). The aged lover is not yet, in literal terms, 'sous la terre et fantôme sans os' (xvii, 266, l. 9). But the fear of becoming a 'fantôme' haunts Ronsard's late verse.

Perhaps the most poignant variation on the poet as ghost appears in the 'Sonets pour Helene'. In one poem, the speaker complains that his beloved no longer tells him of her visits to the capital. 'Pourquoy me caches-tu l'oeil,' he asks, 'par qui tu me plais'? (xvii, 222, l. 4)

> Tu vas bien à Hercueil avecque ta cousine
> Voir les prez, les jardins, et la source voisine
> De l'Antre, où j'ay chanté tant de divers accords.[80]
>
> (xvii, 222, ll. 9–11)

The old poet, he complains, is not invited to the party. But a poignant irony attends upon the speaker's accusation. For while it seems that Hélène does hide her eyes from the poet's famished gaze, the final tercet suggests, perhaps unwittingly, the true cause of her disdain. Maybe his mistress will not see him because he is, literally, *no longer there*:

> Tu devois m'appeller, oublieuse Maistresse:
> Dans ton coche porté je n'eusse fait grand presse:
> Car je ne suis plus rien qu'un fantaume sans corps.[81]
>
> (xvii, 222, ll. 12–14)

It is not the mistress who is hidden from his gaze but the poet—a 'fantaume'—who has vanished out of sight. As Hélène's carriage speeds past the hallowed places of the younger poet's days, she does not—cannot—see that a new ghost now haunts the 'antres' of the 'Élégie à Brinon'. In a move that will culminate in Ronsard's final withdrawal from 'Les Daimons' in 1584, the youthful speaker of that poem has begun to disappear.

Odysseus, Aeneas, Marcellus, Panurge, Ronsard, Taillepied's Lyonnais soldier: this chapter has brought together a number of brothers-in-arms, each of which is intent on showing violence to the ghost. In the early modern examples, the adoption of a material response to the encounter with ghosts finds itself corrected or reformed: this both over the period as a whole, in which the Psellian position was gradually reframed in line with

---

[80] 'Why do you hide from me those eyes that are so pleasing to my sight? You come after all to Hercueil with your cousin to see the meadows, the gardens, and the spring next to that hollow, where I sang my divers strains.'
[81] 'You should call on me, forgetful Mistress. I would not have taken up much room in your carriage: for I am nothing more than a ghost without a body.'

more orthodox doctrine, and, as we have seen, within the specific narratives considered in this chapter. In Rabelais's *Tiers Livre*, the correction is staged as a kind of dialogue, where Panurge's carnal diabology is made to stand as a debased counterpart to Pantagruel's elevated spiritualism. Meanwhile, the aged Ronsard, revisiting the philosophical poems of the mid 1550s, performs his own act of self-revision on his youthful show of violence. This is not to argue that Pantagruel and the later Ronsard should therefore be seen as straightforwardly complicit with the tacit ideologies of Lavater and Taillepied. The comic exaggerations of Rabelais's text and the complex intertextual and biographical threads of Ronsard's verse narrative interfere with such an easy correspondence; for this reason the relation between what we now term literary and theological texts cannot simply be viewed as that of servant to master. Nonetheless, this chapter has shown how their respective Psellian moments are not only to be thought of, in purely literary terms, as instances of romance error, or of the youthful 'errance' of the poet-adventurer; they also mark points in a broader cultural narrative, in which the idea of ghostly bodies was subject to revision and reform.

6

Revenant Lovers

We saw in earlier chapters how sixteenth-century theology, both Catholic and Protestant, tended to proscribe the idea that the dead might return in their own bodies. In so doing it sought to discourage a whole raft of popular superstitions associated with embodied ghosts. In Catholic piety ghosts were not corporeal beings, but rather the disembodied souls of dead men and women; and although Protestant theology rejected ghosts as apparitions of the Devil, these still required not a material but a spiritual response. However, in some early modern narratives, and particularly those that emerge from within humanist rather than theological or pastoral writing on ghosts, the dead do sometimes return in the body. Though the term did not enter French until the eighteenth century, these are early instances of the corporeal 'revenant'.[1]

Late Renaissance demonology offered two explanations for the embodied return of the dead: one divine and the other demonic. The first held that, in certain cases, God himself has occasion to recall dead souls to their bodies, though accounts of divine resurrections are exceptionally rare in the period. Generally confined to the geographical margins, especially the Levant, they are usually played out as conversion narratives, the object of which is the figure of the Turk. The second, more frequently encountered explanation holds that most apparent resurrections are in fact diabolical illusions. Either acting alone, or through the mediating presence of a witch or necromancer, demons can take up and manipulate dead bodies. Though these *corpora peregrina* are of putrefying flesh, the spirit can often mask its appearance, sound, and smell.[2] In narratives of embodied return both divine and demonic, the ghost is most often, though not always, that of a dead woman.

---

[1] On the origins of this word, see above, p. 3.
[2] On the notion of *corpora peregrina*, see above, pp. 183–4.

'REVENEZ QU'ON VOUS REVOYE',
OR THE BRIDE OF CHRIST

Narratives of divine resurrection are exceptionally infrequent in the early modern period. We have already encountered two in this book, namely the stories of Bishop Stanislas of Cracow, which Le Loyer borrows from Martin Cromer's history of Poland, and Bonifinius's tale of the unshriven skull.[3] It is a testament to their status as exceptions that Pierre de L'Estoile, in his hostile reading of the *Discours des spectres*, should have singled these narratives out for especial ridicule.[4] Nonetheless, some writers continue to report cases of dead souls recalled to their former bodies. Like those of Cromer and Bonifinius, narratives of this kind are usually set in far-off lands, and are deemed all the more plausible when the witness to such cases is an infidel or Turk. Three examples stand out. The first is recounted by Simon Goulart, who tells of an annual resurrection in the desert near Cairo. Melchior Flavin, who narrates the second account, this time from Damascus, introduces the motif of the revenant woman. The third and final writer considered in this section, André Valladier, makes explicit a suggestion only latent in Flavin's ghost narrative: that the 'revenant lover' might be devotionalized as the Solomonic Bride of Christ.

Goulart's narrative appears in two slightly differing versions: one is his annotated French version of Philip Camerarius's *Operae horarum subcisivarum*, which he translated in 1608 as *Les Meditations historiques*, the other the first volume of Goulart's own *Histoires admirables et memorables de nostre temps*, first published in 1606. Taken together they provide a highly unusual account of a multiple resurrection thought to occur annually in the Egyptian desert near Cairo.[5] The translation of Camerarius describes how every year for three days in March, body parts can be seen rising from the sand in what is believed to have been the site of an early Christian cemetery:

> Cela commence le Jeudy, et dure jusques au Samedy, que tous disparroissent. Alors pouvez vous voir des corps envellopez de leurs draps, à la façon antique: mais on ne les void ny debout, ny marchans, ains seulement les bras, ou les cuisses, ou autre partie du corps que vous pouvez toucher.[6]

---

[3] See above, pp. 169–70.

[4] See above, p. 170.

[5] Camerarius, *Meditations historiques*, pp. 364–5; Goulart, *Histoires admirables*, I, fols. 32ʳ–4ʳ.

[6] 'This begins on the Thursday, and lasts until Saturday, when they all disappear. During this time you can see their bodies wrapped up in their sheets, in the antique fashion: yet you cannot see them standing up or walking around—only the arms or thighs or another part of the body that you can touch'. Camerarius, *Meditations historiques*, p. 364.

In a note to the text added in the second edition of 1610, Goulart supplements Camerarius's description with a number of eyewitness accounts, communicated to him personally by visitors to the region. One goldsmith from La Rochelle, named Georges Cortin, claims to have seen an entire head 'avec barbe et poil' emerging from the desert; another traveller from Antwerp, Jean Baclé, 'avoit gardé long temps un pied de tels corps sans le corrompre'.[7] According to another report, however, included in Goulart's *Histoires admirables*, local bystanders disapproved of the travellers' impulse to touch the risen bodies. This account is taken from a conversation that had taken place between Goulart and one Estienne Duplais, an 'orfevre ingenieux, homme d'honneste et agreable conversation' who had travelled in the Levant in his youth, and had witnessed the apparition with Claude Rocard, 'apoticaire, de Cably en Champagne', and twelve other Christians. The party also included another goldsmith, named Alessandro Maniotti, who, acting as 'truchement et conducteur', was able to translate the distress of an Arab onlooker present at the scene:

> Il [Duplais] me disoit d'avantage avoir (comme aussi firent les autres) touché divers membres de ces ressuscitans. Et comme il vouloit se saisir d'une teste chevelue d'enfant, un homme du Caire s'escria tout haut, *Kali, Kali, antê-matarasde*: c'est à dire, *laisse, laisse, tu ne sçais que c'est de cela.*[8]

The behaviour of the travellers, and the guarded response among the local inhabitants, are susceptible to a number of different readings. According to Cortin, the Arab population had interpreted the annual miracle in terms of religious conflict, crying out that 'ce sont corps de Chrestiens que la terre ne veut pas recevoir'.[9] But the clash of perspectives dramatized in the scene may have had as much to do with economic as spiritual considerations. The mid sixteenth century had seen an explosion in the trade of Egyptian body parts as a source of the drug *mumia*, used as a cosmetic among the rich of Western Europe. Pierre Belon, writing in 1553, had remarked that 'la momie' had become, in the last four or five years, the most sought after of all exotic goods, thought as it was to combat ageing and decline.[10] Claude Guichard observed much later, in 1584, that cargoes of mummies were still arriving at Venice and Marseilles 'où

---

[7] Camerarius, *Meditations historiques*, p. 365.

[8] Goulart, *Histoires admirables*, I, fol. 33ᵛ: 'Moreover he [Duplais] told me that (like the others) he had touched various limbs of these resurrected bodies. And as he went to grab the hairy head of a child, a man from Cairo shouted out, *Kali, Kali antêmatarasde*: which means *leave it alone, leave it alone, you don't know what you're dealing with.*'

[9] Camerarius, *Meditations historiques*, p. 365.

[10] Cited in P. Delaunay, *L'Aventureuse Existence de Pierre Belon du Mans* (Paris: Champion, 1926), p. 102.

l'on apporte ces corps entiers pour les distribuer çà ou là, le plus souvent par pieces et lopins'.[11] Around the same time, Amboise Paré can be found complaining that bodies were even being stolen from gallows, and passed off as Egyptian.[12] Especially active in the trade were apothecaries, such as Claude Rocard, and goldsmiths, who often doubled as medical suppliers. Within this context, the spectacle of the European witness tugging greedily at the 'resurrected' limbs, along with the distress of local onlookers, presumably hostile to desecrations of this kind, begins to take on a more worldly colouration.

Neither Camerarius nor Goulart make mention of the trade in body parts. The author of the *Operae horarum subcisivarum* instead provides two, more theologically oriented, explanations for the resurrections outside Cairo, although in the end he decides to commit himself to neither:

> Comme je n'ay pas entreprins de maintenir que ceste apparition soit miraculeuse, pour confondre ces superstitieux et idolatres d'Egypte, et leur monstrer qu'il y a une resurrection et vie à venir, ny ne veux non plus refuter cela, ny maintenir que ce soit illusion de Satan, comme plusieurs estiment: aussi j'en laisse le jugement au lecteur, pour en penser et resoudre ce que bon luy semblera.[13]

Camerarius's refusal to decide on the cause of the apparitions, that is to engage in the act of *discretio spirituum*, is typical of a writer who, in this text at least, seeks to avoid choosing between competing theological positions. Goulart, for his part, is less non-committal. Years after his visit to the Levant, Estienne Duplais had told him that the site of the apparitions was not that of a cemetery, but of a massacre: a number of Christians, having assembled in order to worship, had been surrounded by their enemies, 'lesquels taillerent tout en pieces, couvrirent de terre ces corps, puis se retirerent au Caire'.[14] Goulart inscribes these Christian martyrs within a providential framework. Where the Egyptian bystanders had claimed that the ground itself, as it expelled the unwelcome bodies, was the agent of the so-called resurrection, he locates that agency in God's own anger at the killing. The whole episode, he writes, calls for 'esbahissement et reverence de la Sagesse divine'.[15]

---

[11] Guichard, *Funerailles*, p. 477.

[12] Cited in Delaunay, *L'Aventureuse Existence de Pierre Belon*, p. 103.

[13] Camerarius, *Meditations historiques*, p. 365: 'Since I have not undertaken to maintain that this apparition is a miracle wrought to confound the superstitious and idolatrous inhabitants of Egypt, and to show them that there is a resurrection and a life to come, nor to refute that idea or maintain that it is a diabolical illusion, as many think it is, I therefore leave it to the reader to judge, to think of it and resolve it as he pleases.'

[14] Goulart, *Histoires admirables*, ı, fol. 34ʳ.

[15] Ibid.

In Melchior Flavin's narrative, as in Goulart's, God raises the dead for the conversion of the Turk. His *De l'estat des ames apres le trespas* describes a resurrection supposed to have occurred in 1555 at Merula, a small village situated (as befits a narrative of conversion) on the road into Damascus.[16] An unnamed woman died and was buried for six days. On the seventh day, Flavin continues, 'elle commença à crier dessous terre, à la voix de laquelle s'assemblerent une grande multitude de gens' (fo. 17^v). The parents and husband were summoned to the scene, where they saw the dead woman pulled alive from the tomb. Her husband wished to take her home, but she protested that she would prefer to be led to a church, in order to be baptized into the Christian religion. Instead of granting her that wish, her indignant family delivered her into the hands of the religious authorities. When the Cadi, or chief inquisitor, asked the woman why she wished to join 'la foy damnee des Chrestiens', she replied that she had seen those faithful to Mohammed burning in hellfire (fo. 18^r).

The crowd that had gathered to hear the judgement of the Cadi demanded that the woman be sent to the stake. However, he decided on an alternative solution:

> Le Cadi dist qu'il n'en estoit pas d'avis, afin que les Chrestiens n'en glorifiassent, au grand despris d'eux et de leur foy: mais pour nostre gloire traictons la comme folle et insensee, et la renvoyons pour telle, par instrument public. Ce que fut fait, à l'heure ceste bonne femme s'en vint à l'Eglise des Chrestiens et receut la foy, et le baptesme, et despuis vesquit avec les Chrestiens en la religion Chrestienne, et en icelle elle mourut. (fos. 18$^{r–v}$)[17]

As in Estienne Duplais's account of the Cairo resurrections, the voice of the Muslim is heard again here, if only in French, as it emerges from reported ('Le Cadi dit que...') into direct speech ('pour nostre gloire traictons la comme folle et insensee'). But the irony attendant on the Cadi's words, in which he expresses the wish that the story he is part of must not take on the weight of an exemplary tale, would not have been lost on Flavin's readers: this all the more since his decision to spare the resurrected woman, and instead pass her off as 'folle et insensee', is unwittingly complicit with one of the most powerful topoi of Pauline conversions, namely that of Christian folly.

---

[16] Flavin, *De l'estat des ames*, fos. 17^v–18^v. References are incorporated into the text.

[17] 'The Cadi said that he did not agree with this course of action, for fear that the Christians might make of it a source of triumph, to the great detriment of them and their faith: but for the sake of our reputation let us treat her as a mad women quite out of her mind, and send her away as being such using official procedures. This plan was carried out, upon which this good woman went off to the Christian Church and was received in the faith and baptized. From that time she lived among the Christians and according to the Christian religion, in which she died.'

We shall see in a moment how in narratives of demonically engineered, as opposed to divinely sanctioned, 'revenance', the returning wife is often imagined with reference to the mythological story of Orpheus and Eurydice. In those stories the husband, like Orpheus, recovers his wife only fleetingly before going on to lose her for a second, definitive time. Flavin's account constitutes what might be described as a sanctified variation on that theme, since the husband of his narrative is also robbed of his wife: this time, through baptism, to her new Christian faith. Unlike the story of Orpheus and Eurydice, however, the tale that Flavin relates is not offered as one of loss, nor are we at any stage invited to share in the husband's pain. For in renouncing one—earthly—husband, the woman quickly gains another: her newly risen soul is now a Bride of Christ.

André Valladier's *La Saincte Philosophie de l'ame* provides what might be considered a discursive validation of both embodied revenance and the Christ-bride as a figure. That text, probably printed for the first time late in 1612, is an edition of seven sermons delivered by Valladier in Laris in the third week of Advent. In it the preacher revives the possibility of divinely sanctioned corporeal apparitions, and offers the subject an extended theoretical treatment. Tuesday's lesson, entitled 'Des apparitions des ames des trespassez',[18] begins with a passage from the Song of Songs in which the dead soul that returns is likened to the Christ-bride, or 'Espouse'. The typographical layout, reproduced below, underlines the preacher's 'parallèle':

Revertere, revertere, Sunamitis: revertere, revertere ut intueamurte. Revenez, revenez espouse, revenez, revenez qu'on vous revoye. C'est assez demeurer en vos tenebres. C'est une des plus grandes merveilles de reprendre vostre corps, ou quelque autre vous en estant une fois despoüillee, pour vous faire veoir: ô quelle merveille de revenir ça haut, en ceste region soüillee, et marescageuse, pour vous y soüiller les pieds que vous vous estes desia lavez. (p. 673)[19]

Parallele de l'espouse du Cantique avec l'ame

---

[18] Valladier, *La Saincte Philosophie*, pp. 673–713. References are incorporated into the text.

[19] '*Revertere, revertere, Sunamitis: revertere, revertere ut intueamurte.* Come back, come back, bride, come back so that we may see you. You have remained in the shadows long enough. It is one of the greatest marvels that you might take back your body, or some other having once divested yourself of it, to make yourself visible: oh! what a marvel it is to come back from on high, to this sullied mire, to sully your feet there that you had already washed clean. (Parallel between the Bride of the *Song of Songs* and the soul.)

The central notion of Valladier's allegory, that a dead soul might 'reprendre' its body, 'ou quelque autre', in order to '[se] faire veoir', is elaborated in the subsequent sermon. There the preacher argues that aside from being able to take on borrowed bodies, or *corpora peregrina*, some ghosts can appear 'par leur mesme corps':

Vous voudriez sçavoir s'il se peut faire, ou s'il se faict que les esprits pour paroistre se servent non seulement de ces corps fantastiques, mais encores des leurs, les prenans dans leurs tombeaux, ou par les gibets? Pourquoy en douterez vous, puis que l'Escriture Saincte le dit? (p. 691)[20]

By referring to 'l'Escriture Saincte', Valladier is careful to anticipate the most familiar objection to this thesis, namely that dead souls would feel revulsion on re-entering the flesh. This is almost certainly true, he concedes, but the spirit's stay in 'ceste region soüillee, et marescageuse' is only a brief one:

Quand les esprits prennent leurs propres corps, ils ne le prennent pas pour y vivre, et pour l'informer, ains seulement pour y ester cogneus, et pour le mouvoir. (p. 692)[21]

After all, did not the holy men, he asks, rejoin their bodies, however fleetingly, on the day of Christ's Passion on the Cross?[22] 'Revenez qu'on vous revoye': the Song of Songs, rejected by Calvin and many of his followers as apocryphal on account of its vivid sensuality, provides Valladier with a means of devotionalizing, through allegory, the topic of corporeal return.

EURYDICE, OR THE BRIDE OF SATAN

In 1555 the Protestant humanist Georgius Sabinus published a facing-page Latin commentary on various episodes in Ovid's *Metamorphoses*.[23] For the

[20] 'You would like to know whether it is possible or has chanced that spirits, in order to appear, make use not only of those fantastic bodies but also of their own, taking them up from graves or gallows? Why should you doubt it, since Holy Scripture says so?'
[21] 'When spirits take up their own bodies, they do not take them up in order to live in them, and to give them form, but only in order to be recognized, and to move it about.'
[22] Matthew 27:52–3: 'And the graves were opened; and many bodies of the saints which slept arose. And came out of the graves after his resurrection, and went into the holy city, and appeared unto many.' The question of whether the risen men remained alive, or returned to the tomb, had been a subject of theological discussion since Augustine. See, for instance, J. Calvin, *Commentaires de Jehan Calvin sur le Nouveau Testament*, I, p. 722.
[23] G. Sabinus, *Fabularum Ovidii interpretatio tradita in Academia Regiomontana a Georgio Sabino* (Wittemberg: G. Rhaw, 1555); I have consulted a later edition (Canterbury: T. Thomas, 1584), to which references are incorporated into the text.

most part, Sabinus's text belongs squarely in the tradition of the *Ovide moralisé*, aiming as it does to draw out the moral, natural philosophical, and historical implications of Ovid's poem.[24] When Sabinus comes to the story of Orpheus and Eurydice, however, he does not immediately follow the Ovidian 'fabula' with its learned humanist gloss; instead the tale becomes a stimulus for a narrative of his own.

Citing the authority of several noble witnesses, Sabinus recounts the recent story of a Bavarian man who, like Orpheus, is struck with grief at the loss of his young wife. The widower prays ardently for her return until, one day, she miraculously appears. Man and wife renew their marriage vows under the threat of one condition, imposed by the ghost herself, that her husband no longer curses or blasphemes as before. Once this is agreed, the couple continue to live normally; the woman, though pale and sad ('semper tamen fuisse tristem ac pallidam', p. 384) even bears two children. Years pass until, one night, the ghost hears her husband direct curses at a maid. Unfortunately for the husband, the threat was not an idle one: he finds that his wife has vanished, leaving behind only a pile of her clothes. At this point Sabinus proceeds to the commentary proper ('sed Orphei fabulam exponamus . . .', p. 385). The fate of the children is left undisclosed.

Sabinus must have been attracted to the parallel between this recent true report ('historia') and, across the page, its counterpart in fable. Both stories describe a process of loss and temporary recovery, followed by a second, definitive loss. There also reappears the motif of prohibition: just as Orpheus must not look back as he leads his dead wife out of Hades, the ghost instructs her husband that he, too, must not turn back— to the former brutish habits that she endured while still alive. To this extent the narrative serves not as a digression from, but rather a fulfilment of, the commentator's moralizing purpose, providing Sabinus with an opportunity to reflect upon conjugal relations, domestic violence, and loss. Were it not for its supernatural dimension, Sabinus's updated Ovid would tell simply of the breakdown of a marriage. In his interpretation the story of Orpheus and Eurydice becomes—indeed, may never have been anything other than—a tale of separations, second chances, and (with no time to pack the clothes) the final slamming door.

---

[24] On the *Ovide moralisé* tradition in the sixteenth century, see A. Moss, *Ovid in Renaissance France: A Survey of the Latin Editions of Ovid and Commentaries Printed in France before 1600* (London: Warburg Institute, 1982); idem., *Poetry and Fable: Studies in Mythological Narrative in Sixteenth-Century France* (Cambridge: Cambridge University Press, 1984).

Yet the supernatural element remains, and with it a puzzle. Where did this dead woman come from? The child-bearing ghost of Sabinus's narrative raises difficult questions for contemporary demonology. In spite of their Protestantism, neither Sabinus nor Goulart, who would later translate the narrative for the expanded version of his *Histoires admirables et memorables*, chooses to diabolize the ghostly wife in the story.[25] Although neither author is explicit on the matter, the narrative itself rather suggests, through her objection to blasphemy, a divine provenance for this latter-day Eurydice. For the majority of other writers, however, and even for Goulart (as we shall see later), ghosts that one can touch are almost always demonically inspired. As Valladier explained to his congregation in 1612, an evil spirit 'entrera dedans un corps mort, le mouvera, et le fera marcher, mesme parler, non d'un parler propre à l'homme, mais battant tellement l'air qu'on ne pourra nullement y recognoistre aucune difference'.[26] Diabolical agency of this kind was especially to be suspected in cases of dead women who return, since touching enables a new, and far more dangerous, fascination: that of post-mortem sex with the lost spouse or lover.

Several writers on ghosts and (in particular) necromancy seem curiously entranced by ghosts that touch or are touched. Belleforest's *Histoires prodigieuses* makes a discreet reference to the view that ghosts are sometimes able to return in corporeal, palpable form, or 'ainsi que j'ay ouy dire,' he explains, 'à quelqu'un qui avoit experimenté ce qui est de la Necromance'.[27] The possibility of touching ghosts exerts an especial fascination over Goulart, whose *Histoires admirables* includes a number of such cases, mostly German in origin. He tells the story of Estienne Hubener who, having died a wealthy man in 1567, returned as a wrathful revenant.[28] His ghost would stalk the streets, embracing passers-by 'si ferme et roide... qu'aucuns moururent, les autres furent griefvement malades, tous affermans que le riche Hubener les avoit ainsi maniez, et estoit tout tel qu'en son plein vivant'.[29] It is only when the town magistrates slice the head

---

[25] Goulart augmented his *Histoires admirables* in a number of editions between 1610 and his death in 1628. I have consulted the 1628 edition, entitled *Thresor d'histoires admirables et memorables de nostre temps* (Geneva: J. Crespin, 1628). The translation of Sabinus appears on p. 65.

[26] Valladier, *La Saincte Philosophie*, p. 607 'will enter into a dead body, move it around and make it walk, even speak, not using human speech but beating the air at such speed that nobody can recognize any difference'.

[27] Boaistuau, Belleforest, et al., *Histoires prodigieuses* (Paris: veuve G. Cavellat, 1597–8), p. 95.

[28] Goulart, *Histoires admirables*, I, sig. 388ᵛ.

[29] Ibid.: 'so firmly and stiffly... that some died from it, others became seriously ill, all claiming that the rich man, Hubener, had handled them in this way, and appeared as exactly as he was when fully alive'.

from the corpse ('dont le sang rejaillit, comme si Hubener eust esté en plaine vie'), that the dreadful apparitions, which Goulart calls an 'illusion Satanique', are brought to an end.[30] Another of Goulart's anecdotes, taken from the Swiss physician and theologian Thomas Erastus, imagines a less violent form of touching. He tells how Marguerite de Roth, the Abbess of Etesterten, haunted her former home shortly following her death. Goulart writes that 'ce fantosme parloit distinctement de diverses choses', adding further, in a phrase pregnant with sensual possibility, 'et se laissoit toucher'.[31]

The late sixteenth and early seventeenth century produced an increasing number of such tales, the framework almost always that of black arts or illusion. Nicolas Rémy's *Daemonolatreiae* contains a story not unlike that in Sabinus's commentary on Ovid. Rémy tells how a certain German gentleman, 'Aulicus', who is still grieving over the recent death of his wife, one night receives a visit from her ghost. Seeing her undressing in her usual manner, he agrees to let her into his bed. They live together as before until the demon who had raised up her corpse and occupied it in order to deceive and, if possible, destroy the husband, was compelled by an exorcist to depart from it.[32] Goulart's compilation, for its part, alludes to the notorious rumour, especially popular among the enemies of the empire and recently peddled again in Augustin Lercheimer's treatise on enchantments, that the emperor Maximilian had dabbled in necromancy with the help of Johannes Trithemius.[33] The story goes that Maximilian had been left inconsolable following the death of his wife, Marie de Bourgogne. Trithemius, 'homme docte, mais grand magicien', raises up the dead woman who, at his command, walks into Maximilian's chamber:

> Sur ce Marie de Bourgongne entre tout bellement, et vestue à l'accoustumee, en la chambre. L'Empereur la regarde et considere soigneusement, se souvient qu'elle avoit eu en son vivant une verruë sur la nuque du col, laquelle fut veuë lors.[34]

Although, in the manner of the classic recognition scene, the irregularity on Marie's body seems to confirm her identity as the emperor's dead queen, Maximilian soon takes fright and commands his magician to call

---

[30] Ibid., I, fos. 388ᵛ–9ʳ.
[31] Goulart, *Thresor d'histoires admirables*, p. 65.
[32] Remigius, *Daemonolatreiae*, p. 189.
[33] A. Lercheimer (= H. Witekind), *Christlich bedencken und erinnerung von Zauberey* (Heidelberg: J. Müller and H. Aven, 1585).
[34] Goulart, *Thresor d'histoires admirables*, p. 64: 'Upon this Marie de Bourgogne walked straight into the room, dressed in her normal fashion. The Emperor looked at her and examined her carefully, remembering that she had while alive a wart on the nape of her neck, which was also visible now.'

off the illusion. This was a damned art, he concludes, and Trithemius is ordered never to repeat it.

The early seventeenth-century theologian, René Du Pont, writing in his 1602 *La Philosophie des esprits*, is categorical on the illusory nature of revenant wives. Apparitions of this sort are nothing more than demonic 'pourritures'. And since demons cannot contravene nature by engendering a living child in a dead woman's womb, any offspring of such couplings must be illusions or, as he puts it, 'enfans supposez'.[35] Like Sabinus, Du Pont remembers the Eurydice myth, and makes it the archetype of conjugal revenance:

> Et que veulent dire les poëtes par leur fable de la descente d'Orphee aux enfers, pour en retirer sa femme, sinon que par les arts magiques il la resussita, faisant entrer en son corps inanimé quelque diable qui la faisoit sembler vive? mais que le charme fut de si peu de duree, et sa curiosité si grande à la considerer, qu'il la reperdit incontinent?[36]

Where Sabinus had refused to diabolize Orpheus's wife, Du Pont is categorical: Eurydice returns as the bride of Satan.

How can we account for the growing prominence of the revenant lover in late Renaissance France? The witchcraft historian Walter Stephens, writing in his recent *Demon Lovers*, has characterized the problem of demonic corporeality as a primarily intellectual crisis: of an Aristotelian world-view in its late or dying throes. In order to persuade a sceptical population that demons truly exist, Stephens explains, early modern demonology had to grant them bodies—a move its own traditions could not convincingly sustain.[37] An alternative explanation might take us back to the moralizing concerns of post-Tridentine pastoral demonology. For theologians like Du Pont, the story of Eurydice is mobilized as a moral fable about loss. At first she holds out the promise of former fulfilments, as when she is encountered in the bedroom, 'vestue à l'accoustumee' before Maximilian I, or 'disrobing herself in her customary manner' in Remigius's story of Aulicus. In the end, however, she offers only a hollow consolation as she leaves, in Sabinus, her borrowed clothes lying empty on the ground. To this extent Orpheus's catastrophic 'curiosité' provided an

---

[35] Du Pont, *La Philosophie des esprits*, sigs. Evi[r–v].

[36] Ibid., sigs. Ffiii[r–v]: 'And what do the philosophers mean to say through their fable of Orpheus's descent into the underworld, to recover his wife, if not that he resurrected her by means of magic arts, conjuring into her inanimate body some devil who made her seem alive (yet the spell was so short-lived, and his curiosity in examining her so great, that immediately he lost her once more)?'

[37] W. Stephens, *Demon Lovers: Witchcraft, Sex, and the Crisis of Belief* (Chicago: University of Chicago Press, 2002), ch. 3 ('Sexy Devils: How they Got Bodies') and ch. 4 ('Incredible Sex: The Difficulty of Belief').

excellent opportunity to warn against the sexually morbid longings of bereft and lonely men.

But the intellectual and devotional frameworks alone may not do enough to explain the increase in such stories. Many such narratives appear (as in Sabinus or Goulart) without any edifying or intellectual gloss. Another possibility is that the motif's popularity sprang from precisely that ghoulish fascination that clergy like Du Pont were seeking to suppress. Though some of these narratives may ultimately condemn the curiosity of Orpheus, or of Maximilian inspecting 'soigneusement' every inch of his wife's body, they share the necrophiliac fascination of their male protagonists. The following sections of the chapter explore two further avatars of the revenant Eurydice, in which the ghost is gradually eroticized as a figure of both sexual and narrative pleasure. This change is marked, as we shall see shortly, in a shift in the revenant's marital status: she features in these stories no longer as a wife but now as a rebellious adolescent or a stranger in the street. The first of these stories is Phlegon of Tralles's 'Philinnion and Machates', introduced to early modern Europe by Xylander in 1568 and then translated, embroidered, and enlarged in Le Loyer's *Quatre livres des spectres*. The second belongs to François de Rosset, and appears as the tenth narrative in his best-selling *Histoires memorables et tragiques de ce temps* of 1614. Both submit, somewhat in spite of their expressed intentions, to the extraordinary narrative temptations of late Renaissance ghosts.

PHILINNION TRANSFORMED: FROM PHLEGON TO LE LOYER

In 1568 Wilhelm Xylander published a Latin translation of a short text by the then unknown second-century Greek paradoxographer, Phlegon of Tralles.[38] Phlegon's *De mirabilibus libellus*, as Xylander named it, comprises around thirty *faits divers* of varying length, from the single-sentence anecdote or *paradoxon* to the more developed narrative. Subjects range

---

[38] Phlegon of Tralles et al., *Antonini Liberalis transformationum congeries. Phlegontis Tralliani de mirabilibus et longaevis libellus. Eiusdem de Olympiis fragmentum... graece latineque omnia*, trans. and ed. by W. Xylander (Basel: T. Guarinum, 1568). Xylander's text was re-edited by Meursius in 1620 (reprinted again in 1622); see Phlegon of Tralles, *Phlegontis Tralliani, quae exstant opuscula. G. Xylandro interprete. I. Meursius recens* (Louvain: J. Elzevirium, 1620). All references, incorporated into the text, are to Phlegon of Tralles, *The Book of Marvels*, trans. and ed. by W. Hansen (Exeter: University of Exeter Press, 1996).

from monstrous children, homosexual and multiple births, and sex changes, to giants, centaurs, and abnormally rapid senescence. The three longest and most detailed narratives in the collection are all accounts of return from the dead.[39]

Phlegon's most important narrative, and the one we shall focus on here, is the story of Philinnion and Machates. It takes the form of a letter written by the author himself, in his capacity as a local administrator, to another unnamed official. The text discovered by Xylander had only survived as a fragment, so that the report, whose beginning is lost, effectively opens *in medias res*:

> ...[The nurse] went to the door of the guest room, and in the light of the burning lamp she saw the girl sitting beside Machates. Because of the extraordinary nature of the sight, she did not wait there any longer but ran to the girl's mother screaming 'Charito! Demostratos!' She said they should get up and come with her to their daughter, who was alive and by some divine will was with the guest in the guest room. (p. 25)

At first the mother, Charito, does not believe the nurse's story. Her daughter Philinnion, the girl sitting beside the guest, has been dead for six months. At length, however, she is persuaded to check the bedroom for herself. Peering in through the doorway, she cannot make out the female figure and decides to return as dawn breaks the next day. Morning comes, but the girl has disappeared. Charito challenges the guest, Machates, and asks him who was with him in his room the previous night. When he nervously admits that the girl's name is Philinnion, and that it was not the only occasion on which she had visited his room, Charito begins to moan and wail and asks for further proof, revealing that her daughter has long been dead and buried. Machates, stupefied, shows her two love tokens—a gold ring and a breast band—exchanged between the couple the previous night.

The following night Philinnion comes to him again. Waiting for her this time is not only Machates but, now alerted to the ghost's extraordinary visits, the entire household:

> She entered at the usual time and sat down on the bed. Machates pretended that nothing was wrong, since he wished to investigate the whole incredible matter to find out if the girl he was consorting with, who took care to come to him at the same hour, was actually dead. (p. 26)

---

[39] The prominence of this theme may explain why the Danish Protestant historian, Anders Sorensen Vedel, the original owner of the Bodleian copy consulted for this book (Byw. P 2.6), took the decision to bind Phlegon's text with Lavater's *De spectris*.

As the young guest sits with his mistress, eating and drinking, he cannot believe what the others have told him. In order to make sure, he secretly summons the girl's parents:

> They came quickly. When they first saw her, they were speechless and panic-stricken by the amazing sight, but after that they cried aloud and embraced their daughter. Then Philinnion said to them: 'Mother and father, how unfairly you have grudged my being with the guest for three days in my father's house, since I have caused no one any pain. For this reason, on account of your meddling, you shall grieve all over again, and I shall return to the place appointed for me. For it was not without divine will that I came here.' Immediately upon speaking those words she was dead, and her body lay stretched out visibly on the bed. Her father and mother threw themselves upon her, and there was much confusion and wailing in the house because of the calamity. The misfortune was unbearable and the sight incredible. (p. 27)

News of these extraordinary events soon reaches the town officials, including the narrator himself. Crowds begin to gather outside the house. At dawn it is decided that Philinnion's tomb should be opened. In place of the girl's body lies only the iron ring and gilded cup that Machates had given her on the night of her first visit. Having called at the house to examine the corpse, the officials finally take the decision, on the advice of a soothsayer, to burn the dead body outside the city walls. The story ends as Machates becomes despondent and takes his own life.

Phlegon's tale of Philinnion and Machates exhibits many characteristics of a story long known to folklorists as AT245 ('The Search for the Lost Husband').[40] That story would later become, as 'la morte amoureuse', one of the staples of the so-called 'fantastic' literature of early French Romanticism. The central motifs are all there: the young traveller and his mysterious visitor, the sexual encounter, the opening of the tomb, and the discovery of the tell-tale tokens exchanged between the lovers. Also present, and communicated in the narrator's own interventions, is an atmosphere of fearful *admiratio* ('the misfortune was unbearable and the sight incredible') that will reach its apogee in the narrative treatments of writers like Gautier, Nodier, and Potocki. But early nineteenth-century Romanticism was not first to realize the sensationalist potential of Phlegon's letter. Le Loyer had got there first in 1586. For the Angevin demonologist not only translates Phlegon's fragmented original, he completes it, effectively embroidering it into a full-blown erotic melodrama. A close reading of his version will illustrate the point.

---

[40] Using the Arne-Thompson motif index. See Hansen's analysis in Phlegon of Tralles, *Book of Marvels*, pp. 79–85.

Le Loyer's translation from Phlegon's *Book of Marvels* appears in the second book of the *Quatre livres des spectres*, in a chapter entitled 'De l'apparition des demons en cadavres ou charoignes de morts'.[41] There the story of Philinnion and Machates is set out as if what we are reading were a direct translation. This impression is partly an effect of the printer's typography: the episode, one of the longest in the *Quatre livres des spectres*, is recounted over several pages and accompanied throughout by inverted commas in the margin. In spite of its appearance as a faithful replication, however, Le Loyer has made a number of significant alterations. Five in particular stand out: the switch from the first- to the third-person narrative voice; the addition of a long opening passage, entirely the product of Le Loyer's own invention; the emergence, both in this passage and elsewhere in the narrative, of several stylistic and rhetorical features lacking in Phlegon's original; a more pronounced interest in the body of the ghost; and a new and striking stress on the salacious aspects of the tale.

In the first of Le Loyer's alterations to the original, he entirely suppresses Phlegon's first-person narrator. This change has important consequences for the story as a whole, and will to some degree permit the author his further, more far-reaching changes. In Phlegon's narrative, framed as a letter to an official, the narrator signals his presence first of all as an agent in the events. He is entrusted with controlling the crowds who gather at the house; he accompanies other officials to the opening of the grave; he, again with others, sees for himself the body of the dead girl as it lies stretched out on the bed in Machates's chamber; finally, he is instructed by a local soothsayer to perform a series of sacrificial rites in order to appease the angry gods. In addition to being an actor in the story, the narrator is also one of several self-conscious agents in the narrative's transmission. At the end of Phlegon's text, he instructs the recipient of the letter that if he decides to pass the news on to the king, he should send word back to the narrator 'in order that I may dispatch to you one of the persons who examined the affair in detail'.[42] To this extent, the 'I' of Phlegon's text places himself within a hierarchy of expert witnesses, all with differing degrees of access to the original events.

For the incredulous or sceptical reader, however, Phlegon's role as *actant* within the narrative, that is to say as a participant and witness, may present a problem. By including, or embodying, himself as an actor in the events that he relates, and by laying such an emphasis on the process of transmission, the letter-writer in fact signals his own limitations as narrator. His narrative lays claim to a degree of omniscience that effectively

<hr/>

[41] *Quatre livres des spectres*, Book Two, ch. 3. All references are incorporated into the text.
[42] Phlegon, *Book of Marvels*, p. 28.

stands in contradiction to the true, and only partial, view of the events that he recounts. Particularly suspect are those moments in which the narrator reports, or at the very least focalizes, the thoughts and emotions of the unfortunate Machates. How could he have known the details of what passed, in private, between the lover and the ghost? Le Loyer, in ridding himself of Phlegon's epistolographical 'I', removes such disjunctions at a stroke. In his third-person translation, suppositions of this kind are entirely unproblematic, since the narrator of the story can pretend to complete omniscience.

Thanks to this newly omniscient narrator, Le Loyer is able, in a second alteration to Phlegon's original, to provide what in Xylander's edition is left unseen and incomplete, namely the beginning of the story and—crucially—the ghost's first appearance. Thus the narrative begins with an introduction to Philinnion, 'belle et de bonne grace', and to her parents, 'des notables bourgeois et famez de la ville' (I, p. 380). In a fatalistic gloss reminiscent of Boaistuau and Belleforest's *Histoires tragiques*, Le Loyer continues, 'voicy que la fortune ou plustost le destin (qui se plaist de changer les choses tout au rebours qu'elles ne sont pourpensées et proposées en la pensée des hommes) voulut aussi renverser le bonheur de ceste famille et son attente' (I, p. 380). Just as the parents, Demostratos and Charito, are preparing their daughter for marriage, Le Loyer supposes, Philinnion is struck down by a strange and incurable illness. Despite the doctors' best attempts to save her, she dies and is buried in the family vault, along with a number of jewels and other accoutrements dear to her when still alive.

Shortly afterwards, a young man, Machates, pays the family a visit 'en intention de renouveller le droict d'hospitalité que luy et les siens avoient avec Demostrate' (I, p. 381). Despite the friendship between the parents of the two families, Machates knows nothing of Philinnion or her death. He is warmly received, and shown to the best room in the house. Giving his imagination free rein in a passage with no counterpart in Phlegon, Le Loyer imagines Philinnion's arrival:

> Et là comme il estoit prest d'aller soupper et resvoit profondement sur quelques occurrences, voicy que d'une antichambre sort l'ombre de Philinnion, semblable à elle de corps, de face, et de couleur, sinon qu'elle estoit aucunement plus palle que durant sa vie, laquelle voyant Machates estonné de son arrivée inopinée en ce lieu, s'approche de luy et luy commence à dire, 'Mon Gentilhomme qu'avez vous à vous estonner en ceste façon? Je suis la fille de ceans qui pieça advertie de vostre venu et gentillesse, et la voulant connoistre maintenant par espreuve, vous suis venu requerir une chose que bonnement ne me pouvez refuser, aumoins si vous estes celuy que bruit la renommée estre courtois, doux et bien apprins: c'est qu'eu egard à l'affection

et bon vouloir que je vous porte et vous porteray toute ma vie, vous ne soyez dedaigneux de me recevoir par un devoir mutuel, en vostre amour. Et vous puis asseurer au reste que je n'ay peu choisir une heure plus commode que ceste cy, en laquelle aydée et appuyée de la faveur de la nuict, je puisse deceler mon amour sans le sçeu de mes parens qui m'esclairent de pres. Ne me chassez donc point, et ne permettez que contre l'opinion que j'ay euë de vostre douceur et humanitez (vertuz qui vous sont plus familieres) je sorte toute vergogneuse et honteuse (comme fille que je suis) devant vostre face. Ce disant elle luy tend le bras au col, et le baise fort mignardement. Le jeune gentilhomme mis aux alteres, et ne se faisant point par trop tirer l'oreille, la receut aussi de son costé, et la jettant sur un petit lit qui estoit en la chambre, jouit d'elle à son plaisir. Leurs baisers et accolades passées, Machates appella son serviteur, feist couvrir la table, et soupperent ensemble Philinnion et luy. (I, 381–2)[43]

It is at this point—and only at this point—that Phlegon's own fragment begins, as the nurse, peering through the doorway, witnesses the extraordinary sight of her mistress's daughter returned from the dead.

Le Loyer's imaginative completion of the story's opening enables him to introduce, in a third transformation of Phlegon's original, a number of stylistic and rhetorical features that continue to predominate throughout the rest of the translation. The most obvious is the use of direct as opposed to reported speech. Philinnion's invented address to Machates is the work of Le Loyer the playwright. Its carefully turned rhetoric pitches a direct appeal to the young man's 'douceur et humanitez (vertuz qui vous sont plus familieres)' against the shame she would suffer—'vergogneuse et honteuse (comme fille que je suis)'—were he to refuse her advances. The ghost also plays vividly on the contrast

---

[43] 'And then as he was ready to go and dine, and daydreaming deeply about sundry things, behold the ghost of Philinnion emerging from an antechamber, similar to her in body, face, and complexion, except that she was somewhat paler than when alive. Seeing Machates surprised at her unexpected arrival in that place, she approached him and addressed him thus. "My noble Sir why are you so surprised? I am the daughter of the house who, a short while ago warned of your visit and your noble nature, and, now wanting to experience it directly for myself, have come to ask of you something you cannot rightly refuse me, at least if you really are that man reputed to be courteous, gentle, and well brought up. Namely, in view of the affection and good will in which I hold you now—and shall all my life—you will not be so contemptuous as to receive my love, and give me yours. And I can assure you besides that I could not have chosen an hour more appropriate than this one, since being helped and supported as I am by the cover of darkness, I can hide away my love from my parents, who keep watch over me. So do not chase me away, and do not disappoint my high opinion of your gentleness and human qualities by making me leave disgraced and shamefaced (girl that I am)." As she said this she curled her arm around his neck, and kissed him most alluringly. The enraptured young gentleman did not need to be asked twice, received her willingly and, throwing her on a small bed that was in the room, took his pleasure of her. Once their kisses and caresses were over, Machates called his servant, ordered that the table be laid, and dined together with Philinnion.'

between light and dark, knowledge and ignorance: able to visit 'à la faveur de la nuict', she is concealed from her parents who, she claims, '*m'esclairent* de pres' (my italics). A little further on, Le Loyer again has recourse to direct speech in the confrontation between the old nurse and the parents:

> Ô Charito et vous mon maître Demostrate, s'il vous plaist de me suivre je vous montreray la plus grand merveille que vous veistes jamais: c'est vostre fille Philinnion qui est resuscitée et retournée en vie par la volonté des Dieux et souppe en la chambre haute avec vostre hoste Machates. (1, 382–3)[44]

Where in Xylander's edition and translation the conversation is merely reported, the French translation brings it to life as a piece of narrative drama.[45]

In addition to his privileging of direct over reported speech, Le Loyer also betrays a tendency to embellish the affective dimension of the story. This is achieved most straightforwardly by granting prominence to an element already ubiquitous in Phlegon's original narrative: the pathetic body. For instance, when Charito enters Machates's bedchamber and finds that her daughter is no longer there, 'elle devint toute troublée de tristesse, et fondant en larmes se jetta aux pieds de Machates qu'elle embrassa fort estroitement' (1, pp. 384–5).[46] And once the youth has shown her the tokens left to him by Philinnion the previous night, 'Elle commença de s'escrier hautement et se laissa tomber en terre, derompant sa cotte et sa robbe, et arrachant par grand violence son chaperon hors de sa teste, disant mille folies, et tenant et serrant estroittement entre ses mains la bague et le collet qu'elle baisoit mille fois' (1, p. 386).[47] The apogee of the pathetic body comes as the mother and father grieve over the corpse of the newly deceased Philinnion:

> Qui diroit le deuil du pere et de la mere pleurans encore une fois leur fille, et environnans son lict avecques gemissements et pleurs? (1, p. 388)[48]

---

[44] 'Oh Charito and you, my master Demostrate, if it please you to follow me I shall show you the greatest wonder you have ever seen: it is your daughter Philinnion who is resurrected and come back to life by the grace of the gods, and dining in the upper chamber with your guest, Machates.'

[45] Phlegon of Tralles et al., *De mirabilibus et longaevis libellus*, p. 3.

[46] 'She became overcome with sadness and, bursting into tears, threw herself to Machates's feet, which she drew in a tight embrace.'

[47] 'She began to cry out and dropped to the ground, tearing her dress and her skirts, and ripping off her bonnet with great violence, saying a thousand mad things and, in her hands, holding and clutching tight the ring and the bodice, which she covered in kisses.'

[48] 'What words could describe the mourning of the mother and father, grieving for their daughter a second time, and surrounding her bed with wailing and tears?'

The 'Qui diroit?' here, which seems an acknowledgement of the limits of narratability, is in fact a rhetorically productive instance of *adynaton*.[49] Though words fail the narrator, the second half of the sentence, and the grieving gestures of the parents, is enough to provide an answer to his question in the first.

In a further substantive change to Phlegon's original, Le Loyer counterpoises the transparently expressive, pathetic bodies of Charito and Demostratos, with the opaque, uncertain corporeality of the ghost of their dead daughter. That uncertainty, which is of central concern within the theoretical context of Le Loyer's chapter as a whole, is evoked from the perspective of Machates. Is the girl with whom he is consorting truly dead, as Charito claims? Or is she in fact alive, and are her visitations thus susceptible to another, less sinister explanation? As if attempting to answer the young man's question, Le Loyer's narrative gaze, unlike that of Phlegon, lingers long on the body of the girl:

> Voicy que d'une antichambre sort l'ombre de Philinnion, semblable à elle de corps, de face, et de couleur, sinon qu'elle estoit aucunement plus palle que durant sa vie. (I, p. 381)[50]

In Phlegon's story, the youth's suspicions over the mother's story arise from seeing his mistress eat and drink, an activity not usually associated with ghosts.[51] In Le Loyer, by contrast, the same doubts have their origins in the girl's lifelike appearance:

> Machates regardant de plus pres à la contenance, à la face, au corsage, et à la couleur aucunement vermeille de la fille, ne pouvoit se persuader que ce fust un corps mort, ou l'ombre et spectre d'un corps. (I, p. 387)[52]

Machates's bewildered examination might appear to recall that of Emperor Maximilian who, having raised his dead wife with the help of Trithemius, 'la regarde et considere soigneusement' in an attempt to locate traces of imposture. In that episode, however, the emperor's search was for *gnomismata*—in this case the telltale wart—or recognizable signs of a given individual. The use here of the technical 'spectre' suggests that Machates's scrutiny of Philinnion, as narrated by Le Loyer, coincides instead with the sophistication of the specialist enquirer.

---

[49] In the sense described by R. A. Lanham, *A Handlist of Rhetorical Terms*, 2nd edn. (Berkeley and Los Angeles: University of California Press, 1991), s.v. 'adynata'.
[50] 'Behold the ghost of Philinnion emerging from an antechamber, similar to her in body, face, and complexion, except that she was somewhat paler than when alive.'
[51] On the question of whether ghosts eat and drink, see above, p. 53.
[52] 'Looking more closely at the countenance, face, clothing, and at the somewhat ruddy complexion of the girl, Machates could not accept that this was a dead body, or the shade or spectre of a body.'

The undecidability surrounding the body of the ghost, and the resulting
fascination, also survives into later editions of the *Quatre livres des spectres*.
There, in keeping with the prefatory promise of a 'science des spectres', the
breathless hypotaxis, direct speech and rhetorical embellishments of Le
Loyer's first version make way for a sparser, more controlled account of
the narrative in Phlegon. Nonetheless, the translator's fascination with
Philinnion's corporeality persists, and spreads to every quarter of the
town's community. Here, Le Loyer describes the servants' reaction to
Philinnion's second death:

> Ayant dit ces mots elle tomba morte, et son corps fut mis sur le lict, exposé à
> la veuë de ceux de la maison, à qui le vouloit toucher et manier.[53]

Likewise the official investigators who, having found the grave empty, visit
the house to view the revenant:

> Ce faict, le gouverneur et ceux de la ville allerent en la maison de Demostrate,
> et entrerent en la chambre de Machates pour cognoistre si le vray corps de
> Philinnion y estoit. Ils voyent le corps couché à plat de terre, ils le touchent,
> ils le manient, et se retirent.[54]

In both of these cases the fascination of the witnesses is satisfied no longer
only by sight. Acting on an impulse that cannot fail to recall that of those
who bore witness to the resurrected Christ, the company that gathers
around Philinnion's corpse cannot apprehend what has happened without
touching the dead body.

Le Loyer's insistence on the ghost's corporeality is a characteristic
feature of the ghost narratives considered in this chapter. Perhaps most
prominent of all, however, and what separates accounts such as this from
those found in Goulart, Sabinus, and Remigius, is Le Loyer's obvious
interest in the prurient or salacious aspects of the story. That salaciousness
derives in part from an increased emphasis on Philinnion's sexual agency.
Thanks to a number of surreptitious additions to the Greek original, Le
Loyer's ghost kisses, cajoles, and caresses as Phlegon's does not:

> Ce disant elle luy tend le bras autour du col et le baise fort mignardement.
> (1, 382)[55]

---

[53] *Discours des spectres*, p. 247: 'Having said these words she fell down dead, and her
body was placed on the bed for those of the household to see, so that whoever wanted to
could touch and handle her.'
[54] Ibid.: 'This having been done, the governor and townspeople went to Demostrates's
house, and went into Machates's chamber to find out whether Philinnion's true body was
there. They saw the body lying on the ground. They touched it, handled it, and left.'
[55] 'As she said this she curled her arm around his neck, and kissed him most flirtatiously.'

Or devant que le jour commençast à poindre, l'ombre de Philinnion... se leve du lit, et baisant et accollant Machates... luy laissa son collet ou gaze duquel elle estreignoit ses beaux et rons tetins. (I, p. 384)[56]

Elle ne faut pas à venir, et la premiere chose qu'elle faict c'est d'accoller et baiser Machates, et s'asseoir puis apres sur un lict comme elle avoit fait la premiere nuit. (I, pp. 386–7)[57]

The erotic appeal of the ghost's body is only increased when we remember that, aside from the frisson of necrophilia, the story of Philinnion and Machates also offers us illicit love *tout court*. The young girl is consorting with a guest without the knowledge of her parents. Le Loyer insists far more strongly than Phlegon on this element of secrecy attendant upon the trysts between the lovers. As dawn breaks after their first night together, Philinnion, who here keeps up the pretence of the ever-watchful parents, 'prist congé de Machates, craignant que sa mere la voulust venir trouver'. And when, shortly after the passage quoted earlier, in which Machates gazes perplexedly upon the body of his lover, he imagines that Charito may have lied in an attempt to trap her daughter:

Il consideroit... que la fille, au desçeu de ses parens, venoit en cachettes à luy, à une heure propre pour ceux ou celles qui veulent negotier et traiter d'amour familierement, et que sa mere la feignoit morte, afin que par ceste ruze elle les trouvast sur le faict tous deux. (I, p. 387)[58]

In this extraordinary piece of wishful thinking—that the mother might have feigned her daughter's death in order to discover an illicit affair— Machates fleetingly supposes that he may just have been the victim of an elaborate ghost-hoax.

Subsequent events will prove Machates wrong. But there is a sense in which, as is often the case in romance or comedy, the true drama of the story has as much to do with a generational conflict over the fate of female bodies as with the supernatural 'marvel' of the dead returned to life. The theme of parental oppression, and of adolescent rebellion, is strengthened in the beginning that Le Loyer imagines for the story. There, he states, Philinnion had died of her illness 'comme ceste Damoiselle feust en aage

---

[56] 'Now before day began to break, the ghost of Philinnion... got up from the bed, and kissing and embracing Machates... left him her band or bodice, with which she bound her beautiful round breasts.'

[57] 'She did not fail to visit, and the first thing she did was to embrace and kiss Machates, and then sit on the bed as she had on the first night.'

[58] 'He thought... that the girl was coming to him in secret, without her parents' knowledge, at a time of day quite apt for those who want to engage in amorous pastimes, and that her mother was pretending that she was dead, in order that by that ruse she might catch the two of them in the act.'

nubile, et que son pere et sa mere fussent prests de l'apparier et marier selon sa qualité' (i, p. 380).[59] The 'comme' here, capable of meaning not only 'when' but also 'since', carries a strong hint that the girl's death and impending marriage might here too be causally related as, perhaps, does the prohibitive-sounding 'selon sa qualité'. This was certainly the way in which Le Loyer's narrative was read by two later specialists, Delrio and Guazzo. In their summary retellings of the narrative, Philinnion is to wed Machates himself before she died, but pines away in despair when her parents object to the match.[60] In all these versions, the exchange of gold and iron rings between the couple on the night of their first meeting takes on added significance as an act of youthful rebellion. By symbolically marrying Machates as a corporeal revenant, the young girl reclaims her body not only from death but also, and more importantly, from the clutches of her parents. Philinnion is just one of several women in this chapter who enjoy a pleasure unknown while still alive: that is, the extremes of sexual freedom that come with being dead.

Le Loyer's demonological reading of Phlegon's story was not new. Writing in his annotations to the first edition of 1568, Xylander had also raised the possibility of diabolical involvement in Philinnion's return, although in the end he chooses to suspend judgement on the matter ('ego in medio rem relinquo').[61] What is new is the degree of narrative seduction at work in the French version. Taken together, all Le Loyer's alterations to Phlegon's original suggest that the author's interest in the story goes beyond, or at least is not reducible to, its value as evidence for a demonological thesis. The degree of rhetorical interference is such that Le Loyer appears less engaged in communicating 'une science des spectres' than indulging in what he will later condemn, in subsequent editions of the treatise, as 'un conte à plaisir'. The tale is the product of a poet and a playwright susceptible, here as so often in his treatise, to the compulsion to narrate.

That compulsion, and the desire it reproduces in the reader, fulfils in part a moralizing purpose. In a shock reversal characteristic of Counter-Reformation writing, Le Loyer exploits the pleasure that the reader takes in his erotic melodrama in order to spring, at the close of the narrative, an unpleasant surprise. Having indulged the (male) reader's fantasy of illicit sex with a young stranger, he now asks rhetorically:

---

[59] 'as this girl was of marriageable age, and as her mother and father were preparing to find a match for her and marry her according to her status'.
[60] Delrio, *Disquisitionum magicarum*, sig. Zzii^r; Guazzo, *Compendium maleficarum*, p. 77.
[61] Phlegon of Tralles et al., *De Mirabilibus et longaevis libellus*, p. 316.

Or qui voudroit maintenant revocquer en doubte qu'au corps et charoigne de Philinnion ne fust enclos un diable, qui pour estre succube de Machates s'advisa de prendre ce corps freschement mort, et avoir son accointance, de laquelle il se retira si tost qu'il fut descouvert par les parens de la fille deffuncte? (ɪ, p. 391)[62]

This rhetorical question is of a different order to those instances of *adynaton* (e.g. 'Qui diroit le deuil du pere et de la mere?') within the narrative itself. Here, it seems, Le Loyer is no longer indulging the pleasure to be had in erotic spectacle, preferring instead, and as it were retrospectively, to unmask the source of pleasure in the story as repulsive and demonic. This frightening reversal, which consists in turning the reader's pleasure back against him, is one that we shall encounter again. In the final narrative considered in this chapter, from François de Rosset's *Histoires memorables et tragiques de ce temps*, the erotic spectacle of the revenant lover, and the pleasure it induces in both characters and readers, is forced to nightmarish extremes.

PHILINNION'S AFTERLIFE: FRANÇOIS DE ROSSET

By the time the second edition of Le Loyer's treatise appeared in 1605, Philinnion's story had gained a certain independence. In the intervening period, the author would have seen, perhaps with approval, how her narrative had become a prominent commonplace in the demonologies of Crespet, Remigius, Guazzo, and Delrio.[63] He would also have been aware, and possibly less approving, of the extent to which his translation had made Philinnion the subject of less serious writing, or 'propos familiers': the *devisants* of Bouchet's *Sérées* discuss her, for instance; she also features in a late addition to the *Histoires prodigieuses*.[64] It was not until the following decade, however, that Philinnion's popularity, not to say narrative promiscuity, reached its peak. In 1613, a version of the same character appears in a *canard* entitled *Histoire prodigieuse d'un gentilhomme auquel le Diable s'est apparu, et avec lequel il a conversé, sous le corps d'une femme morte*.[65] In that narrative, whose mixture of prurience and disgust is characteristic of the *canards* as a genre, the 'femme morte' is a Parisian

---

[62] 'Now who would be prepared to doubt that a devil invaded Philinnion's corpse, who in order to be Machates's succubus decided to take a newly deceased body, and couple with him, and from which it withdrew the moment it was discovered by the dead girl's parents?'

[63] Crespet, *La Hayne de Sathan*, sigs. 107ᵛ–8ʳ, 294ʳ–5ʳ; Remigius, *Daemonolatreiae*, p. 188.

[64] On these adoptions of Le Loyer's translation of Phlegon, see above, p. 168.

[65] Paris: F. de Carroy.

courtesan who seduces a young man as they shelter from the rain. Transposed to Lyon, that story, along with Philinnion's tale, may have provided the inspiration for the subject of what follows, the tenth narrative of François de Rosset's *Histoires memorables et tragiques de ce temps.*

It is now over a decade since Anne de Vaucher-Gravili edited Rosset's *Histoires memorables et tragiques* for Le Livre de Poche.[66] Her critical work, along with that of Sergio Poli in particular, provides a detailed introduction to Rosset, who now appears to have cemented his place in French literary history.[67] This is not to forget that Rosset's own contemporaries, among them Pierre de L'Estoile, may well have regarded his 'histoires' as only slightly more respectable variants on the popular *canards*, from which the author drew so much of his material. Like the *canards*, these stories were 'nouvelles' in the original sense of that term: that is, texts written, at least in part, to satisfy a desire for sensational news.[68] That said, however, the *Histoires memorables* long outlived their immediate function. First published in 1614 and reprinted, accompanied by varying amounts of new material, in no fewer than twenty-five editions (not counting translations into English, Dutch, and German) over the course of the seventeenth and eighteenth centuries, Rosset's collection has been described as an early modern best-seller.[69] The text's influence was considerable: imitated in the seventeenth century by Camus, Mallingre, and Parival, and revived in the late eighteenth and early nineteenth by Sade, Potocki, Nodier, Barbey d'Aurevilly, Dumas, and Stendhal, Rosset's collection of 'aventures tragiques', 'amours incestueuses', 'horribles excès', and

[66] F. de Rosset, *Histoires memorables et tragiques de ce temps* [1614], ed. by A. de Vaucher-Gravili (Paris: Livre de Poche, 1994). Vaucher-Gravili's text, which uses modernized orthography, is based on the 1619 edition, the last to be published during Rosset's lifetime. All references are to Vaucher-Gravili's edition and are incorporated into the text.

[67] See especially A. de Vaucher-Gravili, *Loi et transgression: les histoires tragiques au XVIIᵉ siècle* (Lecce: Milella, 1992); idem., 'De la transgression et du tragique: les *histoires tragiques* de François de Rosset', in *Tragedia e sentimento del tragico nella letteratura francese del Cinquecento*, ed. by E. H. Balmas (Florence: Olschki, 1990), pp. 164–76; idem., 'Langages et figures de séduction dans les *Histoires tragiques* de François de Rosset', in *Miti e linguaggi della seduzione*, ed. by M. G. Adamo, M. Gasparro, and M. T. Puleio (Catane: C.U.E.C.M, 1993), pp. 97–114; S. Poli, *Histoire(s) tragique(s): Anthologie/Typologie d'un genre littéraire* (Paris: Nizet, 1992).

[68] On Rosset's debt to the *canards*, see M. Lever, 'De l'information à la nouvelle: les "canards" et les *Histoires tragiques* de Rosset', in *Revue d'histoire littéraire de la France*, 79 (1979), pp. 577–93. On the *canards* as news, see J. P. Séguin, *L'Information en France avant le périodique: 517 canards imprimés entre 1529 et 1631* (Paris: G.-P. Maisonneuve et Larose, 1964); R. Chartier, 'Reading Matter and "Popular" Reading: From the Renaissance to the Seventeenth Century', in *A History of Reading in the West*, ed. by G. Cavallo and R. Chartier, trans. by L. G. Cochrane (Oxford: Polity Press, 1999), pp. 269–83.

[69] For a full list of editions, see Vaucher-Gravili's introduction in Rosset, pp. 25–6.

'barbaries estranges' has been cited as a prominent precursor of modern 'fantastic' literature.[70] Of all Rosset's narratives, perhaps that considered below was the most widely read: the tenth in Vaucher-Gravili's edition, it is entitled 'D'un demon qui apparaissait en forme de demoiselle au lieutenant du chevalier du guet de la ville de Lyon, de leur accointance charnelle, et de la fin malheureuse qui en succéda'. The aim here is not to cast Rosset in the role of an early forebear within a genealogy of the fantastic. What follows instead places his *Histoires memorables* as a culminating point on the trajectory traced out over the course of this book: that of the reception, vulgarization, and narrativization of learned writing on ghosts in late Renaissance France. Even without the narrative that we are about to consider, Rosset's contribution to that journey was considerable. Like his precursors in the tradition of the *Histoires tragiques*, François de Belleforest and Bénigne Poissenot, Rosset took a keen interest in demonological matters: his translations of Simon Maiolus's *Dies caniculares* and (with Goulart) Philip Camerarius's *Operae horarum subcisivarum* brought into French a wealth of learned writing about ghosts and other prodigies.[71] Unlike those two authors, however, whose demonological preoccupations never encroached on the *Histoires tragiques* themselves, Rosset placed preternatural phenomena at the very centre of the genre. His narratives are strewn with references to witchcraft, sorcery, and ghosts.[72] The third *histoire* recounts the notorious case of Louis de Gaufridy, a Provençal priest convicted of sorcery, with the Dominican exorcist and demonologist Sébastien Michaëlis making a personal appearance. Mention is made, in the fifteenth narrative, of Plato's authority on the phenomenon of cruentation, where a murderer approaches the body of his victim only to find that 'ses narines et ses plaies s'ouvrent et jettent contre lui un ruisseau de sang dont il est tout souillé' (p. 346). In the tenth narrative, 'd'un demon qui apparaissait en forme de demoiselle', Rosset cites the notorious case of the 'démoniaque de Laon', written up by Jean Boulaese and others. Finally, the same story includes a reference to 'une jeune fille nommée Philinnion de Thessalie qui, après avoir été mise au sepulchre, parut à Machates Macédonien et coucha longtemps avec lui' (p. 261). Though Rosset here accredits only the source in Phlegon, 'affranchi de l'empereur

[70] This is Vaucher-Gravili's view. See Rosset, *Histoires memorables et tragiques*, p. 6.
[71] Rosset's version of the *Operae horarum subcisivarum*, which completed Goulart's unfinished translation, contains a detailed examination of Icelandic ghosts, for example; see P. Camerarius, *Les Heures desrobees*, pp. 109–18.
[72] See Closson, *L'Imaginaire démoniaque*, pp. 297–302.

Adrien', it is clear that he has found the narrative in Le Loyer's *Discours et histoires des spectres.*[73]

The facts of his own story, which Rosset claims to have occurred four or five years previously, are as follows. In Lyons a 'chevalier de guet', La Jacquière, is out patrolling his watch. Well known to suffer from a weakness for 'les garces', he declares to the group of friends walking with him, 'je ne sais, mes amis, de quelle viande j'ai mangé. Tant y a que je me sens si échauffé que, si maintenant je rencontrais le diable, il n'échapperait jamais de mes mains que premièrement je n'en eusse fait à ma volonté' (p. 253).[74] Speak of the Devil: no sooner are these words uttered ('à peine a-t-il achevé de proférer ces paroles') than he spies a young woman, accompanied only by a single lackey, out walking 'en une rue, qui est proche du pont de Saône' (ibid.). Unperturbed by the coincidence of her sudden appearance, La Jacquière approaches her and offers to escort her home. At first she protests, concerned at her husband's response, but relents when La Jacquière reveals his position. Back at her house ('une maison fort écartée') on the other side of town, La Jacquière is admitted along with two of his friends. The husband is nowhere to be seen.

The scene inside is briefly described. The house is 'fort basse', with the upstairs rooms used solely for storing wood 'et autres choses semblables' (p. 255). The remaining rooms, 'une petite salle et une garderobe', are for their part pleasantly decorated in taffeta and serge. However, in what may constitute a hint to the vigilant reader of demonological signs, the dominant shade is a sulphurous yellow. After a lengthy scene of seduction, La Jacquière finally obtains what he desires in the 'garderobe' on a small bed, also of yellow, where 'ils prennent leurs déduits ensemble' (p. 256). Emboldened by the ease of his success, La Jacquière suggests that 'ses compagnons aient part au gâteau', a prospect to which the young woman, after further persuasion, eventually agrees. Shortly after all three men have satisfied their desire, they recline in the next room, admiring the beauty of their latest conquest. At this point the woman gets up, approaches the fire and challenges them as follows:

---

[73] The nationalities of Philinnion and Machates ('de Thessalie', 'Macédonien') mentioned by Rosset are not given in Xylander's edition, but only deduced later, by Le Loyer, from the names of the young couple.

[74] 'I do not know, my friends, what food I've eaten. But I feel so aroused that, even if I now encountered the devil himself, he would not escape my hands until I had used him as I wanted.'

Vous croyez avoir fait un grand gain, d'avoir obtenu de moi l'accomplisse-
ment de vos désirs. Il n'est pas si grand que vous penseriez bien. Avec qui
pensez-vous avoir eu affaire? (p. 258)[75]

No sooner have the men replied, with unwitting irony, that they find her
to be 'la plus belle et la plus galante dame qui vive', than Rosset stages his
coup de théâtre. 'Je veux me découvrir à vous et vous faire paraître qui je
suis', she tells them:

Ce disant, elle retrousse sa robe et sa cotte et leur fait voir la plus horrible, la
plus vilaine, la plus puante et la plus infecte charogne du monde. (pp. 258–9)[76]

At this moment the house vanishes, leaving the three men 'étendus
comme des pourceaux dans le bourbier, sans reprendre leurs esprits'
(p. 259). One of the men is already dead, of fear; La Jacquière dies the
next day, and the third only two or three days later, but not before he
'raconta le succès de cette étrange aventure' (ibid.).

Aside from its ostensible purpose, which Rosset claims to be a refutation of 'les athées et les épicuriens qui nient l'apparition des esprits', the
narrative operates on an equally straightforward level as a misogynist fable
or, more specifically, a warning against the 'puanteur' or (to recall Du
Pont's term) 'pourriture' of female sexuality.[77] The procedure is not subtle
and involves, typically for Rosset, the staging of what one of his many
imitators, Jean-Pierre Camus, would call a sudden 'spectacle d'horreur'.[78]
The critical peripeteia is prepared as the three friends, fresh from their
collective sexual conquest, sit back to gaze on their new mistress. We have
already encountered a number of moments in narratives of corporeal
return where the witness stops to examine, or 'considerer', the body of
the female revenant: Orpheus's 'curiosité si grande à...considerer' his
dead wife Eurydice; Emperor Maximilian who 'regarde et considere
soigneusement' his dead wife, Marie de Bourgogne; and Machates, who,
'regardant de plus pres à la contenance, à la face, au corsage, et à la couleur
aucunement vermeille de la fille', cannot be persuaded that Philinnion is
dead. All of these moments describe a kind of secular *discretio spirituum* in
which the witness attempts to discover, or discern, the true nature of the
body before him. Unlike these characters, however, the three friends in

[75] 'You think you have made a great gain to have obtained from me the fulfilment of
your desires. It is not as great as you think. Who do you think you have been dealing with?'
[76] 'Saying this, she lifts up her dress and her underskirts and reveals to them the most
horrible, the most vile, the most revolting, the foulest carcass in the world.'
[77] See M. Jeanneret, *Éros rebelle: littérature et dissidence à l'âge classique* (Paris: Seuil,
2003), Ch. 4 ('Le Fouet des paillards').
[78] J.-P. Camus, *Les Spectacles d'horreur, où se descouvrent plusieurs tragiques effects de
nostre siècle* (Paris: A. Soubron, 1630).

Rosset's story have not the slightest suspicion that the object of their desire is, or may be, dead: this is not a tale of *revenance* in the strong sense, of a lost lover or family member returning to the living; it is rather a cautionary tale in which careless, lustful words ('si maintenant je rencontrais le diable...') come back to haunt the speaker. Their ignorance permits Rosset to redescribe the male gaze upon the demon in the terms of an unalloyed eroticism:

> Ils ne cessent de la contempler et admirer. L'un loue son front et dit que c'est une table d'ivoire bien polie. L'autre s'arrête sur ses yeux et assure que ce sont les flambeaux dont Amour allume toutes les âmes généreuses. L'autre se met sur la louange de ses blonds cheveux qu'elle déliait, parce qu'il était temps de s'aller coucher et ne cesse de proférer tout haut que ce sont les filets où le fils de Cypris arrête la liberté des hommes et des dieux. Enfin, il n'y a partie de son corps qu'ils ne prisent. Ses mains ne vont jamais en vain à la conquête. Sa gorge surpasse la blancheur de la neige; et les petits amours volettent à l'entour de ses joues pour y sucer les roses, les lys et les oeillets que la nature y a semés. (p. 258)[79]

This prose 'blason du corps aimé' is accentuated, in its parataxis ('l'un.. . l'autre... l'autre'; 'ses mains... sa gorge'), its tired lexis ('Sa gorge surpasse la blancheur de la neige'), and its cloying conclusion ('les petits amours volettent', etcetera) almost to the point of parody. The writing sets up a brutal disabusal of, or contre-blason to, the men's eroticizing gaze. As the demon discovers ('me decouvrir') or shows its true identity ('faire paraître qui je suis'; 'leur fait voir'), the climax of Rosset's narrative, 'la plus horrible, la plus vilaine, la plus puante et la plus infecte charogne du monde', takes the form of a gruesome visual reckoning.

As in Le Loyer's narrative of Philinnion and Machates, neither reader nor narrator is entirely untainted by this sudden reversal of fortune. La Jacquière's aggressive sexuality is described throughout the tale, in a constellation of metaphors that prepares the fireside revelation, in terms of heat ('ardeur excessive', 'sale ardeur', 'le désir qu'il avait d'éteindre le feu qui le consommait'). That heat fires not only his companions on the

---

[79] 'They do not stop looking at and admiring her. One praises her forehead and says that it is a well-polished ivory table. The other lingers over her eyes and claims for certain that they are the torches with which Love lights up every generous soul. The other begins praising her blond hair, which she had loosened because it was time for bed, and says again and again that they are the threads with which the son of Cypris takes away the freedom of men and gods. In the end they do not fail to admire a single part of her body. Her hands always return victorious in their conquests. Her bosom is whiter than the snow; and little cupids flit about her cheeks to taste the roses, lilies, and carnations that nature has scattered there.'

watch. Indulged for a time, through La Jacquière's apparently considerable powers of seduction, in the fantasy of the chance erotic encounter, the reader, like the hero himself, 's'échauffe... en son harnois'; now that his perspective is focalized in line with that of the sexual adventurers, he also comes to enjoy, albeit vicariously, 'sa part au gâteau'. Such pleasure comes at a price, however, since the reader, too, will fall victim to the harrowing reversal. In this sense the question posed by Rosset's succubus, 'Avec qui pensez-vous avoir eu affaire?', though ostensibly addressed to the three men within the story, also constitutes a challenge to Rosset's (male) readers, seduced as they are by the erotic spectacle.

The narrator's own role in casting that spell, in the vernacular, and over (we can assume) a greater number of textual consumers than would have ever read Xylander, or even Le Loyer's *Quatre livres des spectres*, is problematic. All the more so, perhaps, since the question of shared pleasure is so prominent within the *histoire* itself. When the 'chevalier de guet', now inside his quarry's house, moves in for the final seduction, she initially puts on a show of reticence:

> Elle faisait semblant de le refuser, opposant l'honneur pour sa défense, l'infidélité des hommes, qui est si grande au siècle où nous sommes, et leur peu de discrétion qui publie aussitôt une faveur qu'ils ont reçue. (p. 256)[80]

The increasing polysemy of the word 'discrétion' towards the beginning of the seventeenth century here allows the narrator a pun at La Jacquière's expense.[81] On one level, and looking back to the medieval *discretio spirituum*, La Jacquière's 'peu de discrétion' is clear; unlike Goulart's Maximilian I, for instance, he is not able to discern the succubus demon until it is too late. On another level, and bearing in mind the relatively new sense of 'discretion' as tact or the ability to keep a secret, La Jacquière will be found equally wanting. Not only does he immediately publish ('publier') his lady's 'faveur', he goes as far as to insist that she reproduce it for his friends. The demon's pun refocuses the *discretio* of the witness here as specifically sexual indiscretion—elite learning, or the *libido sciendi*, now diffused into animal desire.

Might not a similar charge be levelled at Rosset himself? It is clear from his prefaces to the 1615 and 1619 editions of his work that the author was aware of the problem of narrative indiscretion. Perhaps conscious by this

---

[80] 'She made as if to refuse, citing her honour in her defence, the faithlessness of men (which is so great in our time), and their want of discretion in straight away making known a favour they have received.'

[81] Huguet, *Dictionnaire de la langue française du seizième siècle*, s.v. 'Discretion'. See also M. Maître-Dufour, 'Une anti-curiosité'.

time of the wide range of readers to whom he had gained access, he too identifies a tension between secrecy and publication. He has taken the decision, he claims, to 'déguiser les noms' of his characters, his intention being not to 'publier les hommes pour les rendre déshonorés mais bien plutôt de faire paraître les défauts' (p. 35).[82] And yet Rosset must have been aware that, as amply demonstrated in his own tale of the 'chevalier du guet', only a thin—and therefore titillating—line separates 'déguisement' from its opposite in the desire to 'faire paraître'. This must have been all the more true when writing, as an impoverished translator, for a reading public voracious not only for the secrets of learned demonology (already disseminated through the *canards*) but also, and as evinced by the rapid expansion in pornographic writing in the first twenty years of the new century, for the private indiscretions transacted in the 'garderobe'.[83]

THE HAUNTED WIDOW

So far this chapter has focused on the female revenant as the object of erotic curiosity. But another narrative, this time from a *canard* of 1607, explores the sexual possibilities that arise when a male revenant visits his widow.[84] Here again the ghost allows prurient readers access to private female space, but this time through a series of narrative mechanisms more subtle, and at first sight more ostensibly edifying, than we saw in the sensationalists Le Loyer and Rosset. A close reading of this, our final story, suggests how the feminized spaces of Catholic pastoral demonology might also be eroticized for the pleasure of male readers.

Toulouse, in the early years of the seventeenth century. A woman loses her husband, a country gentleman, after two happy though childless years of marriage. Highly devout, she decides to live out the rest of her days as a widow. In order to bolster her resolve she moves back to town, where she will be near her parents and where, the narrator adds, the divine service is celebrated with greater devotion than out in the villages, 'où le plus souvent les prestres ne se trouvent pas fort sçavans' (sig. Aii').

One day on her way back from church the woman encounters a strange man in the doorway to her house. The first thing she remarks on is his wonderful smell—'un odeur trop plus suave que musc, ambre, civette, et autres tels parfums' (sig. Aii'). Well dressed, yet pale and sad, alone and

[82] See also p. 503 ('Préface' to the edition of 1615).
[83] See Jeanneret, *Éros rebelle*, ch. 5; J. Dejean, *The Reinvention of Obscenity: Sex, Lies, and Tabloids in Early Modern France* (Chicago: University of Chicago Press, 2002).
[84] *Histoire admirable... d'un gentilhomme, qui s'est aparu par plusieurs fois à sa femme, deux ans apres sa mort* [1607] (Paris: J. Le Roy, 1609).

without servants, the figure salutes her in a low, quiet voice: 'je voy bien Madamoiselle que vous ne me recognoissez plus, je prie Dieu qu'il vous console et confirme en vostre resolution' (sig. Aii^v).[85] The woman is amazed at this remark since, in what turns out to be the story's only running joke, she claims she had disclosed her intentions to 'no living person' ('à personne vivante'). Over the coming months, the figure appears twice more, on both occasions—again—in the doorway to the woman's house. Each time he is much altered in appearance, even to the extent that the woman does not connect him with their previous encounters.

On the third meeting the man declares that he will reveal his identity, swearing on his very soul, 'laquelle est sur l'attente et esperance de jouyr en bref de la beatitude eternelle', that what he is about to say will cause her no offence (sig. Aiii^v).[86] He goes on to repeat back to her the words that she and her husband exchanged on the way home from their wedding, as well as before and after the consummation of their marriage, 'qui fut tel jour, en telle maison, et en telle chambre' (sig. Aiv^r). Asked whether she has divulged these details to anybody else, she replies, 'Non... à personne vivante, ce sont choses qui ne se doivent pas dire' (sig. Aiv^r). The stranger then invites her to consider his clothes. Are they not the same garments that her husband was wearing on the day of their wedding? Finally, all is revealed as the figure declares: 'je suis l'homme que vous avez autrefois plus aymé au monde; regardez moy bien je vous prie, vous me recognois-trez à present sans faute' (sig. Aiv^v)[87]. The widow's first reaction is one of pure astonishment: 'Que suis-je! Où suis-je! Quelle merveille?' (ibid.). But no sooner has she uttered these words than her husband replies brusquely, 'Ne me touchez pas!' (sig. Aiv^v). The dead man explains that for what remains of his time in Purgatory, his soul has been allowed to re-enter his body on condition that he commit no human action—eating, drinking, sleeping, and other such things. Only honest desires are permitted him. This said, he promises to visit her the following week, and vanishes once more.

Alarmed, the widow takes the matter up with her confessor. The priest's response is to suspect an elaborate trap, and he warns the woman to arm herself with the weapons of the Church. She must fast, he says, receive confession, give alms, and perform charitable works. Above all, he adds in a commonplace of pastoral demonology, she must show extreme caution, since the demon often 'se transforme en Ange de lumiere'. In spite of such suspicions the ghost, who returns the following week as promised,

---

[85] 'I see Madamoiselle that you no longer recognize me. I pray to God that he console and confirm you in your resolution.'

[86] 'the which is waiting and expecting shortly to enjoy eternal bliss'.

[87] 'I am the man whom you once loved most in all the world. Look at me closely: you will now recognize me without trouble.'

continues to behave in exemplary fashion. The text maintains that the
visits continue without a single dishonest word, that the dead husband
never laughs, never touches his former wife, or demands anything improper. On the contrary, when on occasion he surprises her 'esmeuë de
quelque esguillon', he exclaims 'ha! ne vous esmouvez ma grand'amie, il ne
faut pas penser à cela' (sig. Bi^v).[88] On hearing this the woman blushes
furiously, amazed that he could have known her innermost thoughts.

The visits continue for some six months 'sans que personne vivante s'en
aperçoive' (sig. Bi^v). After a time, trouble arrives in the shape of a wealthy
new suitor. As a consequence of this new development, the ghostly visits
cease abruptly and, under pressure from her family, the woman decides to
remarry. The contract is signed, and the day of the wedding arrives. But
just as the woman steps into the church she, and apparently she alone,
hears a voice warning 'Pensez à ce que vous faictes!' (sig. Bi^v). Such is the
shock of the ghost's unexpected interruption that the woman falls into a
faint. The subsequent attempt to carry out the ceremony proves more
successful, though the ghost does make one final intervention. When the
couple lean forward to kiss at the altar, the voice bids one last farewell: 'je
m'en voy pour ne plus retourner' (sig. Bii^r). The bride, beside herself for
the next two hours, is eventually brought round and the banquet passes off
undisturbed. But during preparations for the after-dinner dance, there is
one last surprise in store:

> Le festin se faict assez joyeusement et apres les tables levees du soir, voicy un
> corps mort et ensevely qui s'aparoist au milieu de la salle descouvert de la face
> et les mains joinctes, rendant une odeur admirablement douce. (sig. Bii^r)[89]

Panic ensues. Most of the women flee, leaving the men to examine the
body, which is soon recognized to be that of the new bride's first husband.
Among the assembled guests is the woman's confessor, 'aussi peu asseuré
que les autres' (sig. Biii^r); he sends for his colleagues, who soon arrive with
holy water and sprinkle the corpse. A councillor at the Toulouse *parlement*
decides, along with 'autres personnages d'auctorité et de lettres' (sig. Biii^r),
to summon some physicians and surgeons, as well as a Doctor of Theology
in order to take advice on what is to be done.

The physicians arrive, declare the body to be a true corpse, and recommend, by way of confirmation, that the husband's grave be searched.

---

[88] 'prickled by desire ... ha! do not become aroused, my love: you must not think of
that.'
[89] 'The banquet went off quite joyfully. After the tables were removed in the evening,
there was a dead body, recently buried, appearing in the middle of the hall, its face
uncovered and its hands joined, giving off a wonderfully sweet smell.'

Finding it empty, yet with a smell identical to that in the banqueting hall, the company determines that a report must be given to the court. Meanwhile, the body is placed under guard. The following day, the woman tells her side of the story. The physicians and theologians present, much amazed, declare that the dead husband's freshness, fragrance, uncovered face, and hands joined as if in prayer, all 'faisoient foy de la beatitude de l'ame' (sig. Biii^v). It is further decreed that the body be solemnly reburied with the married couple in attendance and that the newlyweds must mourn for the space of three months, during which they may not live under the same roof. Only after that time elapses may they 'jouyr du fruict de leur marriage' (sig. Biii^v). The narrator then tells us:

> Cela a appresté de merveilleux discours et disputes entre les Theologiens de deçà, sur le retour des esprits et ces mots, *spiritus vadens et non rediens*, et comme aussi si cela se pouvoit appeler Resurrection de corps, puis-qu'il n'en faict aucune action, je croy que par Messieurs de ceste ville en sera en bref envoyé un certificat à Paris. Mais je le vous ay bien voulu faire sçavoir auparavant, comme le tout s'est passé. (sig. Biii^v)[90]

With this conclusion—or rather promise of conclusions—the *Histoire admirable* draws to a close.

DISCRETION'S INDISCRETIONS

Much of this book has been about how interpretive communities structured late Renaissance responses to ghosts and ghost stories. Broadly speaking, the *Histoire admirable* envisages two such communities. One is constituted by the Toulouse schoolmen ('les Theologiens de deçà') who, at the story's close, are left debating the theological basis for belief in return from the dead. These readers of the story are the Catholic clergy considered in Part I of this study, the legatees of the medieval *discretio spirituum* tradition struggling to maintain their authority in the teeth of Calvinist dissent. The language of their debate would probably have been Latin, its points of reference the various scriptural *loci* in which writers such as Taillepied preferred to discuss ghosts and apparitions. All being well, a 'certificat' would be sent to the capital, thus completing a journey from the rural backwaters the widow left behind ('où le plus souvent les

---

[90] 'This has given rise to some marvellous discourses and debates among the Theologians of these parts, about the return of spirits and on the words *spiritus vadens et non rediens*, and also about whether this could be called a Resurrection of the body (since it performs no bodily action). I believe that the Gentlemen of this town will shortly send a report to Paris. But I wanted to let you know beforehand how the whole thing happened.'

prestres ne se trouvent pas fort sçavans'), through the tribunal in Toulouse, to the great centre of theological learning in Paris. In keeping with
Gersonian tradition, and with the patterns of transmission exemplified by
Adrien de Montalembert's *Merveilleuse hystoire* of 1528, the provincial—
and once more feminine—ghostly experience is brought under rigorous
control, and made to serve the needs of the Counter-Reformation.

And yet, as this study has shown, the theological debate is not the only
show in town. For the *envoi* quoted above gestures to a second, less
defined, interpretive community: an unspecified readership addressed
directly as 'vous'. Although members of this constituency would not
have been ignorant of the theological issues surrounding the tale, there
is a suggestion that the text we ourselves are reading was not meant to be
viewed in this way. The final line of the text, 'mais je le vous ay bien voulu
faire sçavoir auparavant', suggests that the *Histoire admirable*, which
would itself have made the journey from Toulouse to the publisher in
Paris, was meant to pre-empt—even rival—the schoolmen's 'certificat'.
Whereas the theological discussion returns us to Part I, this self-conscious
circumvention repeats the move enacted so often in Part II—a move that
shunts us elsewhere, towards other forms of reading.

One contemporary consumer of ghost stories known to have approached this narrative, and many others like it, in this spirit was the
Parisian diarist Pierre de L'Estoile. L'Estoile, whose *Journal* is testament to
his desire to learn of local and provincial gossip, as it were 'auparavant',
professes himself addicted to the *canards* and the pamphlets he buys from
hawkers in the street. Not that he takes their pretensions to instruct any
more seriously than those of Le Loyer in his *Discours des spectres*.[91] He
writes in his journal that the *canards* are nothing more than curiosities 'qui
vident, sans grand proufit, insensiblement les bourses des personnes qui les
aiment et s'y adonnent comme moy'.[92] Eight months after his encounter
with the *Discours des spectres*, the entry for 30 June 1609 lists his purchase
of three 'balivernes qu'on crioit', including an '*Histoire admirable* (ou plus
tost fable plaisante) *d'un gentilhomme de Thoulouze, qui, deux ans apres
estre mort, est venu souventesfois visiter sa femme et parler à elle*'.[93] The ironic
parenthesis indicates the extent to which this textual consumer, who
elsewhere admits his addiction to *canards* or *occasionnels*, sought not so
much improvement in his reading of the text, as the diversion afforded by
a 'fable plaisante'.

---

[91] On L'Estoile and Le Loyer, see above, pp. 168–72.
[92] L'Estoile, *Journal*, II, p. 471: 'which quietly empty, without great profit, the coffers of
people who like them and get hooked on them, like me'.
[93] L'Estoile, *Journal*, II, p. 466.

We shall look in more detail at those aspects of the text that sold it to
L'Estoile as, above all, a pleasurable tale. But before coming to these, it is
worth pausing to reflect on what the first community of readers, the
theologians of Toulouse, might have made of the young widow's narrative. In terms of the mechanics of *discretio spirituum*, the status of the
spectre is relatively clear. In line with accepted clerical practice the
woman's confessor, whose credentials as an educated, city-dwelling priest
(as opposed to the rural churchman, whom post-Tridentine reformers had
still to reach) are established early in the tale, initially suspects some form
of diabolical illusion, citing the familiar Pauline dictum that the Devil can
take the guise of an 'ange de lumière'. In fact, subsequent indications
suggest that the husband's ghost is not an Infernal, but rather a Purgatorial,
figure. The spirit itself tells his former wife as much, claiming that his soul
stands in wait for the beatific vision. Later on in the narrative, the learned
men who gather around his corpse suppose him to have reached his final
destination, declaring that his odour, posture, and uncorrupted state all
'faisoient foy de la beatitude de l'ame'. It would appear, then, that the soul
of the dead husband has travelled a familiar ghost-narrative trajectory:
having been weaned off his attachment to the things of this world, he has
finally found peace in his wife's remarriage to another.

The status of the text as a Purgatory narrative finds partial confirmation
in the tale's liminal topographies. The site of the parallel trajectories
travelled by the couple—the husband's journey into Paradise, the wife's
into remarriage—is represented throughout the *Histoire admirable* as a
physical threshold. The ghost of the dead husband makes all his visible
appearances in the doorway to his widow's house; she recognizes him
when he reminds her what he told her on their wedding day as they
entered their new home; she hears his voice ('Pensez à ce que vous faites!')
at the very moment she steps into the church; and the newly married
couple are forbidden to 'cross the threshold' until the mourning process is
complete. The text, we might say, is nothing if not a story about transition
between states—most obviously that between widowhood and remarriage
but also, and in parallel, that between the spaces of purgation and beatitude.

If the presiding topography of the *Histoire admirable* makes it legible as
a narrative of Purgatory, that reading is complicated, as the narrator
suggests, by the ghost's corporeality. Purgatorial apparitions, as we saw
in the first part of this book, are generally bodiless in nature. This ghost,
by contrast, belongs in the tiny category of divinely sanctioned resurrections described earlier in this chapter, clearly embodied and susceptible to
touch. Indeed, this problematic 'resurrection de corps', as the narrator
puts it, exhibits certain parallels with the resurrected Christ. It is possible
to identify a number of moments in which the text gestures directly to

episodes in Scripture. Particularly prominent is the gospel of Saint John which, as we saw in Chapter 1, pays especially close attention to the nature of Christ's body. For instance, the ghost's warning to his wife, 'Ne me touchez pas!', finds a clear parallel in the resurrected Christ's 'Noli me tangere', when Jesus urges Mary Magdalene not to touch him in the garden.[94] Christ's explanation for this prohibition, that he has not yet ascended to his father, is echoed in the ghost's own insistence that his soul awaits admission to the beatific vision.

The Christ-like character of the returning husband is further reinforced by the ghost's solemn demeanour. He offers her not one 'parole deshoneste, ains toutes choses vertueuses, saintes et fort beaux enseignemens' (sig. Bi^v) and, as tradition says of Jesus, the ghost never laughs ('jamais elle ne le vid rire'). Another parallel appears late on in the tale, where the body is found under the tables at the banquet. Just as, in John's Gospel, the resurrected Christ had appeared 'in the midst' of the disciples as they hid from the Pharisees inside a locked room, so too the body of the woman's late husband 's'aparoit au milieu de la salle'.[95] And although the smell accompanying the ghost's appearances, and then the body itself, is eventually attributed to 'la beatitude de l'ame', it may also involve an additional scriptural echo. According to John 19:39–40, Nicodemus brought myrrh and aloes to Christ's resting place, where the body of Jesus was 'wound ... in linen clothes with the spices, as the manner of the Jews is to bury'. Of course, the parallels between the dead husband and Christ are not pushed too far. One significant difference, and a profound doubt as to the status of the husband's return as a 'vraye resurrection', lies in the revenant's inability to perform 'des actions humaines, c'est à dire boire, manger, dormir'. Christ certainly eats and drinks with the disciples as a way, precisely, of proving the truth and solidity of his own risen body.[96] In spite of this distinction, however, the *Histoire admirable* works hard to establish a degree of analogical intimacy between the events it describes and the late chapters in John's Gospel. While it must remain a matter for speculation, it seems likely that the theologians of Toulouse would have read the events described in the pamphlet as a revelation of God's will (the truth of Purgatory, the nature of Christ's body), effected through a series of parallels with Scripture.

This is not to claim that such correspondences would have lain beyond the reach of less expert readers, though it is probable that even for learned textual consumers such as Pierre de L'Estoile the text would have been more immediately reminiscent of popular narrative traditions. The *Histoire*

---

[94] John 20:17.   [95] John 20:19. See also Luke 24:36.
[96] Luke 24:41–3.

admirable, whose threefold apparition recalls the most ancient of folk-narrative structures, also shares a number of features—both stylistic and thematic—with medieval storytelling. For instance, the widow's repeated references to 'personne vivante' recall similar *clins d'oeil* in the trickster traditions of the *fabliau* and the romance, in which a supposedly exclusive category (for example, Iseut's public protestation, in Béroul's *Tristan*, that no man but her husband and the leper who carried her across the marshes has been between her thighs) permits a dramatic irony to be enjoyed by all those, including the reader, in the know (namely, aware from the beginning that the leper is Tristan in disguise).[97]

The motif of the jealous ghost is also far from new. For instance, the thirteenth-century judge, Gervase of Tilbury, includes in his *Otia imperialia* a collection of *mirabilia* dedicated to Otto IV of Brunswick, the similar story of Guillaume de Mostiers, who had made his wife swear that after his death she would never remarry. After several years of chastity, the wife reneges on her vow. As she is leaving the church on the day of her wedding, she espies the ghost of De Mostiers wielding a mortar. Remembering her former oath, she cries out, 'Misérable que je suis! J'ai violé la foi de mon mariage et voici mon mari qui va me tuer avec le mortier.'[98] The rest of the wedding party, for whom only the mortar is visible, hovering above her head, see it crash down and kill the new bride. Schmitt, who has written on this story, points out its kinship with the *charivari* tradition, in which those who disapproved of an improper match banged pots, pans, and (very probably) mortars. Certainly, when viewed from the perspective of Gervase the advocate, it is easy to see the attraction of the narrative, in which the remarried woman is punished with an instrument pertaining to her own, forsaken, wifely duties. Stories of ghostly *charivari* were most likely still common in the later oral traditions of the early modern period.

As familiar as these older narrative traditions may have been to an early seventeenth-century reader such as L'Estoile, the most obvious intertext is more specific and more recent. Its signature appears at the moment of recognition:

> Vous souvenez-vous... de tels propos qu'il vous tint au paravant que d'entrer au lit: ceux qu'il vous dit devant et apres la consommation du mariage, qui fut tel jour, en telle maison, et en telle chambre. Et luy ramentevant confessa que ouy, l'avez vous jamais descouvert à nul? Non, ce dit-elle, à personne vivante, ce sont choses qui ne se doivent pas dire. Mais

---

[97] For Iseut's ambiguous oath, see Béroul, *The Romance of Tristan*, ed. by A. Ewert, 2 vols. (Oxford: Blackwell, 1953), I, 125–6.

[98] Cited in Schmitt, *Les Revenants*, p. 107: 'Oh I am a wretched woman! I have violated my vow of marriage and here is my husband who is going to kill me with the mortar!'

comment l'avez-vous peu sçavoir vous mesmes? Il luy raporta d'autres
particularitez de leur mariage, dequoy ceste Damoiselle ravie en admiration
et estonnee outre mesure, reprend ses premieres opinions que c'estoit
veritablement quelque enchanteur ou demon: elle tremble de crainte et
d'apprehension, lors il luy dit: n'ayez peur, Madamoiselle, et n'estimez
aucunement que je sois enchanteur, ny demon: je suis l'homme que vous
avez autrefois plus aymé au monde; regardez moy bien je vous prie, vous me
recognoistrez à present sans faute. (sigs. Aiv^{r-v})^{99}

For the widow, having failed to see the shape of her husband, or hear her
husband's voice, in those of the mysterious visitor, the moment of
recognition—or *anagnorisis*—arrives in the form of a secret: that of the
words exchanged, and deeds done, on the night of the young couple's
wedding.^{100} The wording of that secret, here hidden from the reader in
the titillating imprecision of 'tels propos', 'tel jour', 'telle maison', and
'telle chambre', would have produced a striking instance of intertextual
recognition in readers encountering the tale in the early 1600s. Here the
Histoire admirable no longer gestures to biblical precedent in the Gospel of
Saint John, or to the precedents in medieval narrative traditions. For
canard fanatics such as Pierre de L'Estoile, the ghost of the dead man,
and the process by which he wins the recognition of his spouse, could not
fail to recall a more recent revenant husband: a man who forty years
earlier, in a village not far from Toulouse, had returned to claim his
property, his land, and his wife, as the long-lost Martin Guerre.

In the Guerre case, too, Arnaud du Tilh—the man who posed as
Martin Guerre—is accepted by his wife, Bertrande, precisely on account
of his knowledge of those things only a husband could or ought to know.
And as the investigating judge, Jean Coras, reminds us, Arnaud knew it all:

Mesmes des actes et propos qui interviennent le plus secrettement entre
mariez, et qu'autres ne peuvent bonnement sçavoir, ou entendre: jusques à
luy enseigner les lieux, temps, et heures des actes secrets de mariage (plus

---

^{99} '"Do you remember such and such a thing that he said to you before getting into
bed, what he told you before and after the consummation of the marriage, which was on
such and such a day, in such and such a house, in such and such a bedroom?" And she, now
remembering, confessed that she did. "Have you ever revealed this to anyone?" "No," she
said, "to nobody living: these are things that must not be spoken of. But how do you
yourself know?" He revealed to her other private matters in their marriage, upon which this
woman, struck by wonder and astonished beyond all measure, began to fall back on her first
suspicions: that this was truly some enchanter or demon. She was trembling with fear and
apprehension, when he told her, "Do not be afraid, Madamoiselle, and do not think me an
enchanter or a demon: I am the man whom you once loved most in all the world. Look at
me closely: you will now recognize me without trouble."'
^{100} For a detailed study of *anagnorisis*, see T. Cave, *Recognitions: A Study in Poetics*
(Oxford: Clarendon Press, 1988).

aisez beaucoup à comprendre, qu'honneste à reciter, ou escrire) et les propos qu'avant, apres et en l'acte, ils auroyent tenuz.[101]

This mode of recognition fascinated contemporary commentators on the case and, as suggested by Coras's parenthesis '(plus aisez beaucoup à comprendre, qu'honneste à reciter, ou escrire'), their puzzlement was not without an edge of prurience. Even the most fleeting reference to the affair rarely fails to mention the motif. For instance, the jurist Jean Papon diverges from Coras in maintaining that, initially at least, Bertrande 'ne fut vaincue ny deceuë de la grande affection, qu'elle pouvoit avoir d'ouïr nouvelles de son mari, et de recouvrer sa presence'.[102] But when Du Tilh began to tell of 'infinis petis propos, et faicts secrets, qui sont ordinaires entre mari et femme' she was, Papon claims, entirely won round:

> Tels propos et actes, qui jamais n'avoyent esté ouïs, sceus, ny veus par autres que son mari et elle, dont la memoire luy estoit presentee par ledit accusé, l'asseuroyent probablement et de toutes parts, et ne luy permettoyent d'en douter.[103]

Estienne Pasquier, writing in his *Les Recherches de la France*, tells a similar story. When first Du Tilh presented himself to Bertrande, he writes, 'du commencement elle ne le vouloit en aucune façon'.[104] But quite aside from the physical resemblance between Du Tilh and her husband, 'il luy discourut tant de privautez qui s'estoient passées entr'eux deux, mesmes la premiere nuict de leurs nopces, voire jusques aux hardes qu'il avoit laissées dans un coffre lors de son partement: choses qui ne pouvoient estre sceuës que par le vray mary'.[105] What this recognition narrative offers, and Coras, Papon, and Pasquier appear to be responding to, is something very different from the physical scars, birthmarks, or (in the case of Marie de

---

[101] J. Coras, *Arrest memorable du parlement de Tholose, contenant une histoire prodigieuse d'un supposé mary, advenuë de nostre temps, enrichie de cent et onze belles et doctes annotations* [1561] (Paris: Galliot du Pré, 1572), p. 21: 'Even the most secret actions and words of married couples, and which others could in no way know, or understand: even telling her the places, seasons, and times of their secret marital acts (much more easy to understand than honestly related, or written down), and the words that they spoke to each other before, during, and after the deed.'

[102] J. Papon, *Recueil d'arrests notables des cours souveraines de France* (Lyon: J. de Tournes, 1568), p. 719.

[103] Ibid.: 'Such words and actions, never heard, known, or seen by anyone other than her husband and her, and the remembrance of which was spelled out to her by the accused, were to her probable proof in every respect, and left her no room to doubt it.'

[104] E. Pasquier, *Les Recherches de la France*, ed. by M.-M. Fragonard and F. Roudaut, 3 vols. (Paris: Champion 1996), III, p. 1335.

[105] Ibid.: 'he spoke to her of some many private things that had passed between them, even on their wedding night, and even including the clothes that he had given her to keep in a chest when he had left: things that could only have been known by the true husband'.

Bourgogne) warts that are the stuff of traditional *anagnorisis*. Instead they are left to ponder a proto-Freudian intuition: that identity might be imagined as a unique erotic story—perhaps the only story that confirms us truly as ourselves.

This is not the moment to add to the (already considerable) volume of critical work on the return of Martin Guerre. But the shared motif of the recognition scene, and the intimate narrative through which a revenant husband succeeds in gaining access to his wife's home and—by extension—body, takes us right to the heart of the ghost's erotic charge at the end of the Renaissance. As in the pastoral demonology considered in Chapter 2, domestic space—and especially, in the Counter-Reformation, feminine domestic space—is figured as the privileged site of secure identity. Only this time that space has been eroticized. If ghosts, and our responses to them, throw into crisis the innermost chambers of early modern selves, it is above all because they know—and could say out loud—what women do in bed. To take up the more recent theory of Abraham and Torok, these early modern 'phantoms' signal the presence of a secret.[106] Little wonder that the *canard* parted L'Estoile from his cash.

For not only is the ghost of the Toulouse story able to penetrate the doorway to his widow's inner life. So are those who buy and read the tale. The reader's access to that life is partly a function of the narrative's transmission: the pamphlet records not the proceedings of a criminal trial but (supposedly) the direct report of the widow herself, called upon to explain the dead body at her wedding. The narrative, whose point of focalization thus coincides with that of its female protagonist, proceeds by alternating events with her reactions, offering access as it goes to her deepest thoughts and feelings. The verb 'sentir' in particular, usually expressed as a continuous participle, accompanies her actions throughout the *Histoire admirable*: 'elle sentant une esmotion extraordinaire' (sig. Aiii^v), 'se sentant un peu fortifiee de courage' (sig. Aiii^v), 'se sentant estrangement ennuyé ainsi seule' (sig. Aii^r), etcetera. More striking still are a number of formulae that combine to suggest a powerful sense of psychological interiority: '[elle] rumine et remasche ces propos' (sig. Aiii^r), '[elle] se recommande en son coeur devotement à Dieu' (sig. Aiii^v), 'vous devez croire que ceste demoiselle entra en de merveilleux pensements' (sig. Bi^r).

Remembering Saint Luke's words on Mary ('kept in mind all these words, pondering them in her heart'), we might at first suspect that we are being offered a Gersonian vision of idealized feminine *discretio*. Something

---

[106] On Abraham and Torok's notion of the 'phantom' and its relation to secrecy, see Davis, 'Hauntology, Spectres, and Phantoms'.

of that ideal does persist, residually, in both this and other early seven-teenth-century *canards*.[107] And yet in this tale the widow's interiority is not left intact or undisturbed. Rather, and by way of a series of masculine intrusions, it is imagined as pure transparency. This fantasy is interested more in the widow's sexual appetite than her devotional rectitude. First there is the new suitor who, upon an initial refusal from the widow at a dinner, reads between her words a conscious sexual ruse:

> Privé de ce grand bien, le Gentil-homme se persuade ceste responce estre d'artifice et mignardise, pour l'eschauffer d'avantage, luy dict: Madamoiselle vous y penserez, je ne perds pas l'esperance de vous faire jetter le froc aux horties. (sig. Bii^r)[108]

Even then the suitor's competence as a reader is as nothing when placed alongside the ghost's curious second sight. From their very first meeting, the returning husband is able to divine his former wife's thoughts. He knows of her resolution to remain a widow, an intention, she claims, she has divulged to 'personne vivante'. He knows, too, of her suspicions that he is a devilish impostor and, echoing Gabriel's words to Mary, seeks to reassure her on that score: 'n'ayez peur, Madamoiselle, et n'estimez aucunement que je sois enchanteur, ny demon' (sig. Aiv^v). The dead husband is also, finally, capable of detecting the 'esguillon' that pricks inside her. Here, as in the previous chapter, the ghost's embodiment holds out the promise of a sexual encounter. Unwilling to sully his newly risen flesh, however, it is an encounter that the husband continually resists:

> Quelquefois se trouvant esmeuë de quelque esguillon il luy dit 'ha! ne vous esmouvez ma grand'amie, il ne faut pas penser à cela', dont elle rougit tres-fort estonnee comme il l'avoit peu cognoistre. (sig. Bi^v)[109]

Able to read her innermost thoughts and feelings, the husband's ghost effectively embodies a male fantasy within which women become sexually legible as never before. As in medieval *discretio* the mystery of woman, like

---

[107] See, for instance, the *Discours veritable de l'esprit d'un Advocat qui s'est apparu apres sa mort à son Pere Confesseur, et du despuis en pleine assemblee en la ville d'Orliac en Auvergne, pour faire restituer un doublon à ses Parens, qu'il avoit retenu à son voisin, et en estoit tourmenté en Purgatoire* (Lyon: P. Verrier, 1609); *Histoire miraculeuse, advenue en la Rochette, ville de la Maurienne en Savoye* [1614] in N. Lenglet du Fresnoy, *Recueil de dissertations anciennes et nouvelles, sur les apparitions, les visions et les songes* (Avignon: J. N. Leloup, 1752), II, pp. 82–96.

[108] 'Deprived of this great bounty, the Gentleman was convinced that her response was a mere artifice or flirtation, in order to arouse his ardour further, and said to her: "Madamoiselle you will reflect on this. I still hope you make your jump over the convent wall."'

[109] 'Sometimes when she found herself prickled by desire, he said to her, "Ha! Do not become aroused, my love: you must not think of that." Upon which she blushed furiously, amazed that he could have known about it.'

the mystery of ghosts, is finally brought to heel. But this time it is not just the privileged priest, Gerson or Montalembert, who exercises power. As with Le Loyer and Rosset, and with ghost stories like this on sale in the street, every male reader has had 'sa part au gâteau'. By the end of the Renaissance, the discretion of spirits had never looked less discreet.

Conclusion

'Plus je me hante...'

Halfway through 'Des boiteux' (III.11), an essay more famous for its witches than its ghosts, Montaigne pauses. Up until now the chapter has been a spirited exercise in pyrrhonist debunking. Following a sardonic opening gambit on the newly calibrated Gregorian calendar ('Ny l'erreur ne se sentoit en nostre usage, ny l'amendement ne s'y sent'), Montaigne has been musing that human reason is at best 'un instrument libre et vague' and, by way of illustration, reported the case of a gouty prince—the first of the chapter's many 'boiteux'—who, believing the stories of a priest with miraculous powers of healing, sought out the man and, by the sheer force of his imagination (doubtless coupled with ecstatic mugging from the priest), walked away as right as rain.[1]

Once the fraud was eventually unmasked the authorities found so little cunning in the faith-healer's charade that they thought him unworthy of punishment. But, as Montaigne reminds us, things could have turned out very differently: six or seven more rejuvenated nobles, and his reputation as a miracle-worker might well have hardened into fact. Such is our love of 'causes' ('plaisants causeurs!') that we fail to investigate the truth of things ('choses') themselves. Or, to put the same point not with a pun but with an image, 'nostre veüe represente ainsi souvent de loing des images estranges, qui s'esvanouissent en s'approchant' ('our eyes often show us strange things from afar, which evaporate as they draw nearer'). But despite these ghostly evaporations, still we do not learn. Our thirst for the aberrant will always stand at odds with the true humdrumness of things.

But then comes the pause. One thing still looms large and mysterious to Montaigne, no less strange—in fact stranger—as he draws closer to it. That thing is Montaigne himself:

---

[1] Montaigne, *Essais*, pp. 1025–9.

Je n'ay veu monstre et miracle au monde plus expres que moy-mesme. On s'apprivoise à toute estrangeté par l'usage et le temps; mais plus je me hante et me connois, plus ma difformité m'estonne, moins je m'entens en moy.[2]

Montaigne is well-known for his self-interruption, but there is something especially arresting about this sudden onset of ontological bewilderment, coming as it does in a chapter whose focus until now has been so resolutely outward. For modern readers especially (of Marivaux's *La Double Incon-stance* or André Breton's *Nadja*, for instance) the wording of the final sentence ('plus je me hante…') may gain added force in its resonance with the well-known proverb: 'Dis-moi qui tu hantes, je te dirai qui tu es.'[3] Resonance, but also stark contrast: for whereas the proverb offers the promise of epistemological clarity ('A man is knowable by the society he keeps'), Montaigne's sentence gropes only in the dark. I myself am the society I keep, and yet in spite of that society—or rather *because* of it—I grow stranger to myself. Breton and company have hit upon man the social animal, Montaigne only upon himself… as an unfathomable monster.

Or, should we say, a ghost? To read 'hanter' in this way is tempting, not least because Montaigne would then join Ronsard, his late (and by this time his late late) Renaissance peer, in figuring himself as his own 'fantaume sans os'.[4] Of course, 'hanter' in the French of Marivaux and Breton means simply 'to frequent, associate with', without any connota-tion of the untoward or eerie. And we should probably think the same of Montaigne's verb, were it not that the expression is followed, in the very next lines, by a ghost story.

Passant avant hier dans un village, à deux lieues de ma maison, je trouvay la place encore toute chaude d'un miracle qui venoit d'y faillir, par lequel le voisinage avoit esté amusé plusieurs mois, et commençoient les provinces voisines de s'en esmouvoir et y accourir à grosses troupes, de toutes qualitez. Un jeune homme du lieu s'estoit joué à contrefaire une nuict en sa maison la voix d'un esprit, sans penser à autre finesse qu'à jouyr d'un badinage present. Cela luy ayant un peu mieux succedé qu'il n'esperoit, pour estendre sa farce à plus de ressorts, il y associa une fille du village, du tout stupide et niaise; et furent trois en fin, de mesme aage et pareille suffisance; et de presches domestiques en firent des presches publics, se cachans soubs l'autel de

---

[2] Montaigne, *Essais*, p. 1029: 'I have seen no more evident monstrosity and miracle in the world than myself. We become habituated to anything strange by use and time; but the more I frequent [haunt] myself and know myself the more my deformity astonishes me, and the less I understand myself.' (*Complete Works*, p. 958).
[3] The phrase was already proverbial by the time of Cervantes's *Don Quijote de la Mancha*, where Sancho Panza cites it (in Book II, ch. 23) in the form 'Díme con quién andas, decirte he quién eres.'
[4] On Ronsard as a ghost, see above, pp. 202–3.

l'Eglise, ne parlans que de nuict, et deffendans d'y apporter aucune lumiere. De paroles qui tendoient à la conversion du monde et menace du jour du jugement (car ce sont subjects soubs l'authorité et reverence desquels l'imposture se tapit plus aiséement), ils vindrent à quelques visions et mouvements si niais et si ridicules qu'à peine y a-il rien si grossier au jeu des petits enfans. Si toutefois la fortune y eust voulu prester un peu de faveur, qui sçait jusques où se fut accreu ce battelage? Ces pauvres diables sont à cette heure en prison, et porteront volontiers la peine de la sottise commune; et ne sçay si quelque juge se vengera sur eux de la sienne. On voit cler en cette cy, qui est descouverte; mais en plusieurs choses de pareille qualité, surpassans nostre cognoissance, je suis d'advis que nous soustenions nostre jugement aussi bien à rejetter qu'à recevoir.[5]

Usually passed over by critics as just another instance of limping human reason, this hoax narrative—a relative of the impostures discussed in Chapter 1—is worth a closer look.[6] For as well as lending 'hanter' a ghostly resonance (a possibility to which we shall return), it takes us right to the heart of the questions considered in this book. What drove the circulation of ghost stories in late Renaissance France? And can we read these 'images estranges' without their vanishing as soon as we draw close?

Two forces or energies, minimally present in the rest of 'Des boiteux', come together in this passage with special intensity: light and heat. Elsewhere in the chapter, the vocabulary of light joins with the metaphor of clear visual perception to express the idea of epistemological certainty, most famously in the statement, on the witchcraft prosecutions, that

---

[5] Montaigne, *Essais*, pp. 1029–30: 'Passing the day before yesterday through a village two leagues from my house, I found the place still stirred up about a miracle that had just failed to come off, by which the neighbourhood had been entertained for months; and folk from the adjoining provinces were beginning to get excited about it and to come running up, people of all classes, in great crowds. A young man of the place had amused himself in his house one night by counterfeiting the voice of a spirit, with no more trickery in mind than enjoying a momentary joke. When this succeeded a little better than he expected, in order to extend the scope of the farce he took as an associate a thoroughly stupid and silly village girl; and in the end there were three of them, of the same age and similar ability. And from preaching at home they went on to preaching in public, hiding under the altar of the church, speaking only at night, and forbidding anyone to bring any light. From words tending to the conversion of the world and the threat of judgement day (for these are subjects under whose authority and reverence imposture most easily hides), they proceeded to some visions and actions so silly and ridiculous that there is hardly anything so crude in children's play. Yet if fortune had seen fit to favour them a little, who knows to what point this buffoonery would have grown? These poor devils are at this moment in prison and will probably pay the penalty for the common folly; and who knows but some judge will avenge himself on them for his own stupidity? We see clearly in this case, which is exposed; but in many things of similar quality, surpassing our knowledge, it is my opinion that we should suspend our judgement just as much in the direction of rejecting as of accepting.' (*Complete Works*, pp. 958–9).
[6] A notable exception is Butterworth, 'The Work of the Devil?'.

'A tuer des gens, il faut une clarté lumineuse et nette.'[7] But the difficulty for Montaigne is that, given our 'appercevance grossiere et obscure', the light of certainty is exactly what we lack. The story of the ghost hoaxers plays precisely on this metaphor of light and darkness, even to the point of rendering it literal. Though the children only speak at night ('ne parlans que de nuict') and prohibit others from bringing light ('aucune lumiere') into the church, the trick they try to pull is eventually found out: 'on voit cler en cette-cy, qui est descouverte'. But as with the faith-healer, the outcome might have been different. Had fortune furnished the prank with 'un peu de faveur'—in the sense not only of 'favour' but also, through association with the phrase 'à la faveur de la nuit', of darkness—the villagers would still be talking about the ghosts under the altar. The darkness would have lingered, and the true facts never been known.

Darkness obscures truth. Heat alters it. Montaigne finds the village square still *hot* ('la place encore *toute chaude*') with talk of a miracle. As with light, the vocabulary of heat surfaces at a number of other moments in the chapter, as if kept in motion by a kind of metaphorical convection. It is tacit in the reference to the witch pyres ('c'est mettre ses conjectures à bien haut pris que d'en faire cuire un homme tout vif'). But it also serves to convey, more titillatingly, the recurrent motif of desire for all things strange. Let us not forget that the ostensible purpose of the chapter is to address the question of why 'le boiteux le faict le mieux', the answer to which will also serve to explain why 'les Grecs descrioent les tisserandes d'estre plus *chaudes* que les autres femmes'.[8] That the crowd gathered in the square might be experiencing the excitement of the ghost tale as something close to erotic attraction might seem far-fetched, were it not that 's'esmouvoir', the verb used to describe the response of those in the neighbouring countryside, also carries more than a hint of sexual charge. To this extent narrative desire becomes erotic—even generative—in its force: the miracle, or miracle that nearly was, is engendered less in the antics of the youthful prankster and his friends than aroused in the bodies of those who throng the square.

Perhaps the thematics of light and heat, which is to say knowledge and desire, also attends studies such as this. Those parts of it dealing in intellectual history—that of the *discretio spirituum*, for instance, or the growth of pastoral demonology—rested on the presumption that light can still be shone into the gloom of ages past. As in many previous histories of

[7] Montaigne is here referring to a category of proof ('luce clarior') in Roman law. I am grateful to Ian Maclean for this observation.
[8] Montaigne, *Essais*, p. 1034.

the subject, the guiding assumption of Part I was that the purpose of those who tell ghost stories, and the intellectual context within which they write, will emerge shining in the beam of the scholar's well-directed torch. This is history as diorama, with the historian as projectionist. The idea seems natural enough, and also appears faithful to the purpose of men like Lavater and Taillepied as they themselves sought—through stories—the light of Scripture, or to tell ghosts apart from Satan, the 'ange de lumière'. Even the tales of the *histoires prodigieuses*, or of parts of Le Loyer's *Quatre livres des spectres*, seem to invite readings of this kind. Less concerned with theological polemic, these writers too believed that ghost narratives might shed light on human affairs: on the dynasties of France, on friendship, murder, or the New World. Read in the right way, and with careful attention to their intellectual contexts, their stories still flicker as vanished modes of thought. We can still see some things in the dark, whatever Montaigne says.

But to read only for the light is to fail to feel the heat. In Parts II and III it transpired that many of those who wrote and consumed ghost tales in the period were spurred on less by the search for moral, spiritual, or even intellectual illumination than the very desire for the aberrant described in the pages of Montaigne's 'Des boiteux'. Gradually unyoked from their once natural context of sectarian polemic over Purgatory, and made the autonomous topic of miscellanies and *canards*, ghost narratives were now available to serve more wordly ends. Whereas (but for a few exceptions) post-Tridentine theology disembodied late Renaissance ghosts, these stories produced ghosts that one could touch and take to bed. And while the Counter-Reformation made the haunted house a space of feminine devotion, Le Loyer, Rosset, and the *canards* exploit that space for its high erotic charge. For this reason, always to interpret the ghost stories of this period as the servants of a higher, religio-political function is not only historically po-faced but often just plain wrong. By the late sixteenth century ghost stories circulated less in the light of moral, spiritual, or intellectual exchange than in the strange convection currents of narrative desire. Here the modern scholar must leave his diorama, and switch on instead his thermal-imaging machine.

Not that the storyteller's heat—sexy and edgy though it is—is always a cause for celebration. Montaigne himself feels it, not to mention its strange deforming power. In another confessional moment in 'Des boiteux', he writes:

> Moy-mesme, qui faicts singuliere conscience de mentir et qui ne me soucie guere de donner creance et authorité à ce que je dis, m'appercoy toutesfois, aux propos que j'ay en main, *qu'estant eschauffé* ou par la resistance d'un

autre ou *par la propre chaleur de la narration*, je grossis et enfle mon subject par vois, mouvemens, vigueur et force de parolles, et encore par extention et amplification, non sans interest de la verité nayfve.[9]

When seen in the light—or rather felt in the heat—of this passage, Montaigne does not finally stand philosophically aloof from the crowd in the square: this despite his claim, at the beginning of his ghost tale, that he was only passing through—casually, just the other day, on his way out or on his way home—the space of fevered narrative exchange that is the 'place encore toute chaude'. Rather his speech, like theirs, is inclined to warp or swell, caught up as he is in 'la propre chaleur de la narration'. And what if this applies to the very words that we are reading? Compromised in this crucible of narrative desire would be, in that case, not only truth ('la vérité nayfve') but the very form and shape of his project as a writer. Consubstantial with himself, Montaigne's book would here take on an unsettling aspect. This might then explain the puzzle of the preceding lines. 'Plus je me hante . . . moins je m'entens en moy': whether monstrous or ghostly, perhaps this is the swollen stranger—that is the *Essais*, his own uncanny creation—that looms so foreign, so haunting, in the half-light of his tower.

As it turns out, the taste for ghost narrative identified in Montaigne's 'Des boiteux' survived well into the first half of the seventeenth century, where it continued to flourish in a variety of generic environments. The lasting success of Rosset's *Histoires memorables et tragiques* and, after Rosset, of Jean-Pierre Camus's many and lengthy additions to the genre, is testament to the continued popularity of ghost-talk and ghost tales. Interest in apparitions, broadly understood, was doubtless partly sustained through a series of notorious, and very public, possessions (most notably at Louviers and Loudun). Meanwhile, ghosts remained a prominent feature of the so-called 'baroque' poetry of writers such as Théophile de Viau, Saint-Amant, and Tristan l'Hermite.[10] And although the ghostly prosopopeia of mid-Renaissance dramatists such as Jodelle and Garnier appear to have become the object more of ridicule than of terror by the early 1620s,[11] apparitions of the dead could still be found on the seventeenth-century

---

[9] Montaigne, *Essais*, p. 1028, my emphasis: 'I myself, who am singularly scrupulous about lying and who scarcely concern myself with giving credence and authority to what I say, perceive nonetheless *that when I am excited* over a matter I have in hand, either by another man's resistance or *by the intrinsic heat of the narration*, I magnify and inflate my subject by voice, movements vigour, and the power of words, and further by extension and amplification, not without prejudice to the simple truth.' (*Complete Works*, pp. 956–7).

[10] *Anthologie de la poésie baroque française*, ed. by J. Rousset, 2 vols. (Paris: M. Leclerc, 1961), ii, pp. 69–101 ('Le songe et l'illusion') and 103–67 ('Le spectacle de la mort').

[11] According to Millet, 'L'Ombre dans la tragédie française', pp. 173–4.

stage. Pierre Du Ryer's tragedy *Saül* (1642) restages, some seventy years after La Taille's *Saül le furieux*, the raising of Samuel by the witch of Endor; the other characters in the play argue about the status of Samuel's 'spectre' in terms very similar to those of Lavater and Le Loyer.[12] Furthermore, theatrical apparitions were not limited to tragedy. 'Ombres', for instance, briefly become a feature of the *Ballets de cour*;[13] successfully capturing their light, insubstantial movements seems to have provided an attractive challenge for dancers, and a popular pleasure for those watching in the stalls. The figure of the ghost also arises in comedy and pastoral. There it tends to appear in association with the necromancer's cave: in Corneille's *L'Illusion comique* (1636), for instance, or in Joyel's macabre *Tableau tragique ou le funeste amour de Florivale et d'Orcade* (1633).[14] Finally, in philosophy, it appears that ghosts even survived the Cartesian revolution, at least in the short term. According to Descartes's English detractors, of course, Cartesian dualism had itself reduced the soul to nothing more than 'the ghost in the machine'. But the language of ghosts was sustained not only in the context of philosophical abuse. Alongside the question, 'Qu'est-ce que l'âme?', those attending the meetings of Théophraste Renaudot's weekly think-in at the *Bureau d'adresse* in the 1640s could still be found debating 'l'apparition des esprits, ou phantosmes'.[15] To judge by one of La Rochefoucauld's most celebrated maxims, discussion of ghosts may even have forced its way into the late-century salons. There it seems that talk of apparitions had begun to merge with that of a more recent fashionable delusion: 'Il est du veritable amour comme de l'apparition des esprits; tout le monde en parle, mais peu de gens en ont vu.'[16]

---

[12] P. Du Ryer, *Saül: tragédie (1642)*, ed. by M. Miller (Toulouse: Société de littératures classiques, 1996). On Du Ryer's treatment of the necromancy scene, see L. Zilli, 'Saül: de Jean de la Taille à Pierre du Ryer', in *Le Théâtre biblique de Jean de la Taille*, ed. by Y. Bellenger (Paris: Champion, 1998), pp. 207–21.

[13] See Lavocat, 'Les Fantômes du ballet de cour'.

[14] P. Corneille, *L'Illusion comique*, ed. by J. Serroy (Paris: Gallimard, 2000); Joyel, *Le Tableau tragique ou le funeste amour de Florivale et d'Orcade* (Douai: M. Bogar, 1633). On the ghosts of Joyel's play, see Closson, *L'Imaginaire démoniaque*, pp. 415–18.

[15] *Recueil général des questions traitées és conférences du Bureau d'Adresse, sur toutes sortes de matières, par les plus beaux esprits de ce temps*, ed. by T. Renaudot and E. Renaudot, 6 vols. (Lyon: A. Valançol, 1666), iii, p. 210.

[16] La Rochefoucauld, F. de, *Maximes*, ed. by J. Lafond (Paris: Imprimerie Nationale, 1998), p. 72 (no. 76): 'True love is like the apparition of spirits; everyone talks about it, but few have seen it.'

Bibliography

WORKS PUBLISHED BEFORE 1800

AGRIPPA VON NETTESHEIM, H. Cornelius, *De incertitudine et vanitate scientiarum et artium* (Paris: Ioannes Petrus, 1531)

——*De occulta philosophia libri tres* [1531], ed. by V. Perrone Compagni (Leiden: Brill, 1992)

ANON, *Les Sorceleries de Henry de Valois, et les oblations qu'il faisait au diable dans le bois de Vincennes* (Lyon: P. Chastain, 1578)

——*Discours veritable de l'esprit d'un Advocat qui s'est apparu apres sa mort à son Pere Confesseur, et du despuis en pleine assemblee en la ville d'Orliac en Auvergne, pour faire restituer un doublon à ses Parens, qu'il avoit retenu à son voisin, et en estoit tourmenté en Purgatoire* (Lyon: P. Verrier, 1609)

——*Histoire admirable, nouvellement advenue en la ville de Thoulouse, d'un gentilhomme, qui s'est aparu par plusieurs fois à sa femme, deux ans apres sa mort* [1607] (Paris: J. Le Roy, 1609)

——*Recueil de plaidoyez notables de plusieurs anciens et fameux advocats de la cour de Parlement faicts en causes celebres, dont aucunes plaidées en presence des Roys. Et divers arrests intervenus tant sur lesdicts plaidoyez, qu'en autres affaires publiques et de consequence* (Paris: veuve J. du Brayet and N. Rousset, 1611)

——*Histoire prodigieuse d'un gentilhomme auquel le Diable s'est apparu, et avec lequel il a conversé, sous le corps d'une femme morte* (Paris: F. de Carroy, 1613)

——*Histoire memorable et espouventable, arrivée au chasteau de Bissestre pres Paris, avec les apparitions des esprits et fantosmes qui ont esté veuz aux caves et chambres dudit chasteau* (Paris: N. Alexandre, 1623)

——*Arrest de mort donné au Parlement de Bretagne, contre Damoiselle Marie de Sornin, accusée et convaincue d'homicide par l'estrange apparition de l'esprit de son feu mari* (Paris: P. Mettayer, 1633)

——*La Chasse donnée aux espouvantables esprits du château de Biscestre, près la ville de Paris, par la demolition qui en a esté faite; avec les estranges tintamarres et effroyables apparitions qui s'y sont toujours vus* (Paris: J. Brunet, 1634)

——in N. Lenglet du Fresnoy, *Recueil de dissertations anciennes et nouvelles, sur les apparitions, les visions et les songes* (Avignon: J. N. Leloup, 1752), II, pp. 82–96

AQUINAS, Saint Thomas, *Super evangelium S. Ioannis lectura*, ed. by P. Raphael Cai (Rome: Marietti, 1952)

——*In octo libros physicorum aristotelis expositio*, ed. by P. M. Maggiòlo (Rome: Marietti, 1954)

——*Summa theologiae*, 60 vols. (London: Blackfriars, 1963)

ARISTOTLE, *The Physics*, ed. and trans. by P. H. Wicksteed and F. M. Cornford, Loeb Classical Library, 2 vols. (London: Heinemann, 1929)

——*On the Soul; Parva Naturalia; On Breath*, trans. by W. S. Hett, Loeb Classical Library (Cambridge, Mass.: Harvard University Press, 1957)

ARTIGNY, A. Gachet d', *Nouveaux mémoires d'histoire, de critique et de littérature*, 7 vols. (Paris: Debure l'aîné, 1749–56)

AUBIGNÉ, A. d', *Oeuvres*, ed. by H. Weber (Paris: Gallimard, 1969)

——*Histoire universelle*, ed. by A. Thierry, 11 vols. (Geneva: Droz, 1981–2000)

AUGUSTINE, Saint, *De fide et symbolo…De cura pro mortuis gerenda*, ed. by J. Zycha, Corpus Scriptorum Ecclesiasticorum Latinorum 41 (Section V, Part III) (Prague: F. Tempsky, 1900)

——*How to Help the Dead*, trans. by M. H. Allies (London: Burns & Oates, 1914)

——*Confessions*, trans. by F. J. Sheed and ed. by M. J. Foley (Indianapolis: Hackett, 2006)

BELLARMINE, R., *Disputationes de controversis fidei*, 3 vols. (Ingolstadt: D. Davidi Sartorii, 1590)

BENOIST, R., *Petit fragment catechistic d'une plus ample catechese de la magie reprehensible et des magiciens, pris de l'une des Catecheses et opuscules de M. René Benoist Angevin, Docteur en Theologie et Curé de S. Eustache à Paris* (Paris: J. Poupy, 1579)

——*Traicté enseignant en bref les causes des malefices, sortileges et enchanteries, tant des Ligatures et neuds d'esguillettes pour empescher l'action et exercise du mariage qu'autres, et du remede qu'il faut avoir a l'encontre* (Paris: J. Poupy, 1579)

——*Trois sermons de S. Augustin, ausquels il est enseigné que ceux qui adherent aux magies, sorceleries, superstitions et infestations diaboliques, pour neant sont Chrestiens et abusent de leur foy* (Paris: J. Poupy, 1579)

BÉROUL, *The Romance of Tristan*, ed. by A. Ewert, 2 vols. (Oxford: Blackwell, 1953)

[BÈZE, T. de], *Histoire ecclesiastique*, 3 vols. (Antwerp: J. Rémy, 1580)

——*Sermons sur l'histoire de la resurrection de nostre Seigneur Jesus Christ* (Geneva: J. Le Preux, 1593)

BOAISTUAU, P., *Histoires prodigieuses les plus memorables qui ayent esté observées depuis la nativité de Jesus-Christ jusques à nostre siecle: extraictes de plusieurs fameux autheurs, Grecs et Latins* (Paris: V. Sertenas, 1560)

——*Histoires prodigieuses: MS 136 Wellcome Library*, ed. by S. Bamforth (Milan: Franco Maria Ricci Spa, 2000)

——and BELLEFOREST, F. de, et al., *Histoires prodigieuses, extraictes de plusieurs fameux autheurs, Grecs et Latins, sacrez et prophanes…augmentees outre les precedentes impressions, de six histoires advenues de nostre temps, adjoustées par F. de Belleforest Comingeois, avec les portaicts et figures* [1575] (Paris: C. Macé, 1576)

——and BELLEFOREST, F. de, et al., *Histoires prodigieuses, extraictes de plusieurs auteurs, grecs et latins*, 6 vols. in 2 (Paris: veuve G. Cavellat, 1597–8)

——and BELLEFOREST, F. de, et al., *Histoires prodigieuses et memorables, extraictes de plusieurs fameux autheurs, grecs et latins, sacrez et prophanes, divisées en six livres*, 6 vols. in 2 (Paris: veuve G. Buon, 1598)

BODIN, J., *De la demonomanie des sorciers* [1580] (Paris: J. du Puys, 1587)

BOGUET, H., *Discours des sorciers, avec six advis en faict de sorcelerie, et une instruction pour un juge en semblable matière* [1602] (Lyon: P. Rigaud, 1608)

BOUCHET, G., *Les Sérées de Guillaume Bouchet, sieur de Brocourt* [1584; rev. edn. 1615], ed. by C. E. Roybet, 6 vols. (Paris: A. Lemerre, 1873–82)

BOUFFLERS, A. de, *Le Chois de plusieurs histoires et autres choses memorables tant anciennes que modernes, appariees, ensemble, pour la pluspart non encores divulguees* (Paris: J. Mettayer, 1608)

BOURDIGNÉ, C. de, *La Légende joyeuse de Maistre Pierre Faifeu* [1532], ed. by F. Vallette (Geneva: Droz, 1972)

BRANTÔME, P. Bourdeille seigneur de, *Oeuvres complètes de Pierre de Bourdeille, Seigneur de Brantôme*, ed. by L. Lalanne, 11 vols. (Paris: Veuve J. Renouard, 1864–82)

BUCHANAN, G., *Le Cordelier, ou le Saint François*, trans. by F. Chrestien (Geneva: Jean de L'Estang, 1567)

CAELIUS RHODIGINUS, L., *Lectionum antiquarum libri xxx* [1516] (Basel: A. and A. Froben, 1566)

CALMET, A., *Dissertations sur les apparitions des anges, des démons et des esprits, et sur les revenants et vampires de Hongrie, de Bohême, de Moravie et de Silésie* (Paris: Debure l'aîné, 1746)

CALVIN, J., *Institution de la religion chrestienne* [1536], ed. by J.-D. Benoit, 5 vols. (Paris: Vrin, 1960)

——*Commentaires . . . sur la concordance ou harmonie composee de trois evangelistes, asçavoir S. Matthieu, S. Marc et S. Luc* [1558] (Geneva: Joachin de Contrieres, 1564)

——*Commentaires de Jehan Calvin sur le Nouveau Testament*, 4 vols. (Paris: C. Meyrueis, 1854–5)

——*Ioannis Calvini opera quae supersunt omnia*, ed. by G. Baum et al., Corpus Reformatorum 38 (Brunswick: C. A. Schwetschke, 1863–1900)

——*Three French Treatises*, ed. by F. M. Higman (London: Athlone, 1970)

CAMERARIUS, P., *Les Meditations historiques de M. Philippe Camerarius, docte Jurisconsulte, et Conseillier au Senat de Nuremberg ville Imperiale . . . Nouvelle edition, reveue sur le Latin, augmenté par l'auteur, et enrichie d'un tiers par le translateur*, trans. by S. Goulart [1608] (Lyon: veuve A. Harsy, 1610)

——*Les Heures desrobees ou meditations historiques du docte et fameux jurisconsulte M. Philippe Camerarius Conseiller du Senat de Nuremberg ville Imperiale*, trans. by F. de Rosset (Paris: J. Cottereau, 1610)

CAMUS, J.-P., *Les Spectacles d'horreur, où se descouvrent plusieurs tragiques effects de nostre siècle* (Paris: A. Soubron, 1630)

CARDANO, G., *Les Livres de Hierosme Cardanus medecin milannois, intitulés de la Subtilité, et subtiles inventions, ensemble les causes occultes, et raisons d'icelles*, trans. by R. Le Blanc (Paris: C. L'Angelier, 1556)

——*De rerum varietate libri xvii* (Basel: per Henricum Petri, 1557)

CHAMPAIGNAC, J. de, *Sommaire des quatre parties de la philosophie, logique, ethique, phisique et metaphisique* (Paris: Fleury Bourriquant, 1606)

CHOPIN, R., *De sacra politia forensi libri III* (Paris: N. Chesneau and J. Poupy, 1577)

CICERO, *De re publica; De legibus*, trans. by C. W. Keyes, Loeb Classical Library (London: Heinemann, 1966)

——*De divinatione*, trans. by W. A. Falconer, Loeb Classical Library (Cambridge, Mass.: Harvard University Press, 1996)

CORAS, J., *Arrest memorable du parlement de Tholose, contenant une histoire prodigieuse d'un supposé mary, advenuë de nostre temps, enrichie de cent et onze belles et doctes annotations* [1561] (Paris: Galliot du Pré, 1572)

CORNEILLE, P., *L'Illusion comique*, ed. by J. Serroy (Paris: Gallimard, 2000)

CRESPET, P., *Deux livres de la hayne de Sathan et malins esprits contre l'homme, et de l'homme contre eux où sont par notables discours et curieuses recherches expliquez les arts, ruses, et moyens, qu'ils prattiquent pour nuyre à l'homme par charmes, obsessions, Magie, sorcellerie, illusions, phantosmes, impostures, et autres estranges façons, avec les remedes convenables pour leur resister suyvant l'usage qui se pratique en l'Eglise* (Paris: G. de la Nouë, 1590)

——*Discours catholiques, de l'origine, de l'essence, excellence, fin, et immortalité de l'ame* (Paris: Claude Chappelain, 1604)

DANEAU, L., *Deux traitez nouveaux . . . le premier touchant les sorciers . . . le second contient une brève remonstrance sur les jeux de cartes et de dez* [1574] (n.p: 1579)

DE FERME, S. (= S. da Fermo), *Brief discours de la difference des esprits, recueilly des oeuvres de Reverend Pere Seraphin de Ferme, chanoine regulier et predicateur excellent*, trans. by N. Dany (Rheims: Jean de Foigny, and Paris: Nicholas Chesneau, 1581)

DELLA PORTA, G., *La Magie naturelle ou les secrets et miracles de la nature* [1565] (Paris: Rouvray, 1993)

DELRIO, M., *Disquisitionum magicarum libri sex* (Louvain: G. Rivius, 1599)

——*Les controverses et recherches magiques de Martin Delrio P. et Doct. de la Compagnie de Iesus. Divisées en six livres, auxquels sont exactement et doctement confutees les sciences curieuses, les vanitez, et superstitions de toute la magie . . . Avecques la manière de procéder en iustice contre les magiciens et sorciers, accommodee à l'instruction des confesseurs*, trans. and ed. by A. du Chesne (Paris: Jean Petit-Pas, 1611)

DES CAURRES, J., *Oeuvres morales et diversifiées en histoires pleines de beaux exemples* (Paris: G. Chaudière, 1575)

DES PÉRIERS, B., *Contes ou nouvelles recréations et joyeux devis* [1558], ed. by P. L. Jacob (Paris: Garnier, 1872)

DU BELLAY, J., *Oeuvres poétiques*, ed. by H. Chamard, 8 vols. in 9 (Paris: E. Cornély, 1908–85)

DU CHESNE, A., *Les Antiquitez et recherche des villes, chasteaux et places plus remarquables de toute la France* [1609] (Paris: J. Boüillerot, 1648)

DU PONT, R., *La Philosophie des esprits, divisee en cinq livres et generaux discours Chrestiens . . . Par feu M. R. du P. P. Et mise en lumiere par F. Matthieu le Heurt Docteur en Theologie, Gardien du Convent de sainct François du Mans 1602* (Paris: veuve Guillaume de la Nouë, 1602)

DURAND, C., *Le Purgatoire des fideles defuncts* (Poitiers: Anthoine Mesnier, 1605)

DU RYER, P., *Saül: tragédie (1642)*, ed. by M. Miller (Toulouse: Société de littératures classiques, 1996)

DU TRIEZ, R., *Les Ruses, finesses, et impostures des espritz malins, oeuvre fort utile et delectable pour un chascun, a cause de la varieté des choses estranges contenue en icelui* (Cambrai: N. Lombart, 1563)

DU VERDIER, A., *La Prosopographie, ou description des personnes insignes* (Lyon: A. Gryphius, 1573)

——*La Bibliothèque d'Antoine du Verdier, seigneur de Vauprivas* (Lyon: B. Honorat, 1585)

ERASMUS, D., *Opus epistolarum Des. Erasmi Roterodami*, ed. by H. M. Allen et al., 12 vols. (Oxford: Clarendon Press, 1906–58)

——*Opera omnia* (Amsterdam: North Holland, 1969–)

ESTIENNE, H., *Apologie pour Hérodote* [1566], ed. by P. Ristelhuber, 2 vols. (Paris: I. Liseux, 1879)

FAREL, G., *Traicté de Purgatoire* (n.p., 1543)

FEU-ARDENT, F., *Semaine des dialogues, ausquels entre un docteur Catholic et un Ministre Calvinic sont paisiblement examinez et confutez quatre cens soixante et cinq erreurs des Hereticques* (Paris: Michel Sonnius, 1598)

FLAVIN, M., *De l'estat des ames apres le trespas, et comment elles vivent estant du corps separees et des purgatoires qu'elles souffrent en ce monde, et en l'autre, apres icelle separation* [1570] (Rouen: J. Osmont, 1605)

GARNIER, R., *Marc Antoine; Hippolyte*, ed. by R. Lebègue (Paris: Belles Lettres, 1974)

GERSON, J., *Joannis Gersonii doctoris theologi et Cancellarii Parisiensis opera omnia*, 5 vols. (Antwerp: sumptibus societatis, 1706)

GOULART, S., *Histoires admirables et memorables de nostre temps, recueillies de plusieurs autheurs*, 2 vols. (Paris: J. Houzé, 1606–7)

——*Thresor d'histoires admirables et memorables de nostre temps* (Geneva: J. Crespin, 1628)

GRAVELLE, F. de, *Abbregé de philosophie, physique, metaphysique, morale, et divine: sur la cognoissance de l'homme et de sa fin* (Paris: J. Pcricr, 1601)

GUAZZO, F. M., *Compendium maleficarum* [1608], trans. by E. A. Ashwin, ed. by M. Summers (New York: Dover, 1988)

GUICHARD, C., *Funerailles et diverses manieres d'ensevelir des Rommains, Grecs, et autres nations, tant anciennes que modernes* (Lyon: J. de Tournes, 1581)

GUICHENON, S., *Histoire de Bresse et de Bugey* (Lyon: Jean Anthoine Huguetan and Marc Anthoine Ravaud, 1650)

GUYON, L., *Les Diverses Leçons de Loys Guyon, sieur de La Nauche... suivans celles de Pierre Messie et du sieur de Vauprivaz* [1604] (2nd edn.; Lyon: C. Morillon, 1617)

HARRISON, R. and BROWNE, R., *The Writings of Robert Harrison and Robert Browne*, ed. by L. H. Carlson and A. Peel (= vol. 2 of *Elizabethan Non-Conformist Texts*), 6 vols. (London: Routledge, 2003)

HOMER, *The Odyssey*, trans. by A. T. Murray, Loeb Classical Library (Cambridge, Mass.: Harvard University Press, 1975)

IAMBLICHUS et al., *De Mysteriis Aegyptiorum, Chaldaeorum, Assyriorum* etc., trans. and ed. by M. Ficino (Venice: A. Manutio, 1497)

ILLAIRE, J. d', *Le Purgatoire des âmes catholiques... où est monstré le soin que nous devons avoir des morts* (Paris: C. Rigaud, 1612)

JACOBUS OF CLUSA, *Tractatus de apparitionibus* (n.p., n.d.)

JODELLE, E., *Cleopatre captive*, ed. by K. M. Hall (Exeter: University of Exeter Press, 1979)

JOYEL, *Le Tableau tragique ou le funeste amour de Florivale et d'Orcade* (Douai: M. Bogar, 1633)

JULIAN, A., *L'Art et jugement des songes et visions nocturnes, avec la physionomie des songes, et visions fantastiques des personnes, et l'exposition d'iceux selon le cours de la lune* [1558] (Paris: Nicolas Gay, 1645)

LA CROIX DU MAINE, F. Grudé de, *Premier volume de la bibliothèque du sieur de La Croix du Maine, qui est un catalogue général de toutes sortes d'autheurs qui ont escrit en françois depuis cinq cents ans et plus* (Paris: A. l'Angelier, 1584)

LAMBERT, J., *Discours evangeliques et instructions chrestiennes et catholiques* [1582] (Paris: Guillaume Bichon, 1586)

LANCRE, P. de, *Tableau de l'inconstance des mauvais anges et demons* [1612] (Paris: N. Buon, 1613)

LARIVEY, P. de, *Les Esprits* [1579], ed. by M. J. Freeman (Geneva: Droz, 1987)

LA ROCHEFOUCAULD, F. de, *Maximes*, ed. by J. Lafond (Paris: Imprimerie Nationale, 1998)

LA TAILLE, J. de, *Tragédies*, ed. by E. Forsyth (Paris: Société des Textes Français Modernes, 1998)

LAVATER, L., *Von Gespaenstern, unghüren, faeln, und anderen wunderbaren dingen, so merteils wenn die menschen sterben soellend, oder wenn sunst grosse sachennd enderungen vorhanden sind, beschaehend, kurtzer und einfaltiger bericht* (Zurich: C. Froschauer, 1569)

——*De spectris, lemuribus et magnis atque insolitis fragoribus, variisque praesagitionibus quae plerunque obitum hominum, magnas clades, mutationesque imperiorum praecedunt, liber unus* (Geneva: J. Crespin, 1570)

——*Trois livres des apparitions des esprits, fantosmes, prodiges et accidens merveilleux qui precedent souventesfois la mort de quelque personnage renommé, ou un grand changement és choses de ce monde* (Geneva: F. Perrin for J. Durand, 1571)

——*Of Ghostes and Spirites Walking by Nyght, and of Strange Noyses, Crackes, and Sundry Forewarnynges, which Commonly Happen before the Death of Menne, Great Slaughters, and Alterations of Kyngdomes*, trans. by R. H. (London: H. Benneyman for R. Watkyns, 1572)

——*Trois livres des apparitions des esprits, fantômes, prodiges et accidens merveilleux qui précèdent souventesfois la mort de quelque personnage renommé ou un grand changement ès choses de ce monde, composez par Loys Lavater... traduits d'aleman en françois, conferez... et augmentez sur le latin. Plus trois questions proposées et résolues par M. Pierre Martyr... lesquelles conviennent à ceste matière, traduites aussi de latin en françois; avecques lesquels nous avons de nouveau . . . ajouté un brief discours sur le fait de la magie . . . Le tout recueilli de la Demonomanie de M. Bodin et autres divers livres tant grecs que latins* (Zurich: G. des Marecz, 1581)

—— *Das Buch Job aussgelegt undd erkläret, in CXLI Predigen* (Zurich: C. Froschauer, 1582)

—— *Of Ghostes and Spirites Walking by Nyght*, trans. by 'R. H.' and ed. by J. Dover Wilson and M. Yardley (Oxford: Folio Society, 1929), p. 215

LE LOYER, P., *Les Oeuvres et meslanges poetiques de Pierre Le Loyer, angevin* (Paris: J. Poupy, 1579)

—— *Quatre livres des spectres ou apparitions et visions d'esprits, anges et demons se monstrans sensiblement aux hommes*, 2 vols. in 1 (Angers: G. Nepveu, 1586)

—— *A Treatise of Spectres or Straunge Sights* (London: V. Simmes for M. Lownes, 1605)

—— *Discours et histoires des spectres, visions et apparitions des esprits, anges, demons, et ames, se monstrans visibles aux hommes* (Paris: N. Buon, 1605)

—— *Discours des spectres, ou visions et apparitions d'esprits, comme anges, demons, et ames, se monstrans visibles aux hommes* (Paris: N. Buon, 1608)

—— *Pierre Le Loyer's Version of the 'Ars Amatoria'*, ed. by W. L. Wiley (Chapel Hill: University of North Carolina Press, 1941)

—— *La Néphélococugie, ou la nuée des cocus* [1579], ed. by M. Doe and K. Cameron (Geneva: Droz, 2004)

LE MASLE, *Chant d'allegresse sur la mort de Gaspar de Colligny, jadis Admiral de France* (Paris: N. Chesneau, 1572)

LEMNIUS, L., *Les Secrets Miracles de nature, et divers enseignemens de plusieurs choses*, trans. by A. du Pinet (Lyon: J. Frellon, 1566)

LENGLET DU FRESNOY, N., *Recueil de dissertations anciennes et nouvelles, sur les apparitions, les visions et les songes*, 4 vols. (Avignon: J. N. Leloup, 1752)

LERCHEIMER, A. (= H. Witekind), *Christlich bedencken und erinnerung von Zauberey* (Heidelberg: J. Müller and H. Aven, 1585)

LÉRY, J. de, *History of a Voyage to the Land of Brazil, otherwise called America*, trans. by J. Whatley (Berkeley: University of California Press, 1990)

—— *Histoire d'un voyage faict en la terre du Brésil*, ed. by F. Lestringant (Paris: Livre de Poche, 1994)

L'ESPAGNOL, J. de, *Histoire de la conversion des Anglois . . . avec un Traicté des apparitions des esprits et fantosmes* (Douai: B. Bellere, 1617)

L'ESTOILE, P. de, *Journal pour le règne de Henri IV*, ed. by L.-R. Lefèvre and A. Martin, 3 vols. (Paris: Gallimard, 1948–60)

—— *Registre-Journal du règne de Henri III*, ed. by M. Lazard and G. Schrenck (Geneva: Droz, 1992–)

LUCAN, *M. Annei Lucani Cordubensis . . . Pharsalia libri x*, ed. by L. Hortensius (Basilae: ex off. Henric. Petrina, 1578)

—— *The Civil War (Pharsalia)*, trans. by J. D. Duff, Loeb Classical Library (London: Heinemann, 1977)

LUTZ, R., et al., *Theatrum de veneficis, das ist, Von teuffelsgespenst Zauberern vnd gifftbereitern Schwartzkunstlern Heren vnd Unholden, vieler fürnemmen*

Historien vnd Exempel... sehr nützlich vnd dienstlich zu wissen vnd keines Wegs zu verachten, ed. by A. Saur (Frankfurt am Main: N. Basseum, 1586)

MAGNUS, O., *Historia de gentibus septentrionalibus* (Romae: apud Ioannem Mariam de Viottis Parmensem, 1555)

MAIOLUS, S., *Les Jours caniculaires, c'est à dire vingt et trois excellents discours des choses natureles et surnatureles*, trans. by F. de Rosset (Paris: R. Foüet, 1609)

MALDONAT, J. (= J. Maldonado), *Commentarii in quattuor evangelistas* (Venice: G.-B. and G.-B. Sessa, 1597)

——— *Traicté des anges et demons*, trans. and ed. by F. de la Borie (Paris: F. Huby, 1605)

MARCONVILLE, J. de, *Recueil memorable d'aucuns cas merveilleux advenuz de nos ans, et d'aucunes choses estranges et monstrueuses advenües es siecles passez* (Paris: J. Dallier, 1564)

[MARCOURT, A. de], *Le Livre des marchans* [1534] (n.p., 1541)

MARGUERITE DE NAVARRE, *Heptaméron* [1558], ed. by S. de Reyff (Paris: Flammarion, 1982)

MASSÉ, P., *De l'imposture et tromperie des diables, devins, enchanteurs, sorciers, noueurs d'esguillettes, chevilleurs, necromanciens, chiromanciens, et autres qui par telle invocation Diabolique, ars magiques et superstitions abusent le peuple* (Paris: J. Poupy, 1579)

MÉNARD, J., *Declaration de la reigle et estat des Cordeliers, composée par ung jadiz de leur ordre, et maintenant de Jesus Christ* (Geneva: [J. Michel], 1542)

MENAGIUS, A. (= Gilles Ménage), *Vitae Petri Aerodii quaesitoris andegavensis et Guillelmi Menagii advocati regii andegavensis* (Paris: C. Journel, 1675)

MESSIE, P. de la (= P. Mexía) and Du Verdier, A., *Les Diverses Leçons de Pierre Messie, gentilhomme de Sevile, avec trois dialogues dudit auteur, contenans variables et memorables histoires... Augmentées de la suitte d'icelles par A. du Verdier*, trans. by C. Gruget (Lyon: B. Honorat, 1577)

MICHAËLIS, S., *Pneumalogie, ou discours des esprits, en tant qu'il est besoing pour entendre et resouldre la matiere difficile des sorciers* (Paris: Guillaume Bichon, 1587)

MONTAIGNE, M. de, *Essais*, ed. by P. Villey (Paris: Presses Universitaires de France, 1965)

——— *Complete Works*, trans. by D. M. Frame (London: Everyman, 2003)

MONTALEMBERT, A. de, *La Merveilleuse Hystoire de l'esperit qui nagueres s'est apparu au monastere des religieuses de sainct pierre de lyon* (Paris: G. de Bossozel, 1528)

——— 2nd edn. (Rouen: R. Gaultier, 1529)

——— 3rd edn. (Paris: J. Pinart, 1580)

MORRY, A. de, *Discours d'un miracle, avenu en la Basse Normandie, avec un Traité des Miracles, du pouvoir des Demons, et de leurs prestiges, et le moyen de les recognoistre d'avec les vrays miracles* (Paris: F. du Chesne, 1598)

MURET, M.-A., *Commentaires au premier livre des 'Amours' de Ronsard* [1553], ed. by J. Chomarat, M.-M. Fragonard, and G. Matthieu-Castellani (Geneva: Droz, 1985)

NAUDÉ, G., *Apologie pour tous les grands personnages qui ont estés faussement soupçonnez de magie* (Paros: F. Targa, 1625)

NICÉRON, J.-P., *Mémoires pour servir à l'histoire des hommes illustres dans la république des lettres*, 43 vols. (Paris, 1727–45)

NODÉ, P., *Declamation contre l'erreur execrable des maleficiers, sorciers, enchanteurs, magiciens, devins, et semblables observateurs des superstitions: lesquelz pullulent maintenant couvertement en France* (Paris: J. du Carroy, 1578)

OCHINO, B., *De Purgatorio dialogus* (Zurich: J. and A. Gesner, 1555)

ORIGEN, *Opera Omnia*, trans. by C. and C. V.Delarue, Bibliotheca Patrum Graeca, 7 vols. in 9 (Paris: J.-P. Migne, 1862)

PAPON, J., *Recueil d'arrests notables des cours souveraines de France* (Lyon: J. de Tournes, 1568)

PASQUIER, E., *Les Recherches de la France*, ed. by M.-M. Fragonard and F. Roudaut, 3 vols. (Paris: Champion 1996)

PASSERAT, J., *Recueil des oeuvres poetiques de Jean Passerat . . . augmenté de plus de la moitié, outre les precedentes impressions* (Paris: C. Morel, 1606)

PELTANUS, T., *Doctrina catholica de Purgatorio, animarum sedibus* (n.p.: ex typographia, Weissenhorniana, 1568)

PERREAUD, F., *Démonologie, ou traitté des démons* (Geneva, 1653)

PEUCER, K., *Les Devins, ou commentaire des principales sortes de devinations*, trans. by S. Goulart (Lyon: B. Honorat, 1584)

PHILOSTRATUS, F., *De la vie d'Apollonius Thyaneen en VIII livres*, trans. by B. de Vigenère, ed. by F. Morel and A. Thomas and with a commentary by T. Artus [1599] (Paris: veuve M. Guillemot, 1611)

PHLEGON OF TRALLES, *Book of Marvels*, trans. and ed. by W. Hansen (Exeter: University of Exeter Press, 1996)

——et al., *Antonini Liberalis transformationum congeries. Phlegontis Tralliani de mirabilibus et longaevis libellus. Eiusdem de Olympiis fragmentum . . . graece latineque omnia*, trans. and ed. by W. Xylander (Basel: T. Guarinum, 1568)

——*Phlegontis Tralliani, quae exstant opuscula. G. Xylandro interprete. I. Meursius recens* (Louvain: I. Elzevirium, 1620)

PLINY THE YOUNGER, *Letters*, trans. by W. Melmoth, Loeb Classical Library, 2 vols. (London: Heinemann, 1915)

POISSENOT, B., *Nouvelles histoires tragiques* [1586], ed. by J.-C. Arnould and R. A. Carr (Geneva: Droz, 1996)

PRÉVOST, J., *La Premiere Partie des subtiles et plaisantes inventions. Contenans plusieurs jeux de recreation, et traicts de soupplesse, par le discours desquels, les imposteurs des bateleurs sont descouvertes* (Lyon: A. Bastide, 1584)

PSELLUS, M. *De daemonibus*, in Iamblichus et al., *De Mysteriis Aegyptiorum, Chaldaeorum, Assyriorum* etc., trans. and ed. by M. Ficino (Venice: A. Manutio, 1497)

——*Traicté par dialogue de l'energie ou operation des diables . . . avec les chapitres xxxiii et xxxv du quatriesme livre du Tresor de la foy catholique du venerable Nicetas de Colosses*, trans. by P. Moreau (Paris: G. Chaudière, 1576)

——*Dialogus de energia, seu operatione daemonum*, trans. by P. Moreau (Paris: G. Chaudière, 1577)

RABELAIS, F., *Pantagruel* [1532], ed. by V. L. Saulnier (Geneva: Droz, 1965)

——*Gargantua* [1534/5], ed. by M. A. Screech and R. Calder (Geneva: Droz, 1970)

——*Le Tiers Livre* [1546], ed. by J. Céard (Paris: Livre de Poche, 1995)

——*Le Tiers Livre* [1546], ed. by M. A. Screech (Geneva: Droz, 1964)

——*Le Quart Livre* [1548/52], ed. by G. Defaux (Paris: Livre de Poche, 1994)

——*The Complete Works of François Rabelais*, trans. by D. M. Frame (Berkeley: University of California Press, 1991)

REMIGIUS, N. (= N. Rémy), *Daemonolatreiae libri tres ex judiciis capitalibus nongentorum plus minus hominum, qui sortilegii crimen intra annos quindecim in Lotharingia capite luerunt* (Lyon: ex off. Vicentii, 1595)

——*Demonolatry*, trans. by E. A. Ashwin and ed. by M. Summers (London: J. Rodker, 1930)

RENAUDOT, T. and RENAUDOT, E., *Recueil général des questions traitées és conférences du Bureau d'Adresse, sur toutes sortes de matières, par les plus beaux esprits de ce temps*, 6 vols. (Lyon: A. Valançol, 1666)

RIVET, A., *Sommaire et abbregé des controverses de nostre temps touchant la religion* (La Rochelle: H. Haultin, 1608)

RIVIUS, J., *De conscientia libri III... Eiusdem de spectris et apparitionibus umbrarum, seu de veteri supersitione liber I* (Leipzig, 1541)

RONSARD, P. de, *Oeuvres complètes*, ed. by P. Laumonier, 20 vols. (Paris: Hachette, 1914–75)

——*Hymne des daimons*, ed. by A.-M. Schmidt (Paris: A. Michel, 1939)

——*Oeuvres complètes*, ed. by J. Céard, D. Ménager, and M. Simonin, 2 vols. (Paris: Gallimard, 1993–4)

ROSSET, F. de, *Histoires memorables et tragiques de ce temps* [1614], ed. by A. de Vaucher-Gravili (Paris: Livre de Poche, 1994)

RUBYS, C. de, *Histoire veritable de la ville de Lyon* (Lyon: Bonaventure Nugo, 1604)

SABBATINI, N., *Pratique pour fabriquer scènes et machines de théâtre* [1st Italian edn. 1638], trans. by M. Canavaggia, R. Canavaggia, and L. Jouvet (Neuchâtel, 1942)

SABINUS, G., *Fabularum Ovidii interpretatio tradita in Academia Regiomontana a Georgio Sabino* [1555] (Canterbury: T. Thomas, 1584)

SCAINO, A., *In octo Aristotelis libros de physica auscultatione accuratissima expositio* (Francofurti: apud Claudium Marnium, et heredes Ioannis Aubrii, 1607)

SERCLIER, J., *L'Antidemon historial, où les sacrileges, larcins, ruses, et fraudes du Prince des tenebres, pour usurper la Divinité, sont amplement traictez, tant par le tesmoignage des S. Escritures, Peres et Docteurs de l'Eglise, qu'aussi par le rapport des Histoiriens sacrez et profanes* (Lyon: P. Rigaud, 1609)

SEXTUS EMPIRICUS, *Works*, trans. by by R. G. Bury, Loeb Classical Library, 4 vols. (London: Heinemann, 1933)

SLEIDANUS, J., *Histoire de l'estat de la religion et republique*, trans. by R. Le Prévost ([Geneva]: B. Richard, 1557)

SPRENGER, J., *Malleus maleficarum* [1488], ed. by C. S. Mackay, 2 vols. (Cambridge: Cambridge University Press, 2006)

SURIUS, L., *Histoire ou commentaires de toutes choses memorables, avenues depuys LXX ans en ça par toutes les parties du monde, tant au faict seculier que Ecclesiastic*, trans. by J. Estourneau (Paris: Guillaume Chaudière, 1571)

TAILLEPIED, N., *Brief traicté et declaration de l'an jubilé et efficace des pardons et indulgences données et octroyées par le souverain Evesque de Rome aux fidelles chrestiens, l'an 1576* (Paris: J. Parent, 1576)

——*Histoire des vies, meurs, actes, doctrines et mort de Martin Luther et André Carlostad, hérétiques de nostre temps* (Paris: J. Parent, 1577)

——*Oeuvres de philosophie, à sçavoir: dialectique, phisique et ethique d'Aristote* (Paris: J. Parent, 1583).

——*Histoire de l'estat et republique des druides, eubages, saronides, bardes, vacies, anciens François, gouverneurs des païs de la Gaule, depuis le deluge universel, jusques à la venuë de Jesus-Christ en ce monde* (Paris: J. Parent, 1585)

——*Recueil des antiquitez et singularitez de la ville de Pontoise* (Rouen: G. l'Oiselet, 1587)

——*Recueil des antiquitez et singularitez de la ville de Rouen, avec un progrez des choses memorables y advenues depuis sa fondation jusques à present* (Rouen: R. Petit, 1587)

——*Psichologie, ou traité de l'apparition des esprits. A sçavoir, des ames separees, fantosmes, prodiges, et accidens merveilleux qui precedent quelquefois la mort des grands personnages, ou signifient changements de la chose publique* (Paris: G. Bichon, 1588)

——*Traicté de l'apparition des esprits. A sçavoir, des ames separees, fantosmes, prodiges, et accidens merveilleux qui precedent quelquefois la mort des grands personnages, ou signifient changements de la chose publique* [1588] (Rouen: J. Osmont, 1602)

——*Les Antiquités et singularités de la ville de Pontoise*, ed. by A. François (Pontoise: A. Seyrès, and Paris: H. Champion, 1876)

——*A Treatise of Ghosts*, trans. and ed. by M. Summers (London: Fortune Press, 1933)

THEVET, A., *Les Singularitez de la France Antarctique, autrement nommée Amerique: et de plusieurs terres et isles descouvertes de notre temps* (Paris: Maurice de La Porte, 1558)

THYRAEUS, P., *De variis tam spirituum quam vivorum hominum prodigiosis apparitionibus et nocturnis infestationibus libri tres* (Coloniae Agrippinae: ex off. M. Cholini, sumptibus G. Cholini, 1594)

——*Loca infesta, hoc est de infestis ob molestantes daemoniorum et defunctorum hominum spiritus locis, liber unus … Accessit eiusdem libellus de terriculamentis nocturnis* (Coloniae Agrippinae: ex off. M. Cholini, sumptibus G. Cholini, 1598)

——*De apparitionibus omnis generis spirituum, Dei, angelorum, daemonorum et animarum humanarum liber* (Coloniae Agrippinae: ex off. M. Cholini, sumptibus G. Cholini, 1600)

TOLETUS, F., *Societatus Iesu Commentaria una cum quaestionibus in octo libros aristotelis de physica auscultatione* (Venetiis: apud Iuntas, 1580)

TORQUEMADE, A. de (= A. de Torquemada), *Hexameron, ou six journees, contenans plusieurs doctes discours sur aucuns poincts difficiles en diverses sciences, avec maintes histoires notables et non encore ouyes* [1573], trans. by G. Chappuys (Rouen: R. de Beauvais, 1610)

TYRON, A., *Recueil de plusieurs plaisantes nouvelles, apophtegmes, et recreations diverses* (Antwerp: M. Huyssens, 1596)

VAIR, L. (= L. Vairo), *Trois livres de charmes, sorcelages, ou enchantemens*, trans. by J. Baudon (Paris: N. Chesneau, 1583)

VALLADIER, A., *La Saincte Philosophie de l'âme, sermons pour l'Advant preschez à Paris à St-Médric, l'an 1612, par André Valladier* (Paris: P. Chevalier, 1614)

VERMIGLI, P. M., *In Samuelis prophetae libros duos... commentarii* (Zurich: C. Froschauer, 1564)

VIGNEULLES, P. de, *Les Cent Nouvelles nouvelles*, ed. by C. H. Livingston (Geneva: Droz, 1972)

VIRET, P., *Disputations chrestiennes, touchant l'estat des trespassez, faites par dialogues*, (n.p., 1552)

——*La Cosmographie infernale*, ed. by C. Calame (Paris: Éditions de la différence, 1991)

VIRGIL, *L'Eneide*, trans. by L. des Masures (Lyon: J. de Tournes, 1560)

VIVES, L., *De veritate fidei Christianae libri vi* [1543] (Basel: J. Oporinus, 1544)

WECKER, J. J., *Les Secrets et merveilles de nature, recueillis de divers autheurs et divisez en XVII livres*, trans. by G. Chappuys, ed. by P. Meyssonnier (Lyon: B. Honorat, 1586)

WEYER, J., *Cinq livres de l'imposture et tromperie des diables, des enchantements et sorcelleries*, trans. by J. Grévin [1567] (Paris: J. du Puys, 1569)

ZAMARIEL, A., [= A. de Chandieu] and Mont-Dieu, B. de [= J. Grévin], *Response aux calumnies continues au discours et suyte du discours sur les miseres de ce temps, faits par Messire Pierre Ronsard, jadis poëte, et maintenant Prebstre* (n.p., 1563)

ZIEGLER, J., *Schondia*, in *Quae intus continentur: Syria... Palestina... Arabia Petraea... Aegyptus... Schondia*, etc., ed. by J. Ziegler (Argentorati: apud Petrum Opilionem, 1532)

WORKS PUBLISHED AFTER 1800

ADAMO, M. G., GASPARRO, M., and PULEIO, M. T., eds., *Miti e linguaggi della seduzione* (Catane: C.U.E.C.M, 1993)

ALTENDORF, H.-D. and JEZLER, P., eds., *Bilderstreit, Kulturwandel in Zwinglis Reformation* (Zurich: Theologischer Verlag, 1984)

AQUILON, P. 'Quatre avocats angevins dans leurs librairies (1586–1592)' in *Le Livre dans l'Europe de la Renaissance: actes du XVIIIe colloque international* *d'études humanistes de Tours*, ed. by P. Aquilon and H.-J. Martin (Paris: Promodis, 1988), pp. 502–49

——and MARTIN, H.-J., eds., *Le Livre dans l'Europe de la Renaissance: actes du XVIIIᵉ colloque international d'études humanistes de Tours* (Paris: Promodis, 1988)

ARIÈS, P., *L'Homme devant la mort*, 2 vols. (Paris: Seuil, 1977)

ARNOULD, J.-C., DEMAROLLE, P., and ROIG-MIRANDA, M., eds., *Tourments, doutes et ruptures dans l'Europe des XVIᵉ et XVIIᵉ siècles* (Paris: Champion, 1995)

BACKUS, I. D., *Le miracle de Laon: le déraisonnable, le raisonnable, l'apocalyptique et le politique dans les récits du miracle de Laon, 1566–1578* (Paris: Vrin, 1994)

BALMAS, E., ed., *Tragedia e sentimento del tragico nella letteratura francese del Cinquecento* (Florence: Olschki, 1990)

BATH, J., '"In the Divell's Likenesse": Interpretation and Confusion in Popular Ghost Belief' in *Early Modern Ghosts: Proceedings of the 'Early Modern Ghosts' Conference held at St. John's College, Durham University on 24 March 2001*, ed. by J. Newton and J. Bath (Durham: Centre for Seventeenth-Century Studies, 2002), pp. 70–8

BELLENGER, Y., ed., *Le Temps et la durée dans la littérature au Moyen Âge et à la Renaissance* (Paris: Nizet, 1986)

——ed., *Pierre de Larivey (1541–1619): champenois, chanoine, traducteur, auteur de comédies et astrologue* (Paris: Klincksieck, 1993)

——ed., *Le Mécénat et l'influence des Guises* (Paris: Champion, 1997)

——ed., *Le Théâtre biblique de Jean de la Taille* (Paris: Champion, 1998)

BERTHOUD, G., *Anthoine Marcourt: réformateur et pamphlétaire du Livre des marchans aux placards de 1534* (Geneva: Droz, 1973)

BETZ, J., ed., *Répertoire bibliographique des livres imprimés en France au seizième siècle*, Bibliotheca Bibliographica Aureliana, 19 ('Nantes') (Baden-Baden: V. Koerner, 1975)

BIEL, P., *Doorkeepers at the House of Righteousness: Heinrich Bullinger and the Zurich Clergy, 1535–1575* (Bern: Peter Lang, 1991)

BLUM, C., *La Représentation de la mort dans la littérature française de la Renaissance*, 2nd edn., 2 vols. (Paris: Champion, 1989)

BOLAND, P., *The Concept of 'Discretio spirituum' in John Gerson's 'De probatione spirituum' and 'De distinctione verarum visionum a falsis'* (Washington D.C.: The Catholic University of America Press, 1959), pp. 25–38 (*De probatione*) and pp. 76–145 (*De distinctione*)

BOWEN, B. C., ed., *The French Renaissance Mind: Studies Presented to W. G. Moore* (= *L'Esprit Créateur*, 16 [1976])

BOWYER, R. A., 'The Role of the Ghost-Story in Mediaeval Christianity' in *The Folklore of Ghosts*, ed. by H. R. Ellis Davidson and W. M. S. Russell (Cambridge, N.J.: D. J. Brewer, 1981), pp. 177–92

BRIGGS, K. M., *The Anatomy of Puck: An Examination of Fairy Beliefs among Shakespeare's Contemporaries and Successors* (London: Routledge, 1959)

BRUN, R., *Le Livre illustré en France au XVIe siècle* (Paris: F. Alcan, 1930)

BUCHAN, D. and IVRES, E., 'Tale Roles and Revenants: A Morphology of Ghosts' in *Western Folklore*, 45 (1986), pp. 143–60

BUSE, P. and STOTT, A., eds., *Ghosts: Deconstruction, Psychoanalysis, History* (London: Macmillan, 1999)

BUTTERWORTH, E., 'The Work of the Devil? Theatre, the Supernatural, and Montaigne's Public Stage', *Renaissance Studies*, 22 (5) (2008), pp. 705–22

CACIOLA, N., 'Wraiths, Revenants, and Ritual in Medieval Culture', *Past and Present*, 152 (1996), pp. 3–45

—— 'Spirits Seeking Bodies: Death, Possession, and Communal Memory in the Middle Ages' in *The Place of the Dead: Death and Remembrance in Late Medieval and Early Modern Europe*, ed. by B. Gordon and P. Marshall (Cambridge: Cambridge University Press, 2000), pp. 66–86

——*Discerning Spirits: Divine and Demonic Possession in the Middle Ages* (Ithaca: Cornell University Press, 2003)

CAMPAGNE, H., 'Démonologie ou "Histoires prodigieuses"?: au carrefour de la science et de la littérature', *Studi Francese*, 43 (1999), pp. 496–503

CARNEY, P. *The Structure of Resurrection Belief* (Oxford: Clarendon Press, 1987)

CARR, R. A., *Pierre Boaistuau's 'Histoires tragiques': A Study of Narrative Form and Tragic Vision* (Chapel Hill: University of North Carolina Press, 1974)

CARRÉ, Y., *Le Baiser sur la bouche au Moyen Âge: rites, symboles, mentalités* (Paris: Léopard d'Or, 1993)

CASTOR, G., *Pléiade Poetics: A Study in Sixteenth-Century Thought and Terminology* (Cambridge: Cambridge University Press, 1964)

CAVALLO, G. and CHARTIER, R., eds., *A History of Reading in the West*, trans. by L. G. Cochrane (Oxford: Polity Press, 1999)

CAVE, T., *Recognitions: A Study in Poetics* (Oxford: Clarendon Press, 1988)

——*Pré-histoires: textes troublés au seuil de la modernité* (Geneva: Droz, 1999)

CÉARD, J., *La Nature et les prodiges: l'insolite au XVIe siècle en France* (Geneva: Droz, 1977)

—— 'Dieu, les hommes et le poète' in *Autour des 'Hymnes' de Ronsard*, ed. by M. Lazard (Paris: Champion, 1984), pp. 83–101

CECCHETTI, D. and DALLA VALLE, D., eds., *Il tragico e il sacro dal cinquecento a Racine* (Florence: L. S. Olschki, 2001)

CHAIX, P., *Recherches sur l'imprimerie à Genève de 1550–1564* (Geneva: Droz, 1954)

CHARMOT, F., *Ignatius Loyola and Francis de Sales*, trans. by M. Renelle (London: Herder, 1966)

CHARPENTIER, F., ed., *Les Tragédies de Jean de La Taille* (= *Cahiers Textuel* 18 [1998])

CHARTIER, R., 'Reading Matter and "Popular" Reading: From the Renaissance to the Seventeenth Century' in *A History of Reading in the West*, ed. by G. Cavallo and R. Chartier, trans. by L. G. Cochrane (Oxford: Polity Press, 1999), pp. 269–83

CHESTERS, T., 'Jean de La Taille et la scénographie du "creux": *Saül le furieux* (1572)' in *Dramaturgies de l'ombre: spectres et fantômes au théâtre*, ed. by

F. Lecercle and F. Lavocat(Rennes: Presses Universitaires de Rennes, 2005), pp. 101–18

——'Demonology on the Margins: Robert Du Triez's *Les Ruses, finesses, et impostures des esprits malins* (1563)', *Renaissance Studies*, 21 (3) (2007), pp. 395–410

——'Pierre Le Loyer et la cosmographie du spectre' in *Voyager avec le diable: voyages réels, voyages imaginaires et discours démonologiques (XVe–XVIIe siècles)*, ed. by G. Holtz and T. Maus de Rolley (Paris: Presses Universitaires de Paris-Sorbonne, 2008), pp. 183–92

——and MAUS DE ROLLEY, T., 'Le Diable et le bibliothécaire: la classification des ouvrages démonologiques dans les catalogues bibliographiques aux XVIe et XVIIe siècles' in *Styles et partages du savoirs (1500–1700)*, ed. by F. Lavocat and F. Lecercle (forthcoming)

CLARK, S., *Thinking with Demons: The Idea of Witchcraft in Early Modern Europe* (Oxford: Oxford University Press, 1997)

——'The Reformation of the Eyes: Apparitions and Optics in Sixteenth- and Seventeenth-Century Europe', *Journal of Religious History*, 27 (2003), pp. 143–60

—— *Vanities of the Eye: Vision in Early Modern European Culture* (Oxford: Oxford University Press, 2007)

CLERC, S., 'Un exorcisme à Lyon au XVIe siècle' in *Revue du Lyonnais: esquisses physiques, morales et historiques*, ed. by L. Boitel, 2 vols. (Lyon, 1835), ii, pp. 81–9

CLOSSON, M., *L'Imaginaire démoniaque en France: genèse de la littérature fantastique (1550–1650)* (Geneva: Droz, 2000)

——'Le "Théâtre des spectres" de Pierre Le Loyer' in *Dramaturgies de l'ombre: spectres et fantômes au théâtre*, ed. by F. Lavocat and F. Lecercle (Rennes: Presses Universitaires de Rennes, 2005), pp. 119–39

COHEN, G., *Ronsard: sa vie et son oeuvre* (Paris: Boivin, 1946)

COLEMAN, J. and SCOLLEN-JIMACK, C. M., eds., *Rabelais in Glasgow* (Glasgow: Glasgow University, 1984)

COOPER, R., 'Pierre de Larivey astrophile' in *Pierre de Larivey (1541–1619): champenois, chanoine, traducteur, auteur de comédies et astrologue*, ed. by Y. Bellenger (Paris: Klincksieck, 1993), pp. 97–118

CRESSY, D., *Birth, Marriage, and Death: Ritual, Religion, and the Life-Cycle in Tudor and Stuart England* (Oxford: Oxford University Press, 1997)

CROW, G. D., 'Antonio de Torquemada: Spanish Dialogue Writer of the Sixteenth Century' in *Hispania: A Journal Devoted to the Teaching of Spanish and Portuguese*, 38 (3) (September, 1955), pp. 265–71

DASTON, L., and PARK, K., *Wonders and the Order of Nature (1150–1750)* (New York: Zone, 1998)

DAVIDSON, H. R. ELLIS and RUSSELL, W. M. S., eds., *The Folklore of Ghosts* (Cambridge: D. J. Brewer, 1981)

DAVIS, C., 'État présent: Hauntology, Spectres, and Phantoms', *French Studies*, 59 (3) (2005), pp. 373–9

——*Haunted Subjects: Deconstruction, Psychoanalysis, and the Return of the Dead* (New York: Palgrave, 2007)

DAVIS, N. ZEMON, 'Some Tasks and Themes in the Study of Popular Religion' in *The Pursuit of Holiness in Late Medieval and Renaissance Religion*, ed. by C. Trinkaus and H. A. Oberman (Leiden: Brill, 1974), pp. 307–36

——'Ghosts, Kin, and Progeny: Some Features of Family Life in Early Modern France' in *The Family*, ed. by A. S. Rossi, J. Kagan, and T. K. Hareven (New York: Norton, 1978), pp. 87–114

DEJEAN, J., *The Reinvention of Obscenity: Sex, Lies, and Tabloids in Early Modern France* (Chicago: University of Chicago Press, 2002)

DELAUNAY, P., *L'Aventureuse Existence de Pierre Belon du Mans* (Paris: Champion, 1926)

DELUMEAU, J., *La Peur en Occident (XIVe–XVIIIe siècles): une cité assiégée* (Paris: Fayard, 1978)

DEMERSON, G., 'Apollonios de Tyane chez Rabelais: Christ dans un miroir déformant?' in *Cité des hommes, cité de Dieu*, ed. by A. Meyer (Geneva: Droz, 2003), pp. 503–12

DEMOUGIN, P., 'Étude sur l'oeuvre démonologique de Pierre Le Loyer, 1550–1634' (unpublished doctoral thesis, Université de Paris I, 1994)

DERRIDA, J., *Spectres de Marx: l'État de la dette, le travail du deuil et la nouvelle internationale* (Paris: Éditions Galilée, 1993)

DESGRAVES, L. et al., eds., *Répertoire bibliographique des livres imprimés en France au seizième siècle*, Bibliotheca Bibliographica Aureliana, (Baden-Baden: V. Koerner, 1978–)

DESROSIERS-BONIN, D., *Rabelais et l'humanisme civil* (Geneva: Droz, 1992)

DOVER WILSON, J., *What Happens in Hamlet?* (Cambridge: Cambridge University Press, 1935)

DUBOIS, C.-G., '*Imaginatio phantastica*: le discours des spectres et apparitions d'esprits de Pierre Le Loyer (1586)' in *La Littérature fantastique: colloque de Cérisy* (Paris: Albin Michel, 1991), pp. 73–89

DURANVILLE, L. de, *Essai sur l'histoire de la côte Sainte-Catherine et des fortifications de la ville de Rouen, suivi de mélanges relatifs à la Normandie* (Rouen: Lebrument, 1857)

DUVAL, E. M., *The Design of Rabelais's 'Tiers Livre de Pantagruel'* (Geneva: Droz, 1997)

ELLA, G. M., *Henry Bullinger (1504–1575): Shepherd of the Churches* (Durham: Go, 2007)

ELLIOTT, D., 'Seeing Double: John Gerson, the Discernment of Spirits, and Joan of Arc', *The American Historical Review*, 107 (2002), pp. 26–54

ENGAMARRE, M., *Qu'il me baise des baisers de sa bouche: le cantique des cantiques à la Renaissance* (Geneva: Droz, 1993)

EVANS, R. J. W. and Marr, A. J., eds., *Curiosity and Wonder from the Renaissance to the Enlightenment* (Aldershot: Ashgate, 2006)

FERBER, S., *Demonic Possession and Exorcism in Early Modern France* (London: Routledge, 2004)

FERRERAS SAVOYE, J., 'Doutes et ruptures dans le dialogue humaniste: le *Jardín de flores curiosas* de Antonio de Torquemada' in *Tourments, doutes et ruptures dans l'Europe des XVIe et XVIIe siècles*, ed. by J.-C. Arnould, P. Demarolle, and M. Roig-Miranda (Paris: Champion, 1995), pp. 81–91

FINUCANE, R. C., *Appearances of the Dead: A Cultural History of Ghosts* (London: Junction Books, 1981)

FLORENNE, Y., 'Un quêteur de prodiges', *Mercure de France*, 342 (1961), pp. 657–68

FRÈRE, E., *Manuel du bibliographe normand*, 2 vols. (Rouen, 1858–60)

GALLAGHER, T. M., *The Discernment of Spirits: An Ignatian Guide for Everyday Living* (New York: Crossroad, 2005)

GAUNA, S. M., '*De Genio Pantagruelis*: An Examination of Rabelaisian Demonology', *Bibliothèque d'Humanisme et Renaissance*, 33 (1971), pp. 557–70

GILMONT, J.-F., *Jean Crespin: un éditeur réformé du XVIe siècle* (Geneva: Droz, 1981)

GODET, M., ATTINGER, V., TÜRLER, H., et al., *Dictionnaire historique et biographique de la Suisse*, 7 vols. (Neuchâtel: Administration du dictionnaire biographique et historique de la Suisse, 1921–33)

GORDON, B., 'Malevolent Ghosts and Ministering Angels: Apparitions and Pastoral Care in the Swiss Reformation' in *The Place of the Dead: Death and Remembrance in Late Medieval and Early Modern Europe*, ed. by B. Gordon and P. Marshall (Cambridge: Cambridge University Press, 2000), pp. 87–109

——and MARSHALL, P., eds., *The Place of the Dead: Death and Remembrance in Late Medieval and Early Modern Europe* (Cambridge: Cambridge University Press, 2000)

——and CAMPI, E., eds., *Architect of Reformation: An Introduction to Heinrich Bullinger, 1504–1575* (Michigan: Baker, 2004)

GREENBLATT, S., *Hamlet in Purgatory* (Princeton: Princeton University Press, 2001)

GRIFFITHS, K. and EVANS, D., eds., *Haunting Presences: Ghosts in French Literature and Culture* (Cardiff: University of Wales Press, 2009), pp. 43–59

GUY, H., 'Les Sources françaises de Ronsard', *Revue d'Histoire Littéraire de la France*, 9 (1902), pp. 217–56

HAMPTON, T., *Literature and Nation in the Sixteenth Century: Inventing Renaissance France* (Ithaca: Cornell University Press, 2001)

HIGMAN, F., 'The Reformation and the French Language' in *The French Renaissance Mind: Studies Presented to W. G. Moore*, ed. by B. C. Bowen (= *L'Esprit Créateur*, 16 [1976]), pp. 20–36

HOLTZ, G., and NAUS DE ROLLEY, T., *Voyager avec le diable: voyages réels, voyages imaginaires et discours démonologiques (XVe–XVIIe siècles)* (Paris: Presses Universitaires de Paris-Sorbonne, 2008)

HOUDARD, S. and JACQUES-CHAQUIN, N., eds., *Curiosité et Libido Sciendi de la Renaissance aux Lumières*, 1 vol. in 2 (Paris: ENS editions, 1998)

HOWE, A., 'La Taille's *Saül*: A Play of Two Halves', *French Studies Bulletin*, 19 (Summer 1986), pp. 3–5

HUGUET, E., *Dictionnaire de la langue française du seizième siècle*, 7 vols. (Paris: Didier and Champion, 1923–75)

IMBS, P., 'Le Diable dans l'oeuvre de Rabelais' in *Mélanges de linguistique française offerts à M. Charles Bruneau, professeur à la Sorbonne*, Société de publications romanes et françaises, 45 (Geneva: Droz, 1954), pp. 241–61

JANIER, A., 'Les Sources des *Sérées* de Guillaume Bouchet' in *La Nouvelle française de la Renaissance*, ed. by L. Sozzi (Geneva: Slatkine, 1981), pp. 557–86

JAUSS, H. R., *Towards an Aesthetic of Reception*, trans. by T. Bahti (Brighton: Harvester, 1982)

JEANNERET, M., *Éros rebelle: littérature et dissidence à l'âge classique* (Paris: Seuil, 2003)

JOSEPH, M., 'Discerning the Ghost in *Hamlet*', *PMLA*, 76 (1961), pp. 493–502

JOYNES, A., ed., *Medieval Ghost Stories* (Woodbridge: Boydell, 2001)

KOSLOFSKY, C. M., *The Reformation of the Dead: Death and Ritual in Early Modern Germany, 1450–1700* (Basingstoke: Macmillan, 2000)

KRAILSHEIMER, A. J., *Rabelais and the Franciscans* (Oxford: Clarendon Press, 1963)

LA CHARITÉ, R. C., 'Devildom and Rabelais's *Pantagruel*', *The French Review*, 49 (1975), pp. 42–50

LAFEUILLE, G., *Cinq hymnes de Ronsard* (Geneva: Droz, 1973)

LANGER, U., *Perfect Friendship: Studies in Literature and Moral Philosophy from Boccaccio to Corneille* (Geneva: Droz, 1994)

LANGWEHR, D., 'Gut und böse Engel contra Arme Seelen. Reformierte Dämonologie und die Folgen für die Kunst, gezeigt an Ludwig Lavaters Gespensterbuch von 1569' in *Bilderstreit, Kulturwandel in Zwinglis Reformation*, ed. by H.-D. Altendorf and P. Jezler (Zurich: Theologischer Verlag, 1984), pp. 125–34

LANHAM, R. A., *A Handlist of Rhetorical Terms*, 2nd edn. (Berkeley and Los Angeles: University of California Press, 1991)

LAVOCAT, F., 'Les Fantômes du Ballet de Cour' in *Dramaturgies de l'ombre: spectres et fantômes au théâtre*, ed. by F. Lavocat and F. Lecercle (Rennes: Presses Universitaires de Rennes, 2005), pp. 177–200

——and LECERCLE, F., eds., *Dramaturgies de l'ombre: spectres et fantômes au théâtre* (Rennes: Presses Universitaires de Rennes, 2005)

LAZARD, M., ed., *Autour des 'Hymnes' de Ronsard* (Paris: Champion, 1984)

LECERCLE, F., 'Saül et les effets de spectacle' in *Les Tragédies de Jean de La Taille*, ed. by F. Charpentier (= *Cahiers Textuel*, 18 [1998]), pp. 25–42

——'Les Bénéfices de la trahison: impératifs de foi et exigences dramatiques dans le *Saül* de Jean de La Taille' in *Il tragico e il sacro dal cinquecento a Racine*, ed. by D. Cecchetti and D. Dalla Valle (Florence: L. S. Olschki, 2001), pp. 17–54

LE CHARPENTIER, H., 'Notice sur Noël Taillepied' in N. Taillepied, *Les Antiquités et singularités de la ville de Pontoise*, ed. by A. François (Pontoise: A. Seyrès, and Paris: H. Champion, 1876), pp. 1–55

LECOUTEUX, C. and MARCQ, P., *Les Esprits et les morts* (Paris: Champion, 1990)

LE GOFF, J., *La Naissance du Purgatoire* (Paris: Gallimard, 1981)

LEPREUX, G., *Gallia Typographica ou répertoire biographique et chronologique de tous les imprimeurs de France*, 5 vols. (Paris: Champion, 1909–14)

LE ROY LADURIE, E., *Montaillou, village occitan de 1294 à 1324* (Paris: Gallimard, 1975)

LESTRINGANT, F., *André Thevet* (Geneva: Droz, 1991)

——*Jean de Léry, ou l'invention du sauvage: essai sur l'Histoire d'un voyage faict en la terre du Brésil* (Paris: Champion, 1999), pp. 107–8

LEVER, M., 'De l'information à la nouvelle: les "canards" et les *Histoires tragiques* de Rosset', *Revue d'histoire littéraire de la France*, 79 (1979), pp. 577–93

LEVI, A. H. T., 'Rabelais and Ficino' in *Rabelais in Glasgow*, ed. by J. A. Coleman and C. M. Scollen-Jimack (Glasgow: Glasgow University Press, 1984), pp. 71–85

LEWIS, B. 'Protestantism, Pragmatism, and Popular Religion: A Case Study of Early Modern Ghosts' in *Early Modern Ghosts: Proceedings of the 'Early Modern Ghosts' Conference held at St. John's College, Durham University on 24 March 2001*, ed. by J. Newton and J. Bath (Durham: Centre for Seventeenth-Century Studies, 2002), pp. 79–91

LIAROUTZOS, C., *Le Pays et la mémoire: pratique et représentation de l'espace chez Gilles Corrozet et Charles Estienne* (Paris: Champion, 1998)

LIENHARD, J. T., 'On "Discernment of Spirits" in the Early Church', *Theological Studies*, 41 (3) (1980), pp. 505–29

MACLEAN, I., *Logic, Signs, and Nature in the Renaissance: The Case of Learned Medicine* (Cambridge: Cambridge University Press, 2002)

MAÎTRE-DUFOUR, M., 'Une anti-curiosité: la discrétion chez Mlle de Scudery et dans la littérature mondaine (1648–1696)' in *Curiosité et Libido Sciendi de la Renaissance aux Lumières*, ed. by S. Houdard and N. Jacques-Chaquin, 1 vol. in 2 (Paris: ENS editions, 1998), pp. 333–58

MARCHADOUR, A., *Lazare: histoire d'un récit, récits d'une histoire* (Paris: Cerf, 1988)

MARSHALL, P., 'Fear, Purgatory, and Polemic' in *Fear in Early Modern Society*, ed. by W. G. Naphy and P. Roberts (Manchester: Manchester University Press, 1997), pp. 150–66

——'"The Map of God's Word": Geographies of the Afterlife in Tudor and Early Stuart England' in *The Place of the Dead: Death and Remembrance in Late Medieval and Early Modern Europe*, ed. by B. Gordon and P. Marshall (Cambridge: Cambridge University Press, 2000), pp. 110–30

——*Beliefs and the Dead in Reformation England* (Oxford: Oxford University Press, 2002)

MARTINEZ, C., 'Fantômes, oracles et malédictions: figures du temps tragique' in *Le Temps et la durée dans la littérature au Moyen Âge à la Renaissance*, ed. by Y. Bellenger (Paris: Nizet, 1986), pp. 139–51

MASTERS, G. Mallary, *Rabelaisian Dialectic and the Platonic-Hermetic Tradition* (Albany: State University of New York Press, 1969)

MCGRATH, A. E., *Reformation Thought: An Introduction* [1988] (Oxford: Blackwell, 1999)

MCKENZIE, D. F., *Bibliography and the Sociology of Texts* (London: The British Library, 1986)

MEERHOFF, K., *Rhétorique et poétique au XVIe siècle en France: Du Bellay, Ramus et les autres* (Leiden: Brill, 1986)

MEYER, A., *Cité des hommes, cité de Dieu* (Geneva: Droz, 2003)

MILLET, O., 'L'Ombre dans la tragédie française (1550–1640), ou l'enfer sur la terre' in *Tourments, doutes et ruptures dans l'Europe des XVIe et XVIIe siècles*, ed. by J.-Cl. Arnould, P.Demarolle, and M. Roig-Miranda (Paris: Champion, 1995), pp. 163–77

—— 'Faire parler les morts: l'ombre protatique comme prosopopée dans les tragédies françaises de la Renaissance' in *Dramaturgies de l'ombre: spectres et fantômes au théâtre*, ed. by F. Lavocat and F. Lecercle (Rennes: Presses Universitaires de Rennes, 2005), pp. 81–100

MOREAU, H., 'Les Daimons, ou de la fantaisie' in *Autour des 'Hymnes' de Ronsard*, ed. by M. Lazard (Paris: Champion, 1984), pp. 215–42

MORIN, E., *L'Homme et la mort* (Paris: Seuil, 1970)

MOSS, A., *Ovid in Renaissance France: A Survey of the Latin editions of Ovid and Commentaries Printed in France before 1600* (London: Warburg Institute, 1982)

—— *Poetry and Fable: Studies in Mythological Narrative in Sixteenth-Century France* (Cambridge: Cambridge University Press, 1984)

MUCHEMBLED, R., *Une histoire du diable: XIIe–XXe siècle* (Paris: Seuil, 2000)

NAPHY, W. G. and ROBERTS, P., eds., *Fear in Early Modern Society* (Manchester: Manchester University Press, 1997)

NEWTON, J., 'Reading Ghosts: Early Modern Interpretations of Apparitions' in *Early Modern Ghosts: Proceedings of the 'Early Modern Ghosts' Conference held at St. John's College, Durham University on 24 March 2001*, ed. by J. Newton and J. Bath (Durham: Centre for Seventeenth-Century Studies, 2002), pp. 57–69

—— and BATH, J., eds., *Early Modern Ghosts: Proceedings of the 'Early Modern Ghosts' Conference held at St. John's College, Durham University on 24 March 2001* (Durham: Centre for Seventeenth-Century Studies, 2002)

NORA, P., *Les Lieux de mémoire* (Paris: Gallimard, 1984–92)

OMBRES, R., *Theology of Purgatory* (Dublin: The Mercier Press, 1978)

PASQUIER, E., and DAUPHIN, V., *Imprimeurs et libraires de l'Anjou* (Angers: Éditions de l'ouest, 1932)

PEARL J. L., 'French Catholic Demonologists and their Enemies in the Late Sixteenth and Early Seventeenth Centuries', *Church History*, 52 (1983), pp. 457–67

—— *The Crime of Crimes: Demonology and Politics in France, 1560–1620* (Ontario: Wilfred Laurier University Press, 1999)

PÉRICAUD, M. A., *Notice sur François de Rohan, Archévêque de Lyon* (Lyon: A. Vingtrinier, 1854)

PERRET, D., 'An Avine Cosmography: *La Nephelococugie*, or Aristophanes Gone Cuckoo in the French Renaissance', *The Comparatist: Journal of the Southern Comparative Literature Association*, 18 (1994), pp. 23–38

PIAGET, A., *Les Actes de la dispute de Lausanne, 1536* (Neuchâtel: Secrétariat de l'Université, 1928)

POLI, S., *Histoire(s) tragiques(s)*: *Anthologie/Typologie d'un genre littéraire* (Paris: Nizet, 1992)

PRAT, J.-M., *Maldonat et l'université de Paris au XVIe siècle* (Paris: Julien and Lanier, 1856)

PUES, F., 'La "Silva de varia lección" de Pero Mexía', *Lettres Romanes*, 13 (1959), pp. 119–43

—— 'Les sources et la fortune de la "Silva" de Mexía', *Lettres Romanes*, 13 (1959), pp. 279–92

—— 'Du Verdier et Guyon: deux imitateurs français de Mexía', *Lettres Romanes*, 14 (1960), pp. 15–40

RAFFINI, C., 'Rabelais, Raminagrobis, and the Problem of Censorship, *Tiers Livre*, 21–23', *Romance Notes*, 36 (1996), pp. 35–46

RENAULD, E., 'Une traduction française du *Peri energeias daimonon dialogos* de Michel Psellos', *Revue des études grecques*, 151 (1920), pp. 56–95

RENOUARD, P., *Imprimeurs et libraires parisiens du XVIe siècle*, 5 vols. (Paris, 1964–)

—— *Répertoire des imprimeurs, libraires, fondeurs de caractères et correcteurs d'imprimerie depuis l'introduction de l'imprimerie à Paris (1470) jusqu'à la fin du seizième siècle* (Paris: M. J. Minard, 1965)

ROBERTS, P., 'Contesting Sacred Space: Burial Disputes in Sixteenth-Century France' in *The Place of the Dead: Death and Remembrance in Late Medieval and Early Modern Europe*, ed. by B. Gordon and P. Marshall (Cambridge: Cambridge University Press, 2000), pp. 131–48

ROSSI, A. S., KAGAN, J., and HAREVEN, T. K., eds., *The Family* (New York: Norton, 1978)

ROTH, C., *Discretio spirituum: kriterien geistlicher Unterschneidung bei Johannes Gerson* (Würzburg: Echter, 2001)

ROUSSET, J., *La Littérature de l'âge Baroque en France: Circé et le paon* (Paris: Corti, 1953)

—— ed., *Anthologie de la poésie baroque française*, 2 vols. (Paris: M. Leclerc, 1961)

ROYLE, N., 'Phantom Review', *Textual Practice*, 11 (1997), pp. 386–98

RÜETSCHI, K. J., 'Bullinger and the Schools' in *Architect of the Reformation: An Introduction to Heinrich Bullinger, 1504–1575*, ed. by B. Gordon and E. Campi (Michigan: Baker, 2004), pp. 215–29

SCHENDA, M. R., *Die Französische Prodigienliteratur in der 2. Hälfte des 16 Jh.* (Munich: Max Hueber Verlag, 1961)

SCHMITT, J.-Cl., 'Le Spectre de Samuel et la sorcière d'En Dor. Avatars historiques d'un récit biblique: I Rois 28', *Études rurales*, 105–6 (1987), pp. 37–64

—— *Les Revenants: les vivants et les morts dans la société médiévale* (Paris: Gallimard, 1994)

SCHMITT, P., *La Réforme catholique, le combat de Maldonat, 1534–83* (Paris: Beauchesne, 1985)

SCHOLAR, R., *The Je-Ne-Sais-Quoi in Early Modern Europe: Encounters with a Certain Something* (Oxford: Oxford University Press, 2005)

SÉGUIN, J. P., *L'Information en France avant le périodique: 517 canards imprimés entre 1529 et 1631* (Paris: G.-P. Maisonneuve et Larose, 1964)

SEN, A., *Identity and Violence: The Illusion of Destiny* (London: Allen Lane, 2006)

SHARRATT, P., 'Rabelais, Ramus et Raminagrobis', *Revue d'Histoire Littéraire de la France*, 82 (1982), pp. 263–9

SIMONIN, M., 'Benigne Poissenot: Discours confirmatif de l'authorité des anciens touchant l'apparition du mauvais daemon ou génie', *Anagrom*, 7–8 (1976), pp. 37–44

——'Notes sur Pierre Boaistuau', *Bibliothèque d'humanisme et Renaissance*, 38 (1976), pp. 323–33

——'La Vérité de l'estrange: pédagogie et poétique du fantastique à la Renaissance', *Studi di Letteratura francese*, 212 (1987), pp. 30–44

——*Vivre de sa plume au XVIe siècle, ou la carrière de François de Belleforest* (Geneva: Droz, 1992)

SLUHOVSKY, M., *Believe Not Every Spirit: Possession, Mysticism, and Discernment in Early Modern Catholicism* (Chicago: University of Chicago Press, 2007)

SOZZI, L., ed., *La Nouvelle française de la Renaissance* (Geneva: Slatkine, 1981)

STABLER, A. P, 'King Hamlet's Ghost in Belleforest?' in *PMLA*, 77, no. 1 (March, 1962), pp. 18–20

STEGMANN, A., 'Comment constituer une bibliothèque en France au début du XVIIe siècle: examen méthodologique' in *Le Livre dans l'Europe de la Renaissance: actes du XVIIIe colloque international d'études humanistes de Tours*, ed. by P. Aquilon and H.-J. Martin (Paris: Promodis, 1988), pp. 467–501

STEPHENS, W., *Demon Lovers: Witchcraft, Sex, and the Crisis of Belief* (Chicago: University of Chicago Press, 2002)

SULLIVAN, H. W., *Grotesque Purgatory: A Study of Cervantes's 'Don Quixote' Part II* (University Park, Philadelphia: Pennsylvania State University Press, 1996)

SVOBODA, K., *La Démonologie de Michel Psellos* (Brno: Vydává filosofická fakulta, 1927)

TANNER, N. P., *Decrees of the Ecumenical Councils*, 2 vols. (London: Sheed & Ward, 1990)

TERNAUX, J.-C., *Lucain et la littérature de l'âge baroque en France: citation, imitation et création* (Paris: H. Champion, 2000)

THIERRY, A., 'La Maison de Guise dans l'oeuvre d'Agrippa d'Aubigné: exécration et estime' in *Le Mécénat et l'influence des Guises*, ed. by Y. Bellenger (Paris: Champion, 1997), pp. 81–94

THOMAS, K., *Religion and the Decline of Magic: Studies in Popular Beliefs in Sixteenth- and Seventeenth-Century England* [1971] (London: Weidenfeld and Nicolson, 1997)

TONER, J. J., *A Commentary on Saint Ignatius' Rules for the Discernment of Spirits* (St. Louis: The Institute of Jesuit Sources, 1981)

TOOTHILY, G., 'A Note on Frère Colimant (*Hep* XLIV)', *Bibliothèque d'humanisme et Renaissance*, 33 (1971), pp. 151–3

TRINKAUS, C. and OBERMAN, H. A., eds., *The Pursuit of Holiness in Late Medieval and Renaissance Religion* (Leiden: Brill, 1974)

VOUCHER-GRAVILI, A.de, 'De la transgression et du tragique: les *histoires tragiques* de François de Rosset' in *Tragedia e sentimento del tragico nella letteratura francese del Cinquecento*, ed. by E. H. Balmas (Florence: Olschki, 1990), pp. 164–76

—— *Loi et transgression: les histoires tragiques au XVIIe siècle* (Lecce: Milella, 1992)

—— 'Langages et figures de séduction dans les *Histoires tragiques* de François de Rosset' in *Miti e linguaggi della seduzione*, ed. by M. G. Adamo, M. Gasparro, and M. T. Puleio (Catane: C.U.E.C.M, 1993), pp. 97–114

VOADEN, R., *God's Words, Women's Voices: The Discernment of Spirits in the Writing of Late-Medieval Women Visionaries* (York: York Medieval Press, 1999)

VOVELLE, M., *Les Ames du purgatoire, ou le travail du deuil* (Paris: Gallimard, 1996)

WALKER-BYNUM, C., *The Resurrection of the Body in Western Christianity, 200–1336* (New York: Columbia University Press, 1995)

WANDEL, L. P., *Voracious Idols and Violent Hands: Iconoclasm in Reformation Zurich, Strasbourg, and Basel* (Cambridge: Cambridge University Press, 1995)

WILLIAMS, W., '*Out of the frying pan*...: Curiosity, Danger, and the Poetics of Witness in the Renaissance Traveller's Tale' in *Curiosity and Wonder from the Renaissance to the Enlightenment*, ed. by R. J. W. Evans and A. J. Marr (Aldershot: Ashgate, 2006), pp. 21–42

YARDLEY, M. 'The Catholic Position in the Ghost Controversy of the Sixteenth Century' in L. Lavater, *Of Ghostes and Spirites Walking by Nyght*, ed. by J. Dover Wilson (Oxford: Oxford University Press, 1929), pp. 220–51

ZERVOS, C., *Un philosophe néoplatonicien du XIe siècle: Michel Psellos, sa vie, son oeuvre, ses luttes philosophiques* (Paris: E. Leroux, 1920)

ZILLI, L., 'Saül: de Jean de la Taille à Pierre du Ryer' in *Le Théâtre biblique de Jean de la Taille*, ed. by Y. Bellenger (Paris: Champion, 1998), pp. 207–21

Index